A History of Bicycling in Illinois

A HISTORY OF BICYCLING IN ILLINOIS

160 Years of Booms and Busts

CHRISTOPHER SWEET

3 Fields Books is an imprint of the University of Illinois Press.

Manufactured in the United States of America
1 2 3 4 5 C P 5 4 3 2 1
♾ This book is printed on acid-free paper.

Cataloging data available from the Library of Congress
LCCN 2025027252
ISBN 978-0-252-04698-8 (cloth : alk.)
ISBN 978-0-252-08913-8 (paper : alk.)
ISBN 978-0-252-04863-0 (ebook)

Cover image: Chicago mayor Carter Henry Harrison IV and selected dignitaries pose aboard the ten-man Oriten bicycle, 1897. Carter H. Harrison IV papers, The Newberry Library, Chicago.

Cover design: Jason Gabbert

To my mother who taught me an early love of books,

to my father who taught me how to fix my bicycles,

and to Illinois bicyclists, then and now.

Contents

Acknowledgments

This book is the result of nearly a decade of intermittent research and writing. As a first-time book author, I am astonished at the lengthy list of people to whom I am indebted for their support of this project. It truly takes a village. In 2014, I was considering a number of projects for my first sabbatical at Illinois Wesleyan University. This book never would have come into being if it weren't for the enthusiastic support of my then supervisor, University Librarian Dr. Karen Schmidt. In retrospect, I believe Karen recognized the true scholarly and historical significance of this project before I did. This critical support has been continued by my current supervisor, University Librarian Stephanie Davis-Kahl. Both University Librarians worked with me to try and squeeze some research and writing time for this book into my day-to-day responsibilities as an academic librarian. I am also grateful for the unwavering assistance of Tony Heaton, the former Interlibrary Loan Specialist at The Ames Library. Over the years, Tony tracked down and filled hundreds of interlibrary loan requests for this project. These were often esoteric, difficult to locate items. More recently, Katy Ritter has continued this excellent interlibrary loan work and previously provided administrative support for multiple aspects of the research and composition process. Rick Lindquist, Chief Information Officer at Illinois Wesleyan University and fellow cyclist, provided a wide array of information technology support related to this project. Dr. Andrew Hartman, an accomplished historian and professor at Illinois State University, provided me with much-appreciated practical guidance related to publishing scholarly works of history.

Researching this book consumed my first sabbatical, and then seven years later, the bulk of writing and revision happened during my second sabbatical.

These sabbaticals, as well as multiple internal grants, have been the result of continued support from our Faculty Development Committee. Various phases of this book have been supported by Illinois Wesleyan University Artistic and Scholarly Development Grants. An internal "Recentering the Humanities" grant funded by the Andrew W. Mellon Foundation also supported my work.

My wife, Cara, also deserves a great deal of credit and thanks for her support of this work. During the early research stages, I was often away from home and our family as I visited a variety of Midwest research locations. Later, I would be away for substantial chunks of time for multiple International Cycling History Conferences (ICHC). My wife was often the first proofreader of my draft chapters, and I once persuaded her to join me in scouring a Peoria cemetery for the long-lost headstone of cyclist Thomas W. Davis (we didn't find it).

As a librarian and historian, visiting regional libraries, museums, archives, and private collections was my favorite phase of writing this book. Digitization efforts have made great strides in the last two decades, but much of the material consulted for this book only exists in print form. The Chicago History Museum proved to be the most fruitful for researching this book. I am particularly indebted to Conservator Liz Sorokin, who helped me access an important scrapbook that was not available to the public due to its poor condition. Likewise, Linda Aylward, Special Collections Assistant at the Virginius H. Chase Special Collections Center of Bradley University, was a helpful guide through the holdings of the Peoria Historical Society. Other fruitful research visits were made to the Newberry Library, Henry Ford Museum Archives, Bicycle Museum of America, Chicago Public Library Special Collections, and the Peoria Public Library.

I was thrilled to discover many kindred spirits through ICHC. This eclectic group of historians, museum curators, scholars, and collectors represent the driving force behind the majority of modern bicycle history scholarship. Today, the majority of bicycle history books begin life as presentations at an ICHC conference. In particular, Gary Sanderson does the yeoman's work of editing and publishing both the ICHC *Conference Proceedings* and the American *Wheelmen* magazine. I was frequently the beneficiary of Gary's editorial feedback, and I also drew on his published scholarship for this book. Noted bicycle historians David Herlihy and the late Andrew Ritchie also provided feedback and guidance for this project. Lorne Shields provided some outstanding rare images from his vast collections for this book. The Wheelmen organization, and particularly members of the Illinois Wheelmen delegation, also provided invaluable assistance. Marty Potts, John Traum, and Carey Williams each shared their extensive bicycle history knowledge and personal collections to aid in the creation of this book.

Interviews were key to developing the contemporary portion of this book. Dave Simmons, Executive Director of Ride Illinois (the largest Illinois non-profit bicycle advocacy organization), filled me in on the work of his organization and provided me with valuable connections around the state. My old friend Isabel Reyes-Todd and bicycle advocate Ismael Cuevas joined me for a discussion of contemporary Illinois bicycle advocacy and social justice efforts. In another interview, Tom Limon, founder of Biketropolis, shared his extensive knowledge of Chicago bicycle history and associated locations that appear on his guided bicycle tours of Chicago. Chris Koos, former bike racer and current owner of Vitesse Cycle Shop, provided insight on Illinois bicycle racing during the twentieth century. Likewise, Robbie Ventura, former professional cyclist and founder/owner of Vision Quest Coaching, also assisted me with identifying key Illinois bicycle racers of the twentieth and twenty-first centuries.

In 2017, Daniel Nasset, then Senior Acquisitions Editor at the University of Illinois Press, reviewed my prospectus for this book along with what were, in retrospect, three rather inconsistently written and only vaguely connected draft chapters. Fortunately, Daniel saw the potential for this rough early work to become a compelling piece of historical scholarship. Daniel provided much-needed early guidance that definitively shaped the final book.

Once a complete draft had been completed, a host of new supporters stepped in with editorial help. Most notably, using grant funds, I was able to hire historian and editor Dr. Steven P. Miller. Dr. Miller, himself a published historian and experienced editor, provided detailed and insightful developmental editing and copyediting for the entire manuscript. Very early in this endeavor, I discovered a fellow bicycle historian, Dr. Thomas Burr, at nearby Illinois State University. I consulted with Dr. Burr at all stages of this project and drew on his dissertation work focused on the history of international bicycle markets. Dr. Burr also read and provided excellent edits on my draft manuscript. John Knudson, a good friend from my college days and current Assistant Managing Editor with the Radiological Society of America, was the third and final editor of my draft manuscript.

As part of my composition process, I also sought out feedback on individual chapters. Sometimes I tapped friends with specific bicycle history expertise, while other non-historians provided feedback from the perspective of general readers for whom this book was written. Here again, I am indebted to Amy Bowden, Dr. Meghan Burke, Dr. Caitlin Starr Cohn, Mick Hannah, Dr. Kate Herald-Browne, Sammie Lewis, and Chris Majerczyk.

After this round of editing, my manuscript went back to the University of Illinois Press, this time under the able guidance of Senior Acquisitions Editor

Martha Bayne. Two peer reviewers, who are unknown to me as a condition of the review process, approved the manuscript and offered highly detailed and useful editorial feedback, which further improved the manuscript. Senior Editor Tad Ringo guided me through all the various final components of the book production process.

A Note on Primary Sources

American bicycle history is a rich area for research, since the bicycle boom of the 1890s coincided with an exceptionally productive era of American periodical publishing. Early on in this project, I realized I needed to better understand the full scope of nineteenth-century bicycle periodical literature in order to effectively research this topic. The result of these efforts was a comprehensive bibliography, published in the journal *American Periodicals*, that documents more than one hundred nineteenth-century bicycle periodicals.[1] Unfortunately, only a small fraction of these periodicals can be searched online through Hathi Trust, Internet Archive, and the Smithsonian.

Newspaper coverage of bicycling was extensive during the boom and intermittent throughout the twentieth and twenty-first centuries. Compared to the periodical literature, the majority of historical newspapers from these time periods have been digitized. The Chronicling America historic newspaper database from the Library of Congress is freely available. Subscription-based historical newspaper databases that provided critical research for this book include Newspapers.com, NewspaperArchive, Nineteenth Century U.S. Newspapers, Accessible Archives, and ProQuest Historical Newspapers.

Historians are keenly aware that the vast majority of primary resource material has yet to be digitized, and this certainly holds true for bicycle history. Many visits to regional archives, libraries, and museums were instrumental in writing this book. The single best source for materials related to Illinois bicycle history was the Abakanowicz Research Center at the Chicago History Museum. Beyond the Chicago History Museum, the bicycle historian can find pockets of excellent primary source material at a variety of locations. In Illinois, the Newberry Library, Chicago Public Library, Abraham Lincoln Presidential Library and Museum, and Cullom-Davis Library at Bradley University all have small collections of bicycle material. Outside of Illinois, the Bicycle Museum of America in New Bremen, Ohio, owns the records of the Schwinn Bicycle Company as well as the collections of the former Schwinn Museum. They have a particularly rich collection of bicycle catalogs. The Benson Ford Research Center at the Henry Ford Museum in Dearborn, Michigan, has a substantial collection of bicycle history materials. The University of Michigan's Special Collections Research Center also has a limited collection of bicycle materials. Although most of it is not Illinois-specific, both the Library of Congress and the Smithsonian have been steadily adding to their collections of digitized bicycle materials.

During the course of writing this book, I compiled two important lists based on primary source research. The first is a list of all known nineteenth-century Illinois bicycle brands, manufacturers, assemblers, and jobbers. When available, this list also includes factory addresses and years of active production. This work builds upon the excellent list of bicycle brands maintained by The Wheelmen organization. The second list is a compilation of all known world and American bicycle racing records set in Illinois during the nineteenth century. Both documents are available in the Internet Archive or by contacting the author.[2]

A History of Bicycling in Illinois

Introduction

"No One Can Touch Chicago"

The weather in Chicago on Wednesday, October 6, 1897, was unseasonably warm and dry. In fact, Illinois had suffered under a drought since August, and farmers were concerned about the effect on crop yields. Newspapers that week reported that the dry weather had triggered a fire, which began near the stockyards and burned three city blocks, dredging up painful memories of the Great Chicago Fire of 1871. The upside of the unseasonably warm weather was a pleasant fall day for the recently elected mayor of Chicago, Carter Henry Harrison IV, to take a bicycle ride. This was not unusual for the mayor, who had ridden more than four thousand miles the previous year. The Century Road Club of America (a national cycling organization founded in Chicago and still in existence today) had awarded Harrison eighteen commemorative bars to be worn with his cycling attire, one for each hundred-mile "century" ride that he had completed up to that point.

As a candidate the previous year, Harrison had carefully catered to the influential Chicago bicycle lobby. Under the umbrella of the Associated Cycling Clubs of Chicago, cyclists formed a nonpartisan voting bloc that supported any candidate who backed issues important to "wheelmen." In a testament to the size of the bloc, Harrison had printed 100,000 postcards featuring an image of himself astride a bicycle with the caption "Not the Champion Cyclist but the Cyclists' Champion." His outreach to Chicago cyclists proved effective. Multiple pro-Harrison bicycle clubs were formed before and after the election. The race drew national attention. "The power of the bicycle in politics has recently been manifested in a conspicuous manner," the *New York Journal* declared. "There can be no reasonable doubt that the Mayoralty race in Chicago was run principally on 28-inch wheels with pneumatic tires. Carter Harrison was elected by the bicycle vote."[1]

Illustration of bicyclists in 1895 on Michigan Avenue. (From *50 Years of Schwinn-Built Bicycles*, 1945.)

For Wednesday's ride, Harrison rounded up a who's who of political allies and Chicago bicycling notables. These dignitaries included Si Mayer (president of the Lake View Cycling club and later alderman), William C. Malley (former University of Michigan football player, local attorney, and election commissioner), Granville W. Browning (special commissioner of the Superior Court of Cook County), George K. Barrett (former high-wheel racer and recently editor of the national *LAW Bulletin and Good Roads*), Charles P. Root (bicycle racer who later founded the Chicago Motor Club), and James B. Bowler (bicycle racer and later alderman and United States representative). On most days, Harrison rode a Hibbard bicycle, a popular model made by Chicago's St. Nicholas Manufacturing Company, which just happened to be owned by Harrison's brother-in-law.[2] This day was different, though. As depicted on the cover of this book, all of Harrison's selected associates climbed aboard the Oriten, a ten-person bicycle made by the Waltham Manufacturing Company. A caricature of the excesses of the Gilded Age, this behemoth of a bicycle weighed 305 pounds and was designed to carry up to 2,500 pounds. More than twenty-three feet in length, it was capable of hitting 45 mph with the right set of riders. The bike was produced mainly as a novelty for shows and races, although most racetracks were too small to accommodate its gigantic turning radius. Three hundred Chicagoans showed up to watch Mayor Harrison and his associates ride the Oriten on the cinder path that paralleled Lake Michigan in Lake Front (now Grant) Park. At one point, a spectator stepped in front of the riders, leading to a spectacular crash. "Three inches separated his [Harrison's] head from a sharp-topped iron post," reported the *Chicago Chronicle*.[3]

What might seem like a simple photo op or publicity stunt to twenty-first century readers was anything but. The 1890s were the golden age of cycling in the United States. During this decade, bicycling surged in popularity in both urban and rural areas and from coast to coast. Bicycle races rivaled baseball games as America's favorite spectator sport, churches debated the propriety of cycling, and social elites flocked to join bicycle clubs. Bicycle manufacturing became a major United States industry. Bicycles were one of the top United States exports at the time, and Illinois produced far more bicycles than any other state. In 1898, bicycles ranked ninth among all United States exports at $6.8 million in aggregate value, just behind iron, oil, copper, and leather.[4]

A survey of more than a dozen news stories related to bicycling in Chicago's two largest newspapers in the two days immediately following Mayor Harrison's Oriten ride offers a glimpse of the bicycle mania. The *Tribune* reported that there were 329,818 bicycles in France and that a bicycle tax had generated 329,272,339 francs in the past year. While France was also a major international producer of bicycles, the article noted that well-to-do French citizens preferred the lighter and more comfortable American bicycles; the majority of these would have been manufactured in Illinois. The *Inter Ocean* reported on some drama surrounding the Illinois Cycling Club's Football team's decision to cancel its upcoming football game. In the 1890s, Chicago had more than fifty cycling clubs, the largest of which fielded their own football, baseball, and bowling teams. Cycling clubhouses of the day were lavish affairs with amenities like billiard tables, bowling alleys, cafes, libraries, theaters, parlors, lodging rooms, and weight rooms. One paper reported on a big circuit race taking place in Peoria. Professional racer Tom Cooper of Detroit won the mile in a record time of 2:09⅖ (a rate of about 28 mph), and amateur Earl W. Peabody of Chicago won his seventy-eighth race. A different article reported on a five-mile race in Philadelphia between a team of four "crack" cyclists on a quadruplet bicycle and a team of six thoroughbred horses; the cyclists lost by a mere five meters. In the bicycle slang of the day a "crack" racer was one with exceptional skills who knew precisely when to make a decisive winning move. Clearly, racing was hugely popular. Chicago's Pullman Road Race was the largest in the country, and for a few years attracted as many as 200,000 spectators over the length of the course. For comparison, Chicago's current-day Soldier Field stadium has a capacity of only 61,500. During the winter, six-day races in which individuals or teams of racers rode constantly were all the rage. Many cycling records were set on the Lakeview track in Peoria, with prizes ranging from big cash payouts to gold watches, grand pianos, and even building lots in Chicago.[5] Another article noted that New York's bicycle police squad now included sixty-eight men, including one "scorching" detective. ("Scorchers" were fast riders.) Chicago, likewise, had a bicycle police force, along with more than one hundred bicycle mailmen and even a bicycle ambulance.[6]

These are just a few of the bicycle stories from two days of newspaper coverage in 1897. What is notable from these summaries is that newspapers weren't just covering bicycle racing as a sport, hobby, or fad. During the boom of the 1890s, bicycling transcended sport and had broad impacts on American social issues, politics, and economics.

"Democracy of the Wheel"?

Nineteenth-century bicycle advocates, who aligned themselves with Progressive Era reformers, made a litany of claims in favor of cycling. A few of the benefits they touted included improved physical fitness, reduction of alcoholism, reduction of urban pollution, improved camaraderie, transportation cost savings, reduction in animal cruelty, and improved sleep. A notable number of pundits made even more ambitious arguments about the impact of bicycles on American life. At a time when wealth inequality had soared to new heights, many saw bicycling as an egalitarian force. "As a social revolutionizer it has never had an equal," New York's *Evening Post* editorialized about bicycling. "It has put the human race on wheels, and thus changed completely many of the most ordinary processes and methods of social life. It is the great leveller, for not till all Americans got on bicycles was the great American principle, that every man is just as good as any other man, and generally a little better, fully realized. All are on equal terms, all are happier than ever before."[7] The fact that the writer specifically singles out "every man" is the first indication that this bicycle utopia might not actually be meant for "all Americans."

Similar sentiments were echoed, sometimes in more gender-inclusive terms, by other mainstream publications of the day. In an article published in *The Forum*, Joseph Bishop argued that bicycling "brings all classes together when all are in a condition of healthy enjoyment and physical content. The artisan, the millionaire, the professional man, the laborer, the rich merchant, the lady whose name appears in all the 'society movements' of the day, the shop-girl, the banker and his clerk—all roll along on equal terms."[8] The *Inter Ocean* newspaper painted a rich portrait of cycle-centered urban life:

> The boulevard is crowded with wheels, and their riders are from every walk and avocation of life. The merchant prince, the mistress of fashion, the minister of the gospel, the miller, the milliner, the butcher, the baker,

> and the candlestick-maker, roll along in one grand procession. Indifferent to all social and business distinctions, each feeling a fraternal interest in all the rest and each yielding a cheerful obedience to the code of ethics that governs the democracy of the wheel.[9]

For the moment, bicycles seemed the height of modernity and progress. The bicycle craze even drew the attention of the usually austere Census Bureau, which in a 1900 report opined, "It is safe to say that few articles ever used by man have created so great a revolution in social conditions as the bicycle."[10] An "eminent physician" quoted in the *Evening Post* elevated the bicycle even higher, saying, "Not within two hundred years has there been any one thing which has so benefited mankind as the invention of the bicycle."[11]

The truthfulness and elisions present in these utopian claims suggest how American bicycling history has paralleled the achievements and limits of American democracy as a whole. In many respects, bicycles have served the cause of egalitarianism. On an existential level, as bicycling advocates have long noted, once aboard a bicycle, all riders are equally subject to the same winds, hills, and bad roads as their companions. By the end of the 1890s, mass production of bicycles, coupled with the market power of mail-order companies, made what previously were the playthings of the upper classes accessible to nearly everyone. On a socio-political level, the evidence is strong that bicycles accelerated the push for women's rights, suffrage, and independence, among other important Progressive Era reforms.

Yet a host of contrary evidence punctures this idyllic narrative of American bicycle history. The child laborers employed in Illinois's bicycle factories and the Black cyclists that were blocked from participating in Chicago's many races surely did not see bicycles as "the great leveller." Neither did the medical authorities who argued that women bicycling would lead to infertility or sexual deviance, or the preachers who saw the devil's work in a Sunday bicycle ride. Untangling the utopian myth of the bicycle—in the 1890s, but also in the present—remains a complicated but important task. This book, through the lens of Illinois bicycle booms and busts, traces and interrogates these utopian conceptions of bicycles and bicycling.

If bicycling's relationship to democratic culture remains murky, what is much clearer is the central role that Illinois played in the history of American bicycling. Surprisingly (or perhaps unsurprisingly, for jaded midwesterners in "flyover" country), American bicycle history has often overlooked Illinois and its surrounding states in favor of focusing on the East Coast. To be sure, America's first bicycle ride and first mass-produced high-wheel bicycles indeed originated on the East Coast. As this book shows, however, American cycling culture really took off when its locus moved to the Midwest, specifically Illinois, residing there from the 1890s through most of the twentieth century.

On a quantitative level, the case for Illinois as the country's leading bicycle manufacturer is exceedingly straightforward: From the mid-1890s through the 1990s, the state was the largest producer of bicycles and bicycle parts in the United States. In 1898, a massive 152-page directory of the Chicago bicycling scene boasted that "[t]wo-thirds of this country's output of bicycles and accessories comes from within a radius of 150 miles around Chicago."[12] What might be dismissed as mere Windy City bluster is supported by data from the *United States Census of Manufactures*. This publication showed that in 1900 (shortly after the bicycle boom had peaked), the total value of products for only the *larger* Illinois bicycle manufacturers was $8,960,421, or 28 percent of the national total. New York came in a distant second with $3,842,020; in fact, Illinois's total value of products was greater than that of all the New England states combined.[13] In 1896, during the height of the boom, a cycling periodical called *The Referee* published an annual comprehensive directory of large bicycle manufacturers. The directory listed 110 bicycle manufacturers in Illinois, compared to 80 in New York, 36 in Ohio, and 30 in Indiana.[14] All in all, between 1869 and 1900, more than 500 bicycle companies produced more than 800 different bicycle models in Illinois.[15] Many of these companies were only in existence for a few years, and a good number of them just put their own custom name on bicycles that were actually manufactured by larger companies. Still, no other state came close in terms of the total number of bicycle brands and models produced. While modern bicycle histories have largely neglected Illinois, contemporary bicycle publications routinely recognized the state's bicycle prominence. In 1892, at the beginning of the bike boom, *Bicycling World and L.A.W. Bulletin* (the official publication of the League of American Wheelmen) described Chicago's bicycle industry:

> It is really amazing how Chicago is coming to the front in the cycling trade. Already one of the most active centres of the industry in the United States, she seems destined to leave her competitors so far in the rear in the near future that they cannot even claim to be active competitors. New York and Boston of course will probably always be the centres of the importing business, but in the number and size of the manufactories already in existence and springing up all over the city, no one can touch Chicago.[16]

No one could touch the state of Illinois either. When it comes to American bicycling history, Illinois and Illinoisans can lay claim to the following important American achievements:

- first six-day bicycle race
- first bicycle velodrome with a banked track
- first bicycle world championships
- first back-pedal brake and freewheel system on a safety bicycle

- first safety bicycle with multiple gears
- first commercial safety bicycles with pneumatic tires
- most expensive bicycle ever built
- first prototype of an aluminum bicycle
- first all-wood safety bicycle
- most bicycles produced during the bicycle boom
- most bicycles produced during the twentieth century
- first husband and wife to ride around the world
- numerous world bicycle-racing records
- founding of the influential Good Roads Movement
- first wireless electronic bicycle shifting system

Those already familiar with American bicycle history will surely approach this list with skepticism. For this audience, it is worthwhile to pay close attention to the extensive documentation provided for each of these claims. These feats are just a few of the reasons why Illinois was at the heart of the bicycle boom of the 1890s and then remained a leading center of American bicycle manufacturing and culture in the twentieth and twenty-first centuries. They also suggest why Illinois provides a fitting case study for the promise and limits of the bicycle as a vessel for democratic culture.

An Overview of Bicycle History

The significance of Illinois's contributions to bicycle history can only be established within the context of broader international and American bicycle history and the evolution of bicycle design. Understanding that history, in turn, requires some explanation of the occasionally esoteric terminology related to early bicycle variants. This section provides a high-level overview of global bicycle history from its beginnings through the end of the bicycle boom around 1900. The focus in this section is primarily on international and broader American bicycle history, while the remainder of the book delves into Illinois-specific bicycle history. By necessity, this will be a highly compressed history; several excellent books provide a thorough examination of global and/or American bicycle history.[17]

American bicycle history can be characterized by an ongoing series of extreme boom and bust cycles affecting both production and popularity. While manufacturing is only one aspect of bicycle history, increases in production are a good indicator of the overall health of American bicycling. When demand is up, more people use bicycles for commuting, leisure, and racing. The boom-bust cycles have continued to the current day, with the COVID-19 pandemic driving the most recent bicycle boom. The earliest booms were driven by evolutions in the design of the bicycle itself. By contrast, later booms and busts have been linked to broader forces like changing social tastes, the invention of the automobile, world wars, and the rise of the environmental movement.

A great deal of historical misinformation surrounds the first precursors to the modern bicycle. A clever forgery in a fifteenth-century Italian codex led some to mistakenly believe that Leonardo Da Vinci designed the first bicycle. With scant evidence, others have claimed that a seventeenth-century stained-glass window in Stoke Poges Church (Buckinghamshire, England) depicts the first bicycle. Those wishing to bestow the honors of the first bicycle on France will sometimes point to an inventor named Comte de Sivrac, who they claim developed a pedal-driven machine called a *célérifère* in 1792. That any such contraptions were ever built, or even amounted to human-powered machines that balanced on two wheels, is speculation at best. Without new evidence, these early accounts of the bicycle should remain squarely in the category of bicycle myths.[18]

On much firmer historical footing is the story of a German forester named Karl von Drais, who invented what he called a *laufmaschine* (running machine) in 1817. This wooden device did not have pedals and was instead propelled by the rider's feet in the manner of today's children's balance bikes. The genius of Drais' invention was the inclusion of an articulated front wheel, which allowed a rider to remain balanced and steer the contraption. Contemporaries named this contraption after Drais, labeling his original *laufmaschine*, as well as similar copies, the *draisienne* (or *draisine*). As a few draisiennes spread across Europe, they were given the nickname "hobby-horse." What followed was the first of many booms in bicycle history. Members of the European aristocracy purchased hobby-horses and took to parading around in their finery, resulting in another nickname for draisiennes, "dandy horses." This first boom was short-lived, lasting only a few years (1818–1820). During this time, a few hobby-horses were imported to the United States, but they never really caught on as they did in Europe.

The next major step in the evolution of the bicycle was the addition of cranks and pedals to drive the front wheel. The first pedal-driven velocipedes were invented around 1863 in the Parisian workshop of Pierre Michaux. Some debate remains about who within the Michaux shop was responsible for the addition of pedals. The Michaux velocipede featured a heavy iron frame and iron wheels. Because of these design features, the velocipede soon earned the nickname "boneshaker." Pierre Lallement, a machinist in Michaux's workshop, struck out for America in 1866, taking his bicycle manufacturing experience with him. By 1867, Lallement had secured a very important United States patent for a velocipede.

A number of American improvements to the velocipede helped to ignite the first American bicycle boom. The velocipede craze quickly reached its zenith in 1869. *Galaxy Magazine* reported that there were sixteen thousand velocipedes in New York. "The art of walking is becoming obsolete," exclaimed *Scientific American*.[19] Since the great majority of roads were unsuitable for riding, most people learned to ride in indoor bicycle schools. Like the earlier hobby-horse boom in Europe, the velocipede boom fizzled out very quickly. For all intents and purposes, this boom was over by 1870. Lack of good roads, coupled with the weight, cost, and awkwardness of velocipedes, ultimately limited their appeal.

Another decade passed before the next substantial evolution in bicycle design, the high-wheel. James Starley of England created some of the most successful designs of this new style of bicycle. His 1871 Ariel bicycle featured a large front wheel and a much smaller rear wheel. A front-wheel-mounted crank still propelled these high-wheel bicycles, but they now featured wire-spoked wheels, which reduced overall weight and decreased the amount of road vibrations transferred to the rider. The large front wheel also allowed riders to achieve much faster speeds than was possible on earlier velocipedes.

Advertisement for a velocipede riding school in Chicago. (Courtesy of the Chicago History Museum.)

The frames featured lighter hollow steel tubing instead of solid metal. The English nickname for these high-wheel bicycles was "penny farthing," since the difference in wheel sizes corresponded with the larger British penny and corresponding smaller farthing. Later, the high-wheel earned another nickname: "ordinary." This nickname was used to distinguish "ordinary" high-wheel-style bicycles from the subsequent "safety bicycle," which featured chain drives and wheels of equal sizes. The terms high-wheel, penny farthing, and ordinary thus can be used interchangeably.

In 1876, the Centennial Exposition in Philadelphia commemorated the one hundredth anniversary of the signing of the Declaration of Independence and was the first time that an official world's fair was held in the United States. The fair cost $11 million, covered 450 acres, and was attended by ten million visitors. Tucked away in the British Building were a few examples of the new high-wheel style of bicycles.[20] Among the millions who passed through the fair was Civil War veteran Colonel Albert A. Pope. Following the war, Colonel Pope founded the Pope Manufacturing Company and made a small fortune selling shoe supplies and air pistols. The first storefront for the new company was in Boston, but it was soon moved to nearby Hartford, Connecticut. Always on the lookout for the next profitable endeavor, Pope was particularly taken with the fair's exhibits of English high-wheels. He contracted the following year with a local machinist to build a prototype for an American ordinary. After learning to ride this prototype bicycle, Pope began importing and reselling English ordinaries in 1878. An astute businessman, Pope quickly realized that tariffs and shipping costs were eating into his potential profits, so later in 1878, he contracted with the Weed Sewing Machine Company of Hartford to begin manufacturing his own Columbia brand bicycles. In a crucial move to the development of the American bicycle industry, Pope purchased a handful of the most important American velocipede patents, including the original Lallement patent. Production was slow to ramp up, but Pope Manufacturing Company is recognized as the first successful American commercial manufacturer of adult-sized ordinary bicycles.[21] At this time Illinois manufacturers were still producing the older-style velocipedes and some transitional high-wheels. This is but one example of lopsided bicycle history that favors the New England states.

Bicycle culture evolved with advances in design and production. The Boston Cycling Club was formed in 1878, making it America's first cycling club, and the Chicago Bicycle Club followed soon after, in 1879. The first full six-day bicycle race in America took place in Chicago's Exposition Building that same year, and in 1880, the influential League of American Wheelmen was founded in Rhode Island. Meanwhile, a limited number of women became involved in cycling through the use of tricycles. Many of these tricycles were built for two riders; they earned the nickname "sociables" because riders could sit next to each other. Bicycling celebrities also began to emerge: Thomas Stevens, an English-born American immigrant, expanded notions of what bicycles were capable of when he rode around the world between 1884 and 1886. Unlike previous advances in bicycling, the high-wheel boom was not followed by a bust. Rather, interest in the bicycle continued to grow worldwide.

The final evolution in the basic design of bicycles occurred with the aforementioned safety bicycle. From the late 1870s to the mid-1880s, there were multiple attempts at creating a successful chain-driven bicycle with smaller wheels. Once again, it was a member of the Starley family who created a safety bicycle design that caught on with contemporary cyclists. John Kemp Starley's 1885 "Rover" safety bicycle roughly resembled most modern bicycles. It featured much smaller wheels that were nearly the same size. Crucially, the rear wheel was driven by a chain. This chain drive was a key evolutionary feature, as it enabled high speeds through the use of mechanical advantage. A large front gear, coupled with a much smaller rear cog, enabled safety bicycles to be pedaled as fast as humans were capable of. At the same time, the small wheels kept the center of gravity low, making them much easier and safer to ride, hence the nickname "safety bicycle." Safety bicycles required less material than high-wheels, which meant they were both lighter overall and cheaper to produce. This new design marked a major step toward making bicycles available to the masses, which would now include substantial numbers of women and children. The "double diamond" safety bicycle frame design was refined in the 1890s and has been largely unchanged in the following 130 years.

During the 1890s, America and Europe experienced a bicycle craze that has never been rivaled. In addition to the aforementioned advances in bicycle production, what accelerated the bicycle boom was the first mass-produced pneumatic tire, developed in 1888 by John Boyd Dunlop. Pneumatic tires were much more comfortable to ride than the solid rubber tires they replaced; they also provided better traction. Despite a serious American economic downturn, bicycle ridership grew dramatically. Writing in the *Century Illustrated* in 1896, the president of the League of American Wheelmen estimated that there were two and a half million riders in the United States, and that an additional one million bicycles would be produced that year. He counted "2,530 bicycle-factories, 24 tire-makers, and 600 concerns dealing in bicycle sundries, all representing a combined investment of $75,000,000."[22]

The economic and social effects of the bicycle boom were far-ranging. The price of horses and livery fell drastically. Jewelers and piano makers took a hit, as bicycles became trendy gifts for the affluent. Riders became more health-conscious and spent less time in saloons. Cigar makers claimed that during the boom, one million fewer cigars were smoked per day. Pastors lamented the deleterious impact of long Sunday rides on church attendance.

Then the boom-bust cycle resurfaced. The bust following the boom of the 1890s was deep and long-lasting. By 1899, the United States bicycle industry was in serious trouble. Seemingly everyone and their brother had gotten into the bicycle manufacturing business, and the bicycle market collapsed. Meanwhile, in true Gilded Age fashion, a group of manufacturers and investors got together to form a trust. Similar to steel, oil, and railroad trusts of the time, the idea behind the American Bicycle Company was to consolidate bicycle manufacturing and force the competition out of business. The timing and implementation were all wrong, however, and the trust itself joined hundreds of bicycle manufacturers in failing. In 1899, United States bicycle factories had a total output valued at $31 million. By 1904, this output had fallen to just $5 million.[23]

For consumers, there was a long-term upside to the bust: lower prices. By 1900, any American could order a good-quality bicycle from a Sears or Montgomery Ward catalog for around $20. Less than a decade earlier, safety bicycles had been selling for around $100, a prohibitive amount for most consumers. Affordable bicycles certainly made bicycling accessible to far more Americans. With this affordability, along with the rise of automobiles and motorcycles, bicycle ownership no longer served as a mark of class or status distinction. Bicycling's complicated relationship to democratic culture thus continued apace.

Acrobatic children cyclists on the cover of Chicago's *Wheel Talk* magazine, January 16, 1896.

Two world wars and the Great Depression heavily influenced bicycling in the first half of the twentieth century. Bicycle riding became linked with patriotism as Americans sought to conserve steel, rubber, and gasoline to support the war efforts. After the bicycle bust of the late 1890s, Schwinn slowly but surely rose to prominence as the largest bicycle manufacturer in the country. Where the 1890s only had a nominal children and teen market, these demographics dominated the bicycle industry during the first half of the twentieth century. Relatively lightweight ten-speed bicycles and burgeoning environmental and fitness movements finally reinvigorated the adult bicycle market in the 1970s. Women returned to bicycling in substantial numbers for the first time since the 1890s. Schwinn continued to lead the American bicycle industry during the second half of the twentieth century, but cheaper Asian imports steadily replaced American-made bicycles. During the 1970s and 1980s, off-road bicycling skyrocketed in popularity with the development of mountain and BMX bicycles.

In the twenty-first century, there are still a few large, American-based bicycle companies, but nearly all of their bicycles are manufactured overseas. Venerable component makers Shimano (Japan) and Campagnolo (Italy) dominated the bicycle component market for many decades until challenged by Illinois-based SRAM. Bicycles and bicycle component sales began shifting to e-commerce platforms, forcing the closure of many brick-and-mortar bicycle shops. Mountain bikes and road/mountain hybrid designs now constitute the vast majority of bicycle sales. In the twenty-first century, carbon fiber has become the material of choice for mid- and high-end bicycle frames. At the same time, a resurgent interest in high-quality, American-made products has created a niche for a growing number of small American bicycle companies who hand-build their bicycle frames. The COVID-19 pandemic and social-distancing measures drove yet another major bicycle boom. Road and track racing waned in popularity, while participation in triathlon, cyclocross, and gravel racing increased.[24]

This brief history captures, in very broad strokes, the last 160 years of (primarily American) bicycle history. It provides foundational knowledge critical for understanding the many ways that Illinois bicyclists, bicycle companies, and bicycle advocates have shaped American bicycle history. This book builds on this foundational knowledge by exploring Illinois's many significant contributions to bicycle history.

What Goes Around, Comes Around

A decent cyclist can only produce around a quarter horsepower for a couple of hours. Even so, the mechanical advantage provided by gears, coupled with the low-friction coefficient of bearings and rubber tires, take that meager input and translate it into around 20 mph on a flat road.[25] Compared to walking or running, substantial speeds on a bicycle feel effortless (at least for a brief time). These feelings of power, speed, and momentum have compelled generations of bicyclists. Simple physics often feels like magic.

Bicycle advocates and evangelists have long ascribed additional magical properties to bicycles and bicycling. As in the above example, there is usually a grain of truth to many of these claims. Much of the work of this book, then, is to take these bold proclamations about bicycling's ability to create a more democratic and egalitarian society and hold them up to the light of rigorous historical scrutiny. An 1896 newspaper article proclaimed, "It would not be at all strange if history came to the conclusion that the perfection of the bicycle was the greatest incident of the nineteenth century. When we think of the effect upon the race of endowing practically all of the people with the means of greatly accelerated locomotion, the imagination knows no bounds."[26] One hundred thirty years later, this claim seems rather simplistic and naïve. What has been largely overlooked in the narrative of American history is just how popular and influential bicycling truly was in the 1890s. Bicycles were deeply intertwined with this formative period of American history.

In the 1890s it was commonplace for bicycle advocates to make outsized claims about bicycles' ability to create a more just and democratic society. This sort of bicycle rhetoric largely disappeared until its reemergence during the beginning of the environmental movement in the 1970s. Suddenly, people remembered that bicycles could indeed be part of the solution to saving the planet. During the physical fitness crazes of the 1970s and 1980s, people realized that bikes could also help save our bodies. As the twenty-first century progresses, we have begun to see myriad ways that bicycles can indeed contribute to improving social justice. Twenty-first-century bicycle advocates are adamant that bicycling should be accessible for all, not just the privileged classes that dominated nineteenth-century bicycling. Bicycle co-ops keep old bikes out of landfills and teach underprivileged youth and adults how to repair bikes. The reward for completing these co-op programs is usually your own bicycle. Public bike-sharing systems in large urban areas now log millions of rides per year and help reduce traffic congestion and carbon emissions. Robust bicycle infrastructure has been shown to make riding safer and more accessible to all.

The following pages uncover the people, companies, and events that make up Illinois bicycle history, but they also trace the long arc of bicycles and their complicated relationship to creating a pluralist democratic society. Originally, these ideas were grandiose and selectively applied. In recent decades, bicyclists have revisited these old ideas and have dug into the hard work of making bicycles truly accessible to all. In the case of Illinois bicycle history, what goes around, comes around.

1

Boneshakers and High-Wheels

Bicycles Arrive in Illinois (1867–1889)

It is likely that we will never know the precise date of the very first pedal-driven bicycle ride in Illinois. The most likely candidate is mentioned in an 1898 *League of American Wheelmen and Good Roads* article, which states that Charles Gilbert Wheeler brought a velocipede from the 1867 Paris *Exposition Universelle* to Chicago "as early as the Fall of 1867."[1] The aptly named Wheeler was an 1858 graduate of Harvard University and served as the United States Consul to Nuremberg from 1862 to 1867. Traveling around Europe in 1867, he surely stopped by the hugely popular world's fair in Paris, where it is well known that the Michaux brothers displayed and sold velocipedes.[2] Very probably, someone who brought a velocipede all the way from Paris would have tried to ride it in its new home, but no direct record of such an inaugural spin in 1867 exists. Tantalizingly, one of the earliest histories of Chicago stated that in 1867, a velocipede riding school was opened in an old skating rink located at the corner of Wabash Avenue and Jackson Street.[3] Even so, this later account was likely off by a year, as even more proximate sources first noted riding schools in Chicago in the year 1868.

The first recorded reference to bicycle riding in Illinois came from the *Chicago Tribune* on August 26, 1868, when they reported that Augustus W. Wheeler, Charles's younger brother, had been riding a velocipede around town. "The aristocratic denizens of Michigan and Wabash Avenues are just now experiencing quite a sensation produced by the advent of one of the famous Paris velocipedes," the article stated, adding that Augustus had had the velocipede imported (surely by his brother Charles). Purportedly, even a rider of "mediocre experience" could ride it 15 mph. In truth, as any bicyclist would recognize, it would have taken a good amount of effort to get an ironclad wheel, without the mechanical advantage provided by gearing, up to that speed. "Much is expected of it," the obviously enamored reporter continued, adding their own predictions. "Its adoption in opposition to hacks, buggies, street cars and like vehicles, for the transportation of the human species, will bring about an epoch in the history of science, which will crush these monopolies of the day and give to the people a healthful and invigorating exercise."[4] Save for the lofty Victorian prose, the article's arguments for the benefits of the very first bicycles were not far afield from those made by the staunchest of twenty-first-century bicycle advocates. It is clear that from its very first appearance in Illinois, people recognized the promise of bicycles to improve society. Multiple Illinois papers published a condensed version of Wheeler's ride, simply stating, "The genuine Parisian Velocipede has appeared in Chicago."[5]

The arrival of the velocipede in Illinois came shortly after Parisian mechanic and inventor Pierre Lallement made the very first ride on a pedal-driven velocipede in America. On April 5, 1866, the *New Haven Daily Palladium* reported on the spectacle, describing "a curious frame sustained by two wheels, one before the other, and driven by foot cranks."[6] Later that year, Lallement and his new partner, James Carroll, were awarded United States Patent 59,915 for

Harris, Beebe & Co. Velocipede Tobacco advertisement (Quincy, IL). (From the Library of Congress.)

"Improvement in Velocipedes." However, they were not able to convince a manufacturer to enter the untested business of building velocipedes. By early 1868, Lallement had returned to France, where a velocipede craze was just getting underway. The craze soon spread across the Atlantic from trend-setting France, powered in part by traveling bicycle acts such as the Hanlon Brothers.[7]

Lallement's first ride in the United States is one of many significant anecdotes that, when related in isolation, has contributed to an East Coast–centered telling of American bicycle history. As bicycle historian David Herlihy has contended, Augustus Wheeler's 1868 ride in the rapidly growing city of Chicago was, quite plausibly, the second time a bicycle was ridden in the United States. The Midwest, however, would not stay in second place for long. Illinois soon evolved into the major center of bicycling in America.[8]

The state of Illinois was admitted to the Union in 1819, and Chicago was first incorporated as a town of four hundred people in 1833. As of 1847, there were no railroads in the growing town, but ten years later, 4,000 miles of railroad track sprawled out in all directions from Chicago, making it the railroad center of the country. In 1848, the Illinois and Michigan Canal was completed, thereby opening up a shipping route from the Great Lakes all the way down to the Gulf of Mexico. But what really set the stage for the city's subsequent rise to bicycle supremacy was the installation of a new kind of road pavement in 1856. The Nicolson pavement system utilized blocks of wood, with their harder end grain facing upwards. They were fixed in place with a mixture of coal tar and gravel. Paved streets—of any type—were a rarity in major cities throughout most of the nineteenth century, but they were critical for the growth of bicycling, and Chicago had more than most.[9]

First and second riders quickly became a moot point, as a bout of "Velocipedomania" gripped the country in 1868 and 1869. "The art of walking is becoming obsolete," gushed a writer for *Scientific American*. "It is true that a few . . . who still cling to that mode of locomotion are still admired as fossil specimens of an extinct race of pedestrians; but for the majority of civilized humanity, walking is on its last legs."[10] Sporting crazes that captured the public's rapt attention (and drew overheated rhetoric) were not new in the United States. Before velocipedes, there were crazes for croquet (1860s) and competitive walking, or "pedestrianism" (1860s and '70s). What distinguished bicycling, though, was mass appeal and the economic opportunity it presented to manufacturers.

Manufacturing Velocipedes

New American manufacturers, alongside old firms entering into a new line of business, obliged the velocipede craze in spades. Soon, one could purchase improved American velocipedes from Pickering & Davis, the Hanlon Brothers,

Mercer & Monod, Calvin Witty, William P. Sargent and Company, the Wood Brothers, and the Kimball Brothers.[11] Chicago pipe fitters Loring and Keene briefly got into the velocipede business as well. By 1869, the United States Patent Office was overwhelmed with applications related to velocipedes. One room of the Patent Office reportedly held a backlog of four hundred patent applications, with eighty new ones arriving in the course of one week.[12] New York carriage maker Calvin Witty got into the velocipede business by building Hanlon Brothers–designed models. Upon learning of the earlier Lallement-Carroll patent, Witty shrewdly purchased the rights to the patent and then promptly slapped a $10 fee on every velocipede produced in the country. This same tactic would later be employed by Albert Pope and Pope Manufacturing to control the United States high-wheel bicycle markets. At the height of the boom in 1869, United States manufacturers reportedly were churning out 1,000 velocipedes a week but meeting only one-tenth of orders.[13]

Illinoisans also contributed to velocipede improvements and manufacturing during the years of the craze. The addition of rubber tires to velocipedes marked an important evolutionary step in bicycle design, making the move to taller (and thereby faster) ordinary bicycles possible. Rubber tires cushioned riders from the literal bone shaking while also greatly increasing traction. In this case, as with much of early bicycle history, multiple people were working on the same idea at nearly the same time. Although the Hanlon Brothers received a patent (accepted by the United States Patent Office in July 1868) that included the addition of rubber tires as an improvement, some historians attribute the first actual use of rubber tires on a velocipede to an Illinoisan, the Reverend Arthur Edwards of Chicago. Edwards, a chaplain and veteran of eighteen Civil War battles, became the editor of the Chicago-based *Northwestern Christian Advocate* in 1864. Like Wheeler, he began riding sometime in 1867 or early 1868. In *Riding High: The Story of the Bicycle*, Arthur Judson Palmer credits Edwards with the first ride on a rubber-tired velocipede: "it is definitely on record that he was first to ride a pedaled vehicle equipped with rubber tires . . . This was in 1868, and in 1869 commercially produced boneshakers began coming out with rubber tires, factory equipped."[14] In 1869, the short-lived *Velocipedist* magazine and *Scientific American* both reported on Edwards's earlier use of rubber tires on his velocipede but failed to give specific dates.[15] Looking back on the evolution of the bicycle in 1898, the *L.A.W. Bulletin and Good Roads* noted that C. K. Bradford had often been credited with using rubber tires in the fall of 1868 but that it was possible that the Reverend Arthur Edwards had beaten him to the punch.[16]

Other Chicagoans also got into the velocipede patent game. E. K. W. Blake received United States Patent 84,163, issued on November 17, 1868, for a new style of velocipede tricycle. Blake created an improved system of propulsion and steering, which he described in typically convoluted patent language: "It consists in an arrangement of loose hollow pulleys on the driving-axle, having pawls taking into ratchets within the said pulleys secured to the axle, and belts for operating the pulleys, passing over guide-pulleys at the front of the machine, to the hands of the operator, whereby he may propel the machine by pulling from directly in front of him."[17] If Blake ever succeeded in actually building such a contraption, it certainly never caught on, and no examples have survived. In 1869, John Lauer of Chicago was awarded United States Patent 92,976 for an "Improvement to Velocipedes" that was essentially an elaborate set of training wheels.[18] Meanwhile, the *Detroit Free Press* reported, "A Chicago genius has invented a one-wheeled velocipede." The article went on to predict, "The next improvement will probably dispense with wheels altogether."[19]

Loring and Keene was the only successful commercial manufacturer of velocipedes in Illinois. Edward R. Loring is listed in contemporary Chicago city directories as a plumber and a pipe fitter. The skills required for these trades were certainly applicable to velocipede manufacturing. In 1869, Loring entered into a partnership with Samuel D. Keene. Since there was no city directory category for velocipede manufacturers, they were listed simply as machinists at Calhoun Place between Clark and Dearborn Streets.[20] The Loring and Keene velocipede was a close copy of the popular Pickering & Davis velocipede. A distinctive feature of both velocipedes was a saddle mounted on a spring mechanism, providing some measure of relief from the bone-shaking ride. Newspaper advertisements claimed that the Loring and Keene velocipede had "three distinct patents," so it appears they secured the necessary patent rights to replicate the best velocipede features of the day. The Loring and Keene was a (relatively) lightweight velocipede and sold for the princely sum of $130 (inflation calculators are imprecise tools, but this amount equates to about $2,900 in 2024). For context, in 1869, those working in skilled trades would have made only $600–$800 annually.[21] Also, for a time, the O. E. Merrill Company, based in Beloit, Wisconsin, sold their own velocipedes on LaSalle Street. The *Chicago Tribune* noted that they "are manufacturing a very beautiful velocipede, with several novel improvements of their own." It's likely that these velocipedes were built in Beloit and then sold in Chicago.[22]

Races and Riding Schools

There is an old adage that goes, "The first bicycle race began when the second bicycle was built." Indeed, races followed closely on the heels of the first velocipedes. In addition to manufacturing velocipedes, Edward Loring was an accomplished racer. In April of 1869, a St. Cloud, Minnesota, newspaper reported that Loring had won a half-mile race in one minute and fifty-five seconds. The article goes on to note that among the racers, Loring and Keene velocipedes were "the unanimous choice."[23] The Loring and Keene velocipede won additional honors at a Chicago velocipede event that was billed as "The Championship of America." The event occurred after Walter H. Brown of Boston established a "world" record of five hours and seventeen minutes for fifty miles of indoor riding. Throughout most of the nineteenth century, claims of world record setting should be approached with skepticism, as international bicycle recordkeeping was inconsistent until around 1900. In reality, the Championship of America consisted only of Chicagoan William H. Sexton riding an indoor solo time trial to try and better the standard set by Brown. Sexton rode a Loring and Keene velocipede and was supported by a full orchestra during his attempt. The rink was so small that it required fifteen laps to make one mile, meaning Sexton made a dizzying 750 revolutions around the course during his fifty-mile time trial, a substantial distance even for modern cyclists. He took the championship with a time of 3:55:00 (nearly 13 mph).[24] Historical context reinforces the remarkable nature of this accomplishment. Velocipedes had been in Illinois for less than a year, and someone was already riding a fifty-mile race. For many of the spectators paying fifty cents for a reserved seat, it would have been their first time seeing anyone aboard one of these new contraptions.

Between the races, newspaper ads all over the country, and old-fashioned word of mouth among velocipede enthusiasts, business was apparently booming for Loring and Keene. An April 1869 story in the *Nebraska Advertiser* reported that Loring had just returned from a trip to New Orleans with two hundred velocipede orders.[25] It isn't clear that these orders were all specifically for Loring and Keene models, since they were also dealers for other makes of velocipedes.

Indoor rinks, sometimes called "velocipedromes," and associated riding schools were essential to spurring on the velocipede craze. As previously noted, mid-nineteenth-century roads were rarely conducive to riding a boneshaker with iron rims. Around the country, the solution was creating indoor rinks that drummed up additional bicycle-related profits by providing professional instruction. At the height of the craze in Boston, there may have been twenty rinks and schools. New York claimed to have 10,000 pupils and "graduates" of such institutions. *Scientific American* routinely reported on the opening of new velocipede schools, and in February of 1869, *Harper's Weekly* published a humorous illustration of a velocipede riding school.[26] Velocipedes had rapidly gone mainstream.

As modern bicycle shop workers everywhere can attest, the test ride is often the crucial selling point. Loring and Keene were aware of this and set up their own indoor riding rink, school, and salesroom in Zouave Hall on the

Loring and Keene Velocipede Riding School and Sales Room advertisement. (Collection of Leonard Cary Williams.)

corner of State and Adams Streets. Instruction ran a steep $15 (or $10, if you had your own velocipede). Male spectators were charged twenty-five cents, while women could watch for free. A competing Chicago velocipede rink was set up at 69 State Street by two New Yorkers with the respective surnames Pearsall and Duryea (the latter does not appear to be directly related to Illinois bicycle and automobile pioneers Charles and Frank Duryea).

The velocipede craze inspired the creation of early bicycle music, including Chicago composer Louis Moeser's 1869 "Velocipede March," which he dedicated to Pearsall. A year earlier, fellow Chicagoan Frank Howard composed "Velocipedia." Memorable lyrics from his tune included "In the days of long ago, people were quite satisfied, when they traveled to and fro, after horse, or mule to ride; but they got up steam, and it then did seem, that we'd never need another thing to furnish speed, but a slight mistake, we all did make, for we've now a thing that's called velocipede."[27] Composing and performing bicycle music was one of the ways that Illinois contributed to the growth of American bicycle culture.

"The velocipede fever in Chicago . . . is attaining a remarkable height," wrote a correspondent to *The Velocipedist* in March of 1869, the magazine's only year of publication. The writer described Chicago's velocipede schools and his experiences trying to ride the contraption:

> I tried one the other day. It is a balky kind of steed. To get on is not difficult. To stay on is a labor of genius. I stayed on about three-fifths of one second. It first got me off by lying down on one side. The next time it unhorsed me by lying down on the other. Then it ran away, and threw me through a picket-fence, carrying off four pickets in the operation. Then it ran away again, and shied me off into the gutter. Next, it stuck fast in a crack in the side-walk, pitching me over its head. Then it backed violently down a small hill, throwing me over its tail.[28]

Chicago even had its own magazine devoted to velocipedes, the *Velocipede Messenger*, although unfortunately no copies appear to have survived.[29]

In Illinois, the velocipede craze extended far beyond Chicago. In December of 1868, *The Decatur Weekly Republican* noted that the artist A. Milt Lapham was preparing for a public velocipede performance. The earliest mentions of a Chicago velocipede school are from January 1869, but a school operated by Lyman Ferre in Bloomington was in business by at least February of that year, and thus potentially beat Chicago to the punch.[30] In April, three velocipede riders appeared on the streets of Rockford. That same month, the *Jacksonville Journal* (Illinois) reported on a third-floor velocipede hall in that city run by a "Professor Grove." An article described how a student rider named Dunlap approached a ramp in the rink at full speed: "up he went like a bird [and] away he went, through the window, like a flash, and disappeared." Miraculously, he managed to jump over a ten-foot-wide alley and land, unharmed, on the roof of a two-story drug store. The article concludes, "Mr. Dunlap thinks he is entitled to the champion medal as the most daring velocipede rider in the country."[31] It is not clear how much journalistic liberty was taken with this particular account.

Women and the Velocipede

According to Victorian conventions, it was unladylike and potentially scandalous behavior for a woman to straddle and ride a velocipede. This was an era that promoted constricting whale bone corsets and heavy, multi-layered skirts supported by rings of steel as the ideal dress for fashionable women. Women were instructed to be seen but rarely heard and to always defer to male companions.

Yet women played a prominent, and previously undocumented, role in the velocipede craze. This prominence can be detected in the sneering treatment bicycling women not infrequently received in print media. "The fair sex have the [velocipede] mania," wrote the aforementioned Chicago correspondent in *The Velocipedist*, "but in their case, like consumption, it is incurable. There are a thousand reasons why it is a misfortune to be a woman, but just now, the chief of all of them is, she can't straddle a velocipede. Like shaving, the machine is an exclusively masculine appurtenance."[32] To the contrary, anyone that was even vaguely aware of the 1869 Chicago velocipede scene would have been aware of multiple proficient women velocipede riders. The presence of women riding velocipedes unsettled gender norms in ways that some found inspiring and others found threatening. In 1869, an enterprising author from London published *The Velocipede, Its Past, Its Present & Its Future*. The book described designs for a tandem velocipede, noting that it was the perfect example of wedded life, with the man doing the hard labor and the lady following wherever he leads and "accustom[ing] herself to his direction." The author then went on to note that American women cyclists were having none of that. "They do not believe in looking for guidance and support," the author wrote. The book continued: "They have fought for equality on the platform and the pulpit; in the sick room and at the bar, and they are not intending to allow the velocipede to remain a standing token of the 'subjection of women.'"[33] Bicycles were only a few years old at this point, but already gendered battle lines were being drawn. Well before the Progressive Era picked up steam, the idea of bicycles as vehicles for women's equality and emancipation was in the air. Controversy would follow soon enough.

Edith Shuler was likely the best-known woman velocipede rider (the convoluted term *velocipedestriennes* was often used) in Chicago. Throughout 1869, Ms. Shuler participated in a traveling velocipede act along with rider, instructor, and rink owner George D. Miles. Newspaper advertisements for their show invariably featured an illustration of Edith riding her velocipede. The velocipede act apparently included a variety of "trick" riding skills, including two people balanced on one velocipede. Their show also featured choreographed riding and time trial races. The *Daily Milwaukee News* said that Shuler was the "embodiment of grace" and "one of the most skillful performers in the country."[34]

Edith Shuler, however, was certainly not the only Illinois velocipedestrienne. *The Chicago Evening Post* ran a story about a performance that featured Shuler and Miss May Graves. Riding in large Victorian dresses would have been impossible, so early women velocipedists had to improvise their outfits. As performers, Schuler and Graves improvised in elaborate fashion. The *Post* article went to great lengths to tantalize readers with details about their dress: "The former wore a blue velvet tunic and red Turkish trousers, which were gathered below the knee, showing a glimpse of white stocking encased in high gaiters. The latter was dressed in black, with tight 'pants'—if the word is not too mannish."[35] At a time when a glimpse of a bare ankle was considered risqué and improper, the paper's description of "high gaiters" and "tight pants" probably served to increase male attendance at future shows. In an article promoting an upcoming performance featuring Shuler, the *Evening Argus* (Rock Island, Illinois) took a different approach in order to recruit women spectators, noting Shuler was a "quiet" and "modest girl" and that "nothing will occur to offend the most refined sensibilities, and the ladies are especially invited to attend."[36] Twenty years before women cyclists popularized split-leg "bloomer" pants, velocipedists in Chicago were pushing the boundaries of gender norms.

The performance that included Miss Shuler and Miss Graves also featured a ten-year-old Miss Brainard who "manipulated a velocipede remarkably well." Astonishingly, Miss Brainard was not the only ten-year-old girl velocipede rider in Chicago. Multiple newspaper advertisements in the spring and summer of 1869 tout the riding prowess of Miss Jennie Durkee, also ten years of age. Durkee's specialty seems to have been riding her golden velocipede on a high wire that was up to thirty feet high.[37] These two girl velocipede riders were possibly the first recorded accounts of a child riding a two-wheeled

Jennie Durkee, trick rider. (From the Historic Cycling Photographic Collection of Lorne Shields, Toronto, Canada.)

velocipede in the United States. From the start, Illinois was at the forefront of pushing bicycle boundaries and development.

The velocipede craze was incredibly short-lived. It built slowly in 1868, exploded throughout 1869, and then fizzled away in 1870. The quick demise of "velocipedomania" had multiple root causes. First, there were the velocipedes themselves. They were heavy, uncomfortable, and difficult to pedal due to the rider's orientation well behind the front wheel. Steel rims and poor roads limited riding mostly to indoor rinks, where the novelty of riding around in tiny circles surely wore off after a few thousand revolutions. Exacerbating matters was the steep costs of purchasing a velocipede, limiting ownership to the upper class. Calvin Witty's $10 licensing fee also cut deeply into manufacturers' profit margins. The final straw was a series of bans in multiple large cities that prevented velocipedes from being ridden on city sidewalks, essentially limiting riding to indoor rinks. Americans had gotten a taste of bicycling, but a widespread national boom was still a number of years away.

The High-Wheel Era

By the early 1870s, velocipedes were largely yesterday's news. There were still exhibition races here and there, and used velocipedes could often be found for sale in secondhand stores. Chicagoans, though, had other things to worry about. The Great Chicago Fire of 1871 had wreaked havoc on the city. Three hundred people were killed, and a third of the city was destroyed, resulting in $200 million worth of damages. Surely, many of the velocipedes that were so popular two years before were lost to the flames. Chicago, however, was quick to rebuild. The blank slate resulting from the fire allowed city leaders to reconfigure downtown Chicago based on the best urban planning principles of the day.[38] Much of the fire debris was pushed into Lake Michigan, conveniently creating the prime lakefront real estate that we know today as Grant Park. The geographical stage was set for Chicago to become one of the leading cities in the country.

Bicycles at this time were slowly evolving to overcome the limitations of the velocipede design. Those improvements would, in time, entice more people into riding. Solid rubber tires became ubiquitous, providing some measure of cushioning and traction. The next major advancement was the wire-spoked wheel. Wire wheels could be built both larger and lighter than the wood or iron-spoked velocipede wheels. Another benefit of the wire-spoked wheel was additional suspension, which further enhanced the ride.[39] Wire-spoked wheels helped to usher in what is known as the "transitional" period to the more familiar high-wheel style of bicycle that featured extreme differences in wheel sizes.

High-Wheel Manufacturing and Patent Wars

Even though overall ridership was low compared to what it would be in the 1890s, Illinois inventors and tinkerers were active during this transitional period between velocipedes and high-wheels. It took a number of years and iterations before any of these new-style bikes were sold in large quantities. In 1875, Chicagoan George W. Marble was issued United States Patent 171,623 for "Improvements in Velocipedes" that consisted of making a child's tricycle simpler and cheaper to build. The following year, Marble received another patent (United States Patent 185,401) for improvements to a two-wheeled children's velocipede. Here again, Marble was simplifying earlier designs and also making bicycles easier to ship by rail, which would become an incredibly important feature in only a few years.

While none of the major velocipede manufacturers survived past the early 1870s, there were a small number of Chicago manufacturers who found a market for children's velocipedes, tricycles, and transitional velocipedes for adults. One of these companies was the St. Nicholas Toy Company, which deserves credit for manufacturing the first American-made transitional high-wheel bicycle. George Marble was one of the owners of the St. Nicholas Toy Company, joining brothers Harry and Heaton Owsley. The company, which first appeared in Chicago papers in 1876, later laid claim to "manufacturing bicycles longer than any other factory in the country."[40] Since all the earlier American velocipede manufacturing companies had gone out of business, and the St. Nicholas Toy Company also predated Pope Manufacturing, this appears to be a legitimate claim. A surviving 1878 catalog gives us better insight into the company's early bicycle endeavors. The St. Nicholas Toy Company had manufacturing facilities and a showroom on the 700 block of West Madison Street. The preface to its catalog indicates that bicycles were quickly becoming a focus for the company: "Please especially consider our new girl's velocipede, which for practicability cannot be excelled; also our men's and youth's bicycles, for which there seems to be a revival in demand." The "Boys Three Wheel Velocipede" is clearly based on Marble's 1876 patent. Most significant, though, is the bicycle designed in "the style of the English Machines now so popular in that country." While lacking the lightweight wire-spoked wheels of later models, it was available in a number of sizes, all the way up to a forty-eight-inch front wheel, with a distinctly smaller rear wheel. This new design was the final transitional step between velocipedes and the fully realized high-wheel bicycles that featured wire-spoked wheels. St. Nicholas's contributions to the early American bicycle market have largely been overlooked.[41]

Soon after this St. Nicholas catalog was issued, Pope Manufacturing began enforcing their newly acquired patent rights, forcing other manufacturers to pay a licensing fee for every bicycle that they produced. In 1879, the St. Nicholas Toy Company began paying Pope one dollar for every bicycle they made with a front wheel under forty-two inches and $2 for larger bicycles.[42] The pinch that the patent control put on manufacturers is made clear by an 1882 *Bicycling World* advertisement, where St. Nicholas is offering forty-four-inch and forty-six-inch bicycles for $45 and $50, respectively, but also notes that larger sizes were available "for export trade only."[43] Exporting bicycles circumvented paying royalties to Pope since those applied only to domestic sales.

Despite running a large company, George Marble was actively working on new bicycle design improvements. In 1884, he filed a new patent application (United States Patent 328,499) for a bicycle that superficially looked like the contemporaneous "Star" models made by New Jersey's H. B. Smith Company.[44] Stars were noted for an inverted high-wheel design, with a small front wheel and a large rear wheel. This feature made them less prone to flipping over forward—an accident known as a "header" that was the result of a dangerous flaw in most high-wheel models. Marble's contribution to bicycle design with this patent was the addition of a chain drive for the rear wheel. The use of chain drives would go on to revolutionize the bicycle industry. The mechanical advantage realized by incorporating gearing allowed a move to smaller (and safer) wheels of equal size. A 1900 *Scientific American* article recapping the first fifty years of bicycle development singled out the importance of this Marble bicycle: "The adjoining machine, dated 1884, represents the first rear-driven chain safety in this country. It was built and patented by George W. Marble. While it was never regularly manufactured, great credit is due to the inventor as having built this machine four years before the safety made its appearance in any numbers."[45]

By the mid-1880s, St. Nicholas was producing adult ordinaries with wheel sizes up to fifty-six inches under the model names Centaur and Acme. At some point, they must have stopped or cut back on paying licensing fees to Pope Manufacturing. In 1883, Pope Manufacturing filed a lawsuit against the St. Nicholas Toy Company for license infringement. After years in court, St. Nicholas lost and had to pay $16,000 in damages.[46] (Not long after, as discussed below, a similar Pope case against Chicago's Gormully & Jeffery made it all the way to the Supreme Court.)

In addition to patent litigation, St. Nicholas Toy Company and other Chicago bicycle manufacturers were enmeshed in the era's tense and frequently violent labor conflicts. In fact, they were directly involved in the labor disputes that led to the infamous Haymarket Riot (or Haymarket Affair) of May 4, 1886. Progressive Era labor reformers had been calling on major Chicago employers to increase workplace safety and implement an eight-hour workday. On

May 4, a crowd composed of unionists, reformers, socialists, and anarchists gathered in Haymarket Square. Toward the end of the meeting, police attacked the gathering, and a bomb was thrown into the crowd. In all, seven policemen and four laborers were killed, and martial law was declared in Chicago and other cities around the country. The crackdown on labor union organizers was swift and severe, leaving the labor movement gravely wounded.[47]

Three days before the riot, a story appeared with a prescient title: "Trouble May Come Yet." The *Chicago Tribune* reported that the "employees of the St. Nicholas Toy Company . . . 150 in number, sent a petition . . . yesterday morning demanding ten hours' pay for eight hours' work."[48] Company owners rebuffed the workers' demands and anticipated a strike. The fallout from the Haymarket Riot squashed workers' hopes at St. Nicholas and other major employers around the country. Shortly after the Haymarket Riot, the *Tribune* reported that rival Chicago bicycle manufacturer Gormully & Jeffery had offered their employees an eight-hour workday at eight hours' wages, although they had conceded on extra pay for overtime hours.[49] These anecdotes suggest that the rise and fall of the Illinois bicycle industry did not occur in a vacuum. Rather, it was destined to be closely aligned with, and emblematic of, the rise and fall of Midwestern manufacturing as a whole.

Chicago's Western Toy Company was the city's other claimant to being one of the earliest bicycle manufacturers in the country; it would go on to become the country's largest in the 1890s. German immigrant Adolph Schoeninger founded Western Toy Company in 1866. In the beginning, the company's primary lines of business were toys, carriages, and furniture. Western Toy's factory and warehouse were among the many casualties of the Great Chicago Fire of 1871. Like so many other Chicagoans, Schoeninger began rebuilding his business almost immediately, although it wasn't officially reincorporated until 1876. Early records of the company—particularly before the Great Chicago Fire—are nonexistent, so it is unclear when Western Toy began producing children's velocipedes.[50] One of George Marble's 1875 bicycle patents was partially owned by Schoeninger, so we can assume that they were producing children's velocipedes before then. In an 1891 article about the company, the *Wheel and Cycling Trade Review* noted that "Adolph Schoeninger is among the pioneers if not the pioneer maker of juvenile cycles in America."[51]

A surviving Western Toy Company catalog shows that, by 1879, the company was primarily focused on bicycles and baby carriages. The company's offices, factories, and warehouses were on the 400 and 500 blocks of North Wells Street. The catalog notes that "we have added four sizes of an improved Bicycle, the two largest of which are adapted for men's use."[52] The bicycle for "men's use" was called the Otto and was available with wheel sizes up to forty-two inches, marking it as yet another transitional bicycle made in Chicago. Like the St. Nicholas bicycles, the 1879 Otto did not yet feature wire spokes, but instead utilized wooden hickory spokes. The cost for the forty-two-inch Otto was a very reasonable $20. In addition to the Otto, Western Toy then sold a variety of smaller tricycles.

The Western Toy Company also bowed to pressure from Pope Manufacturing and began paying for licenses to manufacture bicycles in 1879.[53] During the 1880s, Western Toy steadily increased the quality and quantity of its bicycle offerings. In 1887, it launched a new ordinary called the Rival, billed as "fully equal, in some respects superior, to the best Bicycles made." The Rival was available in sizes ranging from forty-six to fifty-four inches and cost between $63 and $73. The 1887 catalog also featured a number of adult tricycles marketed toward women and the elderly.[54]

Gormully & Jeffery (G&J) was another of the early Chicago ordinary bicycle manufacturers that got their start around the same time as the St. Nicholas Toy Company and Western Toy Company. The firm was founded by English immigrants and school friends R. Philip Gormully and Thomas B. Jeffery. Both Gormully and Jeffery were involved in other business ventures before easing their way into bicycle manufacturing. In later years, the company would claim to have begun manufacturing bicycles in Chicago in 1878, but contemporary documentary evidence is lacking to substantiate these claims. *Wheels and Wheeling, an Indispensable Handbook for Cyclists*, published in 1892, cites 1879 as the first year of business for Gormully & Jeffery.[55] They were certainly manufacturing bicycles before receiving a license from Pope Manufacturing in March of 1880.[56] Thomas Jeffery appeared in an 1881 Chicago city directory under the heading of "Velocipedes," while Gormully & Jeffery Manufacturing Company is first listed in 1884. They began operations on Canal Street but had moved to the 200 block of North Franklin Street by the mid-1880s. In later company catalogs, G&J would proudly claim to have established the first factory in the world dedicated purely to manufacturing bicycles. Their claim is plausible, since most factories in the earliest days of the high-wheel era also manufactured other items, such as guns, sewing machines, or agricultural implements.[57]

From the very beginning, Gormully & Jeffery was intent on creating its own distinct, high-grade bicycles. Thomas B. Jeffery was possibly the most prolific of bicycle inventors from this era. Bicycle historian Gary Sanderson has identified an astonishing 212 bicycle-related patents granted to Thomas B. Jeffery from 1882 to 1900.[58] These patents were quickly incorporated into Gormully & Jeffery bicycles. G&J found early success with their Ideal (up to fifty-inch wheel) and Youth's Ideal, and then later in the 1880s with two models, the American Challenge and American Champion, which were available with wheels larger than fifty inches.

It was these two adult ordinaries that Pope claimed ran afoul of their strict licensing agreements, leading to a series of court cases that went all the way to the Supreme Court. Gormully & Jeffery became one of the largest bicycle manufacturers in the world in the 1890s and later transitioned into making Rambler automobiles. Yet its most significant contribution to American bicycling, and American manufacturing rights writ large, was a legal triumph over Pope Manufacturing's attempts to monopolize the American bicycle market.

Multiple fledgling American bicycle manufacturers were skeptical of Pope's continued enforcement of his acquired patent licenses. Jeffery, who had extensive experience with patents, reviewed the patents that Pope's licenses were based on and concluded that "they were worthless and if contested would not be worth the paper they were written on."[59] Under patent law, the original Lallement patent expired in 1886. Chafing at having to pay Pope a $10 fee on every bicycle that it made, Gormully & Jeffery ceased making payments and geared up for the inevitable lawsuit. *Pope Mfg. Co. v. Gormully* would drag on for four and a half years and went all the way up to the United States Supreme Court. The *American Athlete and Cycle Trades Review* ensured that their readers recognized the significance of the case for the American bicycle industry, writing, "this means that the days of the monopoly in the manufacture of high-grade cycles are numbered, and as a consequence bicycles are bound to come down in price . . . this will be good news to all lovers of the sport."[60] In 1891, the Supreme Court found in Gormully & Jeffery's favor and invalidated Pope's licenses. Illinois-based Gormully & Jeffery ending the Pope monopoly and the invention of the safety-style bicycle were the two crucial elements setting the stage for the great American bicycle boom of the 1890s.

Prior to the resolution of this case, manufacturers had learned that one simple way to avoid paying licensing fees to Pope was to import bicycles from other countries. These bicycles would be subject to import tariffs, but since they were made overseas, American patent licensing was not required. This appears to have been the approach of a well-known Chicago-based sporting goods company, A.G. Spalding & Bros. Albert Spalding had made a name for himself as a pitcher with the Boston Red Stockings (1871–75). Next, he moved to Chicago, where he both pitched for and managed the White Stockings (1876–77). In 1876, Spalding and his brother opened a sporting goods store in Chicago, leveraging A.G. Spalding's name recognition as a marketing tactic.[61] A.G. Spalding & Bros. advertisements that include bicycles can be found in the *Chicago Tribune* as early as 1881. An 1883 A.G. Spalding bicycle catalog lists no less than ten different ordinary models and six tricycles. Of these, the catalog states that five (Yale, Harvard, Shadow Light Roadster, Premier No. 0, and Fairfield) were manufactured exclusively for Spalding by four different English firms. In addition to the English models, Spalding also sold a few St. Nicholas and Columbia models. Spalding seemed keenly attuned to public demand, so much so that its 1888 catalog featured only a single ordinary and instead promoted three brand-new safety bicycle models.[62] Like the Western Toy Company and Gormully & Jeffery, A.G. Spalding went on to become a major manufacturer and mail-order seller of bicycles during the boom of the 1890s.

At this early stage of American bicycle history, most of the Illinois action was centered around Chicago—most, but certainly not all. In the 1880s, the industrial and agricultural hub of Peoria was the second-largest city in the state. Rouse, Hazard & Company was established there in 1864 as an agricultural implements wholesaler and distributor. In 1879, the company began importing European bicycles to sell alongside early American models. Harry (H. G.) Rouse was an early bicycle enthusiast. In 1880, as part of the formation of the League of American Wheelmen, he was elected the first co-director for the Illinois division. Rouse, Hazard & Company claimed to be the first major mail-order company to sell bicycles (both new and used) on installment plans, making them more affordable for the average American.

Another significant development from Peoria was the 1884 invention of an ordinary with a novel gearing system. Brothers Arthur and Frank Beavis received United States Patent 318,532, which contained the following important piece of information about their bicycle design: "If it is desired to turn the drive-wheel faster than the pedal, the gear E is made smaller than the pedal-gear D, while if a slower motion is wished the converse relation is made between said gears."[63] While this geared ordinary was never commercially produced, the related patent is one of the earliest in the country to experiment with gearing. F. S. Beavis would go on to work for Rouse & Hazard before manufacturing his own line of safety bicycles in the 1890s.

Nineteenth-century cycling publications frequently recognized the importance of Illinois as a center of American bicycling. Its close geographical proximity to bicycle manufacturers led to a higher concentration of bicyclists and a richer bicycle culture than most other places. In 1883, *The Wheelman* noted, "Chicago has probably more wheelmen than any other city in the country, Boston and Philadelphia excepted; and even they will be left in the rear if they do not wake up, for Chicago is, in this respect, as in all others, the most wide-awake, energetic, progressive city in the land. . . . The time will soon come when Chicago wheelmen can ride around the entire city on the finest boulevards ever constructed."[64] This was far from the last time that Chicago would be singled out for such bicycling accolades.

The Emergence of Bicycle Clubs and Bicycle Culture

Even from the earliest days, bicycling was seen as more than an individual source of recreation or means of transportation. It was a social undertaking that advocates claimed could mitigate a variety of social ills. Bicycle clubs were key to bringing cyclists together and furthering the development of early bicycle culture. An early edition of the *Wheelman* magazine described the impetus to form clubs as "the natural outgrowth of friendly intercourse on the road. It becomes a centre for social meetings, where many, otherwise friendless, find society and a refuge from ennui and loneliness, and from temptation to seek objectionable distractions."[65] Boston and New York City appear to have organized the first official bicycle clubs in 1878. Once again, Illinois was close behind with the founding of the Chicago Bicycle Club on September 1, 1879. The twelve founding members were originally headquartered at 279 State Street but soon after began sharing a clubhouse with the Racquet Club at 185 Michigan Avenue. The club had a $2 initiation fee and $1 annual dues. In a quintessential Chicago entrepreneurial move, the club later reorganized itself as a stock company to increase revenue and fund building projects. By 1885, the club had grown to one hundred members.[66]

Other Illinois bicycle clubs soon formed, many of which should be counted among the earliest in the country. The Peoria Bicycle and Athletic Club, formed in 1880, was the ninth club in the country to register with the League of American Wheelmen, which was also founded that year.[67] Chicago's Elgin Bicycle Club also formed in 1880, and the Hermes Cycling Club was organized the following year. The first documented case of Illinois women being admitted to a cycling club came in 1884 with the organization of the Dearborn Cycling Club, which counted among its members Miss Florence Fuller, Miss Durrell, and Miss J. O. Blake.[68] When interviewed by the *L.A.W. Bulletin* in 1883, Fuller gushed, "I have been for some time very enthusiastic on the subject of tricycling . . . I have ridden a great many miles in the past two years, and take long and frequent rides alone, for there is then a certain feeling of independence. My health has improved wonderfully, and my strength, well—I surprise my brother sometimes." The same article estimated that there were forty women tricyclists in Chicago at the time.[69]

Collectively, Chicago's cycling clubs wielded considerable political power. As early as 1882, Chicago cyclists banded together to ensure the overturning of local laws requiring them to dismount when a horse approached and prohibiting bicycling in Lincoln Park.[70] Allowing cyclists to access the best roads, paths, and boulevards was yet another critical step in setting the stage for a bicycle boom.

Despite its growing popularity, bicycling in the 1880s was largely an elitist endeavor undertaken by middle- and upper-class white men. It remained an expensive undertaking even before club initiation fees and dues were considered. Most high-wheel bicycles cost over $100 at a time when the average unskilled laborer made around $1.40 per hour. Some cyclists actually celebrated the fact that expensive bicycles naturally excluded immigrants and the lower classes. As one rider put it in a candid display of bigotry, "I believe that, while in its infancy, it is for the best that the wheel is something not within the easy reach of all. This very fact, I think, has given us, on the whole, a gentlemanly class of riders that we would not have had were Patsy O'Rafferty and Hans Schneider able to secure mounts without having to make some real effort to that end."[71] Bicycling in the 1880s reinforced class status and signified wealth. In a few short years, the rhetoric surrounding bicycles as egalitarian transportation would come to predominate. However, elitism and class exclusiveness in bicycling have persisted as problems into the twenty-first century.

In 1882, Chicago hosted the third annual meeting of the League of American Wheelmen (L.A.W.). Formed in 1880 by delegates from many state clubs and organizations, L.A.W. existed "to ascertain, defend and protect the rights of wheelmen [and] to encourage and facilitate touring." State L.A.W. divisions then formed in support of the national organization. After the L.A.W. held its first annual meets in Newport and then Boston, Chicago lobbied hard to bring the next meet west. Held from May 30 to June 1, 1882, the Chicago gathering featured organized rides, races, a grand parade, and a business meeting. Quarter-mile, mile, and two-mile races were held at the Driving Park on the West Side of Chicago. According to local papers, the "slow race" was the highlight of the day. Slow races were won by riders with exceptional balance who took the longest amount of time to ride one hundred yards without falling over. Chicagoan Edward Brown won with the slowest time of three minutes and sixteen seconds. A series of "marine bicycle" races also took place in the basin of Lake Front Park, although it is unclear what precisely they entailed. The grand parade the following day was a fifteen-mile tour around the city. The downtown portion was led by thirty Chicago policemen and a band on a bandwagon. A couple hundred wheelmen participated in the parade, and there were dubious (contemporary newspapers were prone to sensationalism) claims of 50,000 spectators in the local press. Mayor Carter Henry Harrison III delivered an evening speech to hundreds of the gathered wheelmen in which he lauded bicycles and pledged his support for future bicycle efforts in the city. His son would later become an avid cyclist who followed in his father's footsteps, winning the 1897 mayoral race with the backing of Chicago's bicycle lobby.[72]

Chicago began embracing bicycle culture in other ways beyond bicycle clubs. Velocipede stage performances, which had been popular in the late 1860s, became more refined in the high-wheel era. Chicago's many theater venues routinely brought in bicycling acts. In 1881, the Academy of Music on Halsted Street advertised a performance of Stirk's Troupe of Male and Female

Marvelous Bicycle Equestrians. According to the program, this English act had appeared "before all the royalty of Europe." In 1882, Sprague's Olympic Theatre on Clark Street featured the Martells, bicycle acrobats touted as "The Greatest Bicycle Act on the Stage."[73]

High-Wheel Racing

The increased wheel sizes of ordinaries made for much more exciting—and dangerous—races. Since the transition from velocipedes to full-size (50–58-inch) ordinaries was gradual, there is no reliable way to mark the exact beginning of the high-wheel racing era. Whereas the top speed of a velocipede may have been 12–15 mph over a short distance, a skilled ordinary racer could attain speeds of over 25 mph. Factor into the equation that the tops of riders' heads were often upwards of eight feet off the ground, and you have the makings of a popular new spectator sport.

In 1879, Illinois hosted the first American six-day race. This race format was another European import courtesy of Harry Etherington, a promoter, journalist, publisher, and all-around bicycle enthusiast who helped to organize the first European six-day races in 1878 and 1879. A six-day race is as simple as it was brutal; the goal was to see how many miles an individual, or team, could cover in six days (Sunday riding was forbidden on religious grounds). In the 1880s, most six-day races allowed racers to compete for "only" twelve hours a day. Later, six-day races would become even more brutal tests of endurance with round-the-clock riding for 144 hours. Having achieved some success with the six-day format in England, Etherington brought a team of the best European riders to the United States in late 1879. Before crossing the Atlantic, Etherington published the following challenge in the *American Bicycling Journal*: "To give our 'cousins' an equal chance, I will handicap my team singly or collectively, to give all comers starts from 75, 100 to 150 or 200 miles in a six days' race, the races to be contested for in any large city in the United States where a suitable building and good track can be found."[74]

First to step up to this challenge was Boston, with the enthusiastic support of the Pope Manufacturing Company. The Boston track was set up inside a large tent, but due to freezing November temperatures and high winds, the event had to be shortened to five days of racing.[75] With a mere two weeks of rest, the Europeans headed to Chicago, where they staged another six-day bicycle race, the first one in American history to actually last the full six days. The race was held on a ⅛-mile indoor track at the Exposition Building. Local papers noted that the track would be lit by electric light and "thoroughly heated."[76] (The presence of electric light was remarkable, since Thomas Edison had only managed to create a reliable incandescent bulb earlier that same year.) Since the Europeans were experienced "professional" riders using the most up-to-date English bicycles, Etherington allowed the American amateurs a one-hundred-mile handicap for the Chicago event. The format of the Chicago race would be fourteen hours a day, beginning at 10:00 a.m. and finishing at midnight, and the winner would be determined by the combined distance of the top two riders from each team.

The race began on November 24 and featured an astonishingly large prize purse of $4,000 ($122,000 in 2024). Several thousand spectators, including a few hundred women, paid fifty cents each to witness the first day of competition. Later in the week, three thousand spectators (based on actual ticket sales) were in attendance. At the end of six days, the two riders on the European team had pedaled a collective 1,665 miles (or 13,320 laps!) while the American team, including their handicap, totaled 1,658 miles. Had a serious accident not taken out Daniel Belard, the top American rider, midweek, the final results would surely have been reversed. The riders had a meager two days off their bicycles before participating in another series of shorter races at the Exposition Building.[77]

Etherington's tour, which continued after Chicago, can be pinpointed as the beginning of the long, rich, history of six-day bicycle racing in America. Six-day races would grow to become incredibly popular events throughout the 1890s and beyond; some are still held to this day.

Although no Illinoisans were part of that first six-day race, the state soon produced many riders who quickly rose through the ranks of American bicycle racing. In 1881, George H. Craig of Chicago established records of 2:55 for the mile, 15:40 for five miles, and 38:25 for ten miles. These were certainly among the top times of the day (although the *Chicago Daily Tribune's* claim that Craig was entitled "to the amateur championship of the United States" was somewhat of a stretch).[78] Taking advantage of the city's many top-notch racing tracks were John S. Prince (an English immigrant living in Boston) and Chicagoan William Woodside. Prince set the American record of 333 miles (14 mph) for twenty-four hours of riding in Chicago on October 23, 1883. He then set another American record of 6:50:55 (14.5 mph) for one hundred miles on the 28th. In Chicago the following year, Woodside set the American record for fifty miles with his time of 2:54:01 (17.2 mph).

The Chicago Bicycle Track Association was formed in 1885 to promote and coordinate races in the city. The association worked with A.G. Spalding to build a top-notch quarter-mile racing track around the ball diamond of a new $30,000 stadium. This stadium was the new home for the Chicago White Stockings, a team with deep historical connections to both the Chicago Cubs and the Chicago White Sox.[79] Located at Congress and Throop, the new West Side Park stadium was described as "without doubt the finest [ballpark] in America, and . . . probably not surpassed by any athletic grounds in the world."[80] At the time, revenues from baseball ticket sales alone were

Mid- to late-1880s high-wheel bicycle race in Chicago. (From the Historic Cycling Photographic Collection of Lorne Shields, Toronto, Canada.)

not enough to fund such a facility, so bicycle races were added to bring in large numbers of paying spectators on days that there weren't baseball games. Conveniently, Spalding's sporting goods store also profited from increased bicycle sales.

Another bicycling first occurred downstate in Springfield. There, in 1886, racer, trainer, and race promoter Tom Eck built the first fully banked indoor racetrack for cyclists and roller skaters.[81] Banking a track all the way around helps to control the substantial centrifugal forces generated while riding quickly around a small oval and thus allows for higher overall speeds. Fully banked tracks became the norm for bicycle racing after Eck's innovation.

Albert Schock

Another of Tom Eck's bicycle endeavors involved training and promoting one of his protegees, Chicago racer Albert Schock. Schock was a nineteenth-century endurance junkie who specialized in six-day races of all sorts. Prior to taking up cycling, Schock had competed in long-distance competitive walking, known as "pedestrianism." In the 1870s and 1880s, pedestrian competitions were hugely popular events with spectators. Schock's specialty was six-day walking contests. In 1877, he won a six-day, ten-hours-per-day contest at Chicago's Tivoli Gardens, covering 421 miles. At a twelve-hours-per-day event in St. Paul, Minnesota, he earned the "Champion of America" title by walking 523 miles. It was his first championship title, but far from his last. Later, having taken up competitive long-distance roller skating, he surpassed 1,000 miles in a six-day contest held in New York's Madison Square Garden.[82]

Schock gained worldwide fame when he took up six-day bicycle racing. In 1884 he earned one of his first wins as a cyclist in Memphis, Tennessee. Despite having only learned to ride the year before, Schock challenged a team of five horses to a six-day race. The race was neck and neck, but Schock won out, finishing with 611 miles to the horses' 600.[83] The next major milestone in Schock's cycling career was a six-day, twelve-hours-per-day race in Minnesota. In March of 1886, Schock amassed 1,009 miles over six days, breaking the previous world record of 1,007 miles, set in 1880 by Englishman Fred J. Lees. This works out to an astonishing average of fourteen miles per hour, including any breaks he might have taken. This feat clinched the "Championship of America" title for Schock and was also a world record. The *Saint Paul Globe* gushed that Schock was "truly the wonder of the country."[84]

Schock was not inclined to rest on his laurels. His next big six-day race, held at the end of December 1886, was a showdown with up-and-comer W. J. Morgan. The format for this race was changed to the even more grueling "come-as-you-go" model, meaning that the race went on continuously for twenty-four hours a day, with riders taking breaks only when they felt it was absolutely necessary. Racing a Gormully & Jeffery American Champion, Schock ground out 1,405 miles over the course of six days, soundly defeating Morgan by 240 miles. At this time, the design and utility of safety-style bicycles was rapidly improving, and in short order, racers started migrating to those lighter and faster machines. For this reason, Schock's 1886 record of 1,405 miles remains the world record for a six-day race on a high-wheel.[85]

As impressive as Schock's ride was in this new come-as-you-go format, many of the newspaper headlines went to another Chicagoan, who finished third in the same event with 1,050 miles. Her name was Louise Armaindo.[86]

Louise Armaindo

Mlle. Louise Armaindo was a French-Canadian, who moved to Chicago in the 1870s. Like so many riders before her, Armaindo cut her sporting chops in weightlifting and competitive walking before finding success on the bicycle. Armaindo had a compact and strong build. Standing a mere five feet, three inches tall and weighing 135 pounds, she was nonetheless able to lift 760 pounds at the Chicago Athenaeum in 1878.[87] Since there were only a handful of competitive women cyclists at the time, Armaindo often ended up racing against men. For some of her first races in 1882, she was given small handicaps while competing against serious professional male cyclists like Thomas Eck and Fred Rollison. She easily won these handicapped events. Next, Armaindo was the main attraction for a six-day, twelve-hours-a-day event in St. Louis, Missouri. This race was held in March of 1882 in Armory Hall, which contained a dizzyingly small seventeen-laps-per-mile track. Her stated goal was to ride at least one hundred miles a day for each of the six days. In an era where medical doctors warned women that riding at all might cause infertility or permanent physical damage, Armaindo's unprecedented attempt attracted large paying crowds. True to her goal, she completed 617 miles (or 10,489 laps) over the course of the event.

The only other woman rider with a resume to match Armaindo's was New Yorker Elsa Von Blumen. In 1881, Von Blumen had managed to ride 1,000 miles in a six-day, go-as-you-please event. She had numerous wins at shorter events, so an eventual matchup with Armaindo was inevitable. In July of 1882, the two champion women cyclists met in Philadelphia for a six-day short-distance event featuring an intense series of five two-mile heats each day. On

Louise Armaindo, champion high-wheel bicycle racer. (From the Historic Cycling Photographic Collection of Lorne Shields, Toronto, Canada.)

the line was a $1,000 purse and the Female Champion of America title. The result was a rout, with Armaindo winning twenty-one of the thirty heats. A fifty-mile rematch was held in August at Coney Island, New York, with the same result; Armaindo finished twelve miles ahead of Von Blumen.

Male racers had begun to take Armaindo seriously, although many refused to race her. Beginning on May 21, 1883, Chicago hosted a six-day, twelve-hours-a-day, long-distance "Championship of America." Armaindo's competitors were professional racers William Woodside and William Morgan. Well aware of Armaindo's abilities, the men granted her no handicap in this race. Armaindo had grown to be a crowd favorite wherever she went. She began the Chicago championship race wearing a flamboyant "ultramarine-blue outfit, 'splashed' with scarlet, knit fitted body tights, and a jockey cap."[88] The racing was close the first few days, but Armaindo slowly built up a lead. The final results were Armaindo 843 miles, Morgan 829, and Woodside 723. In a head-to-head competition with talented male riders, she had proved herself, and her sex, superior. Through methodical riding, she eventually built an insurmountable lead. "No one can have any idea how I had to punish myself to hold to the end," she said at the end of the race, "but I had determined to beat those two men, and I did it."[89] The country took notice. An article published in an Arizona newspaper opined, "The Belt has always been willing to concede to the gentler sex, bigger hearts and clearer brains than men—in view of the fact that Louise Armaindo won the championship, as a bicyclist against the best men . . . we'll have to concede to them stronger limbs and greater endurance."[90] Two years after the Chicago championship, a cycling record book still listed Armaindo as the record holder for most miles ridden over the course of forty-eight and seventy-two hours.[91] This wasn't some one-off race with poor performances from the men; Armaindo's mileage record held up as the best in the country—for both genders—for years after.

Frustrated, Woodside issued a challenge for a rematch at any distance. Only a week later, Armaindo again beat both Woodside and Morgan, this time at a 120-mile race in Janesville, Wisconsin. In 1886, she lost a New York six-day race to Morgan by the margin of one mile. Apparently, the two competitors were on good terms, since they teamed up two weeks later to shatter a number of tandem records. The end of 1886 saw the six-day race in Minneapolis in which Armaindo lost to Albert Schock and Morgan but managed to surpass the one-thousand-mile mark.[92]

In 1888, Armaindo married twenty-one-year-old Norman Stewart, who sometimes found work as a traveling salesman. Little is known about their brief courtship and wedding. What we do know is that not long after their nuptials, Norman stopped working and instead followed Louise around the country, living off of her earnings. In 1889, Armaindo fell ill and attempted to recuperate in Omaha, Nebraska. Norman had been nagging her to return to racing and bring in more money. Eventually, he turned abusive. A local paper reported the result:

> Norman dropped in and began worrying her and concluded by striking her as she lay in the bed. Forbearance has ceased to be regarded by the little Frenchwoman as a virtue, and after a season of abuse she rose from her bed, and seizing the stripling husband by the scruff of the neck, she slammed him against the wall, and across the bed and over the trunk, and down the stairway to the ground floor.[93]

Throughout her career, Louise had challenged prevailing Victorian gender and social norms. She did not sit back and take abuse from any man, let alone her husband.

By 1889, the high-wheel era was quickly drawing to a close; however, a marquee event showcased the twelve best women racers in the country. The location was Madison Square Garden, and the format was a six-day race with eight hours of riding per day. This race featured old rivals Armaindo and Von Blumen, along with several younger, up-and-coming racers. Armaindo was the favorite and she let it be known, but a bad crash on the first day took her out of serious contention. On the final night, 6,000 spectators witnessed Lottie Stanley complete 624 miles to win the women's six-day title.

The presence of twelve women competitors racing for six days challenged adages about hard physical exercise causing women permanent damage. By this point, many women ordinary racers had competed for years and were no worse for the wear; some had become mothers without complications. Ideas about women's rights and autonomy were slowly beginning to change, but many Victorian men (and a considerable number of women) adamantly maintained that a woman's place was still the hearth and home. Critics of women's bicycle racing simply deemed it scandalous. The conservative editor of *Bicycling World and L.A.W. Bulletin* wrote against the spectacle of women racers, "when it comes to a question of women bestriding an ordinary, and riding around a track for the purpose of being guyed [i.e., ridiculed] by a curious public." He added, "I had thought that this type of cycling disgrace met its birth and death in the performance of Louise Armaindo, but alas I was mistaken."[94]

A generation of Progressive reformers would soon champion the bicycle as an agent and symbol of women's liberation. Many of the twelve women who competed in the famous six-day ordinary race at Madison Square Garden went on to compete on a new type of bicycle: the safety. This was the bicycle that launched a boom like no other. As the statistics and stories shared above indicate, the bicycle boom was deep and broad, not least in Illinois. The full scope of the bicycle boom was much larger and permeated American culture to a far greater degree than most histories have recognized. As the decade progressed, Illinois became the clear leader of the boom.

2

The Great Bicycle Boom of the 1890s

How Illinois Became the Center of American Cycling

Bicycling was bad for horse riding. More precisely, it was bad for the horse trade and the many businesses that supported the use of horses as a major form of transportation. The bicycle boom led to a precipitous decline in horse-related industries, with the annual losses estimated at as much as $20 million ($722 million in 2024). Many carriage and harness makers, breeders, livery stables, and farriers went bankrupt. Some chose to adapt by converting their former stable spaces into bicycle storage. One source in 1895 estimated that Chicago's horse population had declined by 75,000 over just a few years. When asked about the state of his Chicago-based livery business in 1898, one proprietor responded, "Do you remember what a horse looks like? . . . Very few people do, I believe. Bicycling has killed the livery business. Killed it as dead as Moses."[1]

As contemporary newspapers and magazines pointed out, horses were expensive to purchase, with saddles, harnesses, carriages, and stabling consuming additional funds and time. The new style of "safety bicycles," on the other hand, were getting cheaper every year. They also required a relatively small amount of maintenance; for starters, they didn't need to be fed. Late nineteenth-century transportation options were quite limited. In rural areas, walking, riding a horse, or riding in a horse-drawn carriage were the only real options. City dwellers had access to railroads, electric streetcars, and carriages, but each of these came with a cost as well as inflexible schedules and routes.

The decline of the horse trade was one of many ways that the bicycle boom of the 1890s impacted the larger American economy. This was to be expected, given the size of the boom. By the late 1890s, contemporary sources estimated that there were four to five million bicycle riders in the United States out of an overall American population of around only seventy million and an urban pop-

Illinois Cycling Club members and clubhouse, circa 1890. (Courtesy of the Chicago History Museum.)

ulation of around thirty million. Serious riders and racers joined the L.A.W., which reached a peak of 103,000 members in 1898. (In 2018, by comparison, the distantly related League of American Bicyclists had 17,000 members.)[2] In 1896, the president of the L.A.W. valued the total bicycle economy in the United States at $75 million ($2.7 billion in 2024). This figure included thousands of factories, which employed 60,000 workers combined, churning out more than a million bicycles per year (many of which were destined to be exported around the globe). There were around 30,000 bicycle dealers spread across the country. From 1892 to 1896, an astonishing one-third of all patents filed in the United States were related to bicycles, an average of 25,000 per year.[3]

The economic impacts of the bicycle during the mid-to-late 1890s were broad and deep. In an 1896 article on "The Ravages of the Bicycle Craze," *Scientific American* reported that theater ticket sales were the worst in years. During prime cycling season, Chicago theaters were forced to close on Sundays due to lack of interest. Many watchmakers and jewelers were forced out of business or (as was the case for Elgin's Illinois Watch Case Company and Peoria's F. F. Ide Manufacturing Company) turned to bicycle manufacturing instead. Tobacco manufacturers attributed their losses to bicyclists smoking seven hundred million fewer cigars annually. Brewers, distillers, and saloonkeepers bemoaned $2.5 million in lost profits due to cyclists needing to maintain a clear head while riding. The piano trade had been reduced by half, to the tune of $13.5 million in annual losses. Shoemakers claimed they were the worst off of all, since bicyclists "buy cheap shoes for the bicycle, they do not even wear these out, and they refrain from walking much in any kind of shoes whatever."[4]

An important variable in all these economic travails was the fact that the peak of the bicycle boom coincided with a severe economic depression that affected most of the country. The Panic of 1893 was, in the words of the Federal Reserve, "one of the most severe financial crises in the history of the United States." From 1893 to 1897, falling gold reserves triggered the failure of five hundred banks. The bank failures in turn led to the failure of 15,000 companies and an unemployment rate that rocketed to between 15 and 19 percent. In the midst of this depression, it was easy for some to make an economic scapegoat out of bicycles. Clearly, though, the concurrent rise of the bicycle and economic depression worked in tandem to decimate the profits of certain industries. In an era of squeezed disposable incomes, the American middle class still spent millions of dollars on bicycles, bicycle accessories, and bicycle services—money that was not available to be spent elsewhere.[5]

The fact that the American bicycle industry managed to grow by leaps and bounds during a serious economic depression is a testament to the true depths of the bicycle craze during the 1890s.

The Bicycle Boom in Context

Chicago during the last decade of the nineteenth century was one of the fastest-growing cities in the country. From 1890 to 1900, its population nearly doubled in size, growing from around one million to 1.7 million and becoming the second-largest city in the country, behind New York. Chicago was growing spatially as well. Between 1880 and 1890, it quintupled in size from 35 to 178 square miles.[6]

Illinois, and Chicago in particular, was the center of a surge of interest in bicycling that remained unmatched in the United States until the 1970s. As early as 1890, other parts of the country were acknowledging Illinois as one of the most important centers of cycling in the country: "As a cycling centre Chicago is, as in most other things, away ahead. Talk to the riders here and they laugh at you if you pretend to believe that Boston, New York or Philadelphia go ahead of the great Lake City in anything that appertains to cycling." The writer noted, based on firsthand observation, that Chicago's "magnificent roads" were "away ahead of that of Philadelphia."[7] "Chicago is the bicycle center of the United States," the *Chicago Tribune* confidently declared in

1896, backing up the claim with nearly a full page of bicycle-related statistics and stories. The paper estimated that Chicago had 200,000 riders, including 40,000 women and 2,000 children. Chicago's total investment in bicycling (including consumer goods, factories, racing, and repair) was estimated at $33 million ($1.2 billion in 2024). The *Tribune* also noted that the city led the country in bicycle manufacturing, producing an estimated 250,000 bicycles annually (25 percent of the total national output). Bicycle manufacturing was quickly becoming one of Chicago's top industries, with the city's twenty-five largest bicycle manufacturers employing between 5,000 and 8,000 workers. As described in the next chapter, Chicago's Western Wheel Works had grown to become the country's leading bicycle manufacturer. Even as the boom crested around 1897, Western Wheel Works was able to produce and sell an astonishing 100,000 bicycles in 1898 and 1899.[8]

When attempting to capture the full magnitude of the bicycle boom across a state or across the country, estimates are inevitable. Fortunately, due to a wager between two Chicagoans that was covered in the *Chicago Daily Tribune*, we also have relatively reliable counts of how many bicycle commuters entered downtown Chicago in both 1896 and 1898. The wager hinged on a disagreement over the number of Chicagoans utilizing bicycles to commute to work. To settle the bet, counts were made by observers stationed at the main downtown thoroughfares, including Michigan Avenue, Jackson Boulevard, Washington Boulevard, Clark Street, and Dearborn Street. In May of 1896, between 6:00 and 9:00 a.m., 4,943 riders were counted entering downtown Chicago. Two years later, at the peak of the bicycle boom, the counts were repeated, and it was discovered that bicycle commuters had more than doubled in number to 10,522. In 1898, ridership peaked between 7:30 and 8:00 a.m., when an "irresistible tidal wave of men and women, ten or more abreast" yielded an astonishing count of 211 riders per minute on Jackson Boulevard. (For context, the busiest bike paths in the twenty-first century bicycling mecca of Copenhagen, Denmark, total a mere 38 riders per minute). The 1898 Chicago count also found 521 women and 300 boys under the age of twelve. Black bicycle commuters totaled 134, representing a 300 percent increase over 1896. These actual counts for Black and women cyclists have particular historical significance since they provide a reliable snapshot of the participation of these two demographics in bicycling. The paper was careful to note that the actual numbers would have been even higher since "many an uncounted rider slipped through in the scrimmage."[9]

Urban streets weren't the only ones filling with bicycles. While the bicycle boom originated in major cities on the East Coast and in the Midwest, the phenomenon also quickly spread to smaller cities and rural areas. By 1898, an estimated two-thirds of all vehicles on rural country roads were bicycles.[10]

Why did Illinois become the top manufacturer of safety bicycles and the heart of the American bicycle culture? At the most fundamental level, the answers lie in topography, geography, proximity to natural resources, and urban planning. The topography of central and northern Illinois consists of flat farmland or rolling prairies. Critically, Chicago's lakefront topography was also highly conducive to early bicycles. The vast majority of safety bicycles made before 1900 had only a single gear. This was problematic in the mountainous, or even moderately hilly, terrain found in many other parts of the country. A cyclist in the 1890s could easily install a set of low gears designed for hill climbing, but riding over flat land with the same set of gears would have been an exercise in frustration. Conversely, larger gears that enabled fast speeds over flat terrain would often require dismounting and pushing one's bike up a hill. All safety bicycles at the time were what we would now call a "fixed-gear" bicycle. On a fixed-gear bicycle, the pedals have to turn with the wheels; there is no ability to coast without taking your feet off the pedals. Fixed-gears combined with rudimentary braking systems made descending a particularly dangerous endeavor. The flat land covering much of Illinois was therefore very friendly to novice bicyclists.

An older transportation innovation of the nineteenth century, the railroad, made Chicago a logical manufacturing center. A vast rail network radiated out from Chicago, connecting it to the rest of the country and making it the hub of the nation west of the Appalachians. This rail network was instrumental in the success of Illinois's many bicycle manufacturers. The railroads allowed finished bicycles to be shipped out from Illinois, but they also brought the necessary raw materials into the state. The Lake Superior region of Michigan, Michigan's Upper Peninsula, and Wisconsin were all nearby sources of iron ore. This ore was critical, as the production of Illinois bicycles rose into the hundreds of thousands annually by the late 1890s.

Lastly, forward-thinking urban planners in Chicago facilitated the boom. By 1892, Chicago could boast of an amazing 774 miles of "paved" streets. Road engineering was still in its infancy, so a variety of materials were used with varying degrees of success. Far and away the most common road surface was the aforementioned wood-block Nicolson pavement. Lumber was cheap and plentiful, so it is no surprise that in 1892 Chicago had 481 miles of Nicolson pavement. Ideally, the Nicolson system utilized rot-resistant cedar blocks, but other hardwoods, or even pine, could be used in a pinch. The blocks were dipped in tar and oriented with their much harder end grain facing up. Fine gravel or sand was then used to lock the blocks into place. A square yard only cost about one dollar, including installation. When constructed to Nicolson's specifications, these wood-block streets proved to be very durable and easy to maintain. In fact, a few sections of nineteenth-century Nicolson pavement have survived in Chicago to this day. The other pavement options utilized in Chicago were 256 miles of macadam (a crushed gravel system), 23 miles of stone, 9 miles of sheet asphalt, 3 miles of asphalt brick, and a half mile of brick. By 1897, Chicago's "paved" streets had exceeded the 1,000-mile mark. Cedar block was still the most popular surface with 726 miles, followed by 332 miles of macadam.[11]

Another one of Chicago's forward-thinking urban planning decisions was the establishment of the country's first boulevard system. Beginning in the 1860s, Chicago planners laid out a series of large public parks that encircled downtown Chicago and were connected by boulevards. Boulevards were city streets that only allowed the use of pleasure vehicles, a designation that included bicycles, horses, and personal carriages. The heavy and noisy commercial teamster wagons that snarled traffic on other downtown streets were prohibited, as were streetcars. Much to the chagrin of speeding cyclists, known as scorchers, most boulevards also enforced an 8-mph speed limit. The streets that were originally designed as boulevards (as opposed to being converted at a later time) were very wide and featured one-way traffic lanes divided by a substantial amount of landscaped green space. All of the original boulevards were managed by local park commissions rather than the city itself. The boulevard system originally provided safe routes between Chicago's parks, which were extremely popular with cyclists. At one point during the bicycle boom, 2,000 bicyclists per hour were counted passing a single point in Lincoln Park. Some of the Chicago streets that were designated—at least in part—as boulevards included Drexel, Michigan, Van Buren, Garfield, Grand, Jackson, and Washington. By 1897, two miles of Grand Boulevard (now Martin Luther King Drive) had been designated for use only by bicycles, surely making it one of the country's first dedicated urban bicycle lanes. *The Chicago Chronicle* reported, "No city in the United States can boast of so many streets, boulevards and parks suited to cycling as Chicago, and in no city are these advantages so universally taken advantage of."[12] Chicago's bicycle-friendly topography, coupled with hundreds of miles of paved roads and its boulevard system, proved instrumental in setting the stage for the bicycle boom.

The history of Chicago cycling may have been drastically different without the contributions of Aaron Montgomery Ward and his efforts to preserve the city's open lakefront. As detailed in chapter eight, both Montgomery Ward and Sears drastically changed the American bicycle market by introducing very low-priced bicycles sold on small profit margins through their mail-order catalogs. During the 1890s and early twentieth century, Aaron Montgomery Ward was a tireless crusader for maintaining Chicago's lakefront as an open public space. The full story dates back to 1829, when the federal government granted land to Illinois for the construction of the Illinois and Michigan Canal.

Part of this land grant was the lakefront area that borders downtown Chicago. An 1836 map created by the Illinois and Michigan Canal Commissioner clearly designated the lakefront area "PUBLIC GROUND [—] A Common to remain forever Open, Clear & free of any buildings, or other Obstructions Whatever."[13]

Over the years, the grant for an "open, clear & free" lakefront was conveniently ignored by successive generations of Chicago aldermen and business promoters. By 1890, multiple illegal buildings, asphalt factories, and railroad storage areas had encroached on the lakefront. Ward, who owned property along the lakefront, filed a lawsuit against the city of Chicago in 1890 for violating the original designation of the lakefront. Ward's desire to keep the space open for all to enjoy put him at odds with many city council members and industrialists. In 1896, the Illinois Supreme Court ruled in Ward's favor, and the buildings were removed. The *Chicago Record* called Ward "the watchdog of the lakefront." He fought additional successful legal battles to keep the lakefront open, but later said, "Had I known how long it would take me to preserve a park for the people against their will, I doubt if I would have undertaken it . . . Here is a park frontage on the lake, comparing favorably with the Bay of Naples, which city officials would crowd with buildings, transforming the beauty spot for the poor into a showground of the educated rich." Ward's tireless efforts to preserve the lakefront were a defining moment in Illinois history. The downtown Chicago of today, with its panoramic lakefront views and miles of bike lanes, would have been impossible without his foresight.[14]

Outside of urban downtowns, one of the lasting legacies of the bicycle boom was the work done by the Good Roads Movement. At the time, upkeep of rural roads mostly fell on the landowners of the adjacent property. A common complaint was that rural roads were:

> Wholly unclassable,
> Almost impassable,
> Scarcely jackassable.[15]

The Good Roads Movement was created by bicyclists in 1880 to address these kinds of concerns. The National League of Good Roads was then founded in Chicago in 1892, and roads were the primary focus of the L.A.W. during the decade. With bicyclists leading the way, the Good Roads Movement eventually led to state and federal funding for road creation and maintenance. Bicyclists were directly responsible for agitating for better roads. Sometimes they worked with county commissioners or individual landowners on these efforts—and sometimes they just funded the work themselves.

With each success, bicyclists' road-building ambitions continued to grow. As early as 1892, a serious proposal was put forth to create a twenty- to thirty-foot-wide asphalt road between Chicago and New York. This effort had the backing of major bicycle manufacturers. An industrial magazine called *The Manufacturer and Builder* praised the proposal, noting that "a highway of this character would be indeed an object lesson in propagating the gospel of good roads." This same idea was revived by the L.A.W. in 1900. The idea was to establish bicycle "trunk lines," similar to the major railroad thoroughfares, that would connect New York to Chicago to Minneapolis to Denver, and finally to San Francisco. By this time, however, L.A.W. had lost much of its membership and political influence. While hundreds of miles of dedicated bicycle side paths were constructed along these routes, the grand vision of a transcontinental bicycle path was never realized.[16]

Elevated bicycle paths were another favorite preoccupation of bicycle fanatics. In 1895, an Illinoisan named E. J. Pennington proposed the construction of an elevated wooden bicycle path that would connect Chicago and Milwaukee. His plans called for a sixteen-foot-wide path with wooden walls that would serve as windbreaks. At regular intervals cyclists would be able to stop to rest and purchase refreshments at stands built into the structure. He estimated that 20,000 cyclists per week would use the path and that it could be funded with a ten-cent toll. A novel, and slightly more practical, plan for an elevated bicycle path in Chicago was suggested by D. A. Engstrom. His proposal was to construct a wooden bicycle path on top of all of Chicago's existing elevated railroads. This manner of construction would require no additional land or right-of-way agreements and would allow cyclists unimpeded travel across the city. The entire path was to be illuminated by electric lights and, according to Engstrom's calculations, could be built for a mere $40,000. In 1899, one final elevated bicycle path was proposed for Chicago's North Shore area. Proposals called for an initial eight miles of dedicated bicycle path that were to be constructed at a height of sixteen feet. The sides were to be of ornamental ironwork, and, like the earlier proposal, the structure would be lit by electric lights.[17]

As fantastical as these projects may seem now, all were serious proposals at the time. In fact, 1.4 miles of an elevated, electrically lit, wooden bicycle path were successfully constructed in Pasadena, California, in 1899. The California Cycle-Way was intended to provide cyclists with a direct connection from Pasadena to Los Angeles. The bicycle boom ended before this project could be completed. The idea for elevated bike paths endured, however, with Chicago finally getting one (The 606) in 2015.[18]

Bicycle Rows and Bicycle Shows

Chicago's masses of commuters and recreational riders during the 1890s needed somewhere to purchase a bicycle or new riding outfit, or to get a tune-up. For many, that destination was Bicycle Row, known across the country for its dense concentration of bicycle-related businesses. In 1894, the *Chicago Tribune* located Bicycle Row on the north side of West Madison Street.

> Bicycle row is at the height of its glory at night. Apparently every man, woman, and child on the West Side fortunate enough to own a wheel mounts that wheel and rides straight to Bicycle row as soon as supper is swallowed. . . . The rider not only goes there to meet his friend or his best girl, but he goes there for any minor repairs he may need and to pump up his tires. . . . About all the business of Bicycle Row is transacted between 7 and 9 p.m.[19]

In actuality, Chicago had multiples places designated as "Bicycle Row" at overlapping periods of time—a fact that has been a source of confusion for historians. In 1897, nearly two miles along Jackson Boulevard consisted primarily of bicycle-related businesses and was often referred to as Bicycle Row. Chicago's many bicycle manufacturers could be found scattered across the city, but the highest concentrations were on the bicycle rows along Clark and Canal Streets. Wabash Street was also called Bicycle Row during the mid-1890s.[20]

Along with manufacturing facilities, Chicago's bicycle rows featured many dealers and repair shops. The 1890 *Chicago Directory* listed only twenty-five bicycle dealers and a single bicycle repairer. A mere seven years later, that count reached a peak of 472 dealers and 126 repairers (increases of 1,788% and 12,500%, respectively). Bicycle historian Evan Friss has calculated that in 1898 Chicago, "there was one bicycle shop per every 4,235 residents," a better ratio than found in the twenty-first century cycling meccas of Amsterdam (1:5,571) and Copenhagen (1:4,546). In 2024, based on available business directories, that same ratio is now closer to one per every 73,000 residents.[21] In the 1890s, bicycles dominated the life of Chicago and similar cities in a way that has rarely been equaled.

Even with hundreds of bicycle dealers, Chicago's various bicycle rows were not the only place to purchase a new or used bicycle. Chicago was also known for pioneering the department store concept, where, for the first time, consumers could find goods of all types under one roof. Marshall Field & Company was the best-known nineteenth-century department store, but others included Carson Pirie Scott & Company, Mandel Brothers, and the Fair Store. The Fair Store was founded in Chicago in 1874 and earned its name from the idea that "the store was like a fair because it offered many different things for sale at a cheap price." Located at State and Adams, the Fair Store was, at 677,500 square feet, the largest in the world when it was built in 1897. Incredibly, during the peak of the bicycle boom, the Fair Store sold as many as one thousand bicycles per day.[22]

Massive winter bicycle shows helped fuel consumer demand for the newest bicycle models and the dizzying array of bicycle-related goods. Held in January, to take advantage of the cycling offseason, the bicycle shows grew to be elaborate affairs featuring live bands, opportunities to mingle with top racers, trick-riding demonstrations, and souvenir giveaways. Chicago launched its first national-caliber bicycle show in January of 1895. This initial effort garnered praise from industry insiders, with one newspaper declaring, "So far as is known, every manufacturer and dealer in the country who visited the Chicago show, with the exception of Col. Pope of Boston, have voted it the greatest thing of the kind ever held on this side of the Atlantic."[23] (Pope, of course, had vested personal and professional interests in the rival New York show that was held in Madison Square Garden a few weeks after Chicago's show.) Chicago's 1896 bicycle show was held during the peak of the bicycle boom and exceeded all expectations. The show was held in Tattersall's exhibition hall, which was Chicago's largest indoor space at the time. A total of 250 different exhibitors showed off more than one thousand bicycles, which covered 60,000 square feet of floor space. Even a blizzard and subzero temperatures on the show's opening night could not keep away the droves of cyclists who traveled from all over the Midwest to visit the show. The 11,000 tickets sold on the first night led to such a severe crush inside the building that four women fainted. A bicycle pump was used to smash open a window, and the women were assisted to the street outside using a ladder. The show ran for a full week and filled Chicago's hotels beyond capacity. Many reported adding cots to hallways and ballrooms to accommodate the surge. Chicago's famous Palmer House hotel reported, "There are almost as many people sleeping here tonight as we had during the big days of the [World's] Fair and the biggest crowd for this [winter] season the hotel has ever held since it was built."[24] Bicycle agents made an estimated $10 million in advanced sales at the show for the coming season. Two weeks later, *Bearings* would report that attendance at the rival Madison Square Garden bicycle show was significantly lower than Chicago.[25]

If American bicycling had a center, it was squarely located in Illinois by the 1890s.

Bicycle Politics

In 1883, Lewis Bates, president of the League of American Wheelmen, authored an article entitled "Political Power of the L.A.W." Even in those early days of American bicycling, the organization was cultivating the political potential of cyclists. The L.A.W. was adamant that the organization remain nonpartisan. Bates wrote, "Let us, by all means, keep the L.A.W. and all its branches and clubs entirely aloof from politics in the ordinary sense; but let us, whenever our just rights are assailed through politics or politicians, be ever ready as an organization to wield our political power, strongly and efficiently in self-defense."[26] The L.A.W. remained nonpartisan in the sense that it did not automatically back candidates from any specific party; instead, it organized to elect candidates that supported issues important to bicyclists, such as the development of good roads, bicyclists' rights on urban streets, and free transportation of bicycles on railroads.

Below the national L.A.W. were individual state chapters that provided delegates to the national organization, clubs officially registered with the L.A.W., and finally dues-paying individual members. Much of the political organizing occurred at the local club level. In 1890, the leading Chicago bicycle clubs banded together to form the Associated Cycling Clubs of Chicago. The stated objectives of the new organization were to collectively advance issues important to wheelmen, improve city streets, promote racing, encourage communication between clubs, and support the goals of the L.A.W.[27] In 1890, the organization claimed to have "1,500 political votes." Soon, fifty-four bicycle clubs joined up, representing more than 10,000 voters.[28] One of these clubs, the Viking Cycling Club, bluntly asserted that the "club and its associates control 1,800 political votes and will support those candidates favorable to wheelmen and wheeling."[29] The Associated Cycling Clubs held enough sway in city hall that the superintendent of streets provided the club with official postcards that were to be used for identifying problems with city streets. Such was the respect for Chicago's bicycle lobby that, whenever the cards were sent in, the repairs were made immediately.[30]

In the 1896 presidential race, Republican William McKinley faced off against Democrat William Jennings Bryan. Sterling Elliott, the president of the L.A.W., claimed that "if every wheelman in the country was a member of the league we would hold the balance of power, so that even the president of the United States could be elected or defeated by the united forces of bicycle riders."[31] While not decisive, the wheelmen vote ultimately helped McKinley. On August 5, the National Wheelmen's McKinley and Hobart Club was organized in Chicago, and other branches throughout the country soon followed. The Republican National Committee was also headquartered in Chicago. In a nod to the growing political power of wheelmen, a room in the headquarters building was designated specifically for cyclists. In an October rally, 3,000 wheelmen paraded throughout Chicago in support of McKinley. Celluloid buttons were all the rage at the time, and many McKinley campaign buttons featured bicycles. One button depicted McKinley on a bicycle in full cycling attire, while another featured McKinley and running mate Garret Hobart on a tandem bicycle; in both cases, the two were traveling the road to the White House. Democrats made fewer overtures to the country's wheelmen. On the night of the election, a special relay of cyclists traveled from Indianapolis to Canton, Ohio, in order to be the first to inform McKinley of his win.[32]

Carter Henry Harrison IV mayoral campaign photo. (Courtesy of the Newberry Library.)

Carter Henry Harrison IV's win in the 1897 Chicago mayoral race can be attributed—at least in part—to the coordinated efforts of Chicago's bicycle lobby, led by the Associated Cycling Clubs of Chicago. Following his win, the self-proclaimed "Cyclists' Champion" did not wait long to reward the city's cyclers, 6,000 of whom joined him in a parade as part of the annual "Union Run" of the Associated Cycling Clubs.[33] During periods of dry weather, it was common for city contractors to sprinkle water over the city streets. Sprinkling was necessary to cut down on the clouds of dust that would otherwise arise from dry streets. The practice, however, created slippery conditions for cyclists. In June, the new mayor issued an order to the sprinklers to leave four feet of dry road next to both curbs for the use of cyclists.[34]

That same month, Harrison made good on the City Council's earlier decision to convert Jackson Street into a boulevard. In 1896, prior to Harrison's election, the Associated Cycling Clubs had made a concerted effort to defeat proposals from two streetcar companies to install tracks along Jackson Street, which was a major cycling thoroughfare. The Associated Cycling Clubs instead proposed protecting Jackson Street for the long term by converting it into a boulevard. The organization printed 100,000 yellow ribbons that read "Jackson Street Must Be Boulevarded." Anyone in favor of the new boulevard was asked to wear the ribbons to show their support. On March 2, 1896, when the City Council consented and declared Jackson Street a boulevard, the new legislation was referred to as the Yellow Ribbon Ordinance. By the time Harrison took office, little actual work had been done toward the Jackson Street boulevard conversion. Harrison promptly rewarded the city's cyclists for their loyalty, contracting to have the new Jackson Boulevard pavement finished within two months.[35]

The "Cyclists' Champion" did not stop there. In the summer of his first term, Mayor Harrison proposed a plan to pave every street in downtown Chicago. The idea was met with enthusiasm from the city's cyclists, but the costs far outstripped the city's budget. Alderman Charles Martin put forth a plan to collect an annual one-dollar tax on every bicycle ridden in the city. Those who paid the tax would be given a metal license tag that would be affixed to the owner's bicycle. Cyclists generally, if not universally, favored the tax, since all proceeds were to be used for street improvements. By this time, the construction of good roads had become the primary focus of the L.A.W. The Associated Cycling Clubs and Chicago Cycling Club soon fell in line and came out in favor of the bicycle tax: "Cyclists will be in favor of such an ordinance, as they are willing to do what they can for the improvement of the streets." The captain of the large and influential Chicago Cycling Club echoed these sentiments: "The tax is a good thing. It will assure us good streets, and that is what the cyclist wishes most of all."[36] Mayor Harrison signed the new Martin Ordinance into law on July 19, 1897. However, the ordinance was on shaky legal ground from the start, as only the state of Illinois had a right to collect license fees. It was declared unconstitutional less than a month later.[37]

Even without the funds from the bicycle tax, Mayor Harrison continued to repay his political debts to Chicago's cyclists, a fact he was not shy about bringing up when he ran for reelection in 1899: "Being a wheelman myself, I am cognizant of all the wheelmen's needs, and a glance back at the past two years during my occupancy of the mayor's chair will show that the wheelmen's interest have not suffered at my hands."[38]

Civil Service Take to the Wheel

Beyond the realm of electoral politics, bicycling began playing a role in the work of public servants who kept the city functioning. Despite many improvements targeting bicyclists, Chicago's streets remained highly congested. Accidents were bound to follow. An 1897 *Chicago Tribune* article, entitled "Woe Follows the Trail of the Bicycle," documented one hundred bicycle-related accidents for just the months of June and July, noting that only about one-third of all accidents were reported to the police. Causes of accidents included falling from a bicycle (ten), colliding with horse teams (twenty-one), and attempting to cross tracks (eight). Other, less predictable causes included catching clothing in a bicycle (three), colliding while racing (six), and riding into the river (one). The paper went on to report that in terms of the total number of street-based accidents, no other cause rivaled bicycles. A survey of major American newspapers for the month of 1897 found 1,450 bicycle accidents, leading to 46 deaths, 244 fractures, 224 cuts, 420 contusions, and 297 head injuries. The same article estimated that there were between 700 and 1,000 cycling-related deaths per year in the United States.[39] For all of its health benefits, cycling in the 1890s was a dangerous endeavor.

For Chicago physician John T. Binkley Jr., bicycle accidents required a bicycle solution. In 1896, Binkley designed a bicycle ambulance, which was then built by Chicago's Iroquois Cycle Company. His first bicycle ambulance design consisted of two tandem bicycles with a framework in between that supported an enclosed stretcher. The stretcher was suspended by springs, and a pneumatic mattress further reduced vibration. Reportedly, the bicycle ambulance could maintain speeds of up to 16 mph "without discomfort to the patient." It is unclear how many actual patients were surveyed before drawing this conclusion. The whole contraption weighed over 150 pounds and cost more than $1,000 to build. It was reported to be the only bicycle ambulance in America at the time.

Over the course of a few months, the bicycle ambulance delivered more than one hundred patients to the Chicago Hospital on Cottage Grove Avenue. Appropriately, its first test run involved transporting injured racers from Chicago's 1896 Bicycle Derby, a series of bicycle races held on the Fourth of July.

Chicago's bicycle ambulance as depicted in *The Times* (Philadelphia) (November 15, 1896).

Drawing hundreds of riders and tens of thousands of spectators, the road race through the rough streets of Chicago resulted in many crashes and injuries. The most seriously injured riders were transported to the hospital via the bicycle ambulance.

What might strike readers now as a gimmick or a mere novelty made some sense at the time. Traditional ambulances were carts pulled by one or more horses. Horses were expensive to maintain; a contemporary newspaper calculated the cost of stabling and feeding a four-horse team for an ambulance at $168 per month. Moreover, horses couldn't remain harnessed to the ambulance carriage at all times, so they had a relatively slow response time. The bicycle ambulance was far smaller than its horse-drawn counterpart, making it more maneuverable in crowded streets. It was even small enough to be driven straight into the hospital, thereby transporting the patient directly to a room.[40]

Not to be left behind, the Chicago Post Office also got in on the bicycle craze. In 1894, Postmaster Washington Hesing devised a real-world experiment to test the efficacy of bicycles for urban mail delivery. Two special delivery messengers were given seven letters each to deliver along the same route. One messenger would use street cars and the elevated railway, while the other would use a bicycle. Delivery by bicycle was the clear winner, and the post office soon after entered into a contract with Chicago's Derby Cycle Company to supply mail-delivery bicycles. A year later, 115 Chicago postmen were using bicycles, resulting in a savings of $5,000 per year.[41]

Chicago also instituted some of the earliest bicycle police in the country. Already in 1892, a few Chicago police officers were mounted on bicycles. The *Chicago Tribune* reported that in two months' time, they recovered forty-eight stolen bicycles and were able to reach the scene of burglaries, fights, and fires ahead of the horse-drawn patrol wagons. As the boom progressed, bicycle police were frequently used to cut down on dangerous bicycle scorchers who rode haphazardly through the streets at high rates of speed. Captain Murphy of the Lincoln Park Police noted that an officer on foot couldn't catch a bicyclist, "but nine times out of ten he can throw his club so as to tangle it up in the wires of the wheel and bring the rider to grief." Other Chicago officers resorted to slingshots and lead balls, which broke a scorcher's spokes and brought him to a quick halt. In 1897, bicycle police officers arrested eleven scorchers in one evening for violating South Park's speed limit of 8 mph.[42]

Military Cycling

Around the same time that the first bicycle police officers appeared, the United States Army also began to experiment with military applications for bicycles. At the time, much of the army was heavily reliant on horses. Advocates for bicycles in the military were quick to point out that horses required transporting a great deal of food and water, needed frequent rests, were easily killed by the enemy, could be noisy at inopportune times, and could cause injuries to their riders if they panicked during combat situations. Bicycles, on the other hand, could cover greater distances than horses in a much shorter time, were cheaper, required less maintenance, were nearly silent, and could even be hidden underwater and retrieved later if necessary. "A bullet hitting a cycle only requires the gunsmith's aid," noted one commentator, "but a horse cannot be carried to the repair shop."[43]

One of the military's earliest experiments with bicycles occurred at Fort Sheridan, just north of Chicago. In 1891, General Nelson A. Miles established an experimental bicycle detachment consisting of ten soldiers who were part of the Fifteenth Infantry. The following year, this detachment undertook a fifteen-mile "march" from Pullman to Chicago. Riding bicycles loaded down with a complete soldier's kit, the group easily completed the ride in only an hour and twenty-five minutes, far faster than the same trip could be accomplished on foot. That same year, the detachment's commander, First Lieutenant William T. May, authored the first United States field manual for infantry cycling, *Cyclists' Drill Regulations*.[44]

Soon, a far more ambitious demonstration of the bicycle's military capabilities was organized. In May of 1892, General Miles approved an experiment that was called "The Great Bicycle Relay Race." The Great Bicycle Relay Race would evaluate how fast cyclists could deliver a message between the Headquarters Department of the Missouri, located in Chicago, and Headquarters of the Department of the East, located in New York; this was a distance of 975 miles. Instead of soldiers, the relay race featured around two hundred of the fastest civilian bicycle racers in the country. On May 18, in front of more than one thousand spectators, General Miles handed a message for General O. O. Howard to a pair of Chicago's best racers, Arthur E. Lumsden and E.C. Bode. Along the length of the route, cyclists rode in pairs to ensure timely delivery of the message even if a mishap befell one of the riders. This strategy proved effective since heavy rains and winds plagued most of the ride. At times, the mud on some rural roads became knee-deep, forcing the riders onto railroad tracks or into adjacent fields. Fighting against challenging conditions, the final rider completed the last relay leg into New York 109 hours after the endeavor had begun. This time was faster than the Pony Express over the same route and, as General Miles pointed out, faster than infantry or cavalry. The result, he said, "goes beyond confirming my previous opinion of the military value of the bicycle. . . . A regiment of infantry could not make over ten miles a day under similar circumstances."[45]

The first time that bicycles were used in an actual military action in the United States was in response to the Lemont, Illinois, quarry strike of 1893.

The Panic of 1893 had caused a steep loss in profits for the Western Stone Company, which managed a large quarry in Lemont. In June, the company cut wages, which led to a strike. After strikebreakers were brought in, the conflict turned violent, resulting in at least three deaths. The militia was ordered to Lemont, including the Second Regiment Bicycle Corps under the command of Colonel L. S. Judd. During the conflict, the regiment was split into two camps, separated by two miles. Strikers repeatedly cut the telegraph wires between the two camps, forcing reliance on the bicycle soldiers to carry messages back and forth. Eventually, Governor Altgeld traveled to Lemont to mediate an agreement between the strikers and their employer.[46]

Nationally, the best-known use of bicycles in the military during the 1890s was the Twenty-Fifth Infantry Bicycle Corps, stationed at Fort Missoula. Lieutenant James A. Moss requested permission to form the Bicycle Corps in 1896; the approval was granted by General Miles, who had maintained his interest in military cycling. Moss formed the Bicycle Corps from the all-Black "Buffalo Soldiers" who made up the Twenty-Fifth Infantry. Chicago-based A.G. Spalding provided the Army with ten bicycles at no cost, but certainly with the hope of securing future lucrative contracts. A key member of the new Bicycle Corps was Private John Findley, a Black soldier from Chicago. Findley was instrumental in the success of the Corps, as he was an experienced rider who had also worked for the Chicago bicycle manufacturer Ames & Frost, maker

The Buffalo Soldiers of the 25th Infantry Regiment Bicycle Corps standing on Mammoth Hot Springs, Yellowstone National Park. Pvt. John Findley, front left. (Courtesy of Montana Historical Society Research Center Photograph Archives, Helena, Montana. Photographer: Frank J. Haynes.)

of the Imperial brand of bicycles. Findley was tasked with the maintenance and repair of the Corps's bicycles. In 1896, the Bicycle Corps undertook a grueling trial expedition from Fort Missoula to Yellowstone and back. Each soldier traveled with a complete infantry kit that included a rifle or revolver, extra ammunition, tent, blanket, clothing, cooking utensils, and food. Private Findley's total load, including this standard equipment, the bicycle itself, and spare parts and tools, totaled seventy-seven pounds. It took the Corps sixteen days to cover 790 miles of rough terrain over poor roads and trails.[47]

The Yellowstone trip was deemed a success, so Moss proposed a more ambitious expedition from Missoula to St. Louis, a distance of 1,900 miles. The size of the Bicycle Corps was increased to twenty soldiers, who left Fort Missoula on June 14, 1897. Crossing the Continental Divide, they faced blowing snow and freezing temperatures. On the plains, they encountered searing heat, high winds, and terrible road conditions. Forty days later (a total that included six rest days), they reached St. Louis on July 24. Summarizing the trip in the *Army and Navy Journal,* Moss wrote,

> The trip has proved beyond peradventure my contention that the bicycle has a place in modern warfare. In every kind of weather, over all sorts of roads, we averaged fifty miles a day. At the end of the journey we are all in good physical condition. . . . The practical result of the trip shows that an Army Bicycle Corps can travel twice as fast as cavalry or infantry under any conditions, and at one third the cost and effort.[48]

Following the completion of the trip, the *Kansas City Star* published portions of an interview with Private Findley from the Bicycle Corps. When queried about how well the bicycle had held up to the rigors of traveling over western roads, he replied that the Corps had worn out seventeen tires but only experienced eight flat tires. When asked about how a horse would have fared over the same route, he responded, "No horse on earth could make such a trip in the same length of time."[49]

Despite the hopes of military bicycle advocates such as General Miles and Lieutenant Moss, and manufacturers like A.G. Spalding and Pope Manufacturing, bicycles never became widely used by the United States military. Worldwide, bicycles saw limited military use in the Boer War and both world wars. With the twenty-first century invention of quiet and efficient e-bikes, military units are again considering the use of bicycles in modern warfare.[50]

The Church or the Wheel

The addition of bicycles to civil services and the military, while remarkable, was largely uncontroversial. Whatever criticisms there were paled in comparison to the bitter divides about bicycles that were present in some American religious institutions. More than a century later it seems quaint—even bordering on absurd—that American churches were ever threatened by something as innocuous as a bicycle. During the bicycle boom of the 1890s, many clergymen saw the bicycle as a threat to the spiritual well-being of their congregations. Those who chose to embrace bicycling often met fierce opposition from more conservative members of their congregations. A few lost their jobs as a result of bicycling.[51] Some clergymen, such as the Rev. Thomas B. Gregory of Chicago, seemed to attribute all the ills of society directly to the bicycle:

> It is a menace to the domestic virtues. It breaks up and destroys the home. The children are turned into the street or left at home to look out for themselves, while father and mother go spinning. It is a menace to morality. It makes women immodest... There is no telling what a woman will do after she has lost her womanliness . . . It is a menace to religion. The churches are being emptied of the young and middle aged. The Sabbath bells call in vain . . . sooner or later we will learn that, of all the foes of our Christian civilization, the bicycle is the most uncompromising and the most deadly.[52]

The clerical reaction against bicycling drew from a deep-seated distrust of technology among many Christian denominations. The European scientific revolution of the sixteenth and seventeenth centuries had dealt a major blow to the authority and influence of the church. In the context of the late nineteenth-century bicycling boom, bicycles were exemplars of modern technology—that is, of advances that were often seen as subversive to the traditional interests of the church.

The sheer popularity of bicycles during the 1890s appears to have drawn the attention of church leaders, who had not expressed similar concerns during the velocipede and high-wheel eras. That bicycles would be a target of clerical ire was more than a little ironic in light of contemporaneous trends within Protestant Christianity. The American rural-to-urban migration that occurred throughout the nineteenth century resulted in far greater exposure for everyday Americans to the classic urban ills of disease, overcrowding, poverty, alcoholism, and prostitution. The many forms of mass entertainment available in large cities appeared to be a cause of declining church attendance. In England during the 1860s, the concept of "Muscular Christianity" was championed as a strategy for combating modern social ills and keeping the church strong. In his 1861 novel *Tom Brown at Oxford*, Thomas Hughes defined the basic precepts of this new movement: "The least of the muscular Christians has hold of the old chivalrous and Christian belief, that a man's body is given him to be trained and brought into subjection, and then used for the protection of the weak, the advancement of all righteous causes, and the subduing of the earth which God has given to the children of men."[53] Many believed the church had become slothful and overly tolerant of physical weakness and effeminacy. The establishment and growth of the YMCA (Young Men's Christian Association) in the mid-nineteenth century was probably the most recognizable early result of the Muscular Christianity movement, but it was far from the only outcome. Given the widespread interest in Muscular Christianity, it would seem that bicycles should have been readily embraced by Christians as a means to greater physical health and as an aid to evangelism efforts. But this was far from the case.

The major points of contention concerned the competition for Sunday schedules. During the bicycle boom of the 1890s, long Sunday bicycle rides became one of the most important social events of the week. This was the era of six-day work weeks, so Sunday was a logical day for such excursions, which church leaders saw as desecrating the Sabbath in two respects. First, many decided to just skip church services and go for a ride instead. Moreover, per the Ten Commandments, the Sabbath was supposed to be a day of rest, not cycling. In 1895, Rev. David Beaton of Unity Church in Dearborn, Illinois, spoke for many conservative clergymen across the country when he told reporters at the *Chicago Daily Tribune*, "No greater crime against civilization can be committed than the action of bicycle clubs to hold meets, parades, races, and other sports on Sunday. It is a question of health and civic virtue. For to trample upon the religious use of Sunday as a day of rest and worship is to poison the lifeblood of our American civilization."[54]

As the ranks of cyclists swelled, they increasingly came into conflict with church leaders. Sermons against the evils of cycling came not only from small conservative rural parishes, but also from some of the most notable religious leaders of the day, including the famed evangelist Dwight Moody. His evangelistic career had begun in Chicago, after he came to the city in 1856 as a shoe salesman. Moody then began working for the Chicago YMCA in 1861 and served as its president from 1866 to 1869. In the latter years of the nineteenth century, Moody became one of America's foremost evangelists; he also founded Chicago's Moody Bible Institute and Moody Press.[55] Famous for holding large urban revivals, Moody saw the bicycle as a threat to good Christians everywhere. He lamented, "I don't believe any one can see the vast throng of young men in our cities—and I am sorry to say, bad women, too—on their bicycles going off into the country and fields and woods to spend the Sabbath, and trampling the law of God into the dust." Moody recounted a visit to Brooklyn, where he saw a bicycle club starting a Sunday morning ride directly across from the church where he was about to preach. "It wasn't the scum of Brooklyn that were there," he said, "but some of the leading young men. And in that church where I preached there hardly seemed to be twenty-five young men."[56]

One bicyclist was able to return the favor, using Moody's fame to raise her own profile as a racer. Tillie Anderson actually had been a member of Moody's Chicago congregation before she found success as the most dominant woman bicycle racer of the 1890s. In 1897, Anderson was participating in a six-day race in Cincinnati's Music Hall. During the middle of the week, Dwight Moody arrived to preach in another section of the same venue. Anderson, who was known in racing circles as Tillie the Terrible Swede, had a particular knack for using the press to her advantage. She let it slip to local reporters not to tell Moody that she was racing right next door: "If he knew I was riding a wheel in the very building in which he is preaching, he'd be angry and would come and take me off my wheel—and I can't afford to lose a lap. I would not have him know I was riding for anything, and don't you dare say anything about it." The reporters, of course, did precisely that and were rewarded with a provocative statement from Moody about bicycle riding: "Of course I believe in wholesome exercise, but we Americans are so apt to overdo anything that it often results in lasting injury. Where women overdo it, especially, I should think it would lead to troubles particular to woman; and then that is not the worst of it. I think the bicycle and the Sunday newspaper are doing an incalculable injury. They keep people from church services." One local paper published a full-page article on the Anderson –Moody bicycle controversy, complete with sketches of both.[57]

Moody, of course, did not speak for all clergy of the day. Clergy who were more in tune with Progressive reform often advocated for bicycling. Their approach sometimes created deep divisions within their parishes. In 1894, the Rev. F. M. Johnson of the Swedish Congregational Church in Rockford, Illinois, took up cycling. Conservative members of his congregation thought this behavior unbecoming of a minister and called for his dismissal. In such cases, the bicycle question often exposed a divide between more conservative rural areas and larger urban cities that was echoed in debates within Protestant denominations. "If Pastor Johnson occupied a Chicago pulpit," the *Chicago Daily Tribune* opined, "he could hump himself over a wheel to his heart's content, for none of the clergymen or people of his nationality [in Chicago] appear to think that the gates of heaven are closed to all except pedestrians."[58] Reporters from the *Sandusky Register* (Ohio) were even more blunt in their assessment of the case, writing that "Probably the disgruntled prefer that he should ride the foal of an ass."[59]

One leading pro-bicycle clergyman was Rev. Jenkin Lloyd Jones, a Unitarian minister who founded the All Souls Church on Chicago's South Side. (He was also the uncle of Frank Lloyd Wright.)[60] In 1896, Jones garnered headlines for encouraging cyclists to ride to services at All Souls Church. Not only did Jones encourage cyclists to ride to his church, but he also provided valet bicycle parking in the church basement. Reporting on these events, the

Chicago Daily Tribune pointed out the growing popularity of cycling and the inevitable conflicts with Sunday services. They noted, "if it is 'the church or the wheel' one needs no prophetic eye to see which will win in thousands of lives. All Souls' Church, Chicago would fain avert the conflict by saying 'the church and the wheel'."[61]

Although clergymen were primarily concerned about how the bicycle was impacting church attendance and cyclists riding on the Sabbath, these were not the church's only point of contention with bicycling. Some Church leaders and Christian organizations also claimed that the bicycle led to alcoholism, while others contended that bicycling kept men from the bottle. Alcoholism had always been a problem in American society, but during the nineteenth century, as drinks with high concentrations of alcohol like whiskey and rum became cheaper and easier to buy at a local store or pub, alcoholism received more attention as a national problem. As for any connection between bicycling and booze, it was true that a common practice among wheelmen was to ride to some distant country inn or tavern, enjoy a meal and possibly a few drinks, and then return home. Yet even for the most adamant preachers and teetotalers, connecting the bicycling craze with increased alcoholism was something of a stretch.[62]

Progressive reforms instead drew a positive connection between bicycling and temperance. The bicycle, Rev. J. W. Fifield told the *Chicago Tribune*, "has a moral glory. It is emptying the billiard halls and saloons and filling the country roads. It has one great virtue—a drunken man cannot ride it. Had the devil tried to invent his own gallows he could have done no better than to have made the bicycle."[63] The numbers appear to support his point. At the crest of the bicycle boom in 1897, the United States Commissioner of Internal Revenue noted that in the previous year, whiskey consumption was down by six million barrels and beer down by nearly 1.5 million barrels. As noted above, the Panic of 1893 and the ensuing nationwide economic depression certainly accounted for some portion of this decrease, but most also attributed the decrease to the bicycle craze.[64] Aiding the temperance movement was yet another way that bicycling advanced the goals of Progressive reformers and contributed to a more equitable society.

Eventually, as safety bicycles grew in popularity during the early 1890s, many churches realized that rather than fight a losing battle to keep people from riding, they should instead embrace the bicycle to further their evangelism efforts. This approach ultimately won out over Dwight Moody's criticism of bicycles as a threat to Sabbath-keeping. In fact, bicycles were a boon to evangelists for the same reason they were wildly popular among the urban American middle-class: they were far cheaper to own and operate than horses. One contemporary clergyman estimated the cost of keeping up a carriage and feeding a horse at $150 per year, compared to only $2.50 per year for the bicycle. His estimate for bicycle maintenance may have been on the low side, but even so, the cost difference was massive.[65] The lower cost of bicycles allowed preachers and their parishioners to more easily undertake evangelism efforts, particularly in the expansive rural areas of nineteenth-century America that were not accessible by train or streetcar. Some members of a Baptist church in Chicago exhibited admirable resourcefulness in their evangelism efforts when they mounted sails on their bicycles to take advantage of prairie winds.[66] As the Muscular Christianity movement gained in popularity, it was easy to make the case for the bicycle as an aid to greater physical fitness and therefore greater capacity to spread the word of God.

Among the most eccentric of the bicycle evangelists were the Morrill Twins of Chicago. Revs. Herbert and Horace Morrill were identical twins committed to a life of Baptist evangelism. Among their many schemes was the construction of a "Gospel Ship" building on Chicago's West Side. The "ship" was one hundred feet long and twenty-five feet wide, with forty porthole windows. It was made of iron and designed to seat five hundred people. The twins were better known for their use of the bicycle for evangelism. In 1895, *The Daily Republican* (Monongahela, Pennsylvania) reported, "The Rev. Morrill Twins, the evangelists, probably attract more attention when they go forth on their wheels than any other of Chicago's great army of bicycle riders. Wherever they go on their 'bike' people line the streets to watch them pass by; wherever they stop is a crowd. It is rather unusual to see two men in silk hats, Prince

The evangelizing Morrill twins and their tandem bicycle. (Author's collection.)

Albert coats, and looking as much alike as two peas in the pod . . . "[67] The twins sometimes rode a tandem bicycle and sometimes rode matching safety bicycles. In addition to preaching, they would often sing together while riding.

Other Christian organizations slowly began to embrace bicycling. The Salvation Army formed bicycle brigades that were led by founder William Booth's daughter, Evangeline. These bicycle brigades traveled from city to city seeking converts. The Salvation Army even commissioned its own line of bicycles (including both men's and women's models) that were sold at reduced rates to Salvation Army members.[68] The Young Men's Christian Association saw tremendous growth during the 1890s. The YMCA exemplified the Muscular Christianity ethos with its emphasis on developing a healthy body, mind, and spirit (even today, these are the three points of the YMCA triangle). During the bicycle boom, various YMCAs formed bicycle clubs and offered bicycle storage to their residents. In 1892, the YMCA Chicago Central offered indoor storage of more than four hundred bicycles for their dormitory residents.[69]

Clergymen in other states certainly encountered fevered opposition and support for bicycling. Illinois, however, had far more examples of these religious debates over bicycling than other states in the nation. As the nineteenth century came to a close, bicycling had become commonplace in American culture. The tidal wave of cyclists that had swept the country forced the resolution of debates about the religious propriety of cycling. Churches could not continue to condemn an activity that so many of their upstanding members participated in. The idea of Muscular Christianity continued in popularity and was directly aided by bicycling.

Scope of the Boom

The basic elements of the bicycle boom of the 1890s are well-known facts among historians. As the statistics and stories shared above indicate, the true scope of the bicycle boom was much larger, and it permeated American culture to a far greater degree than most past historians have realized. Historians who study the Progressive Era always give at least a nod to bicycling as aiding dress reform, suffrage, and the temperance movement. As evidenced by the chapters that follow, bicycling during the 1890s was truly an economic, social, and cultural force to be reckoned with. As the decade progressed, Illinois became the clear leader of the boom.

3

"Two-Thirds of All Bicycles"

Illinois Bicycle Manufacturing

Charles Edgar Duryea was born in 1861 on a rural farm south of Canton in central Illinois. Charles and his brother James Frank Duryea, born eight years later in Washburn, Illinois, achieved fame and modest fortunes through their roles in building the first mass-produced American automobile. Long before then, the Duryeas—Charles, especially—were heavily engaged in bicycle manufacturing and design. In 1879, a young Charles saw pictures of the first American high-wheel bicycles that Pope Manufacturing had begun producing the previous year. Coming from a poor family, Charles had no hope of purchasing one, so he decided to make one himself. After finishing his farm chores, Charles worked on assembling a working bicycle using wheels from a corn cultivator and a seat made from a block of wood covered in carpet. The crude bicycle was functional, and Charles proceeded to ride it all over town and at the local fair. In 1882, Charles graduated from Gittings Seminary in La Harpe, Illinois, where he wrote a prophetic thesis on the future of transportation, predicting a "time . . . when the humming of flying machines will be music over the lands; when Europe will be distant by a half-day's journey." Shortly after graduation, Charles moved to St. Louis, where he purchased a second-hand Columbia bicycle and even tried his hand at racing.[1]

Charles proved to be a much better inventor than racer. In 1883, he filed his first patent (United States Patent 293,725) for a new two-rail, hammock-style bicycle saddle. His design bears a striking resemblance to modern bicycle saddles, even featuring the anatomical cutouts popular in twenty-first-century saddles. Elements of his design would be widely adopted by the industry, but due to an unscrupulous solicitor during the patent process, he lost out on potential profits. Sometime before 1888, Gormully & Jeffery purchased Duryea's saddle patent and used the design for their bicycles. An 1891 Gormully

Photograph of a young Charles Duryea with a high-wheel bicycle. (Courtesy of the National Automotive Collection, Detroit Public Library.)

& Jeffery catalog offered a "Duryea" saddle for sale, describing it as "the first hammock bicycle saddle patented in this country. It sets very low on the backbone and is a prime favorite with scorchers and racing men."[2]

In 1886, Charles moved his family to Washington, DC, where he went to work at the Herbert S. Owens bicycle shop. Owens was doing good business importing and selling Psycho Cycles, made by Starley Bros. in England. His shop was also near the United States Patent Office, where Charles spent his free time poring over the most recent developments in cycling. It was time well spent, as between 1884 and 1895 Charles patented at least fifteen different inventions or improvements related to bicycles.[3]

Charles was among the earliest pioneers of women's bicycle frame design, an important historical marker that would eventually expand cycling to better include women riders. Soon after the appearance of the first commercially successful chain-driven safety bicycle, the 1885 English Starley Rover, tinkerers and machinists in both the United States and England began working on designs for women's bicycles. Duryea appears to have been interested in women's bicycle designs even before the invention of the safety bicycle, although direct evidence of his earliest work is lacking. In 1892, *The Bearings* published a brief article on an earlier Duryea ladies' bicycle that he designed while living in St. Louis (1882–1885). The design is radical, with a low seat position and the small front wheel running on rollers inside a much larger hoop.[4] An 1892 Rouse-Duryea Cycle Company catalog alluded to a different early ladies' safety design: "As early as 1880 he designed and built a horizontal frame, rear driven, crank movement Safety, suitable for both sexes and adjustable in size. . . . In 1883 he began publicly advocating the use of bicycles for both sexes and in 1887 perfected the designs and built for a prominent company the drop frame ladies safety, claimed to be the first in the United States."[5] The "prominent company" was surely his former employer, H. S. Owen. In a letter to historian Parker Morell written in the early 1930s, Duryea recounted the story of his early women's bicycle designs for Owen and Starley,

> I had repeatedly tried to show him that a sport for males could be sold to females, but he laughed at me. . . . Then, one day, some time later, he came hustling across the yard to the shop I was using to repair cycles in, shouting: "Duryea, I've got a BIG idea!" . . . "If a few girls would take up cycling, every old buck in town would buy a machine. Can't you make something like this?" And he handed me a rough sketch. "No, not that way," I told him, "this way." And with a bit of chalk I sketched a curved reach "drop" or "loop" frame ladies' safety on the floor. "Make one!" Owen ordered me. I did. I rode it much, then Owen got his two nieces to riding it and ordered Starley to make a lot of them. This was about 1888.[6]

Given the multiple contenders for designer of the first women's frame, a little more precision than "about 1888" is desirable. According to the Smithsonian Institution, H. S. Owens gave them what he claimed to be the first American women's safety, which he made in October of 1887, but he later withdrew it to use as evidence in legal proceedings and never returned the bicycle.[7] A series of articles on the evolution of the bicycle in 1897–98 issues of the *L.A.W. Bulletin and Good Roads* concurred that H. S. Owen made and sold Duryea-designed women's safety bicycles in 1887.[8] On firmer historical footing, we know for certain that Duryea applied for United States Patent 357,819 on another radical "sociable" (side-by-side seating) bicycle design in November of 1886, but no one would mistake this contraption for a safety bicycle. In June of 1887, he applied for United States Patent 387,631 for a sort of recumbent tricycle for ladies. Finally, in June of 1888, Duryea got around to submitting United States Patent 402,313 for an actual women's safety bicycle.

In 1889, with a growing number of patents to his name and refined manufacturing skills, Duryea founded the Duryea Wheel Company in Washington, DC.[9] Around this time he also began contracting with other established manufacturers for small numbers of Sylph "spring truss frame" safety bicycles of his own design. His spring truss frames had pivots built into the frame on either side of the crank arms that were matched with front and rear springs that were both under tension. According to an 1892 bicycling handbook, "It is obvious that a frame trussed as is that of the Sylph is an exceptionally strong one, and as the springs take the shock, our machine, light though it is, can be ridden with impunity up and down curbs and would surely 'smash' a stiff frame machine of the same weight."[10] Duryea's spring truss frame was likely the first full-suspension safety bicycle design in history. In 1890, he contracted with the Ames Manufacturing Company in Chicopee Falls, Massachusetts, to build his Sylphs. By then, Frank had joined his brother, first working at Owen's, then at Ames. During their time in Massachusetts, Charles and Frank began collaborating on a prototype of a gasoline-powered automobile. Charles, though, was still primarily focused on bicycles.

Unhappy with the slow progress on his bicycles at Ames, Charles headed to Peoria in 1892. He already had a history in Peoria, having formed Rouse-Duryea Manufacturing there with Henry Rouse in 1889.[11] Rouse, Hazard & Company was one of the largest bicycle mail-order companies in the country but was looking to branch out into manufacturing its own line of bicycles. In 1892, Charles applied for yet another patent (United States Patent 493,488), this time for one of the first American pneumatic tire designs (the other contender, also from 1892, was Chicago's Gormully & Jeffery).[12] An 1891–92 Rouse, Hazard & Company catalog describes Duryea's Sylph bicycles as still being made by Ames, but by 1893 Rouse was selling three Sylph models, including a redesigned dual-suspension frame and the Sylph Model D, which featured a more traditional diamond frame without suspension. Rouse and Duryea took a number of their bicycles to Chicago for the 1893 World's Columbian Exposition, where many American and international bicycle companies had elaborate displays in the Transportation Building. Duryea's Sylph Model D racing bicycle was selected for an award during the juried bicycle competition.[13] By 1895, Rouse-Duryea had moved into a new factory in Peoria Heights with the capacity to produce 20,000 bicycles per year. The factory employed "between 300 and 400 expert mechanics, the majority of whom draw the highest salaries." The factory needed to implement day and night shifts to meet demand.[14]

By 1893, there was a wholesale shift in the American bicycle industry to pneumatic tires, which created new opportunities for tire manufacturers. To take advantage of this demand, Charles convinced Monroe Sieberling of Kokomo, Indiana, to build a tire, bicycle, and automobile manufacturing factory, also in Peoria Heights. Peoria Rubber and Manufacturing Company was formed in 1896. The new business quickly ramped up to employ 600 men, who manufactured 10,000 Patee and Atalanta bicycles and 25,000 pairs of bicycle tires annually.[15]

Charles Duryea's story is significant both because of his connection to the first Duryea mass-produced American automobile and because it is a microcosm of American bicycle manufacturing in the 1890s. To wit, anyone in the Midwest or Northeast with access to a little bit of capital and some general manufacturing knowledge would have had an excellent chance of building a successful bicycle manufacturing company in the early or mid-1890s. Charles's bicycle manufacturing efforts, while extensive, were not even close to being the largest operations in Illinois during the bicycle boom of the 1890s.

The 1890s United States Bicycle Industry

Illinois bicycle manufacturing in the 1890s was thoroughly a part of the second industrial revolution in the United States. The first American industrial revolution began around 1800 with what later became known as "the American System," or more simply, "the Factory System." The factory system concentrated labor and assembly of goods in one large building, or buildings, as opposed to the older model of piecemeal work being done in a variety of artisan shops and family homes. Early factories of the first industrial revolution first relied on water power from streams and rivers, then later adopted steam power. Drop forging, a relatively slow and imprecise manufacturing technique, was widely used. Increasingly, drop forged parts were finished to tighter tolerances with machines as opposed to being hand finished. The concept of interchangeable parts was also developed by American arms manufacturers and shipbuilders during this period and was then adopted by other industries. Cyrus McCormick and William Deering became leading Illinois manufacturers of agricultural implements during the first industrial revolution.[16]

The second industrial revolution is closely associated with steel. The Bessemer process, invented in 1856 by Sir Henry Bessemer of Great Britain, was a new method for making steel that was both cheaper and stronger than iron. Plentiful steel, in turn, enabled the rapid expansion of American railroads and bridges. Railroads would be a key element for the rapid rise of Midwest manufacturing. Midwest railroads allowed coal from Illinois, Indiana, and Ohio, along with iron ore found along Lake Superior, to be transported to cities, and then for the resulting finished manufactured goods to be exported out to the rest of the country. The widespread use of steam power, and later, electricity, in factories was also characteristic of the second industrial revolution. The increase in industrialization spurred a massive rural-to-urban migration, as Americans moved from farms to big cities to find work. Competition for manufactured goods, such as sewing machines and agricultural implements, also increased drastically.

Amid this period of growth and competition, many factories began diversifying their output by producing new items. For Illinois manufacturers like John Deere and the National Sewing Machine Company, those other items were bicycles. By 1890, Chicago had risen to prominence as the top meatpacking, lumber-milling, and furniture-building city in the country. Significantly, Chicago was also a top producer of iron and steel. By the mid-1890s, bicycles joined the list as one of Chicago's nationally leading industries. The shift in Chicago, as elsewhere, followed the 1885 appearance of the first safety bicycle, which quickly spread across the Atlantic. In the last few years of the 1880s, the number of American firms either making or importing bicycles jumped from around a dozen to more than seventy. Over the same period, it was estimated that the number of cyclists in the United States doubled to 150,000.[17] Chicago's manufacturers would help meet this surging demand.

The 1890 census data on bicycle manufacturing provided a decent—although not comprehensive—statistical overview of the United States bicycle industry at the time. The census data focused only on larger manufacturers whose sole line of business was bicycles, of which it found only twenty-seven across the country. The total annual value of bicycles manufactured by these companies was $2.6 million. By 1895, *Harper's Weekly* estimated the total bicycle trade (which encompassed more than just bicycle production) at $50 million, and *Bicycling World* reported that there were 3,000 American bicycle factories.[18] The United States bicycle boom reached its zenith between 1897 and 1898. In 1896, the *Century Illustrated* estimated that 2.5 million United States cyclists spent in the aggregate an astonishing $75 million ($2.7 billion in 2023) on bicycles and bicycle-related products and services.[19] In 1898, *Bicycling World* reported that nationwide there were 316 large manufacturers (that is, companies that produced at least 500 bicycles annually), and around 2,500 small manufacturers (which produced fewer than 500 bicycles annually).[20]

United States bicycle export statistics are another reliable indicator of the scope and importance of the American bicycle industry. In 1896, $3.4 million worth of bicycles were exported. *The Referee* cycling magazine provided a one-week snapshot of the bicycles and bicycle accessories exported from New York in July of that year. The bicycle boom was raging in cities around the globe, creating huge consumer demand. Predictably, many bicycles were being sent to larger European cities, including 108 cases of bicycles to Genoa, 543 cases to London, and another 100 to Southampton. Bicycle demand, however, was truly global in scope, as indicated by some of the other export destinations, including the British West Indies (one case), Cuba (three cases), New Zealand (five cases), and Newfoundland (three cases). In 1897, bicycle exports peaked at a massive $7 million ($255 million in 2024); then as the boom slackened, they decreased to $3.5 million by 1900.[21] It has been estimated that during the peak of the bicycle boom, between a quarter and a third of all United States bicycles left the country as exports. In 1898, bicycles ranked ninth among all United States exports, coming in behind American export stalwarts such as iron, oil, copper, and leather.[22]

Between 1895 and 1900, bicycles were a leading segment of the United States economy as a whole, with Illinois as the leading bicycle manufacturing state. Worldwide, Europe—and England in particular—were the early leaders in the production of high-wheel bicycles. During the safety bicycle boom of the 1890s, United States manufacturing leapt ahead due to advances in manufacturing technologies. In 1895, legendary French bicycle and tire manufacturer Adolphe Clément toured American bicycle manufacturing plants to see "the marvelous machinery that has already enabled American mechanics to compete successfully against the Old World." His American tour certainly included stops at Illinois bicycle manufacturers.[23]

The Illinois Bicycle Industry in the 1890s

As the high-wheel era came to an end, three Chicago firms (Western Wheel Works, St. Nicholas Toy Company, and Gormully & Jeffery) were producing a large number of that style of bicycle. The 1890 census data revealed that five Illinois factories (representing 18 percent of the national total) were producing $2.6 million worth of bicycles. Chicago city directories provide a clearer snapshot of what was happening bicycle-wise within the city. The 1890 city directory listed thirteen companies under the general heading "Bicycles" and nine under "Bicycles and Tricycles." As the bicycle boom began to ramp up, all the major Illinois manufacturers were offering one or more hard-tired safety models by 1890. As the *American Athlete and Cycle Trades Review* reported that year, "There is a certain fever in the Chicago air which is striking down our local cyclists right and left, and that is the go-into-business-for-myself fever."[24]

By the mid-1890s, according to bicycle historian David Herlihy, "the center of the American Industry had . . . shifted to the Midwest."[25] By 1895, the Chicago city directory listed 144 companies under "Bicycles" and 52 under "Bicycle Repairers."[26] These numbers for the general "Bicycle" heading represented a 1,000 percent increase over five years earlier. For a number of years, the cycling magazine *The Referee* published a nationwide bicycle trade directory. In 1897, the directory showed Illinois leading the country with 106 bicycle factories; New York was second with 88; and Ohio came in a distant third with 39.[27] Based on city directories, the bicycle boom in Chicago peaked during 1897, when there were 447 listings under "Bicycle" (an astonishing 3,338 percent increase in just seven years). In 1898, a comprehensive directory of the bicycle trade in Chicago listed one hundred manufacturers, along with more than four hundred bicycle dealers and repairers. "Two-thirds of this country's output of bicycles and accessories comes from within a radius of 150 miles around Chicago," the publication boldly claimed, "and the bulk of the trade is handled in the city proper."[28] A 150-mile radius would have included all the factories in the Chicago suburbs; Peoria; Milwaukee and Beloit, Wisconsin; and a few more in northwest Indiana. This area represented the core of American bicycle manufacturing at the end of the nineteenth century.

Even correcting for the bravado and boosterism endemic to the directory, the "two-thirds" claim was probably not far off the mark. By the time the *Census of Manufactures* was conducted again in 1900, the boom had become a bust; even then, Illinois still led the nation with 4,388 bicycle factory employees producing $9 million worth of bicycles. New York was a distant second at $3.8 million. As a special census report pointed out, Illinois's bicycle product value outstripped that of all the New England states combined.[29]

All told, Illinois was home to nearly 500 different bicycle brands during the 1890s that produced more than 800 different bicycle models.[30] To be clear, there were not 500 separate vertically integrated bicycle manufacturers in the state; it was common practice for the major manufacturers and specialty bicycle "jobbers" to sell unbranded bicycles to smaller firms or local shops, which then put their own head badge on the bicycle and perhaps added a few small customizations. Another common practice was for small bicycle shops and "manufacturers" to purchase all the individual parts needed to make a bicycle, including frame tubing, frame lugs, and crank hangers, then assemble their own "shop bicycles." They weren't making the parts, so they technically weren't bicycle manufacturers, but they were certainly bicycle assemblers.

In other respects, though, the total number of bicycle brands and models does not capture the full picture of bicycle production. The 1900 *Census of Manufactures* special report on bicycles noted that its total reported bicycle production numbers did not include the output of 6,328 bicycle and tricycle repair shops from across the country, since those were a different classification than companies whose sole line of work was manufacturing bicycles. In 1899, *The Cycle Age and Trade Review* observed the role of these small builders in the bicycle industry: "The greater part of the bicycle repairers in large cities, and a goodly number of those in smaller towns, have become recognized in their respective vicinities as cycle builders as well as repairers."[31] By that year, it has been estimated, these small batch "shop bicycles" accounted for around one-third of all bicycles produced in the country.[32] *The Sporting Goods Dealer* recounted a story about how quickly and easily these small shops sprang into business during the mid and late 1890s:

> A sales representative for a maker of sundries remembered visiting a Chicago store when a well dressed older gentleman bought a bicycle and asked to be taught to ride. Two months later, after recruiting a lawyer and a grocery-

> man to join his project, he had started a bicycle company, bought parts and material on credit from jobbers, and had a wheel on the street. The old man was still the only one of the three who could ride . . . adding that "they did not even know who made the Rambler, the Victor, the Columbia or any of the old makes."[33]

In short, the scope of Illinois bicycle manufacturing during the 1890s was massive.

Major Illinois Bicycle Manufacturers

Nearly 500 bicycle companies existed at some point in Illinois during the 1890s. The following section highlights the largest manufacturers that had a national or international presence in the industry, while a later section documents several smaller manufacturers or builders of particular significance to Illinois bicycle history.

A. Featherstone & Co.

The roots of the A. Featherstone & Co. date back to 1871, when the Henry Will & Co. was founded in Chicago. Henry Will & Co. was a leading manufacturer of children's carriages and toys. Alfred Featherstone moved from New York to Chicago in 1881 and quickly rose through the ranks at the company, assuming control of it and changing its name in 1886. A Chicago history published in 1887 described the company as manufacturing children's carriages, rocking horses, toy wagons, children's sleighs, velocipedes, and bicycles. A year later, it was reported that "their attention is now devoted exclusively to the manufacture of high grade wheels."[34]

Featherstone became a significant player in American bicycle history when they secured the rights to manufacture pneumatic tires based on John Boyd Dunlop's patents. Dunlop, a Scottish veterinarian, invented a pneumatic tire in 1887 and patented it the following year. While not the first to invent a pneumatic tire, Dunlop was the first to successfully bring one into commercial production. He secured United States patents for his designs in 1890 and 1891 and entered into an exclusive licensing deal with A. Featherstone sometime late in 1890. Early the following year, Featherstone ran full-page advertisements in multiple cycling periodicals, letting the industry know that his company had secured United States rights to Dunlop's patents and that any future American pneumatic tire manufacturers would be required to pay licensing fees. Featherstone was never as successful in cornering the tire market as Pope was with the high-wheel bicycle market, but their early adoption of pneumatics made the company highly profitable.[35]

By March of 1891, Featherstone was running advertisements for $135 ($4,500 in 2024) pneumatic tire-equipped bicycles, marking the beginning of a new era in American bicycling. These bikes were clearly still luxury items, as annual salaries for skilled laborers were only around $600.[36] In later catalogs, Featherstone would boast of being "the first to manufacture pneumatic tires for bicycles and fit them to wheels in America." Pneumatic tires decreased rolling resistance while increasing comfort. These tires, coupled with the new style of safety bicycle, set the stage for making bicycling accessible to the masses. Anticipating massive demand, Featherstone claimed to have 1,200 men working on pneumatic tire production and an expected capacity of 500 Featherstone bicycles per week. Their most popular models were the "Road King" and "Road Queen." The Featherstone factory at Clark and 16th Street was five stories tall and covered half a block. Cutting-edge machinery was used throughout, including 50 lathes, 75 drill presses, 50 turret machines, and 135 other machines, all powered by a 500-horsepower Corliss Engine. Featherstone was one of the top producers in the country from 1895 to 1899, churning out 60,000 bicycles per year while employing between 1,100 and 1,400 workers. In 1899, as the bicycle boom was rapidly coming to an end, Featherstone sold out to the new American Bicycle Company trust formed by Albert Spalding and Albert Pope.[37]

Gormully & Jeffery Manufacturing Company

Gormully & Jeffery (G&J) was easily the most successful of the Illinois high-wheel manufacturers. The company's Ideal and American Champion models were sold through dealers and bicycle shops around the country and in Europe. This success allowed G&J to invest heavily in its manufacturing facilities and equipment. In 1886, G&J established a new five-story factory on North Franklin Street in Chicago. According to *The Cycle*, the new factory was "the largest and most comprehensive bicycle manufacturing plant in the world, with a capacity of turning out seventy-five perfect bicycles a day, and will furnish employment to four hundred skilled mechanics." Unlike other manufacturers that outsourced many of their parts, G&J claimed to make everything in-house other than tires, rubber handles, and saddle leather.[38] It would not be long before they would make these remaining items in-house as well. In 1887, *Frank Leslie's Illustrated Newspaper* ran a full page of illustrations featuring different parts of bicycle assembly at the G&J factory while declaring it the "largest establishment" in the country.[39]

In 1888, G&J produced its first safety-style bicycle, the American Rambler. Its radical design distinguished it from everything else on the market. The frame consisted of a large "C" shape with no seat tube. This unconventional design provided some degree of built-in suspension to compensate for the rough ride of the hard rubber tires and small wheels. When describing the American Rambler to the cycling press, G&J claimed, "We do not care to be original for oddity's sake, but neither do we believe in following blindly the lead of other makers because the form and type are accepted ones."[40] The first version of the American Rambler weighed forty-four pounds and sold for $120 ($3,800 in 2024). In 1888, G&J also developed and patented a hollow steel rim that reduced the weight of their ordinaries and new safeties. A year later, a redesigned American Rambler incorporated a spring between the top of the seat tube and the seat stays, again to provide suspension. The design, although rudimentary, was conceptually the same as the first attempts in the 1980s and 1990s to build rear suspension into mountain bike frames.

Front cover of an 1891 Gormully and Jeffery bicycle catalog. (Author's collection.)

Soon, G&J was offering multiple styles of spring-frame Ramblers for both men and women. The illustration on the cover of their 1891 catalog featured a graphic and complicated attempt to cast bicycles as a symbol of progress; it showed a Native American man who has shot his horse and is riding away on a Rambler. Progress and bicycles had become synonymous, at least according to G&J advertising. Confident in the quality of their bicycles, G&J became one of the first American bicycle companies to offer a one-year warranty against all manufacturing defects. In 1891, G&J also discreetly published a pamphlet titled *Bicycling for Girls from a Medical Standpoint*. This short document provided health advice and physician testimonials designed to demonstrate that bicycling was indeed safe for women and provided a dignified riding experience. Physician Robert N. Tooker testified, "I would especially recommend such bicycles as I understand are made with spring frames, so constructed that the vibration is entirely eliminated from the saddle or seat." An asterisk at the end of this testimonial leads the reader to a note stating, "Such a machine is the American Rambler, manufactured by Gormully & Jeffery Manufacturing Co."[41]

G&J was certainly keenly aware of Featherstone's introduction of pneumatic-equipped safeties in 1891. Recall that, at the time, G&J was still in the final stages of multiyear litigation over bicycle patent rights with Pope Manufacturing, making it disinclined to start paying a competing Chicago bicycle company for every set of pneumatic tires they installed. As soon as Thomas Jeffery realized the potential for pneumatic tires to revolutionize the bicycle industry, he began working on his own design. Between 1891 and 1892, Jeffery filed, and then was awarded, three tire patents (United States Patents 454,115, 466,565, and 466,789). To circumvent Featherstone's Dunlop patent, Jeffery created a substantially different pneumatic tire. His design had external cords that hooked into grooves cut into the rim. It did not require glue and was therefore relatively easy to install and uninstall. In essence, Jeffery designed a single-tube (his inner tube and tire casing were all one piece) version of a clincher tire. Modern clincher bicycle tires are not all that different from Jeffery's 1891 design.[42]

Even though G&J and Pope had spent an estimated half a million dollars litigating against each other in court, their interests converged when it came to tires. In 1893, Pope approached G&J to provide their tires for his Columbia bicycles. R. Phillip Gormully was quoted as saying, "My dealings with Colonel Pope have been entirely friendly and I am pleased to think that, from this time forward the most cordial relations will exist between the two houses. The colonel is a fair fighter and a good one. When we fight, we fight; but when we have finished we have finished."[43] Pope was the earliest American manufacturer of wire-spoked high-wheel bicycles, but he was quickly ceding ground to multiple Illinois companies in the safety-era.

G&J's new pneumatic tires meant that in 1892 it could begin selling a traditional "double-diamond" Rambler without the heavier spring-frame components. G&J set up an elaborate display at the 1893 World's Columbian Exposition in Chicago, where it was awarded five medals of merit for their Men's and Women's Ramblers, pneumatic tire, unbrazed bicycle frame, and parabolic bicycle lamp.

The following year, the company claimed that twenty-five world records were broken using Rambler bicycles, which had produced an additional 1,000 first-place finishes.[44] G&J's increasingly light racing frames, coupled with their industry-leading tires, were certainly partially responsible for their racing accolades. In their 1895 catalog, G&J wrote, "Hundreds think themselves undeveloped world wonders, only to find themselves defeated on the track by men either physically better or *mounted better* . . . To this class of riders we offer our Rambler Number 10, 'our racing machine.'" The Rambler Number 10 was truly a manufacturing marvel, with the complete wood-rimmed version weighing an astonishing 14 ¾ pounds (a weight on par with the lightest commercially available carbon bicycles in 2024). A thirty-two-pound racing tandem was also available. To achieve these weights, G&J pioneered (and patented) lap-brazing techniques that used flared tubes that overlapped smaller tubes, a significantly lighter system than traditional lugged frame designs. The Number 10 was also the first example of what modern cyclists would call a "compact frame." Compact frame design features steeply sloping top tubes, compact rear triangles, and longer-than-usual seat posts. In 1997, the Giant bicycle company claimed to have created the first compact frame (Total Compact Road, or TCR), but they needed to look back one hundred years earlier to find the true origins of the design.[45]

Business was good during the mid-1890s, and G&J went on a spending spree. In 1895, it opened an additional eight-story factory "with a full complement of expensive automatic machines and testing apparatus, comprising the latest improvements . . . to maintain the superiority of the Rambler." The factory covered one and a third acres and employed 650 workers.[46] In 1896, G&J offered $1,000 in gold ($32,000 in 2023) to any rider that was able to lower the one-mile world record using a Rambler and G&J tires. In a classic example of Gilded Age excess, G&J built a $1,000 Rambler for the 1896 National Cycle Exhibition that featured silver embossing, amethysts, pearls, and gold components.[47]

Like many of the top producers in the country, G&J was bought out by the American Bicycle Company trust in 1899. Through the trust, Pope gained rights to the Rambler name and would continue to produce Rambler bicycles into the early 1900s. R. Phillip Gormully died in 1900, and Thomas Jeffery would go on to produce Rambler automobiles in Kenosha, Wisconsin.[48]

Monarch Cycle Manufacturing Company

The Monarch Cycle Manufacturing Company was notable not for its technical innovations, but rather for the savvy marketing and high-quality bicycles that made it one of the country's top producers during the boom. Like so many other 1890s bicycle companies, Monarch's roots can be found in another industry—in this case, sewing machines. John William Kiser rose through the ranks to become president of the Chicago Sewing Machine Company, but he saw a more profitable future in the bicycle industry. In 1890, the company established a small bicycle division, which a year later employed thirty-five people and only produced 150 bicycles. Monarch Cycle Manufacturing Company was officially incorporated in 1892. The company saw phenomenal growth during the mid-1890s and moved into a new six-story, 90,000 square-foot factory on north Halsted Street. By 1896, 1,500 Monarch employees were annually churning out 50,000 bicycles (worth a combined $2 million). In the late 1890s, "chainless" bicycles that used a shaft-drive and bevel gears were all the rage. Monarch patented their own shaft-drive system, but it never caught on. Monarch, too, was targeted for acquisition by the American Bicycle Company trust in 1899. Even as the bicycle boom was coming to an end, the Monarch brand appeared to thrive. Their 1900 catalog reported the company making 60,000 bikes per year, having made a grand total of 300,000 by that point.[49]

A substantial portion of Monarch's success was attributable to their massive investments in advertising. A study of Gilded Age advertising found that Monarch spent a few thousand dollars in 1893 to sell 1,200 bicycles. The following year their advertising expenditure was $20,000, resulting in 5,000 bicycle sales. By 1896, the company spent $125,000 ($4.5 million in 2024) to sell 50,000 bicycles, which they boasted "were marketed in every civilized country in the world." With hundreds of competing bicycle brands in Illinois and thousands across the country, bicycle manufacturers needed some way of distinguishing themselves. Monarch invested in lavish catalogs with color lithograph covers that featured beautiful original artwork. Likewise, its magazine and newspaper advertisements stood out from competitors through their frequently changing original designs, many of them featuring some version of the Monarch lion trademark. The artwork was a product of Monarch's marketing strategy. Rather than contracting with artists, the company advertised for art design competitions, where winners were awarded cash or free bicycles.[50]

Arnold, Schwinn & Co.

Today, Schwinn is widely recognized as America's most iconic bicycle brand. The company dominated the American bicycle market for most of the twentieth century. Schwinn's origins in 1890s Chicago were comparatively humble, however. Ignaz Schwinn's bicycle career began in the late 1880s in Germany, where he worked as a machinist in a small shop producing bicycle parts before emigrating to Chicago in 1891. Per the Schwinn Company history published for its fiftieth anniversary, Ignaz "went to work for the firm of Hill & Moffat."[51] By 1893, Moffatt Cycles was bankrupt, and Hill, along with Frank Fowler, had incorporated Hill Manufacturing Company, which made the popular Fowler line of bicycles. Ignaz worked for the new Hill Manufacturing Company for a brief time and then left to help set up a new factory for the Chicago-based International Manufacturing Company, maker of the "America" brand of bicycles. While working for International, the diminutive Schwinn posed next to an America bicycle and 500-pound Baby Bliss, a five-hundred-pound bicycle celebrity from Bloomington who advertised for the company. After establishing the factory, Ignaz served as superintendent for a time but found that the company "was not managed to his liking" and departed sometime in 1894.[52]

Around this time, Ignaz made the acquaintance of Adolph Frederick William Arnold, a fellow Chicagoan and also a German immigrant. Arnold had amassed a small fortune through his part ownership of the Arnold Bros. meatpacking business and the Haymarket Produce Bank. Ignaz convinced Arnold to invest in a new bicycle company, and Arnold, Schwinn, & Co. was founded in September of 1895 with capital stock of $75,000.[53] Their corporate charter gave the new company wide leeway in their future endeavors, allowing them to "manufacture, buy, sell and deal in bicycles, sulkies, wagons, carriages, vehicles, and parts for the same." The company established a factory on the corner of West Lake Street and Peoria Street and announced plans to build 5,000–7,000 bicycles in its first year. By the 1896 January Chicago Cycle Show, Arnold, Schwinn, & Co. had a few models ready for display and sale. The company remained quite small. Ignaz was a master German craftsman, however, and his "World" model bicycles became known for their quality and racing capabilities. The 1898 Schwinn catalog boasted that World bicycles were embraced "from Klondike's glacial realms to South America's Horn, from Iceland's icy shores to Africa's end of Hope, from Siberia's snowy fields over China's Wall of Stone, under Japan's balmy skies to the Land of the kangaroo . . . wherever man may roam, 'WORLD Cycles' have found a home and are synonym for BEST." Models that year included Men's and Women's Roadsters, a nineteen-pound Track Racer, a tandem, a triplet, and a $350 quad bicycle.[54]

In 1896, to further promote the company and its World bicycles, Schwinn bankrolled the "World Team," for which he recruited top trainer Tom Eck and champion cyclist John S. Johnson. Schwinn also built a special quintuplet pacing bicycle, which they shipped to France for a series of international races and world-record attempts.[55]

Schwinn family on a Schwinn-built tandem, 1896. (From the Historic Cycling Photographic Collection of Lorne Shields, Toronto, Canada.)

In 1899, Schwinn was too small to interest the American Bicycle Company trust, which targeted only the largest bicycle manufacturers in the country. Despite flagging bicycle sales across the country, Schwinn was doing well enough in that year to purchase the bankrupt March-Davis Cycle Co. at a receiver's sale. Schwinn survived the bicycle bust, in part, by securing lucrative contracts to supply Chicago-based Sears, Roebuck & Co. and Montgomery Ward with large numbers of low-priced bicycles to be sold in their catalogs under Sears' and Ward's own model names. In 1901, Schwinn moved their corporate offices to North Kostner Avenue, where they would remain for nearly a century. Schwinn weathered the end of the bicycle boom better than most, partially through early investments in motorcycle manufacturing. From these humble beginnings in 1890s Chicago, Schwinn went on to create one of the world's largest and most successful bicycle companies.[56]

Western Wheel Works

In 1895, Chicago's *Inter Ocean* newspaper ran a series of articles under the heading "Greatest in the World." One of these articles profiled a company "located in Chicago on the north side of the river not more than a mile from the busy center of the city": the Western Wheel Works, "the greatest" of "the great bicycle manufactories of the world."[57] The evolution of Western Wheel Works into America's largest and most innovative bicycle manufacturer during the boom began at the end of the high-wheel era, when it was known as Western Toy Company. Recall that the company had been a major American producer of high-wheel bicycles, second in Illinois only to Gormully & Jeffery. As the safety bicycle burst onto the scene in the late 1880s, Schoeninger went all-in on bicycles, reincorporating his company as Western Wheel Works in 1889. That same year, the new company invested heavily in its manufacturing capabilities by building a new 375,000-square-foot factory on the corner of N. Wells and Schiller Streets in Chicago.[58]

The pivotal move for Western Wheel Works came in 1890, when it embraced the emerging manufacturing technique of stamping metal parts for bicycles. Western Wheel Works was the first large bicycle manufacturer to implement and then improve industrial stamping techniques. By 1890, the Western Wheel Works factory extended across nine buildings and counted 650 employees. That year, the company purchased materials to build 25,000 bicycles. Notably, Pope Manufacturing, the country's largest manufacturer at the time, purchased 1,000 bicycles from Western Wheel Works (which they presumably re-badged and sold as Columbias).[59] In 1893, Rand, McNally & Co.'s guide to the World's Fair and the surrounding city provided fairgoers with generous details about the company's factory. According to the guide, Western Wheel Works employed 1,200 people, produced 38,000 bicycles, and had the largest bicycle factory in the country. The company installed its own electric dynamos to power 1,200 incandescent lights.[60]

By 1894, Schoeninger had retired from Western Wheel Works and founded the Home Rattan Company, which manufactured children's carriages, chairs, and toys. Home Rattan would soon add children's bicycles to its output. Reuben Lindsay ("R. L.") Coleman, who had overseen the East Coast sales and warehouses for Western Toy and the Western Wheel Works, took over as president of the company. By 1895, the company had grown to 1,500 employees, and its factories had the capacity to churn out up to 300 bicycles per day. Total production for the year was reported at 57,000 bicycles. For some international context, the combined output of all bicycle manufacturers in France was only about 60,000 in 1895.[61]

In 1896, Western Wheel Works became the clear leader of the United States bicycle industry, producing 70,000 bicycles, at least 10,000 more than Pope Manufacturing. The company that year claimed to have "made more high-grade bicycles than any other two factories in the country." The same company bulletin provided an astonishing look at the sheer amount of materials that went into producing Crescent bicycles in 1896. The list of raw materials included 350 miles of frame tubing; 780 miles of spoke wire; 50 miles of

Color lithograph of an 1899 Crescent bicycle advertisement created by Fredrick Winthrop Ramsdell. (Author's collection.)

brass rod for spoke nipples; 35 miles of steel for crank axles, wheel axles, and pedal axles; 19 miles of steel for seat posts; 1 ¼ acres flat steel stock for the steel stampings for sprockets, head clamps, and seat post clamps; 13,997,300 steel ball bearings; 246 ½ miles of cord for chain and dress guards; 1,606,742 bolts; 1,488,975 nuts; 16 ¼ miles of spring steel for saddle springs; and 4 acres of leather for saddle and tool bags. Finished products included 10 miles of cork grips; 70 miles of chain; 72,718,668 individual pieces; and 1,191 tons of bicycles.[62]

The company's sales spanned the continent and globe. Five railroad cars full of bicycles per week were shipped to the company's eastern warehouse. A record-breaking single shipment of 3,685 bicycles once filled fifteen railroad cars. According to the *New York Times*, this represented "the first time in the history of the industry that these popular pleasure vehicles have been transported by train load." The company's "Crescent" brand bicycles were sold in "all the principal cities of Europe, Asia, and South America." European sales were so strong that Western Wheel Works had its own exhibit space at the 1896 Exposition Internationale de Vélocipédie et d'Automobiles in Paris.[63]

Western Wheel Works increased its bicycle sales every year from 1884 to 1900.[64] In 1897, the company sold 83,000 bicycles and set a one-day record by completing 750 bicycles in ten hours. For the 1898 season, shaft-driven, chainless bicycles were offered for sale by the major manufacturers as a novel "improvement" that they hoped would stimulate slumping bicycle sales. Western Wheel Works offered its own high-grade chainless but surely made no friends in the industry when it severely undercut the competition by selling its version for $75 instead of the $100 or $125 other manufacturers were asking. Chainless sales, plus the sales of regular Crescent bicycles priced between $30 and $50, enabled Western Wheel Works to sell more than 100,000 bicycles in both 1898 and 1899.

Western Wheel Works thus was a logical target for the American Bicycle Company trust. After some negotiations, R. L. Coleman agreed to sell Western Wheel Works for a reported $2.5 million ($90.6 million in 2024). In 1900, Coleman succeeded A.G. Spalding as the president of the trust.[65]

Western Wheel Works' success during the 1890s can be attributed to its adoption and refinement of industrial stamping techniques. To understand the broader significance of stamping to American manufacturing requires a baseline understanding of metallurgy and the metalworking techniques that predated stamping. Throughout most of the nineteenth century, American manufacturers of metal goods relied heavily on drop forging. As a manufacturing technique, forging involves pouring liquid metal into a die. Drop forging, then, involves heating a solid piece of metal that is placed into or over a die and submitted to high-pressure "drop" blows to shape and strengthen the metal. The end product is quite strong. However, if a final part of even mild complexity is needed, a great deal of additional wasteful and time-intensive machining is required.[66] The Pope Manufacturing Company largely followed manufacturing techniques derived from New England arms manufacturers. At bicycle shows, Pope sometimes displayed a complete set of the forgings needed to build a regular bicycle. The unfinished set weighed fifteen-and-a-half pounds and required intensive machining to remove 68 percent of the metal, resulting in a finished weight of about five pounds.[67] With this display, Pope was essentially touting its dated, time-intensive manufacturing techniques.

Western Wheel Works, on the other hand, followed a tradition of nineteenth-century Midwestern companies that developed innovative new manufacturing processes. Before the bicycle era, large Midwestern manufacturers focused their innovations on agricultural implements, railroad cars, sewing machines, toys, and furniture. Increased productivity became a badge of regional honor. "I never saw a job where the Western man would not beat the Eastern man out every time," exclaimed a Chicago mechanic in 1890. "You [Eastern men] know too much about tool making, and not enough about making money."[68]

Illustration of Western Wheel Works punching presses from their 1897 catalog. (Author's collection.)

As early as 1890, Western Wheel Works began incorporating some stamped parts into their bicycles. It initially imported stamped parts from Germany but soon switched to manufacturing its own parts.[69] In contrast to drop forging, stamping uses flat steel stock. Large presses or punches, powered by either steam or electricity, apply tremendous force to steel to cut or bend it into the form of the desired end product. As a manufacturing process, stamping is much faster than drop forging. David Hounshell, who wrote the definitive history of American manufacturing, pointed specifically to Western Wheel Works' development and implementation of stamping as critical to mass production: "bicycle makers outside the armory tradition and located primarily in the Midwest developed an important new method of metalworking. This technique—stamping or pressing—has played a fundamental role in mass production industries of the twentieth century."[70] To be clear, Western Wheel Works did not invent the stamping process. However, it was the first American company to embrace the technique and successfully scale it up in a large industrial setting. In doing so, they invented and patented multiple new stamping machines and processes. The *Inter Ocean* reported on these innovations, "I was informed that several of the most ingenious and useful of these machines could be seen nowhere else in the world, the patents being owned exclusively by the Western Wheel Works. All of these are the invention of Mr. Otto Unzicker, company vice president, who certainly ranks among the most scientific men of his profession." The same article noted that there were 325 machines that did the work of "ten times as many men" in use at the Western Wheel Works factory. These machines were run by a 600-horsepower engine powered by steam boilers.[71]

Western Wheel Works figured out how to automate the process of crank hangers, one of the most complex components of nineteenth-century safety bicycles. Crank hangers needed threaded fittings on both sides to hold the cranks and bearings in place. Radiating out from the hanger were four different, precisely placed lugs for attaching the frame downtube, seat tube, and two chainstays. Drop forged crank hangers normally required a great deal of milling work before they could be used. Western Wheel Works' process was much more efficient. A newspaper account described it thusly:

> A piece of steel is fed into a machine and after passing through twenty-six distinct operations it assumes the shape of a finished hanger with the tube lugs perfectly formed and feathered so that only the surface polishing is necessary. Machining and drilling are quite unneeded, as it comes from the dies true and perfect, ready for the brazing-room.[72]

Western Wheel Works also helped to pioneer the assembly line, well ahead of Henry Ford's celebrated automobile factories. The company learned early on that maximum manufacturing efficiency required runners to continuously supply parts to the various machines. According to Hounshell, "In almost every process using machines, the Western Wheel Works employees sat to operate the machines and did not have to move any material before or after carrying out the operation." This is an apt description of an assembly line. Likewise, multiple American bicycle companies were utilizing early assembly lines fifteen years or more before Ford did the same. Ford himself was a former bicycle mechanic, and he visited bicycle factories to study their assembly processes before setting up his Model T assembly line. His essential contribution to the assembly line was not inventing it but rather mechanizing the process so that parts moved on a belt to the workers.[73]

Stamping and highly efficient assembly line processes allowed Western Wheel Works to make bicycles quickly and cheaply. Western Wheel Works was largely responsible for bringing down the price of high-grade bicycles from a luxury item costing $100 or more in the early 1890s to only $35 in 1899. This drastic decrease in cost enabled larger socio-economic classes of American society to afford bicycles, which inadvertently hastened the end of the bicycle boom. Nearly every American manufacturer that produced metal goods eventually adopted some of the stamping processes developed by Western Wheel Works. The development and refinement of industrial stamping should be remembered as one of Illinois bicycling's greatest legacies.

Significant Smaller Bicycle Builders

As noted above, hundreds of small bicycle shops and factories across Illinois assembled and customized their own bicycle models. Few had the resources to actually manufacture their own parts, but all could easily cut and braze frame tubes, lace hubs to rims, and assemble a finished bicycle that would then carry their own head badge. The output of these small shops should not be underestimated. While most produced a few hundred to a few thousand bicycles per year, their combined output was responsible for around one-third of all bicycles by the end of the nineteenth century.[74] The following section documents a few significant smaller Illinois bicycle builders.

Deere & Company

In 1868, John Deere incorporated Deere & Company in Moline, Illinois, to expand the manufacturing of his successful self-scouring plow design. The company grew rapidly over the next two decades, opening multiple manufacturing branches and dealerships. One of these branch houses was the Minneapolis-based Deere & Webber Company, which was incorporated in 1893. Charles C. Webber, a grandson of John Deere, was in charge of the branch, and the bicycle boom had piqued his interest. "If there is anything in this bicycle business," Webber wrote to another branch manager in 1893, "any money to be made, we want to take hold of it."[75]

Charles D. Velie, another of Deere's grandsons, was put in charge of John Deere's emerging bicycle business. In 1894, Velie placed an order for 1,000 bicycles that would bear the John Deere name, while the company also sold Tribune (Black Manufacturing Company, Pennsylvania) and Peerless (Peerless Manufacturing Company, Ohio) bicycles. The earliest John Deere bicycle models were the Deere Roadster, Deere Leader, and the Moline Special. Like so many others around the country, Deere turned to Chicago to manufacture bicycles to their specifications. Surviving company records do not indicate which specific companies they contracted with, but *Farm Implement News* reported that "C.D. Velie has gone to Chicago to look after the factory end of the company's wheel business."[76]

The Deere bicycle business thrived as the bicycle boom ramped up. Company catalogs featured their bicycle offerings alongside their agricultural equipment. For 1895, Deere upped their bicycle order to 2,000 machines.

In the summer of 1895, Velie organized the first "Deere Road Race" in Minneapolis. The twenty-mile race featured $2,000 in prizes and attracted 127 entrants. In 1896, Velie unveiled a new company logo that featured a deer riding a bicycle. At the highly attended Minneapolis bicycle show, Deere & Webber displayed a Tiffany-crafted, pearl-inlaid bicycle that was worth more than $5,000. Another highlight of the Deere exhibit was a Tribune bicycle weighing a mere eight pounds. Deere & Webber paid the Minnesota State Agricultural Society $1,000 to secure August 31, 1896, as "Deere & Webber Co. Bicycle Day" at the Minnesota State Fair. Deere & Webber Co. Bicycle Day featured races, club contests, contests for "lady bicyclists," and a parade. For both 1895 and 1896, Deere bicycle sales topped $150,000 ($5.4 million in 2023).[77]

As the bicycle boom waned at the end of the nineteenth century, John Deere slowly extracted itself from the bicycle business. In 1897, it was reported that John Deere was seeking to either purchase or build a bicycle factory in the Chicago area. Instead, they ended up contracting "for the entire output of one bicycle factory, the wheels to be made according to Deere specifications." The last Deere bicycles were sold off in 1902, although John Deere would briefly return to selling Deere-branded bicycles during a different bicycle boom, this time in the 1970s.[78]

Elgin Cycle Company

During the 1890s, Elgin, Illinois, was home to at least four bicycle companies: C. H. Woodruff, Elgin Cycle Company, Elgin Sewing Machine Company, and Seuberth-Leach Manufacturing. Of these, the Elgin Cycle Company is the most notable. Here, again, the story was of industrial conversion. In establishing the Elgin Cycle Company, the successful Illinois Watch Case Company saw an opportunity to leverage their manufacturing abilities to get in on the bicycle boom. This subsidiary was set up sometime in 1895 and shortly after began marketing and selling Elgin Specials for racing, Elgin Kings and Queens, Elgin Princes and Princesses, and Elgin Double Diamond Tandems.

As a promotional gimmick, the artisans at the Illinois Watch Case Company helped the Elgin Cycle Company build an elaborate $5,000 ($179,000 in 2024) Elgin King that was displayed at bicycle shows around the country. The bicycle featured 820 pennyweights of twenty-two karat gold that were crafted into intricate images of branches and leaves. Inlaid with the gold were more than fifteen karats of diamonds and eight additional gemstones. This bicycle helped the company generate additional sales for similar, but less elaborate, custom bicycles, which they sold for $500 to $5,000. The following year, the Elgin Cycle Company crafted a similar tandem bicycle valued at $10,000. According to the 1897 Elgin Cycle Company catalog, the tandem was the most expensive bicycle ever manufactured and featured "8 ⅓ lbs. of fine gold[,] one hundred and seventy-six genuine diamonds, ranging in size from one to eight carats each, several hundred rubies, pearls, emeralds and other precious stones." Images carved in solid gold included a bicycle track with riders and grandstand, a baseball game, a hunting scene, the Washington Park bicycle track in Chicago on Derby Day, and horse races. The tandem also featured two L.A.W. emblems that were encrusted with diamonds. The catalog claimed that the bicycle was not just for exhibiting but was perfectly rideable. Conspicuous consumption characterized America during the Gilded Age, and these Elgin bicycles were truly emblematic of the era.[79] Beginning in the late 1920s, Sears, Roebuck and Co. revived the Elgin brand name with a series of boldly designed bicycles. These Elgin bicycles were big sellers for Sears in the 1930s and 1940s but had no relationship to the earlier Elgin bicycle companies. The Sears Elgins were all built outside of Illinois.

Hirsch Aluminum Bicycle Company

The development of the first aluminum bicycle was an important "first" in the history of American manufacturing. Aluminum is lighter than steel, but it is also more brittle and much harder to work with. Bicycle histories generally credit the St. Louis Refrigerator and Wooden Gutter Company with the invention of the first aluminum bicycle, named the "Lu-mi-num" in 1893.[80] However, there are multiple references to an earlier aluminum bicycle made in Chicago. What can be confirmed is that the Hirsch Aluminium [*sic*] Plating Company was incorporated in Chicago in 1890 with $5 million in capital stock.[81] The following year, the Hirsch Aluminium Bicycle Company also was incorporated in Chicago with $250,000 in capital. The company's namesake, Joseph M. Hirsch, was a German immigrant and chemist who specialized in aluminum plating. In October of 1891, the *Wheel and Cycling Trade Review* reported on the Hirsch aluminum bicycle, noting that people "claim to have seen a thirty pound road wheel built by the firm which is a model of beauty and strength, the frame of which is constructed in such a manner that each brace acts as part of another brace, etc. The frame and larger parts are all of aluminium. Their racing wheel will weigh but fourteen pounds, all on, so reports say." In January of 1892, the *Bearings* asked, "Will Professor Hirsch ever succeed in riding a fourteen pound aluminum 'Snow Flake?'" Later in 1892, Luther Porter's *Wheels and Wheeling: An Indispensable Handbook for Cyclists* included an extensive directory of American bicycles that have "been sold at any time in this country." Notably, Porter's directory included the Snow Flake manufactured by Hirsch.

A few Hirsch Snow Flakes might have been sold, or they may have only existed as prototypes. There are no known surviving examples of these bikes. The best that can be said with historical certainty is that Joseph Hirsch was working on an aluminum bicycle in Chicago around 1891 and 1892.[82]

Stover Bicycle Manufacturing Company

The Stover Bicycle Manufacturing Company was founded in Freeport, Illinois, in 1889. Stover built popular Iroquois and Phoenix model bicycles, but their real claim to fame was inventing the first American coaster brake and freewheel system. There were earlier English patents for coaster brake/freewheel systems on high-wheel bicycles, but in 1889, Daniel C. Stover and William A. Hance were awarded United States Patent 418,142 for bicycle improvements that included a freewheel mechanism for coasting without the pedals moving and with a back-pedal brake system. In their patent application, Stover and Hance explained their new back-pedal brake system: "The principal element of the brake-operating mechanism has heretofore been a hand-lever, but as the

Cover of a Stover Bicycle Manufacturing Company catalog featuring mischievous brownies. (Collection of John Traum.)

first movement when it is desired to stop the machine is naturally the reversal of the motion of the cranks of the driving-sprocket, we have embodied in this machine a brake mechanism adapted to be operated by such reversal of the crank motion." By the end of the nineteenth century, coaster brakes were becoming more popular; they would be nearly ubiquitous in the first half of the twentieth century. At some point in the 1890s, the Eclipse Manufacturing Company purchased the rights to the Stover brake patent to produce their highly-successful Morrow coaster brake hubs.[83]

In an era when there were thousands of different bicycle brands across the country, manufacturers went to great lengths to distinguish themselves. Stover produced some of the most beautiful color lithograph catalogs of the day. Its 1892 catalog, in particular, featured "brownies" most likely created by the Canadian illustrator and author Palmer Cox. The brownies were small, mischievous sprites popularized in Cox's children's books. The striking rear cover of the 1892 catalog features brownies taking joy rides on Stover bicycles while others launch fireworks in the background.[84]

Tonk Manufacturing Company

German immigrant Max Tonk cofounded the Chicago furniture manufacturing company Seaon & Tonk in 1873. In 1884, he took over as president, and Tonk Manufacturing was officially incorporated. In 1895, a Tonk employee named Phineas York submitted a patent application for a wooden bicycle frame made from hickory. By 1896, Tonk Manufacturing had brought their "Old Hickory" line of bicycles to the market, marking the first successful production bicycle made completely out of wood. Earlier attempts, such as those from the Elliott Hickory Cycle Company, utilized a combination of wood and metal tubing, and M.D. Stebbins "Chilion" wood frame bicycles were not sold until 1897. According to an Old Hickory catalog, second-growth hickory and rock elm were cut into ⅛-inch thick strips, then ten strips were laminated together with glue. The company claimed that the resulting frame was ten times as strong as steel and had better vibration-absorption properties. A unique feature of the Old Hickory frame was that both the front and rear triangles of the frame were steam-bent into continuous loops of wood before the two loops were joined together. In addition to the frame, the fork, rims, handlebar, fenders, and chain guard were all made of wood. The initial 1896 model sold for $90, with newspaper advertisements proclaiming, "It's springy though it has no springs." Tonk Manufacturing's Old Hickory bicycles were some of the most artistic and innovative bicycles ever manufactured.[85]

Two-Speed Bicycle Company

The development of variable-speed gearing was a significant innovation that made bicycles even easier to use and allowed them to travel over more varied terrain. Patents had been granted for variable-speed gearing for earlier velocipedes, high-wheels, and transitional bicycles, but only a few had made it into production. Recall that all safety bicycles at the time used a fixed-gear system. After the safety bicycle frame design opened up cycling to the masses, the addition of variable-speed gearing made cycling even more convenient and comfortable.

Illinois was home to the first commercially available American safety bicycle with variable-gearing, the "American Hill-Climber," manufactured by the Two-Speed Bicycle Company of St. Charles. First offered for sale in 1892, the American Hill-Climber two-speed bicycle predated other variable-speed bicycles that have been erroneously identified as the first in the United States.[86] Newspaper ads stated, "The gearing is so arranged that by merely moving a switch lever it can be instantaneously shifted from a 40[-inch gear] to 60, or vice versa. The makers think they have solved the secret of hill climbing."[87] The design featured two different-sized gears mounted between the cranks and utilized a type of clutch system to switch between them. In addition to variable speeds, the bicycle offered another innovation—the ability to disengage the pedals and coast. An *Iron Age* article provided more detailed information on both the two-speed system and the coasting mechanism: "The machines are shifted from one gear to another without taking the feet from the pedals by turning a small switch lever. The larger sprocket is used when riding on good roads and the smaller one for hill climbing. The sprocket not in use runs idle, and for coasting the cranks stand still if desired. It is remarked that there is no jerk when the gear is changed."[88] Quite possibly, the coasting feature was the first example of a "freewheel" mechanism in a commercially produced safety bicycle.[89]

The Two-Speed Bicycle Company was officially incorporated in Chicago in 1893. Frank M. Goodhue and James E. Goodhue (both part-owners of the Two-Speed Bicycle Company) received United States Patent 512,637 for their two-speed bicycle design in 1895, having submitted the application the previous year. The bicycle was no mere novelty, as Chicago bicycle racer H. L. Dodson used a twenty-two-pound version for competitions in 1894 and 1895.[90]

In the early 1900s, rudimentary derailleur systems and freewheel hubs became more common. The roots of these important innovations extend back to the Two-Speed Bicycle Company's American Hill-Climber nearly a decade earlier.

William Wrigley Jr. and Company

Bicycles sold by William Wrigley Jr. and Company were significant not for any particular technical innovation, but rather for their famous company president and his innovative marketing schemes. William Wrigley Jr. moved to Chicago in 1891 and started a business selling soap. To incentivize his soap sales, he often included other items, such as baking soda and chewing gum. The gum turned out to be more of a hit with customers than the soap, leading Wrigley in 1893 to form the Chicago-based Wm. Wrigley Chewing Gum Manufacturing Company. Wrigley's new company focused on selling Wrigley's Spearmint and Juicy Fruit Gum.

Ever the entrepreneur, Wrigley sought to cash in on the bicycle boom. His first spin-off company was the Bicycle Gum Co., which he based out of Chicago's Masonic Temple. In 1897 this company began to run magazine and newspaper ads that promised, "Boys and girls can earn a high-grade bicycle during vacation by advertising our Chewing Gum."[91] By 1898, William Wrigley Jr. & Co. was selling men's and women's "Wrigley" and "Kinzie" model bicycles (the company's headquarters were on Kinzie Street). Bicycle prices were falling nationwide by this time, but Wrigley drove them down further by selling bicycles via mail order with a small profit margin. The '98 Wrigleys sold for only $27, and the bargain-priced Kinzie went for $19. The company's cost for the Wrigley model was $19.40, leaving a profit margin of $7.60. This margin was one of the slimmest in the industry, but the strategy enabled Wrigley to sell as many as two hundred bicycles a day, touting "economical methods" that were "consistent with good workmanship and material."

Unfortunately for Wrigley, the company's production levels proved less than economical. Left with far more bicycles than it could sell, Wrigley used surplus bicycles as incentives for chewing gum sales for several years afterwards. The company's continued success with gum sales allowed William Wrigley to become a majority owner of the Chicago Cubs in the 1920s. Wrigley Field bears his name to this day, and you can still buy Wrigley's Spearmint and Juicy Fruit gum.[92]

All That Glitters

The term "Gilded Age" derives from the novel *The Gilded Age: A Tale of Today*, written by Mark Twain and Charles Dudley Warner in 1873. With biting satire, the authors exposed the rampant corruption and suffering that lay just beneath the thin gilded layer of late nineteenth-century American society. Around the turn of the century, numerous Progressive Era "muckraking" journalists began to peel back these gilded layers to expose the corruption beneath. Upton

Sinclair's *The Jungle* (1906) was nominally a work of narrative fiction, but the horrors of the meatpacking industry that it documented would have been all too real for large swaths of Chicago's population. The bicycling industry was not exempt from these ills. Any celebration of the many accomplishments of nineteenth-century Illinois bicycle manufacturers should be tempered with an acknowledgment that these bicycles were produced in highly dangerous factories that routinely exploited immigrants and children while leaving a legacy of environmental pollution in and around Chicago.

In 1893, Illinois's Progressive governor, John Peter Altgeld, successfully shepherded the Workshop and Factories Act through the state legislature. The new law limited the number of hours women and children could work and provided funding for factory inspections. The law was the first of its kind in the nation and a major milestone for the Progressive reform movement. It was implemented quickly, as the first factory inspections took place the same year the law passed. The resulting report documented children younger than sixteen years old working for Illinois bicycle manufacturers. In 1893, Featherstone employed twenty such child workers; Gormully & Jeffery nineteen; and Western Wheel Works thirty-one. In 1897, even in the aftermath of massive overall growth of employment numbers at those companies, the numbers were twelve, eight, and thirty-four, respectively, indicating that the new law was having some influence on the use of child labor.[93]

During the boom era, newspapers and the bicycle press tended to praise the bicycle industry rather than uncover its abuses. An account from Louisiana suggests the kinds of problems most outlets were overlooking. In 1897, the *New Orleans Medical and Surgical Journal* reported a case of four poisoning deaths at a bicycle factory. The factory in question used a solution of India rubber and benzine, likely for tire manufacturing. Four women reported headache, vertigo, and vomiting. Examination found hemorrhaging from the skin, gums, stomach, and genitals. It was further noted that the factory lacked adequate ventilation.[94] Although these deaths did not occur in Illinois, the report offers a rare glimpse of the dismal working conditions inside some contemporary bicycle factories.

Conclusions

In 1900, the *Inter Ocean* newspaper published *A History of the City of Chicago: Its Men and Institutions*. This celebratory (and clearly gender-biased) history included a lengthy section on Chicago manufacturers. Featured were well-known Chicago manufacturing giants such as Cyrus Hall McCormick (McCormick Harvesting Machine Company), David Bradley (David Bradley Manufacturing Company), and John Warne Gates (American Steel and Wire

Company). What might be surprising to a twenty-first century reader is the book's profiles of Chicago bicycle manufacturers such as Alfred Featherstone (A. Featherstone and Co.) and Frank Thomas Fowler (Fowler Cycle Works) right alongside the better-remembered Chicago industrialists.[95] Their inclusion, however, would have made complete sense to anyone from Chicago who lived through the bicycle boom of the 1890s. Clearly, bicycle manufacturing and repair were major contributors to the economies of Illinois and the United States at the end of the nineteenth century.

At the time, Illinois had the largest bicycle industry of any state in the country by a wide margin. The bicycle economy generated tens of millions of dollars annually in the state and employed tens of thousands of Illinoisans. Illinois bicycle manufacturers, particularly Western Wheel Works, helped to usher in a new era of American manufacturing with the development and refinement of industrial-scale metal stamping. They also exemplified the importance of nimbleness and rapid innovation in American manufacturing. Many Illinois bicycle companies had roots in other product lines, such as sewing machines, agricultural implements, watches, or toys. Skilled engineers and machinists were able to rapidly adapt to changing consumer demands, often retooling a factory to start producing bicycles in a matter of months. In the 1890s, Illinois bicycle manufacturers were on the cutting edge of industrial production.

4

All the World Awheel

Bicycles at the 1893 World's Columbian Exposition

The Chicago World's Fair Exposition Committee had a big problem. In 1890, Chicago had beaten out bids from Washington, DC; New York City; and St. Louis to host the Columbian Exposition. The grandeur and scale of Paris's 1889 *Exposition Universelle* had set a daunting new standard. The highlight of the Paris Fair was the colossal Eiffel Tower, an engineering and aesthetic masterpiece that soared 984 feet in the air, drawing crowds from all over Europe and abroad. Famed Chicago architect Daniel Burnham, who served as director of works for the Columbian Exposition, was keenly aware that Chicago needed a signature attraction to match or exceed the Eiffel Tower. The 1893 World's Fair ultimately became a watershed moment in Chicago and American history. It was a significant moment in bicycle history as well.

In 1892, however, the outlook was not promising for Burnham and the Exposition Committee. Congress had agreed to delay the start date until the following year, even though the Fair was supposed to mark the four-hundredth anniversary of Columbus's 1492 "discovery" of America. The committee had to wade through a host of outlandish proposals that were fiscally infeasible, mechanically impossible, or both. There were proposals to build an amphitheater to hold 100,000 people, a one-thousand-foot-tall building in the shape of an eagle; a half-mile-tall tower topped with a globe and a statue of Columbus; a forty-story-high re-creation of the Tower of Babel; an aerial island suspended by six balloons; a 1,000-foot-tall mountain with a glass palace on top; and a 1,200-foot-high pyramid covered in statues and electric lights.[1] Grandeur was not lacking in these proposals, but feasible completion before the Fair was scheduled to open in May of 1893 was certainly a pertinent consideration.

One intriguing proposal was for a gigantic rotating wheel that would carry fairgoers high above the Chicago skyline. The idea barely survived doubts

SCIENTIFIC AMERICAN

A WEEKLY JOURNAL OF PRACTICAL INFORMATION, ART, SCIENCE, MECHANICS, CHEMISTRY, AND MANUFACTURES.

NEW YORK, JULY 1, 1893.

THE WORLD'S COLUMBIAN EXPOSITION—THE GREAT FERRIS WHEEL, 250 FEET IN DIAMETER, 36 CARS, 40 SEATS PER CAR.—[See

Chicago World's Fair Ferris Wheel, as depicted by *Scientific American*, July 1, 1893.

about whether it could be built, never mind operated, safely. Nothing might damage the reputation of the Fair, and by extension Chicago, as much as a faulty or dangerous main attraction. The rotating wheel proposal came from an Illinois native, George Washington Gale Ferris Jr. The young but accomplished engineer submitted and resubmitted detailed plans to the Exposition Committee. Ferris would later recall Burnham criticizing his plans and saying, "Your wheel is so flimsy it will collapse, and even if it doesn't the public will be afraid to ride in it." Ferris replied, "You are an architect, sir, I am an engineer. The spokes may seem flimsy, but they are more than strong enough. I feel that no man should prejudge another man's idea unless he knows what he is talking about."[2] Burnham relented, and Ferris was awarded a contract for his wheel. The timeline was incredibly tight; approval came in November of 1892, and construction began in February of 1893.

Remarkably, the Ferris wheel was ready for passengers by June. It was an engineering marvel, standing twenty stories high. Its axle extended forty-five feet and weighed forty-five tons, making it the world's largest single piece of forged steel at that time. The wheel carried thirty-six lushly appointed railroad cars, each of which could hold sixty passengers. The whole thing weighed 1,200 tons fully loaded and was powered by a 1,000-horsepower engine.

What made the whole thing possible, though, also made bicycling possible: the spoke. Each spoke was two and a half inches in diameter and eighty feet long. Significantly, George Ferris had taken his inspiration directly from bicycles, which were the latest fad around the country, but especially in Chicago. The official 1893 press packet from the Ferris Wheel Company makes the connection to the bicycle wheel explicit:

> The Ferris Wheel—at least inside the smaller crowns—is constructed on the principle of the bicycle Wheel. The lower half is suspended from the axle by the spoke rods running downward, and the upper half of the wheel is supported by the lower half. All the spoke rods above the axle, when it was in any given position, might be removed, and the Wheel would be as solid as it would be with them. The only difference is that the Ferris Wheel hangs by its axle, while a bicycle Wheel rests on the ground, and the weight is applied downward on the axle.[3]

Put another way, a gigantic bicycle wheel became the signature attraction of the Chicago World's Columbian Exposition. Passengers paid fifty cents for a two-revolution ride, leaving every twenty minutes. The Ferris wheel made an estimated 10,000 revolutions, providing 1.5 million rides to fairgoers. Gross earnings totaled more than $700,000 (around $23 million in 2023). Shortly after the Fair, the American-Ormonde Bicycle Company, based in New York City, capitalized on the popularity of the Ferris Wheel by selling a bike of the same name.[4] Looking back on the success of the Ferris Wheel, a 1901 *Report of the Committee on Awards of the World's Columbian Commission* noted that it had run on time without "delays or halts of any kind" for the duration of the Fair.[5]

Preparing for the Fair

While the Ferris wheel loomed large over the Chicago World's Fair, the bicycle wheel played a prominent role on the fairgrounds even before the formal festivities had begun. Over the course of three days in October of 1892, a grand dedication was held. One hundred and fifty thousand people gathered in the mostly completed Manufactures and Liberal Arts Building for dedication ceremonies featuring a veritable who's who of American dignitaries, including Vice President Levi Parsons Morton and former President Rutherford B. Hayes, as well as cabinet members and Supreme Court justices. The World's

Fair Dedication Parade, held on October 20, included uniformed members of the First Regiment Cycle Corps of Chicago riding in formation. *The Bearings*, a top Chicago-based cycling magazine, reported that Toledo, Grand Rapids, and Denver also had bicycle soldiers in the parade. It noted that the Chicago Cycle Corps "excelled in being able to climb the viaduct grade near the World's Fair grounds."[6]

On the following two days, the Chicago Bicycle Club hosted a "World's Fair Dedication Tournament" bicycle race. According to the official race program, written with a bit of Chicago bravado, "We have arranged for one of the greatest race meetings ever held in the West, and are assured of the presence of many of the speediest men in the country. Being the last great tournament of the Western Racing Circuit adds much to the importance of this event. The races will be of the highest order, likewise the prizes."[7] Over the course of two days, "World" records were set at the Washington Park course in the two-mile handicap, quarter-mile, and half-mile flying start triplet races. The dedication races were officiated by Colonel Albert Pope. Referees also included Fred Patee (Patee bicycles) and H. G. Rouse (Rouse & Hazard bicycles), both of Peoria.

The race largely lived up to the hype. Total prizes were valued at a lofty $2,354, with a $650 Conover upright piano, donated by the Chicago Cottage Organ Company, featured as one of the top prizes. There was a $500 Walker Challenge Cup, in addition to seven diamond ornaments and five watches. American short-distance racing star Arthur Augustus (known as A. A.) Zimmerman was present at the race; much to his fans' disappointment, though, he sat out due to illness. Top competitors who did race included A. E. Lumsden, W. A. Rhodes, C. W. Dorntage, and J. P. Bliss. The Dedication Tournament was deemed a success, attracting 15,000 people for the first day of racing.[8]

Bicycle Exhibits and Awards

Bicycles were an integral part of the Chicago World's Fair, even though they were banned from the crowded fairgrounds. Chicagoans rode to the Fair in the thousands and flocked to the bicycle exhibits. Covering 633 acres along the Chicago lakefront and containing 65,000 exhibits, the Fair drew 130,000 visitors on its first day. A contemporary guide to the Fair cautioned that if a visitor truly wanted to see everything, they should allot three weeks and plan for 150 miles of walking.[9] Despite the fairgrounds bicycle ban, Fair organizers went to great lengths to ensure that local wheelmen and wheelwomen would feel welcome at the Fair. Rand McNally's official guide to the Fair highlighted the bicycle facilities: two glass-covered bike parking buildings, constructed at Jackson Park, that could accommodate 16,000 wheelmen daily. Attendants provided valet parking and safeguarded the bicycles.[10] As the *Inter Ocean*

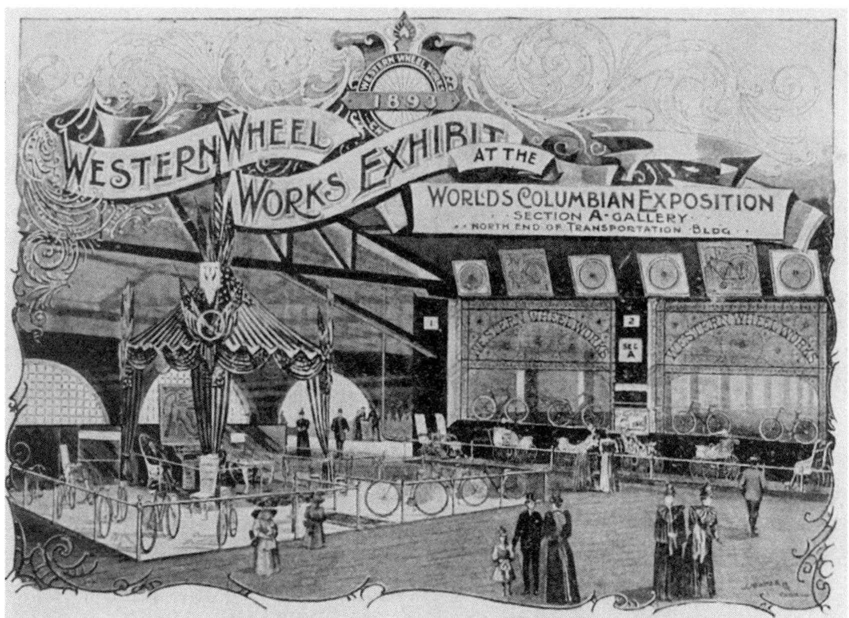

Illustration of Western Wheel Works bicycle exhibit at the World's Fair. (International Cycling Tournament program, August 1893.)

assured readers, "No person without a bicycle will be permitted to enter the wheel courts. They will be maintained sacred to the bicycle enthusiast."[11]

The Fair touted bicycles as yet another sign of American progress and ingenuity. Inside the fairgrounds, wheelmen headed to the massive Transportation Building to see the bicycle exhibits. The transportation building was 960 feet long by 256 feet wide. One of the architectural highlights of the Fair, the Romanesque Transportation Building, was designed by famed Chicago architect Louis Sullivan. Painted a vibrant red, it stood out from the rest of the "White City." Particularly notable was the elaborate "Golden Door," also designed by Sullivan. Facing the central lagoon, the Golden Door featured a series of five receding arches covered in intricate bas-relief sculpture. Sullivan here again used bright red, orange, muted greens, and copious amounts of gold leaf. Western Wheel Works, the largest of Chicago's many bicycle manufacturers, later featured a depiction of the Golden Door on the cover of its 1893 catalog.

Like everything else at the Fair, the bicycle displays were both elaborate and costly. The Pope Manufacturing Company led the way with a $10,000 brass and bronze pavilion adorned with eagle sculptures. Along with the most up-to-date Columbia bicycles, Pope also featured historic bicycles from his personal collection, including a Pierre Lallement–designed velocipede. The

Overman Wheel Company from Massachusetts went with a solid mahogany display covering an area of about 1,500 square feet. In all, *The Bearings* listed fifty-eight American bicycle manufacturers with displays in the Transportation Building.[12]

While visiting the Fair, two ambitious and entrepreneurial brothers from Ohio carefully studied the bicycles on display in the Transportation Building. In the previous year, they had opened their own bicycle shop, but their time at the Fair convinced them that they could also build their own bicycles. They began this endeavor shortly after returning home. Soon, their new line of bicycles was successful enough to allow the Wright brothers to take the proceeds and invest them in their newest interest: airplanes.[13]

The World's Columbian Exposition was intended as a testament to American technological progress and ingenuity. As such, it featured the relative novelty of electrical power on a grand scale. The entire Fair was illuminated at night with tens of thousands of electric lights. One Chicago cyclist was so inspired by the lights of the White City that he would later use it as the inspiration for his fictional Land of Oz. Before Frank Baum's release of *The Wonderful Wizard of Oz* in 1900, he published a series of bicycle poems in his 1898 collection, *By the Candelabra's Glare*.[14] The Fair also featured electric motors in a wide variety of usages. The H. A. Lozier Company from Cleveland used electric motors to keep four of its bicycles in constant motion. Similarly, the United States Government Building included a uniformed postal service delivery rider propelled by electric motors.[15] Another unique bicycle on display was a 10½-pound ultralightweight racing bicycle built by racer and bicycle manufacturer P. J. Berlo. At that weight, his steel-framed, wood-rimmed bicycle bests the lightest production carbon fiber bicycles made today. Berlo Bicycles were known for their sub-seventeen-pound "Racer" model that was available to the public. Berlo, however, took one of these bicycles and drilled out material from any place that would not weaken the bike, and he also had small, twenty-two-ounce tires made specially for this bicycle. It was not just a showpiece; Berlo routinely raced and set records on this machine.[16]

Anyone who has visited a county or state Fair will be familiar with the wide range of judged competitions that take place at these events. The World's Columbian Exposition took judged competitions to a whole other level. The official *Report of the Committee on Awards of the World's Columbian Exposition* ran over 1,600 pages and required two volumes. There were judged competitions for everything under the sun. Pabst beer was just plain Pabst until it won its iconic "blue ribbon" at the World's Fair. Awards were given out in thousands of categories that included collections of raisins, mounted specimens of fishes, toilet soap, grindstones, improved policeman's club, lard, curios made from the stomachs of animals, and thousands more.[17] Bicycles were, of course, not to be left out of the potential honor of being able to claim an award at the World's Fair. Even before the judging could begin, there was a major controversy that found its way into the Chicago papers. John Boyd Thacher, chairman of the executive committee on awards, had appointed Irving Miller, a Chicago patent lawyer, to be the juror for the bicycle awards. Word soon surfaced that Irving worked for a Chicago bicycle manufacturer, Gormully & Jeffery, who would have bicycles in the competition. The majority of the other manufacturers appealed to Thacher for Miller's removal. The scandal was significant enough to make its way onto the front page of Chicago's *Sunday Inter Ocean*. The paper reported Thacher's response "that he would see the manufacturers of bicycles in a mighty warm locality before he would comply with their request."[18] Eventually, a second judge was appointed, and Miller promised to forgo judging his employer's bicycles. This seemed to settle the matter.

The judging covered both complete bicycles of various styles and individual bicycle components. A selection of the awards that went to Illinois manufacturers included Kenwood Manufacturing (Chicago) for the Ladies Special bicycle; Rouse, Duryea, and Co. (Peoria) for the Sylph Model D scorcher bicycle; Freeport Manufacturing Co. (Freeport) for their bicycle stands; Rouse, Hazard & Company (Peoria) for their children's bicycle seats; Monarch Cycle Co. (Chicago) for their Road Racer bicycle; and A. Featherstone and Co. (Chicago) for their bicycles overall. Even without Irving Miller, Gormully & Jeffery Company (Chicago) received awards for their pneumatic tires, unbrazed bicycle frames, men's and ladies' Rambler bicycles, and parabolic bicycle lamps.[19] For years following the Fair, these companies' advertisements would capitalize on these awards by reminding potential buyers of their success at the World's Fair.

First Bicycle World Championship

Awards of another sort entirely would later be given out at the first-ever bicycle world championships. The races and their associated social events were held during the peak of the World's Fair, August 7–12. To be sure, race promoters in both Europe and the United States had previously tried to lay claim to hosting a "World Championship," but, more often than not, these races were mostly domestic affairs with perhaps a sprinkling of international competitors. Chicago's International Tournament aspired to attract the best riders from around the globe. What made this arguably the first true world bicycling championship, however, ultimately had less to do with the caliber of the competitors and more to do with the event's sanctioning body, the newly formed International Cyclists' Association.

The International Cyclists' Association was formed in 1892 during the influential and highly attended Stanley Cycle Show in London. Prior to the show, draft rules and objectives had been shared with all active national cycling organizations. Under the leadership of Englishman Henry Sturmey (later one of the inventors of the popular Sturmey-Archer three-speed hub), the nascent International Cyclists' Association's founding members included the national cycling organizations of England, France, Germany, Holland, Italy, Ireland, Belgium, Canada, and the United States. As bicycle historian Andrew Ritchie has observed, the initial meeting of the International Cyclists Association had two goals: to "institute a universally recognized series of world championships" and to create an organization that would establish "a common amateur definition."[20] At the time, unpaid amateurs who participated simply for the love of the sport were held up as the Victorian ideal of manhood. Professional athletes were respected for their accomplishments, but what captured the public's imagination was the amateur gentleman-athlete who held down a regular job and raced when he could. The general rule of amateurism was that you couldn't be paid explicitly to race. Racers across many countries had been stripped of their winnings based on (sometimes dubious) accusations of violating this rather fuzzy standard. Some successful racers, like A. A. Zimmerman, brazenly exploited the ambiguity. While he didn't receive any cash payments, his reported winnings in 1892 included "twenty-nine machines [bicycles], several horses and carriages, half a dozen pianos, a house and a lot, household furniture of all descriptions, and enough silver plate, medals and jewelry to stock a jewelry store."[21] Obviously, the rules surrounding amateurism needed clarification.

Organizing a world championship proved the easier task. After Sturmey's motion for the new organization to organize "championships of the world" was passed unanimously, the honor of hosting the first world championships went to the United States, with the races to be held in conjunction with the World's Columbian Exposition. There would be a wide range of races for local riders as well as national championships races. The marquee events, however, would be world championship races contested for the mile, ten kilometers, and one hundred kilometers.[22] In July, an advertisement appeared in *The Referee and Cycle Trade Journal* touting "the first races ever run for the Championship of the World" and noting $10,000 in prizes. The new one-third-mile track, which cost $8,000, had been constructed at the South Side Ball Park, located at Thirty-Fifth Street and Wentworth Avenue. Its partially covered grandstands were designed to accommodate 15,000 spectators. As the Fair had progressed, word had spread around the country of price gouging at some Chicago hotels. These rumors (which probably had some substance to them) were prevalent enough for the advertisement to address them head on: "As To Hotel Rates.

Reports of extortion are absolutely false."[23] To further drive up attendance, the world championship was held in conjunction with the fourteenth annual League of American Wheelmen meet. In all, forty-seven different races (some including many separate heats) were spread out over the course of six days. In addition to the three world championship titles, state and national championship winners were recognized.

As the start of the races drew near, America's best racers and a few international contestants descended upon Chicago. Most observers predicted A. A. Zimmerman from New Jersey to win one, or both, of the shorter world championship events. The New Jersey resident had dominated recent short distance races in the United States. In 1892, he won seventy-five out of the one hundred races he entered.[24] Other champion riders scheduled to race included J. P. Bliss (Chicago), J. S. Johnson, W. W. Windle, and W. C. Sanger. For months, the gossip at Chicago's many cycling clubhouses and bicycling magazines was over which international competitors would make the trip to Chicago. Just before the start of the world championship races, *The Bearings* summarized the situation:

> WHERE ARE THE CHAMPIONS? Well, well, the international championships are on, but America seems to have almost a complete monopoly of the champions. England, after all her activity in organizing the International Cyclists' Association, has but a single representative here.... The Mexican champion came, and after seeing the riders with whom he would have to compete, silently packed his grip and as silently stole away ... The Italian champion, who was reported on his way to Chicago, has failed to materialize. The South African champion is here to ride; but he does not represent a country which is a member of the International Cyclists' Association, and this leaves the Canadian champion as the only fair representative of the foreign countries and a member of the International Cyclists' Association to compete at the meet.[25]

In the end, travel costs and stiff competition kept most of the international competitors away.

Unsurprisingly, the Americans—and Zimmerman in particular—dominated the races. On the first day of competition, Monday, August 7, 1893, Walter Sanger, the new mile record holder and a local favorite from Milwaukee, was badly injured during a heat of the one-third mile. With Sanger out, Zimmerman easily won this particular race. Julian P. Bliss won the two-mile Illinois championship. The following day, Zimmerman showed he was in top condition, winning the quarter-mile and two-mile "lap" race. The races were designed to build in importance over the course of six days. Following this model, Wednesday's races featured multiple national championship races. In the first national championship race, the quarter-mile, Zimmerman won by the astounding margin of twenty-five feet. The next national championship was the one-mile "ordinary" race. In this event, the newer-style safety bicycles were not allowed. Zimmerman had begun his career racing his Star high-wheel bike; apparently, he had not forgotten how to ride it, as he took another win. He may have been feeling some fatigue from his efforts, as he was beaten in the five-mile national championship by John S. Johnson of Syracuse. The first of the world championship races, the ten kilometer, was contested on Friday. Five American riders faced off against Canadian William Hyslop and South African L. S. Meintjes. Chicagoan J. P. Bliss was neck and neck with Zimmerman to the finish line, narrowly losing the first-ever world championship race. Saturday, the last day of racing, saw 8,000 spectators in attendance and featured two more world championship events: the mile and the one hundred kilometer. Zimmerman, the strong favorite in the mile, capped off a banner week with another world championship title, besting Bliss and Johnson by twenty feet. The one hundred kilometer, the only endurance event contested, featured a number of pacemakers for the leaders to draft behind. The pace was so fast that new American records were set for every mile between twenty-five and

Illustration of A. A. Zimmerman with World Championship trophies published in the *Wheel and Cycling Trade Review*, August 18, 1893.

sixty. After mile forty-two, Meintjes, the South African, came to the lead and held it. He finished one hundred kilometers in two hours and forty-six minutes (about 22½ mph).[26]

The Chicago Fair's world championships marked the beginning of standardized championship events. After Chicago, world championship races were held in Antwerp (1894), Cologne (1895), Copenhagen (1896), and Glasgow (1897). In Cologne, professionals competed alongside amateur racers. The world championships eventually were organized by the Union Cycliste Internationale (UCI) and became increasingly European affairs. They would not return to the United States until 1986.[27]

Wheeling Around the Fair

In addition to the world championship, there was also a full agenda of social events held for cyclists. After the races on Tuesday evening, 1,500 wheelmen boarded the steamship *Nebraska* for a moonlight excursion on Lake Michigan. The boat anchored adjacent to the fairgrounds so that passengers could thoroughly enjoy the electric lights and the firework display. The next night, the headliner was Chicago Mayor Carter Henry Harrison III, who spoke to the 2,000 cyclists who had gathered to enjoy libations at Trocadero Hall.[28]

The social highlight of the week was "Wheelmen's Day" on Thursday, August 10. Officially designated days at the Fair were highly sought after. Many states and some foreign countries had their own days at the Fair; there was also College Fraternity Day, Chicago Day, Colored People's Day, and Stenographer's Day. Chicago's bicycle clubs had applied early and lobbied hard for their own day, a wish that was eventually granted. Only on Wheelmen's Day were bicycles allowed on the fairgrounds. The Transportation Building was kept open late for wheelmen to visit the bicycle displays after attending the day's races. The highlight of Wheelmen's Day was an evening bicycle parade that featured over a thousand riders. The parade was to be led by soldiers from the Bicycle Corps of the Second Regiment, but they were late in arriving. When all were assembled, the full procession of cyclists was twenty-three minutes long. The *Chicago Tribune* described the spectacle as "a dancing river of fire rushing along at breakneck speed. . . . They rolled away under towers of lights and banners and highly-colored coverings like phantoms in the night." A competition for the best-decorated wheel resulted in bicycles adorned with an array of Chinese lanterns. The standouts from the evening were a lighted ten-foot-tall revolving Ferris wheel replica pulled in a wagon behind a bicycle and another bicycle outfitted with a fifteen-foot-tall pagoda with sixty lights. The paper also reported that more than a hundred women associated with the local Chicago cycling clubs participated in the parade.[29]

Bicycles also played supporting roles in other official days and events of the Fair. September 19, 1893, was designated as Regatta Day, featuring a huge range of boat-based events in the Fair's lagoons. The parade of boats included a "water bicycle," which went around Wooded Island in the lagoon. *The World's Fair Album*, published in 1893, described the scene: "The water bicycle competed with the South Sea catamaran, the gondola of Venice with the dug-out of the Southern Pacific, the modern American shell with the West Indian surf-boat; all nations, and colors, and creeds meeting in friendly rivalry."[30]

All was not as it seemed in the White City, however. A darker underside of the Fair lay just beneath the technological, artistic, and cultural showcases. Building the Fair in such a short time frame led to the exploitation of minority and child laborers. The nearby Levee District drew destitute young women to serve the Fair's after-hours clientele.[31]

Erik Larson's hugely popular *The Devil in the White City: Murder, Magic, and Madness at the Fair That Changed America* interweaves the story of the World's Fair with that of H. H. Holmes, a prolific serial killer and Chicago businessman. During the Fair, he lured unsuspecting victims to his "murder castle" hotel, where he asphyxiated them with gas and then murdered them in a soundproof basement room. The smooth-talking and persuasive Holmes had capitalized on the city's bicycle boom. He would purchase bicycles on credit and resell them without ever paying off the original purchases. After some of his murders were uncovered, the *Chicago Daily Tribune* featured an interview with Chicago bicycle manufacturer Charley H. Sieg. Sieg recounted Holmes's con:

> I do not believe it is generally known that he worked a pretty smooth swindle on a number of dealers. At that time he started out with a systematic scheme to obtain his bicycles from each of the dealers in Chicago. He came in here and represented he wanted to get a wheel for himself and one for a woman. He was so particular about the wheels I thought it best to look him up before trusting him, and I found his securities worthless. A few days later we found other manufacturers had been approached and had made deals with him, and that he sold the wheels thus obtained from his drug store. I think he succeeded in fleecing seven firms, some of which have since gone out of business. He was one of the smoothest talking individuals I have ever had anything to do with, and had he not overdone the matter a little, we, too, would have been taken in by him."[32]

Before he was caught for murder, Holmes managed to defraud some of the major Chicago bicycle manufacturers, including Gormully & Jeffery, Taylor Bicycle Company, James Bicycle Company, and Spalding Brothers.[33]

Buffalo Bill and Annie Oakley

Bicycles turned up in another surprising place: Buffalo Bill's Wild West shows. The tremendously popular performance ran throughout the Chicago World's Fair (and, to some extent, competed with the Fair's main displays). As it turns out, the show's most famous acts, Buffalo Bill and Annie Oakley, had both caught bicycle fever.

William Frederick Cody spent his early years as a Pony Express rider, Civil War soldier, buffalo hunter, and Indian fighter. He is better remembered as Buffalo Bill, organizer and headliner for Buffalo Bill's Wild West Show. The shows featured action-packed recreations of wild West events such as a buffalo hunt, the Deadwood stagecoach robbery, Custer's Last Stand, and a Pony Express ride. City dwellers were enthralled with displays of sharpshooting, wing shooting, roping, and trick riding. By the time of the World's Fair, Buffalo Bill's Wild West Show was known worldwide and featured a globally sourced cast of hundreds.[34]

Ever the entrepreneur and master promoter, Cody applied to the Fair Committee to secure space on or near the Fair's Midway Plaisance. The committee, perhaps worried about the massive loans they were now on the hook for, demanded 50 percent of Cody's gross profits. Unwilling to hand over such large margins, Cody instead secured a lease of fifteen acres of land adjacent to the Fair. He even took advantage of the many delays that plagued the opening of the Fair by hosting Wild West shows that began four weeks before the grand opening of the Fair.[35]

Without question, the star attraction of Buffalo Bill's Wild West Show was Annie ("Little Sure Shot") Oakley. In 1884, at age twenty-three, Oakley once shot 943 out of 1,000 glass balls thrown into the air. The following year, over the course of nine hours, Annie broke 4,772 out of 5,000 glass balls using a shotgun.[36] Her notoriety as a sharpshooter led to her being recruited by Buffalo Bill for his Wild West Show in 1885. While on tour in London in 1892, Oakley bought a "Premier" model safety bicycle manufactured by Hillman, Herbert & Cooper. At first, she rode her bike around the streets of London for exercise. It wasn't long before she would claim of her bicycle, "I am equally as fond of it as my horse." By the time Annie arrived at the World's Fair, she was the second-highest paid performer (behind only Cody himself) and an ardent wheelwoman. Some enterprising employee of Chicago's Sterling Bicycle Company recruited Annie to advertise their bicycles. A contemporary trading card shows Annie aiming her rifle while astride a Sterling bicycle. The cards featured Sterling's slogan "Built Like a Watch." For the Wild West shows, Annie taught herself how to ride without hands and shoot at the same time. In 1894, *The Bearings* reported that "she now has something more attractive

Annie Oakley riding and shooting from a Sterling bicycle. (The National Annie Oakley Center at the Garst Museum, Greenville, Ohio.)

in her performance[;] mounted on a twenty-seven-pound ladies' Sterling, she astonishes large audiences by performing wonderful feats of marksmanship while on her wheel. Miss Oakley is an ardent wheelwoman, and takes a daily ride of twenty miles."[37] Oakley included the bicycle shooting act as part of her World's Fair performance.[38] Photographs of her at the World's Columbian Exposition show her sitting in front of her tent with a bicycle and rifle at her side and promotional posters depict her shooting from her bicycle.

In many ways, Oakley typified the "New Woman" of the Progressive Era. She was a successful, self-made businesswoman and bested nearly everyone at the male-dominated sport of shooting. Like Progressive stalwarts Susan B. Anthony and Frances Willard, Oakley advocated for bicycling as healthy exercise for women. However, she had strong opinions about the new style of bloomer cycling pants. "I don't like bloomers or bloomer women," she opined, "but I think that sport and healthful exercise make women better, healthier and happier."[39] Instead of adopting bloomers for riding, Annie came up with her own more modest and practical design. In her book, *Life and Legacy of Annie Oakley*, historian Glenda Riley documents Annie's design:

> On her legs, she laced gaiters about six inches above the knees. She then added a pair of knickerbockers (short, loose trousers gathered at the knee), a skirt extending halfway below the knee, a loose-fitting bodice of white silk, and an Eton-style jacket . . . Although this outfit may not sound unusual, Annie's special contribution to it lay hidden beneath the skirt. She sewed an eyelet to each gaiter and a corresponding elastic with a hook on the underside of the skirt. When mounting her bike, she gracefully hooked her skirt to the gaiters. While she rode, the elastic provided sufficient room for movement of the skirt but prevented it from rising above Annie's knees.[40]

Annie wasn't the only one to ink a bicycle endorsement deal with a Chicago bicycle company. During his time performing at the World's Fair, Buffalo Bill partnered with Chicago's Gormully & Jeffery to promote their Rambler bicycles. Whether he ever actually rode a Rambler is unclear, but an 1896 newspaper advertisement depicts an illustration of Buffalo Bill on a Rambler bicycle followed by the Native Americans that were part of his "Rough Riders" troupe. The Buffalo Bill Museum in Cody, Wyoming, also has a photograph of Cody and his two children standing behind a "triplet" three-man bicycle.

While Buffalo Bill would never deign to ride a bicycle during one of his Wild West Shows, he did share his opinion about the bicycle craze on multiple occasions. Like Annie, he was a study in contrasts when it came to bicycling and women's rights. In an 1896 newspaper interview, he remarked, "I think that women can do everything as well as men, except ride a bucking pony, but they ride the bicycle a great deal better, at least they look better, for they sit up straight. I always want to hit a fellow when I see him bending down to the handle bars."[41] In regard to women and tests of endurance, Cody observed, "A woman always has more pluck, when it comes to endurance, than a man. I believe she would die rather than give in once she has set out to do a thing. In comparison to her strength, a woman has twice the endurance of a man. She has something more than endurance. I think it must be her will power. This forces her to go through with a thing when men drop it." Yet, moments later in the same interview, when asked about women working, Cody falls back on a very traditional Victorian male perspective: "If a woman has some nice occupation which is artistic and one which won't make her unwomanly or unfit to make a nice domesticated home, I do not see why she should not continue her work right straight along."[42]

The Wild West Shows and bicycles were not entirely without conflict. The rope work of the cowboy performers inspired many young boys. As the

Rambler bicycle advertisement featuring Buffalo Bill. (*Chicago Times Herald*, June 7, 1892.)

Jacksonville Daily Journal (Illinois) reported a few days after the Wild West Show passed through town, "Various bicycle riders complain that they are greatly annoyed these days by small boys with lassos who persist in trying 'The Buffalo act' on them. Several wheelmen have been dragged from their machines in this manner."[43]

Although not officially part of the World's Columbian Exposition, Buffalo Bill's Wild West Show was wildly successful. During the Fair, shows ran twice daily, totaling 318 performances. Average show attendance was 16,000 spectators, amounting to an overall attendance of over five million people. This was the most prosperous year for the Wild West Show, with Cody making a million dollars (roughly $30 million in 2024) in profit.[44]

Good Roads and the Fair

Arguably, the most far-reaching impacts of bicycles and the World's Columbian Exposition was further advancement of the Good Roads Movement. The Good Roads Movement was founded by bicyclists in 1880 with the express goal of developing and improving roads in the United States. Progressive Era reformers were interested in the social uplift of American citizens, and improved roads would lead to less isolation of rural towns, more opportunities for healthy recreation, and improved inter- and intra-state commerce. Astutely, Good Roads advocates saw the World's Columbian Exposition as a potential watershed event for the movement. Colonel Albert Pope (Columbia bicycles) was one of the early leaders in the push for good roads. Securing recurring funding from the federal government for road building, research, and development was instrumental to the success of the movement. Earlier efforts to sway Congress had failed, but Pope and other League of American Wheelmen officials saw the World's Fair as a prime opportunity to make the case for good roads to an audience of millions.

A meeting to create a National League of Good Roads was advertised far and wide to coincide with the World's Fair dedication ceremonies. On October 20 (the night before the World's Fair Dedication Tournament bicycle races), a crowd of over one thousand gathered at Chicago's Central Music Hall to discuss this new endeavor. Bicycle enthusiasts made up the majority of the crowd, but the idea of improved roads impacted large swaths of the American public; as such, officials from boards of trade, farmers' organizations, universities, and state road improvement associations were also present. After speeches by a number of dignitaries, a constitution for the National League of Good Roads was approved unanimously. The constitution specified that the goals of the new organization were "to awaken general interest in the improvement of public roads, determine the best methods of building and maintaining them; secure the legislation, State or National, that may be necessary for their establishment and support, and to conduct or foster such publications as may serve those purposes."[45] Chicago's meatpacking giant, Philip Armour, was among those elected to the new organizations executive committee.

Shortly following the establishment of the National League of Good Roads, Pope printed and distributed, at his own cost, tens of thousands of Good Roads petitions, sending them all over the country. The petition called on Congress both to establish a federal department tasked with constructing and maintaining roads and to fund a Good Roads exhibit at the World's Fair. Cyclists around the country were recruited to the cause and helped disseminate and collect petitions. Eventually, seventeen state governors, the entire Massachusetts state legislature, and 150,000 citizens signed Pope's petition. To drive home his point about the popularity of the Good Roads Movement, Pope had all of the petitions he received pasted together, resulting in a 1,400-yard-long sheet of paper that was then loaded onto a pair of seven-foot-high oak spools. This promotional gimmick became known as the "Monster Petition" and created a memorable spectacle before Congress. The Monster Petition is still held by the United States National Archives in Washington, DC. While Congress chose not to fund the Fair exhibition, it did set aside $10,000 in the Department of Agriculture budget for making "inquiries and investigations into the condition of roads in the United States." These funds led the Secretary of Agriculture to create a new "Office of Road Inquiry," which would eventually become the Federal Highway Administration.[46] Funding for the Good Roads display in Chicago ultimately came from the League of American Wheelmen and the National League of Good Roads.

Pope's initial ideas for a Good Roads exhibit at the World's Fair were grandiose. He wanted various models of roads connecting all the major venues at the Fair, and a building that housed machinery for road building. French, German, Italian, and English methods of road construction were all to be on display. The timeline, however, had grown incredibly short by the time the new National League of Good Roads finally appropriated $10,000 for the Fair exhibit in May of 1893. In the end, the League and Pope had to settle for a model road, stretching one thousand feet between the Agriculture Building and the Forestry Building.[47] Rand McNally's promotional guide to the Fair described it as follows:

> Manufacturers of brick used in paving, producers of granite blocks, owners of gravel-beds, contractors of cedar-block work, asphaltum, and other forms of road-construction material take sections of the road and prepare them in the manner most approved by each. Then, to add a touch of realism to the work, one section of the road is left in a condition of original depravity, and in the center of it a country wagon is carefully installed with mud and mire up to the hubs. If a picture so familiar is not sufficient to stir up slothful State legislators to a consideration of the needs of their constituents their case is indeed hopeless.[48]

Today's expansive federal interstate system can be traced back to the efforts of nineteenth-century wheelmen and the Chicago World's Fair.

Over time, the efforts of wheelmen to improve roads in the United States began to pay off. In the late 1890s, the federal Office of Road Inquiry took over the reins for road research and eventually road construction. Ironically, a system of improved roads hastened the rise of the automobile, which in turn played a role in the end of the bicycle boom.

The World's Columbian Exposition finally came to an end on October 30, 1893. By all measures, the Fair was a raging success for Illinois bicyclists, Chicago, and the nation as a whole. Over the course of the Fair, more than twenty-seven million people purchased tickets. To put this into perspective, the population of the United States at the time was only sixty-three million.[49] Traditionally, world's fairs had run up a deficit for host cities. In Chicago, though, revenues from ticket sales, concessions, and exhibits totaled $35 million, netting a profit of $2 million for investors. The architectural legacy of the World's Fair left Chicago with the Palace of Fine Arts, which became the Museum of Science and Industry, and the World's Congress Auxiliary Building, which became the Art Institute of Chicago. The anthropological, geological, and botanical collections that were on display at the Fair formed the original collection of Chicago's Field Museum.[50]

The bicycle boom of the 1890s was beginning to gain some serious steam as Chicago hosted the World's Fair (recall that the boom peaked between 1897 and 1898). The ubiquity of bicycles by this time might explain why contemporary accounts of the Fair and later scholarly histories have largely ignored their role in the months-long spectacle. That role was significant, however, and left a lasting mark on bicycle history. Chicago can lay claim to the first bicycle world championship, however poor the international attendance. The Good Roads Movement picked up momentum and nationwide exposure at the fair. Manufacturers who displayed their bicycles in the Transportation Building would go on to leverage their World's Fair awards into future sales. A few of them would later go on to manufacture motorcycles and automobiles, another example of the intertwined early histories of both means of transportation.

5

The Great Emancipator

Women Take to the Wheel

The best-known woman cyclist from Illinois during the 1890s was not famous for being a wheelwoman. Frances Willard was born in New York in 1839 and graduated from the North-Western Female College in Evanston in 1859. In 1871, she was named president of the new Evanston College for Ladies, and when this school was absorbed by Northwestern University in 1873, she became dean of women. During that time, Willard became involved in the growing temperance and women's suffrage movements. In an era of rampant alcoholism and domestic abuse, temperance and prohibition became one of the foundational goals of the Progressive Movement. In 1879, Willard became president of the large and influential Women's Christian Temperance Union (WCTU), a position she would hold for the rest of her life. The WCTU was the largest women's organization in the country, with over 200,000 members by 1893. Although temperance and prohibition were the organization's primary goals, Willard raised the WCTU's profile and expanded its scope to include a host of other Progressive reform causes including prison reform, the eight-hour workday, women's suffrage, and an issue of particular importance to women cyclists: dress reform.[1]

Willard's experience as a cyclist began relatively late in her life. At age fifty-three, she made up her mind that she needed to learn how to ride a bicycle. In 1895, she turned her bicycling trials and tribulations into a short, bestselling book, *A Wheel Within a Wheel: How I Learned to Ride the Bicycle*. The whole work can be read as a metaphor of women's independence. Even before learning to ride, Willard was a strong advocate of the bicycle in her temperance reform writings, arguing that "the bicycle was perhaps our strongest ally in winning young men away from public-houses, because . . . the skill required in handling it obliges those who mount to keep clear heads and steady hands."[2]

Frances Willard learning to ride a bicycle, from her book *A Wheel Within a Wheel.* (Photo courtesy Frances Willard Memorial Library and WCTU Archives, Evanston, IL.)

Bicycles were the darling of the temperance movement, based on the simple assumption that it was difficult and impractical to ride while inebriated. Willard was once asked if it might be true that cycling actually led men to drink, to which she responded, "Oh folly! In Chicago there is nothing so hated by the saloon keeper, the cigarette dealer, and the proprietor of the low theater as the bicycle. They say the people are all scurrying for the parks." For Willard, the bicycle was "the greatest agent of temperance reform."[3]

Willard drew parallels between the persistence and dedication required to learn to ride and the hard work necessary to move Progressive reforms forward. Despite breaking an elbow in the process, Willard eventually mastered the bicycle. "I found a whole philosophy of life in the wooing and winning of my bicycle," she wrote, and "I finally concluded that all failure was from a wobbling will rather than a wobbling wheel."[4] The bicycle she learned to ride on was a British model given to Willard by her friend Lady Henry Somerset. Willard named the bicycle "Gladys." The original Gladys can still be seen today at the Frances Willard House Museum in Evanston.

Women's Cycling during the Bicycle Boom

Willard's story was emblematic of the middle- and upper-class women in Illinois and around the country who took to the bicycle in substantial numbers during the 1890s. Bicycle historian Ross D. Petty has estimated the number of women cyclists during those years as between 600,000 and 2,000,000 nationwide.[5] The advent of the lower-to-the-ground safety bicycle design greatly increased ridership for women. In an 1888 article titled "A Cycling Prima Donna," the *Evening World* reported that noted opera star Pauline Hall rode an early hard-tired women's safety bicycle "all over Chicago" with members of the Illinois and Douglas bicycle clubs.[6] In an 1890 *Chicago Daily Tribune* article, Mrs. Van Sicklen was credited with being the first woman in Chicago to ride a bicycle, although the specific year during which the ride occurred is not mentioned. The article, of course, was referring to safety bicycles and ignoring the many earlier Chicago women who had ridden velocipedes, high-wheels, and tricycles . The same article also estimated that there were already five hundred women riders in 1890.[7]

By the early 1890s, Chicago was already recognized around the country as a center of women's bicycling. "Bicycling is a favorite diversion of the Chicago girls," a San Francisco newspaper noted in 1892. "No other city in the country has developed so many expert lady riders. There are no less than half a dozen of them . . . that have covered 100 miles within 16 hours."[8] In a few short years, the number of Chicago women finishing a century would number in the hundreds, and their best finishing times would be close behind the fastest men.

Once manufacturers of bicycles and accessories began to build bicycles for women and target them with specific advertising, women's cycling really took off. In 1891, the *Chicago Tribune* estimated that one thousand women's bicycles had been sold in 1890 and that Chicago riding schools were teaching fifty women to ride per week.[9] The first women-only cycling club in Illinois, the Ravenswood Club, was also formed in 1890.[10] Some of the earlier cycling clubs founded in the high-wheel era had admitted women, but it is likely that nearly all of them were riding tricycles rather than high-wheel bicycles. Several additional women's cycling clubs and auxiliaries to the male clubs were formed later in the 1890s. The progressive Knickerbocker and Unique cycling clubs embraced dress reform, specifying that members must wear knickerbockers or bloomers during club rides. The Woman's Cycling Club was popular enough to be able to afford its own clubhouse at 31 Lincoln Ave. When the club was formed, Mr. Cloon of the nearby Lincoln Cycling Club offered to pay dues of $50 per year for the privilege of overseeing a men's auxiliary to the Woman's Cycling Club. There were already women's auxiliaries to the Chicago Cycling Club, the Ozark Club, the Sylph Club, and the Pizen Club.[11]

The public presence of women on bicycles set up a clash with prim and proper Victorian rules and etiquette. As women ventured beyond their domestic spheres into contested public spaces, conflict was inevitable. Oftentimes, these conflicts amounted to nothing more than parlor gossip and parents forbidding their daughters to ride on public streets. Occasionally, women's incursions into traditional male spaces were met with more vehemence, such as in this 1896 *Chicago Tribune* article:

> The practice of running down women riders is not as general as it should be, for they are, with a few exceptions, the greatest nuisance ever met with on the boulevards. One woman on a bicycle will cover the entire boulevard, zig-zagging back and forth, and will effectually prevent any one from passing unless he does succeed in running her down. . . . It would be safer to attempt to pass a circus parade than a woman on a wheel; but when this road-coverer is multiplied by two, three, or four it is a foregone conclusion that they have possession of the earth.[12]

In all likelihood, this diatribe was written in jest, but it is certainly possible that the author was completely serious. The streets had always been the purview of

An example of contemporary imagery featuring The New Woman as a bicyclist. (Author's collection.)

carriages, teamster wagons, and streetcars—all driven by men. Women moving boldly and sometimes en masse onto the streets presented a direct challenge to the established gender norms and Victorian social order.

During the bicycle boom era, the concept of the "New Woman" became increasingly prominent in American society. The New Woman prioritized education, often seeking out a college degree. She also asserted her economic independence by entering the workforce. She lived alone. She was not beholden to anyone (particularly men) and did what she wanted. The New Woman was emblematic of Progressive Era reformers, particularly in her advocacy for women's suffrage. While the New Woman was not strictly a product of the bicycle boom, she was frequently depicted as a bloomer-wearing cyclist, including on the covers of major magazines like *Scribner's* and *Harper's Weekly*. A series of satirical stereographic images showed New Woman cyclists admonishing their henpecked husbands: "Have lunch ready at one dear" and "Sew your own buttons, I'm going for a ride." The middle- and upper middle-class demographics of the New Woman aligned closely with the demographics of cyclists at the time. The New Woman ideal was emulated by young women drawn to Progressive reform but was derided by much of the male population.

Questions about women's cycling extended far beyond whether they should ride on the roads. Appropriate women's cycling attire was discussed ad nauseam. Others wondered if cycling could permanently damage young women's reproductive systems, or if riding hard for extended periods of time permanently locked a woman's face into a twisted grimace known as "bicycle face." These contentions invited retorts, and the subsequent debates were an important aspect of Illinois bicycle culture during the 1890s.

Women and the Bicycle Industry

Advances in bicycle design set the stage for the phenomenal growth in women's cycling. The decisive innovations were safety bicycles and, shortly after, women-specific bicycle frames. Overwhelmingly, these were designed by men. Even by the patriarchal norms of the time, inventing and patenting were thoroughly male-dominated endeavors. By one count, only 1 percent of patent filings in the United States came from women.[13]

A few notable Illinois women broke with convention to design bicycles and even patent their own inventions. The list included Chicagoan Kate Parke, who patented a bicycle lock in 1890, and Elgin resident Alice A. Bennitt, who patented a bicycle canopy in 1896.[14] In 1895, the *Detroit Free Press* ran a fascinating story about Cassie Jorgensen of Chicago. Cassie and her husband Emil operated a bicycle shop on Halsted Street. Like many owners of small shops, they made their own bicycles in addition to selling parts and making repairs. After helping to manage the shop for a few years, Cassie decided that it was important for a woman to make her own bicycle. The newspaper story recounts how she went on to build a new frame from scratch, cutting and brazing the tubes, filing the sprocket, and lacing up a set of wheels. Cassie had intended the bicycle for herself, but after seeing it, a customer quickly purchased it for $100.[15] A growing middle class of consumers and changing attitudes toward women in the workplace led to the employment of significant numbers of women and young girls in Chicago's bicycle factories. In 1897, Gormully & Jeffery employed fifty-one women, while Chicago-based bicycle parts maker George L. Thompson employed thirty-four women along with four girls under the age of sixteen. Chicago's Cash Buyers Union, a bicycle manufacturer and mail-order company, employed more women (fifty-five) than men (thirty).[16] Women's roles in the workplace and American society were evolving, and women cyclists were often at the forefront of this evolution.

The Rational Dress Movement

In 1896, journalist Nellie Bly asked the famed suffragist and abolitionist Susan B. Anthony about her views on bicycling. Anthony's reply amounted to a manifesto for women's cycling in the 1890s:

> I think it has done more to emancipate women than anything else in the world. I stand and rejoice every time I see a woman ride by on a wheel. It gives women a feeling of freedom and self-reliance. It makes her feel as if she were independent. The moment she takes her seat she knows she can't get into harm unless she gets off her bicycle, and away she goes, the picture of free, untrammeled womanhood.

This oft-cited quotation also showed how closely intertwined cycling was with the burgeoning Progressive Era movement.

In a less commonly quoted portion of the interview, Bly asked Anthony about bloomers, the baggy pants preferred by many women cyclists. Anthony was a fan. Bloomers were "the proper thing for wheeling," she stated. "A woman doesn't want skirts and flimsy lace to catch in the wheel. Safety, as well as modesty, demands bloomers or extremely short skirts. You know women only wear foolish articles of dress to please men's eyes anyway."[17] Anthony saw the bicycle as a vehicle for women's emancipation and suffrage, with dress reform playing an important role in both causes. Elizabeth Cady Stanton, the eighty-year-old matriarch of the suffrage movement, agreed. Stanton made a pointed case for bloomers in an interview given the same year as Anthony's. Referring to Victorian-style skirts, Stanton quipped that a woman actually "does not run, as she seems to the ordinary observer, like a churn on casters, a pyramid in shape from waist downward. A being with two legs, for free motion, must of necessity have bifurcated garments. This revelation of legs has been a great shock to some sensitive souls, and the debates on the question of what women should wear have been as hysterical as on the first point, should she be permitted to ride at all?" Stanton was confident that, having already chosen to ride, a woman will "wear what she pleases."[18]

The "revelation of legs" that Stanton joked about became a serious point of contention as bloomers gained in popularity among women cyclists, connecting their cause with the dress reform movement. Amelia Bloomer, and the pants for women that came to share her name, predated all forms of the pedal-driven bicycle. Bloomer attended the first 1848 Seneca Falls Convention on Women's rights and shortly after founded a temperance newspaper called *The Lily*. It was in this paper in 1851 that Bloomer first began arguing that women should wear bifurcated baggy pants. Bloomer and some of her readers (including Elizabeth Cady Stanton) took up this style of dress for a few years, but they met with much resistance and ridicule and eventually gave up the endeavor. The name "bloomer," however, became synonymous with this style of women's clothing. As Victorian culture took root and progressed during the second half of the nineteenth century, women's dress became increasingly restrictive, unwieldy, and dangerous. A Victorian corset included a stiff front busk made of wood or steel. Whalebone was incorporated in the back and sides. This structure was cinched down to augment the bust and slim the midriff to create an idealized figure. There were many layers of clothing either over or under a corset, including a chemise, drawers, and petticoat. Exceptionally large dresses were supported, in part, by these undergarments. Crinolines and hoop skirts were also used to provide additional structure.

The dress reform movement was reignited in 1881 with the formation of the Rational Dress Society in England. The group was quite explicit regarding its dress reform goals. According to guidelines laid out in an 1888 issue of the *Rational Dress Society Gazette*, women's dress should not deform the body or impede movement. This standard ruled out tight corsets, high-heeled shoes, and weighted skirts. In an indication of how heavy and cumbersome Victorian women's attire had become, the Rational Dress Society set as its goal that the upper limit of the weight of undergarments be no more than seven pounds, still hefty by any standard. The Rational Dress Society's ideas slowly began to take hold in Europe and were soon adopted by American reformers.[19]

The advent of the safety bicycle and a surge in women's cycling brought issues of dress reform into the limelight. Heavy dresses and skirts made riding a bicycle impractical, if not impossible. Dresses were liable to get caught up in the chain or spokes and swinging a leg over the bicycle would risk showing far more undergarments—and possibly a bare ankle—than was proper for a Victorian lady.[20]

Dress reform debates played out in Chicago streets and newspapers. Chicago was considered a progressive city by the standards of the day, and Chicago women cyclists could often be found heading out for a morning ride and attending a suffrage or temperance meeting in the evening. Some of them started wearing bloomers. The *Chicago Tribune* credited Lucy Porter as the first Chicago woman cyclist to wear bloomers in public. (To be sure, this attribution ignores the earlier women racers such as Edith Schuler and Louise Armaindo, who would have, by necessity, worn some form of pants or tights.) In Porter's 1894 account to the *Tribune*, she described being very nervous during her initial bicycle ride while wearing bloomers, even though she had the support of the male riders in the local club. People stopped and stared, but she didn't receive any harassment, save for some young boys on the edge of town. According to Porter, the bloomer outfit allowed her to double her speed, and she swore to never ride in skirts again.[21]

Porter's interview did not indicate what year she began riding in bloomers, but by the mid-1890s they were increasingly popular among Chicago's women cyclists. The Chicago Correct Dress and Physical Culture Club even started selling patterns that allowed women to sew their own bloomers for cycling.[22] In 1894, another *Tribune* reporter stood on the corner of Jackson and Ashland and counted seventy-three women riders between seven and nine o'clock on a Thursday evening. Fifty-eight of them had adopted the bloomer outfit. Bloomers became so popular among Chicago's young women that they began wearing them both on and off the bike.[23] This newfound independence in dress and freedom of movement was met with resistance on many fronts.

Some bicycling clubs embraced dress reform. The all-women Unique Club stipulated in its bylaws that all members must ride in the new bloomer pants when on official club "runs." One of these weekend runs, consisting of about fifty members, met in Chicago's Union Park. The president and the captain noted two members had arrived wearing skirts over their bloomers. The members were asked to remove the non-conforming garments. When they refused, the captain ordered the other members to strip off the offenders' skirts, leaving only the bloomers. When asked about the incident, the president, Mrs. Langdon, responded: "It was done in all seriousness. The club's rules are made to be kept and not to be broken. Why did we take off the skirts in public? For no other reason but to make examples of the offenders."[24] Whether this was a well-choreographed publicity stunt or a true clashing of old and new social norms cannot be ascertained. In any case, it is clear that appropriate dress for women cyclists was far from a settled issue.

Hurrah for the Girls in Bloomers: Spirited March Song with Chorus. Published by the S. Brainard's Sons Company, Chicago, 1894. (The Lester S. Levy Sheet Music Collection, Johns Hopkins University Library.)

The reaction against bloomers was not long in coming. Managers of the Chicago Telephone Company were so perturbed with bloomers that they issued an edict barring women operators wearing bloomers to, at, or from work.[25] The Chicago police and even city hall began cracking down on bloomer-wearing cyclists. In 1894, Hattie Strage rode her bicycle down Dearborn Avenue in a sweater and tights. Apparently, the tights were too much of an affront to Victorian (male) standards. The police arrested Strage on a charge of disorderly conduct and fined her a substantial $25.[26] Another scandal occurred in July of 1895 when a ball was thrown in the pavilion in Jackson Park. The catch was that both men and women were required to attend in cycling attire. The ball was a tremendous success, with 400 attendees and 5,000 onlookers. Still, someone at the *Tribune* took offense, writing, "A bloomer on a 'bike' may be apologized for on the plea of convenience and cleanliness, but for a bloomer on a dancing floor there is neither rhyme nor reason. It is the essence of ugliness, the concentration of hideousness, the climax of suggestiveness." Even the Chicago-based bicycling periodical *The Referee* was critical of the event: "The bloomer is a hideous thing. When the wearer is on a bicycle her posture and motion help to disguise the garment's ugliness. But when she stands or walks the baggy shapelessness of her lower limbs spoils her entire figure. The bloomer, in fact, brings out all the defects in a woman's appearance and diminishes all the perfections." This public sentiment against the bloomer was on full display when a second bloomer ball was attempted a few weeks later and was broken up by Chicago police on the grounds of indecent behavior.[27] A Chicago police captain was quite blunt in his disdain for women cyclists:

> I am not an advocate of the use of the bicycle among women, when viewing it from a morality phase. Women of refinement and exquisite moral training addicted to the use of the bicycle are not infrequently thrown among the uncultivated and degenerate elements of both sexes whose coarse, boisterous and immoral gestures are heard and seen while speeding along our streets and boulevards . . . A large number of our female cyclists wear shorter dresses than the laws of morality and decency permit, thereby inviting the improper conversations and remarks of the depraved and the immoral. I most certainly consider the adoption of the bicycle by women as detrimental to the advancement of morality.[28]

Some critics associated women bicyclists with the perversive flip side of Victorian prudery: prostitution. Chicago at this time was well known for its expansive "red light" district that housed many brothels, gambling houses, and taverns. The *Denver Evening Post* reported on Chicago's "Nymphs du pave," who took to the streets on their bicycles when police cracked down on their traditional haunts. Some of these women were said to have scandalized their more proper fellow cyclists by riding around the city at night "in black silk tights and vests that cling to the body like the skin itself." This led *The Post* to speculate that the term "street walker" would soon be obsolete and would need to be replaced with "solicitation on wheels."[29]

Chicago alderman John Coughlin, aka "Bathhouse John," knew something about the red-light district, which was in his ward. In return for some graft and promised political support, Bathhouse John tended to look the other way regarding the sins of this part of his district. Interestingly, though, he introduced an Anti-Bloomer Ordinance to the City Council in 1895. His ordinance specified that it would be "unlawful for any female person within the corporate limits of the City of Chicago to ride or attempt to ride any bicycle or tricycle or to publicly promenade in the streets, avenues, or public highways of said city while dressed or arrayed in costumes commonly known as 'bloomers,' 'knickerbockers,' baseball attire, or trousers."[30] Perhaps Bathhouse John was willing to tolerate "scandalous attire" only if it were kept contained in his red-light districts? The ordinance appears never to have been passed by the council, but that wasn't the case everywhere. South of Chicago's borders at the time, the company town of Pullman barred women from riding in anything other than skirts.[31]

By the end of the century, the public furor over bloomers had mostly subsided. The bicycle craze had come along at a point in history when the dress reform movement was gaining steam in Progressive circles. Dress reform, like women's suffrage, was an idea whose time had come. Within two decades of the end of the boom, women gained the right to vote, and the flapper fashions of the Roaring Twenties were worlds away from the Victorian corsets and hoop skirts. The contributions of women cyclists to this revolution in women's dress have been noted by previous historians, but the sheer magnitude of the boom has been routinely underestimated and underappreciated. Women cyclists, with Illinois leading the way, were instrumental in the success of the dress reform movement that helped make this later progress possible.

Health and Medical Issues

American industrialization and the great nineteenth-century rural-to-urban migration raised concerns about personal health. City life was comparatively sedentary and rife with pollution, and cycling was championed by many as a healthy counterbalance to urban dwelling. Like the issue of bloomers, however, the question of whether cycling was a healthy activity for women was highly contentious. Even by the 1890s, the relationship between modern scientific principles and the medical profession was often murky. The preceding fifty years had seen advances in vaccinations, germ theory, and surgical hygiene. Yet this was also a period when charlatans sold patent medicines, some of them toxic, that they claimed could cure anything from kidney disease to obesity and "female disorders."

The question of the impact of cycling on women's health thus existed within this mixture of science and superstition. The debate within the medical community regarding women's cycling was extremely politicized. If a throughline existed, it was that a male-dominated medical profession sought to further exert social pressure on women to maintain control over women's bodies, regulate with whom they associated, and restrict where they were allowed to go.

As the bicycle boom progressed, the list of maladies specifically attributed to the bicycle grew exponentially. A condition called "bicycle face" received a great deal of attention. The purported symptom of bicycle face was a permanently strained and haggard expression caused by excessive riding and effort. Newspaper accounts said that it could affect either sex but was more likely to cause permanent harm in women. Those afflicted with "bicycle walk," on the other hand, rode so much that their legs were said to continue mimicking pedaling motions even off the bike. "Bicycle hump" was an unnatural curvature of the spine caused by hunching over the bars. If those weren't bad enough, riders were also cautioned against "bicycle gums." This particular malady was said to be caused by fast riding in cold air, the combination of which could cause teeth to fall out. These specious diagnoses all highlighted the potential threat of disfigurement in an era of Victorian idealized feminine beauty.

Physicians arguing against women riding the bicycle cited a variety of more familiar but no less worrisome ailments and diseases that might result. One of the most serious was infertility. Doctors approached this issue from a variety of angles. Without providing any evidence, some argued that the general exertion of cycling would deplete the energy needed for reproduction. Others claimed it was the dangerous shaking and jarring of riding that could leave women infertile. At this time, only a few women were physicians. Even those few were not unanimous in their support of bicycling, as evidenced by Arabella Kenealy of Great Britain. Kenealy was a prominent woman physician who came out strongly against women cycling or participating in any strenuous athletics. Her argument testified to just how rigid and deeply entrenched gender norms were in Victorian society:

> One cannot possess all the delicately evolved qualities of woman together with the muscular and mental energies of man. In debasing her womanhood, in becoming a neuter, she descends from the standpoint whereat life was interesting . . . She no longer preserves and brews. She no longer weaves and fashions. Her children are nursed, fed, clothed, taught, and trained by hirelings; her sick are tended by the professional nurse, her guests are entertained by paid performers. What truly remains which may be called her duties? . . . All that I would warn her against is the terror into which she has been temporarily led, the error of supposing there is any nobler sphere than that of home.[32]

The medical profession's concerns about women cyclists were profoundly connected to sexuality. They were particularly worried that cycling provided women with a new means for masturbation. This claim was not made by a few outliers here and there, but, rather, was a serious topic that was discussed at length in (male-dominated) medical journals and at medical conferences. The premise that cycling could be a form of masturbation and something that male physicians needed to concern themselves with was a pervasive concern in the nineteenth century. Writing in the *Brooklyn Medical Journal* in 1897, Dr. E. D. Page asserted outright that bicycling "teaches masturbation in women and girls. The saddle resting against the labia majora, as it does by a slight inclination forward, it is easy to accomplish it."[33] Recall that a proper Victorian lady did not even straddle a horse; she was expected to ride sidesaddle. As Amy Drake explains in "Rubbing the Pommel: Women and Bicycling in the 1890s," "Many believed that masturbation caused insanity. Women were particularly susceptible to mental instability due to their reproductive systems. . . . The act also sapped the 'vital force' and weakened the individual. This fear permeated society."[34] The concern over masturbation is important not for shock value or sensationalism, but for understanding the multifaceted threats that women riding bicycles presented to the Victorian patriarchy. If women discovered their own sexuality through cycling, would they even need men? If women put on pants, rode to work, and made their own living, then what was the role of men? Buttressing these fears were concerns that cycling could also cause male infertility. Ironically, modern scientific evidence has shown that infertility can be a real concern for some high-mileage male cyclists, but no similar evidence has been found for women.[35]

The proffered solutions to the alleged connection between bicycling and self-pleasuring were many and varied. Some traditionalists argued that women simply shouldn't ride at all. Others offered specific advice on how to adjust a bicycle to avoid this issue: saddles should be level, not tilted, and the handlebars should be of a design and height that encouraged a proper upright posture. Manufacturers, unsurprisingly, saw an opportunity for a new product line and designed a variety of women-specific saddles. These saddles invariably featured some form of channel or cutout designed to relieve saddle pressure while riding. One of the most successful models was the Christy Anatomical saddle. The Christy Anatomical—available in both men's and women's styles—became very popular and was included on many new bicycles. The spring-supported Duplex Safety Saddle was another popular model made in Chicago.

A major argument in favor of women's cycling was the growing recognition that a fully sedentary lifestyle was not healthy for women either. Industrialization and urbanization had for the first time in American history created a middle class that actually had leisure time. Yet many of them—and even more so, working-class Americans—had to contend with the poor air and sanitation and few options for safe outdoor physical exertion that characterized city life. Famed Chicago social worker and reformer Jane Addams recognized the potential for bicycles to improve health. In an 1899 interview with the *Chicago News*, Addams extolled the virtues of cycling for the poor and middle classes: "I think the bicycle is a good thing for the workingman. . . . It gives him recreation and exercise and while riding to and from his work he enjoys the open air."[36] One of Chicago's legions of women cyclists ridiculed the idea that women could not handle the physical demands of cycling, noting the inconsistencies in concerns about women's welfare:

> When a woman wants to learn anything, or do anything useful or even have any fun there is always someone to solemnly warn her that it is her duty to keep well. Meanwhile in many states she can work in factories ten hours a

> day, she can stand behind counters in badly ventilated stores from 8 o'clock to 6, she can bend over the sewing machine for about 5 cents an hour and no one cares enough to protest. But when these same women . . . find a cheap and delightful way of getting the fresh air and exercise they need so sorely there is a great hue and cry about their physical welfare.[37]

Many physicians also saw bicycling as one of the best responses to the health crisis. Even then, some of them tempered their recommendations, warning about the risks of overexertion for women riders. A great deal of hand-wringing went into debates about the best frame designed for women bicyclists (heavier, more flexible, drop-frame models were always recommended) and how they should position themselves on a bicycle (upright, not hunched over the bars), among other concerns.

As the bicycle craze progressed, there were as many physicians championing bicycling as there were naysayers. On the extreme end was Dr. Francis Nash. Writing in *The American Journal of Obstetrics* in 1896, Nash offered an extensive list of conditions that could be improved or remedied through

From *"Bicycling for Girls from a Medical Standpoint: A Paper Read Before the Chicago Academy of Homeopathic Physicians,"* 1891.

cycling, including dilated heart; varicose veins; hemorrhoids; pulmonary affections; nervous diseases such as organic and functional paralysis; neurasthenia and hysteria; migraine; neuralgias; anemia; chlorosis; amenorrhea; dysmenorrhea; uterine congestion; ovarian congestion; pelvic lesions; dyspepsias; constipation; obesity; torpid liver; gout; diabetes; mellitus; spinal curvatures; and ankylosed joints.[38] While Dr. Nash was certainly onto something regarding the health benefits of cycling, his ambitious list of ailments relieved by riding reads suspiciously like the labels found on some of the patent medicines of the day. Unsurprisingly, bicycle manufacturers sought to highlight bicycling-friendly medical perspectives. In 1891, Gormully & Jeffery printed a pamphlet entitled "Bicycling for Girls from a Medical Standpoint." In the pamphlet, Professor Robert Tooker extoled the virtues of cycling for women and girls and provided testimonies from leading physicians regarding the general safety and health benefits of cycling for women. The pamphlet, of course, ends with a nice lithograph advertisement for a Gormully & Jeffery American Ladies Rambler bicycle.[39] Such perspectives represented a concession to Elizabeth Cady Stanton's point that women were going to ride regardless of what the critics said.

Women Centurions

While the papers and medical journals debated the effects of cycling on women's health, a large contingent of women cyclists in Illinois settled the debate simply by continuing to ride long distances with no ill effects. Chicago was a hotbed for American century-riding during the 1890s due in part to the popularity of the Century Road Club of Chicago (later renamed the Century Road Club of America), which was founded in 1891. Another factor in Chicago's favor was the relatively flat and fast Elgin-Aurora century course. At the time, century riding existed in a liminal space between recreational riding and racing. Times and places were recorded for officially sanctioned century rides, but most serious racers focused on track racing. Additionally, a cyclist could set a century record anytime they wanted, provided that they followed the proper protocols, which included following an established course and checking in at official stops along the way where their name and the time of day was recorded.

Illinois had the greatest concentration of women century riders in the country. At the beginning of the 1890s, only a daring few had attempted a century, but their numbers swelled over the course of the decade. Lizzie Hegerty was one of the early century-riding pioneers of the safety bicycle era. She completed her first century on a hard-tired safety bicycle in 1891 and had finished a total of twenty-six century rides by 1894. Most of her century rides were on the well-established Elgin-Aurora course. Also in 1894, Mrs. M. J. Kelly of Chicago accomplished the spectacular feat of finishing two centuries in one day. Those two centuries were among the twenty centuries she would complete that year. Thirteen-year-old Inez Whittaker, a member of Chicago's South Side Cycling Club, completed a century in 1894, leading *The Bearings* to speculate, "She is probably the youngest century rider in the world."[40]

One of the first Illinois women centurions to gain some national attention was Annis Burr Porter of Chicago. In 1894, Porter beat most of the male riders when she finished eighth out of 132 riders with a time of 8:22 for the Elgin-Aurora century course. In 1895, she shattered her own record for the same course, this time finishing in 7:18. Porter was an unabashed advocate for riding in bloomers, which she attributed to helping set her century records. Papers reported that Porter "scorns obscurity and declares that she is the champion lady century rider of the world."[41] Whether or not her time rose to world-champion level, it was likely the fastest for an American woman on a road century course. Her record would be short-lived, as a new generation of Chicago women racers were beginning to dominate on both the track and the road.

Porter gained additional notoriety in 1896 when she rode her bike down a west Chicago water slide attraction called "Shoot the Chutes." The Chutes featured a massive 320-foot-tall ramp set at a steep 45-degree angle. Under normal operation, Shoot the Chutes was a water slide attraction that featured large boats filled with paying passengers. Annis, however, had other plans for the chutes. She went to the top of the chutes with her bicycle while five hundred people watched from below to see what her fate would be. Since nearly all bicycles at the time had fixed gears, Porter could only raise her legs and let the pedals whir below her as she flew down the ramp. Her descent took around four seconds, after which she was launched forty-five feet from the bottom of the slide into the water where she dove "like an eel and came up smiling." *The Chicago Chronicle* took care to detail her pink and blue outfit for their readers and then coyly noted that "there were other things that she didn't wear, but that is a matter of detail."[42] Annis reportedly gave multiple repeat performances on the water slide that fall.

The next year, Annis undertook a 1,100-mile, non-competitive bicycle ride from Chicago to New York. Porter rode with male escorts, and her preferred attire was a "white duck bloomer suit" (duck fabric is a form of heavy cotton). Porter completed the ride to New York in nineteen days, finishing nine full centuries en route.[43]

As the bicycle boom gained steam around the country, more and more women attempted a century. In 1895, a Chicago woman who went by the name Mrs. George Bunker broke Porter's century record with a time of 6:56

(14.4 mph) on the Elgin-Aurora course. Mrs. Bunker, however, was just getting started, as the following year she amassed an astonishing 15,515 miles, a total that included 78 individual century rides. In 1897, she rode 11,000 miles and 60 centuries.[44]

Notable Women Racers

As outlined in chapter 1, only a small number of women participated in races during the high-wheel era. Still, the many racing successes of high-wheel riders such as Louise Armaindo began to change assumptions about what women racers were capable of. With the advent of the safety bicycle, women began riding in far greater numbers. Once again, would-be women racers were met with a social double standard. Many in Victorian society enthusiastically believed in moderate, discreet exercise to maintain women's health (partially for childbearing reasons), but the line was often drawn at racing, which was seen as degrading and unwomanly. An 1896 newspaper article summed up attitudes towards women racers among those who wanted to maintain the status quo: "A woman of any age as a scorcher is so manifestly out of her proper sphere that it would seem unnecessary to even refer to it, and no amount of skill or grace can excuse, in our humble opinion, any modest young woman's making such a spectacle of herself."[45]

In its early days, the L.A.W. had mostly looked the other way when it came to a small number of women's bicycle races being contested across the country. As the sport grew in popularity, the L.A.W. felt the need to take a stance on women's racing. In a similar vein to regulating amateurism in men's racing, the L.A.W. took a very traditional stance toward women's racing. In 1894, Abbot Bassett, the secretary for the L.A.W., stated, "It has come at last. Heaven save the mark. Women on the race track... In riding the wheel, as in everything else, our fair sisters should not forget to be womanly. We look to them to elevate the sport, not drag it down." Apparently, the rest of the League's leadership agreed with Bassett. Its bylaws were changed the following year to ban women's racing at all *sanctioned* events. Following this bylaw change, a track or race promoter could be permanently blacklisted for hosting a women's bicycle race. However, women's races were popular with spectators, and there was money to be made. Unsanctioned women's races continued throughout the 1890s.[46]

One way Illinois women cyclists responded to hostility from the male-dominated bicycling establishment was to form their own organizations. Founded in 1898, Illinois Women's Cycling Association "was formed to promote female cycling and its interests." As a standalone cycling organization, it was free to sanction its own track races. Likewise, some of Chicago's women's cycling clubs took it upon themselves to create their own events. The Women's

Auxiliary of the Ravenswood Club put on a series of charity bicycle races that were for women only and that were completely organized by women.[47]

The fact that the L.A.W. had never been able to fully control the road-racing scene opened some opportunities for women to race and establish records. Many of the best women track racers of the 1890s got their start riding centuries against the clock. This was certainly true of two of the most dominant women racers of the era, Tillie Anderson and Lizzie Glaw, both of whom hailed from Chicago.

Tillie the Terrible Swede

As detailed above, in the early 1890s, a number of Chicago's women cyclists had contributed to lowering the Elgin-Aurora century record. The next woman to do so was another Chicagoan, Tillie Anderson. Anderson, whose competitors would later give her the nickname "Tillie the Terrible Swede," emigrated to Chicago from Sweden in 1891. She settled in Chicago's Swede Town neighborhood, found work as a seamstress, and quickly became intrigued by all the women partaking in Chicago's bicycle boom. Shortly after learning to ride, Anderson set her sights on the women's record for the Elgin-to-Aurora century. In 1895, after a few attempts, her promise as an endurance racer was apparent when she set a new course record of 6:52 (14.6 mph).[48]

Anderson had a crash-course introduction to professional racing when she was encouraged to enter a six-day, three-hours-per-day women's race at Chicago's Second Regiment Armory. At the beginning of 1896, Anderson was just nineteen years old, and she would be racing ten of the best women riders in the country. Her first day of training on the steeply banked, seventeen-lap-per-mile track resulted in multiple crashes and nearly got her removed from the event before it started. She was allowed another day of training, and she began to get a feel for riding on the short and steep track. On the first day of competition, Anderson managed to hang with the leaders until near the end of the allotted time, at which point she surged to the lead. On the second day of competition, Anderson established a new women's record for one hundred miles with her time of 5:09:40 (19.4 mph). Although the racing remained close, Anderson eventually triumphed in her debut race, finishing with a new women's six-day record of 344 miles. A *Chicago Tribune* reporter gushed, "The finish was the most exciting of any event of its kind ever held in Chicago, and showed the winner to be the speediest woman rider in America." In an apt comparison, the *Chicago Dispatch* called Anderson "the second Louise Armaindo."[49]

Anderson's next big race was another six-day held in March in Chicago, this time on a track inside of Tattersall's exhibition hall. Proving that her debut professional race was no fluke, Anderson again finished first, nearly six miles ahead of second place. With these two major wins to her name, the press and other riders began to call her "The Terrible Swede." Throughout her career, Anderson developed a keen sense for self-promotion and blistering one-liners that made good newspaper headlines. In the spring of 1896, Anderson learned that a fellow Chicago cycling Swede, John Lawson, had been calling himself "The Terrible Swede." Flying in the face of Victorian social norms that called for humility and deference to men, Anderson told the *Chicago Chronicle*, "It's not exactly because I want to be known as the 'terrible,' but I don't like to see John Lawson parading himself as the champion of Swedish riders living in Chicago. What has John ever done to deserve all this credit he takes to himself? I never heard of him winning a race nor did anyone else, I guess. He has no right to tell me that I am not in his class." She abruptly challenged Lawson to a race. Lawson, perhaps anticipating the outcome were this race to occur, demanded an indoor track of no less than five laps per mile and a $5,000 purse. Since there were no indoor tracks of that size in Chicago and no one willing to put up $5,000, Lawson managed to escape with some of his dignity. History, however, only remembers one Terrible Swede bicycle racer: Tillie.[50]

Having failed to get a race against Lawson, Anderson next dropped the gauntlet on hundreds of the best amateur male riders, who were eagerly awaiting the 1896 Chicago Road Race. A woman had never been allowed to race in either the Pullman Road Race or its successor, the Chicago Road Race. Anderson defeated the best women riders in her first two track races and was hungry to test her abilities against men. In a letter to the *Chicago Chronicle*, she directly connected her ambition with the broader cause of Progressive reform. "Women can vote occasionally," she said, so "why shouldn't they be permitted to race with men? . . . I have so easily won in the different races in which I have entered that I am fired with the ambition to speed with men cyclists. The Chicago road race offers a splendid opportunity . . . I think I could set an example to some of the boys in the way of training.[51]

If the dress reformers and women's rights advocates of the Progressive Era were looking for an unabashed champion, Anderson may have been it. Unfortunately, she never got a chance to participate in the Chicago Road Race. The Associated Cycling Clubs, who managed the event, rejected her entry on the grounds that the race was only for amateurs and added, "No matter how good a rider she may be, and even though her character may be in other respects like that of Caesar's wife, she is too man-like (and that is a great sin) if she participates in races."[52]

The 1896 season was a banner professional debut for Anderson. She raced at least twenty-four times, including eight six-day races, and had an overall win/loss record of 21–3. Her performances helped her secure a lucrative

Tillie the Terrible Swede poses on her Thistle racing bicycle. ("Tillie Anderson Team Thistle," Alice Olson Roepke, https://commons.wikimedia.org/wiki/File:Tillie_Anderson_Team_Thistle.jpg, CC BY-SA 4.0.)

sponsorship deal with the Excelsior Supply Company of Chicago. Excelsior manufactured the Thistle brand of bicycles. Thistle bicycles soon became synonymous with Anderson, as they launched a nationwide "Tillie Rides a Thistle" marketing campaign that included photographs of Anderson with her Thistle bicycle. It was rumored that Anderson earned $25 a week from Excelsior, with bonuses of $200 or more for winning large races. This was on top of her winnings from the actual races. All told, it is likely Anderson cleared $5,000 ($178,000 in 2024) in her first year of full-time racing, worlds away from her seamstress's salary the year before.[53] As the 1897 season dawned, Anderson was clearly the top long-distance woman cyclist in the country and, arguably, the world.

Never one to sit back and demurely let men make decisions for her, Anderson took a vocal stance against the L.A.W.'s refusal to sanction women's racing. In a letter to the *Chicago Chronicle*, she wrote, "Women riders have no sympathy for the League of American Wheelmen. The officials of this organization have done everything in their power to hurt our interests and kill our game . . . Are women speedy enough to compete with men riders? My answer to The Chronicle is yes and records made during the past indoor season will prove my assertion."[54] Anderson wasn't far off the mark with these claims. It is difficult to make an apples-to-apples comparison between men's and women's six-day events because the men were usually riding for twelve or twenty-four hours a day. Nevertheless, Anderson pointed out that she had ridden 21.7 miles in the first hour of a six-day, whereas the men's record on the same track was 21.9 miles.[55] These narrow margins between the best male and women riders were forcing society to reconsider the physical capabilities of female athletes.

In March, another women's six-day race was held at Tattersall's in Chicago. In the first hour of this event, Anderson was only two laps behind the top male rider from a few weeks prior on the same track. In 1897, the bicycle boom was nearing its zenith, and women's races continued to be incredibly popular. The back-to-back men's and women's Chicago six-day races provided a controlled experiment to accurately gauge spectator interest. As reported in the *Chronicle*, women "proved better attractions than men in six day races last night. . . . Twelve thousand people crowded into the big building to see Tillie Anderson and seven women competitors break records and win the handsome purses put up by the Cycle Carnival Company."[56] Competition was heating up in the women's professional ranks as more and more women riders took to the racetracks. In the Tattersall's six-day, a couple of unfortunate crashes broke Anderson's winning streak, pushing her to fourth. Illinois women riders maintained their dominance, however, since the new champion, Lizzie Glaw, was also a Chicagoan. A recap of the race in the L.A.W.'s *American Wheelman* reminded readers that women's racing was unethical. A few sentences later, however, the author did an about-face: "But to the spectator who can appreciate good racing without regard to the personality of the racers, the riding which has attracted large crowds at Tattersall's every evening during the past week was by far the most spirited and interesting that Chicagoans have had the opportunity of witnessing on an indoor track."[57] High praise indeed for a city that was one of the premier American bicycle racing destinations of the 1890s.

Anderson came back with a vengeance after being defeated in Chicago. In 1897, she went on to compete in thirty races, only losing two to Lizzie Glaw. In December of 1897, Anderson and Lizzie were among the headliners for another six-day race, this time in St. Louis. The race was perhaps more memorable for the borderline-lascivious local newspaper coverage than it was for yet another win on Anderson's resume. During the races, Anderson consented to allowing a doctor and a reporter from the *St. Louis Republic* to examine her naked leg. Women's cycling was already a provocative endeavor, as women's racing attire usually consisted of form-fitting tights and shirts, scandalous by Victorian standards. The *Republic* capitalized on this fetishization of women cyclists by publishing a large sketch of Anderson's leg along with extensive commentary about its anatomical features: "The thigh is beautifully shaped, the flesh and muscles are soft, there is an absence of superfluous fat. . . . The skin is pure white, soft and smooth . . . from the thigh to the knee joint is artistically and anatomically well-proportioned, possessing the grace and desirable curvature of . . . a woman accustomed to hard, healthy, rejuvenating exercises." Anderson seemed to revel in the press coverage and even used the opportunity to take a jab at one of her opponents: "Three years ago I was very fat in the legs . . . almost as much so as Miss Peterson, one of my competitors in the St. Louis race, is today."[58]

A rival paper, the *St. Louis Post-Dispatch*, took a decidedly different approach. An article by the journalist Fanny Darling featured a page-wide sketch of five of the top women competitors at both the beginning and the end of the race. The post-race caricatures of the riders are haggard, gaunt, and wide-eyed in comparison with the fetching portraits from before the races. The headline read "Bicycle Racing Transforms Lovely Woman from a Pale Beauty into a Perfect Fright," and the article quoted a local woman who had watched the race: "It pained me to see them forfeiting health for gain in such a way. . . . God intended women to be better than horses."[59] None of this deterred Anderson in the slightest. She won the race and then, in an exhibition ride, set a new women's record for the fastest paced half-mile, with a time of fifty-two seconds (34.6 mph).

Her record-breaking continued in 1898, when she set a record for twenty-five miles in a time of 57:44 (26.0 mph). Comparisons with cyclists of today are inevitable. Using a single-speed, steel-framed bicycle with wooden wheels,

16 SUNDAY MORNING—ST. LOUIS POST-DISPATCH—DECEMBER 5, 1897.

BICYCLE RACING TRANSFORMS LOVELY WOMAN FROM A PALE BEAUTY INTO A PERFECT FRIGHT.

Dr. George L. Kearney and Mrs. Frazer Deprecate the Practice of Bicycle Riding as a Profession for Girls.

The Women Themselves Admit That They Will Break Down, but They Are Determined to Race for the Money They Win.

Tillie Anderson
Dotty Dayton Farnsworth
Lizzie Glaw
Lillie Williams
Ida Peterson

THE GIRLS AT THE FINISH OF THE SIX DAYS BICYCLE RACE IN THE COLISEUM.

"Bicycle Racing Transforms Lovely Woman from a Pale Beauty into a Perfect Fright." (*St. Louis Post-Dispatch*, Dec. 5, 1897.)

Anderson had a personal record of 26.5 miles for one hour (she was likely assisted by pacers).[60] In 2024, with the advantage of modern equipment and training, the women's unpaced hour record was 31.2 miles. Anderson continued to dominate long distance racing through 1902, after which women's racing faded away along with the bicycle boom. Along the way, she soundly defeated Amélie Le Gall (who raced under the name Lisette Marton), the French champion, and managed to win eighteen out of nineteen races in her final full year of competition. Over the course of her career, she had entered 130 races and managed to win all but seven.[61]

Lizzie Glaw

If not for Tillie Anderson's dominance of 1890s women's bicycle racing, Lizzie Glaw would have been the one in the limelight. Glaw emigrated from Germany to Chicago in the early 1890s and learned to ride shortly after. She was a determined and consistent competitor, as evidenced by her early attempts at the women's record for the Elgin-Aurora century course. Tillie Anderson had attempted the course eight times while establishing her record time of 6:52. Glaw was right on the cusp and completed thirty-six attempts before finally lowering the record to 6:48 in October of 1895.[62] Glaw competed in the two above-mentioned women's six-day races held in Chicago in the spring of 1896, finishing behind Anderson in sixth and third places, respectively. Unlike Anderson, Glaw did not immediately dive into the professional racing circuit, preferring to race close to home in her first year.

In 1897, Glaw secured a sponsorship with Cleveland Bicycles and began racing in earnest. Anderson and Glaw were a study in contrasts. Glaw mostly eschewed the spotlight and employed patient, calculated tactics in her races. When asked about her motivations for racing, she once succinctly replied, "I like this business because I make money."[63] Since they were both from Chicago, Anderson and Glaw often found themselves traveling together. If you believe the newspaper accounts of the day, they were the bitterest of rivals. The *Toledo Blade* once reported that "one calls the other an ignorant Swede and the other is a German lobster." Both women, however, knew how to work the press to drum up big audiences for their races, and there is some evidence that the animosity they exhibited in the papers was simply good show business. As mentioned, one of Glaw's biggest wins was the six-day race in March of 1897 at Tattersall's in Chicago. In that event, she set a world record of 240 miles for twelve hours and earned the title of "women's world champion." In the process, she defeated Tillie Anderson and a deep roster of the best women racers. When she wasn't up against Anderson, Glaw usually triumphed.

With the pair so closely matched, the bicycling world was clamoring for a head-to-head matchup. In July of 1897, race promoters in Toledo, Ohio, got both women to agree to race a best two out of three series of one-hour races for a $300 prize purse. Glaw played up the rivalry for the local papers, first refusing to be in the same room as Anderson when they signed the race contract, and then muttering as she signed, "I'll make her wish she never saw a bicycle."

To increase the speed and excitement of the matchup, each hour race was to be paced by male cyclists, who would leave the track in the final minutes to let the women duke it out to the finish. Promoters ran into problems on the first night of the races when teams of men were unable to match Anderson and Glaw's pace for the full hour, even though the men only rode one-half mile at a time. For miles five through ten, the women averaged an impressive 25.5 mph. Anderson led almost the entire hour, with Glaw glued to her rear wheel. In the final minutes, Glaw unleashed her sprint and pulled ahead of Anderson by a quarter of a lap. Asked later if she expected to win the following night, Glaw boasted, "Well, just watch my smoke. I'll try as hard as any woman who ever donned a sweater, and if I lose it will be because Anderson is the best rider, and I don't think she is."[64] The second night of racing played out much like the first, with Glaw conserving her energy behind Anderson and biding her time. This night, two top women racers were brought in as additional pacers since the men had trouble maintaining the necessary speeds. This time, Anderson was ready for Glaw's big sprint and stuck with her when she made her move. Nearing the finish, Anderson rode high up the banks and swooped down towards the finish line. The judges called it a dead heat—a tie—meaning the overall winner would be decided on the final night of racing. On the final night, much to Anderson's frustration, Glaw again stuck to her strategy of waiting until the last minute to make her move. A minimum total distance was often specified in the race contract to avoid riders plodding along until the final sprint. The third day was certainly no plodding affair, with the women exceeding 24 mph at times. With three laps to go, Glaw threw everything she had into her final sprint. Anderson made a gallant effort to come past her at the finish, but, true to her word, Glaw was the better rider on that night.

Anderson and Glaw were in the same races a few times during the remainder of the 1897 season and then again throughout 1898, with Anderson taking most of the wins. Both returned home to Chicago for a Thanksgiving week seven-day women's race at Tattersall's. The race featured some of the world's best women cyclists. In addition to Anderson and Glaw, there were Dottie Farnsworth from Minnesota and the Frenchwoman, Lisette Marton. Unlike previous events where the winner was determined by highest mileage covered, this race would be won by whomever amassed the highest score in a convoluted—and controversial—point system. Glaw came out swinging and was the top finisher on the first two nights. The point system resulted in furious races to the finish but also resulted in some dubious finish-line calls by the judges. Going into the final evening, Glaw held a slim lead according to the point system, but she was contesting the scoring from the previous evening. Glaw eventually withdrew from the race in protest, and Anderson claimed another victory.

More telling than the controversy over the scoring system was the lagging attendance. Back in March of 1897, the women's six-day at Tattersall's was a raging success, with 10,000 spectators in attendance. Now, a year-and-a-half later, the women's final barely brought in 2,000 spectators. The bicycle boom had peaked, along with interest in bicycle racing. The *Chicago Journal* summed up the situation: "Female bicycle races do not seem to be a drawing card in any city any longer."[65]

Bicycle racing did not dry up overnight, however. Anderson and Glaw found a number of events to compete in through 1902. Glaw won one last six-day in Troy, New York, in April of that year. At some point, she contracted typhoid fever, leading to her death in August. In a testament to how quickly the bicycle boom had come to an end, none of the Chicago papers ran any sort of remembrance of the hometown girl they had celebrated as a world champion only a few years earlier.[66] As historian Roger Gilles has written of Anderson and Glaw, "The pair of them were, without question, the two greatest women racers of the 1890s."[67]

Over the course of the 1890s, Illinois women bicycle racers helped to undermine broader patriarchal arguments about hard exercise being detrimental to women's health. Moreover, Illinois racers like Anderson and Glaw forced the very issue of presumed male physical superiority. The two weren't quite as fast as the best male racers of the day, but they were clearly faster than the average male bicycle racer. Over the decade, women bicycle racers forced society to reconsider the physical abilities of women athletes and, by extension, women in general. They were also instrumental in advancing the dress reform movement, as traditional Victorian attire was shown to be completely incompatible with bicycle riding and racing.

"Don'ts For Women Riders"

In 1895, the *Illinois State Journal* published a lengthy list of "Don'ts for Women Riders." As the negative phrasing of the title epitomized, Victorian social rules and etiquette for women were prescriptive and overbearing, often to the point of absurdity:

Don'ts For Women Riders

Don't be a fright.
Don't faint on the road.
Don't wear a man's cap.

Don't wear tight garters.
Don't forget your toolbar.
Don't attempt a "century."
Don't coast. It is dangerous.
Don't criticize people's "legs."
Don't boast of your long rides.
Don't wear loud hued leggings.
Don't cultivate a "bicycle face."
Don't refuse assistance up a hill.
Don't wear clothes that don't fit.
Don't "talk bicycle" at the table.
Don't neglect a "light's out" cry.
Don't wear jewelry while on a tour.
Don't race. Leave that to the scorchers.
Don't imagine everybody is looking at you.
Don't go to church in your bicycle costume.
Don't wear laced boots. They are tiresome.
Don't keep your mouth open on dirty roads.
Don't converse while in a scorching position.
Don't go out after dark without a male escort.
Don't contest the right of way with cable cars.
Don't wear a garden party hat with bloomers.
Don't wear white kid gloves. Silk is the thing.
Don't chew gum. Exercise your jaws in private.
Don't tempt fate by riding too near the curbstone.
Don't ask, "What do you think of my bloomers?"
Don't use bicycle slang. Leave that to the boys.
Don't discuss bloomers with every man you know.
Don't think you look as pretty as every fashion plate.
Don't go out without a needle, thread and thimble.[68]

This list of bicycling "don'ts" that women needed to adhere to actually continues past what is cited here. While the list was more than likely written as humorous satire, any woman cyclist in the 1890s would have recognized the absurdity of the Victorian social and gender norms that they were expected to uphold. A proper Victorian woman did not wear bloomers, nor did she venture out without a chaperone. A proper Victorian woman certainly didn't race her bicycle or attempt a century.

Yet women cyclists in Illinois routinely flouted social norms and did all of these things. The bicycle was a fin de siècle icon and a rallying point for Progressive reformers who were passionate about advancing women's rights and independence. Those causes were advanced by the bicycle craze of the 1890s.

6

Larger than Life

Bicycle Characters and Bicycle Culture

Baby Bliss

When Baby mounts his wheel,
The folks all stop upon the boulevard,
And stand and look and wonder long and hard.
He mounts so straightly the pneumatic tire,
That all his pigmy friends can but admire.
As Cassius said of old, "He doth bestride
(His wheel) like some colossus." See him ride!
And lo, it seems when his fair form has flown,
As if a section of the town had gone,
When Baby rides his wheel.

When Baby rides his wheel,
His striped stockings radiate before a
Fellow like the northern lights aurora;
Bicycle pants of such a modest size
To take them in requires two pairs of eyes.
A sweater, cut to hold four hundred weight,
And jaunty cap, the girls to captivate.
They all admire, and murmur as they see,
"He'd look so well in bloomers, O dear me,"
When Baby rides his wheel.
—Edward Wilson, 1895[1]

The man known as "Baby Bliss" was an Illinois cyclist who was truly larger than life. Baby Bliss was one of only a few people who bridged the world of the cyclist and that of the circus sideshow act. Along with vaudeville acts and minstrel shows, traveling circuses were especially popular sources of

Illinois cyclist "Baby Bliss" with Ignaz Schwinn, founder of Schwinn bicycles. (The Bicycle Museum of America, New Bremen, Ohio.)

entertainment during the Victorian Era. At a time when sideshow acts faced exploitation by circus managers, Baby Bliss was apparently able to leverage his great size to make a good living while traveling the world promoting various bicycle manufacturers.

Leonard H. Bliss was born in rural central Illinois on May 4, 1865, and weighed twelve pounds at birth. By age eleven, Bliss was six feet tall and weighed 190 pounds. Six years later, he had reached 280 pounds. As he continued to grow—purportedly reaching a weight of around 500 pounds by the mid-1890s—his girth became central to his work as a pitchman. After a short course of study at Illinois Wesleyan University, Leonard began working as a traveling salesman for the wholesale Chisholm Gray Company. In this role, he also sold locally made cigars packaged in a box that carried his image and the name "Our Baby." This seems to be the earliest mention of the nickname "Baby Bliss."[2]

Baby Bliss's rising fame coincided with the early years of the safety bicycle boom. The sheer number of bicycle companies during this period led to intense competition among brands to distinguish their particular bicycle from everyone else's. Assembling teams of professional racers was a common strategy for those companies that could afford it. Others hired famous artists to create elaborate catalogs, posters, and advertisements. Perhaps inevitably, someone had the idea to put the heaviest cyclist they could find on their bicycle for visual proof of durability.

In an era of shoddy manufacturing from some smaller companies, durability and strength were important selling points. Enter Baby Bliss. How Baby Bliss initially became connected with the International Manufacturing Company in Chicago is unclear, but by the summer of 1895, newspapers and cycling publications were abuzz with stories about Baby Bliss on a bicycle. In May, he served as one of the "limit men" in the nationally known Chicago Pullman Road Race. Limit men were the first starters in a handicapped event; they often started ten or more minutes ahead of the "scratch men," who started last with no time advantage. By most accounts, Baby never finished any of these longer events; it was less about racing and more about spectacle and advertising. *The Referee* noted that he successfully rode a twenty-four-pound America bicycle in the Pullman race.[3] Accounts over the next few years differed on whether Baby rode a stock America bicycle or one specially reinforced to hold his weight. The bicycle he rode is always listed as weighing between twenty-two and twenty-six pounds, so a stock frame is quite likely. In July, *The Referee* noted that Baby Bliss was traveling the country riding Morgan and Wright tires. Morgan and Wright was a large Chicago-based tire company that also tapped Baby Bliss to help prove the durability of their tires.[4]

Someone of Baby's size riding a bicycle was a novelty similar to those promoted by the circus sideshows of the time. In 1896, an Iowa newspaper gave a colorful account of one young boy's perceptions of Baby Bliss:

> W'en he gets onto his wheel you ought to see 'im. He's a sight. No, the wheel ain't any bigger'n any other . . . when he gets on you wouldn't believe it would hold him. But it does . . . I tell you, he's a sight. He's 23 years old, an bigger'n you, an' papa, an' gramma all put together. He's good natured, too, an' he likes to have th' kids foller him. I follered 'im all th' afternoon an' he never said a word to me excep' when I got too near, an' he says to me, he ses, "get out o' th' way, kid, er I might fall on ye an' squash ye," an' I got out o' th' way, you bet.[5]

During the following year, it was reported that Baby Bliss attended every major bicycle show in the country. By the summer of 1896, the International Manufacturing Company started using Baby Bliss to help expand their export market. Along with Mr. F. A. Hastings, who managed the company, Baby headed to Europe on the steamship *Umbria*. The pair stayed in London for two months, during which time Baby Bliss took daily rides through the streets and participated in some exhibition races. One county history recounted that Bliss had a personal record of 1:42 for the half mile and that he won a gold medal at Stanford Hill, London, for a race between "the American giant and the English midget."[6] After his stay in London, Baby went on an extensive European excursion, visiting "Birmingham, Manchester, Glasgow, Edinburg [*sic*], Brussels, Utrecht, The Hague, where he rode in the parade with representatives of the royal family of Holland; Dover, Copenhagen, Stockholm, Christiana, Hamburg, Berlin, Vienna, Paris, Belfast, Dublin, Londonderry, Cork and Queenstown." The International Manufacturing Company likely did not regret using Bliss as an advertising gimmick across Europe, as it inked a contract with a London company for the purchase of 500 bicycles.[7]

Between 1896 and 1897, the International Manufacturing Company changed its name to the American Cycle Manufacturing Company. Apparently, the change came about to put more focus on their most successful model, "The America," which Baby Bliss promoted. As the bubble burst on the bicycle boom, the price of the America quickly fell from $100 to $35. Yet Baby Bliss continued to make the rounds in 1897, attending major bicycle shows and riding at least the first mile (in 8:30) of the Pullman race in July.[8] His cycling career came to an abrupt end with the failure of the American Cycle Manufacturing Company later that year.

Baby Bliss's success as an advertiser derived from the same sort of human spectacle that circus sideshows and fairs relied on to attract crowds. Many of these acts featured people with extreme physical deformities, who were exploited by circus managers and promoters. College-educated Baby Bliss actively marketed himself to these venues and was able to leverage his weight into a livelihood. As evidenced by the volume of contemporary newspaper and magazine references, putting Baby Bliss on a bicycle was certainly an effective marketing strategy for the International Manufacturing Company. Baby Bliss is only one of many fascinating characters from this era in Illinois bicycle history.

Charles Tripp and Eli Bowen

There were other Illinois cyclists with ties to the circus scene, where bicycle acts were becoming increasingly popular. Charles Tripp was born in Canada without any arms. He spent his childhood in Olney, Illinois, where he learned to handle many everyday tasks, such as writing and eating, using only his feet. He was also an expert woodcarver and furniture builder. In 1873, Tripp was hired by P. T. Barnum and was given the sideshow nickname "The Armless Wonder." From all accounts, this was a mutually beneficial relationship that saw Tripp work for Barnum and Bailey for more than thirty years. During his time with the circus, his most memorable act was riding a tandem bicycle with the "Legless Acrobat" Eli Bowen. Bowen steered, while Tripp pedaled. The two performers developed their tandem act into something of a comedy routine with Tripp yelling to Bowen, "Watch your step," and Bowen replying, "Keep your hands off me."[9] Later in his career, Tripp helped to form a sort of early union representing the interests of sideshow performers. "The Protective Order of Prodigies" provided healthcare, death benefits, and advocacy for its members. In a letter to his employer, James Bailey, Tripp and the Protective Order demanded that the circus cease using the term "freaks" to describe the sideshow performers and instead use the preferred term of "prodigies." The *New York Times,* reporting on this meeting, quoted Tripp: "We can't endure this. We are all ladies and gentlemen, and we act so. None of us are frights. We are greeted courteously when we go out into the street."[10] After his death in 1930, Tripp was buried in Olney, where some of his furniture remains on display at the Heritage House.

Bicycle Bank Robbers

Bicycle-related spectacles were common fodder for newspaper articles during this period. In one extreme case, a bicycle served as a getaway ride for a pair of would-be bank robbers. Brothers Karl and Joe Kloppenburg achieved notoriety for utilizing a bicycle as part of their bank robbery scheme. Karl Kloppenburg worked as a cashier at the bank in the small town of Buffalo, Illinois (about twenty miles east of Springfield). His brother Joe worked in a Springfield drugstore. On May 14, Karl was working alone at the bank when two men entered it, bound and gagged Karl, and took an estimated $7,000. Notably, the robbers sped away with the loot on bicycles. For a few days, the robbery made headlines, but there were no clear leads on the thieving wheelmen. After repeated questioning, Karl's account of the robbery had not stayed consistent. Eventually, he confessed to concocting the whole robbery scheme with his brother. As it turned out, he had accumulated substantial gambling debts and had been skimming money from the bank. The robbery was planned to cover his theft from the bank. The original idea had been for the robbery to occur a few days earlier, when there was more money in the bank vaults, but Joe was slow in riding over from Springfield and they missed their opportunity. On the day the robbery did take place, Joe bound and gagged his brother, as they had planned, and left town on his bicycle. In one regard, the choice of getaway vehicle was wise. Word of the robbery quickly spread, leading to patrols on the local roads. Joe was noticed, but it was assumed he was just a cyclist out for a leisurely ride, and he was let go without a search. A rainstorm later in the day of the robbery turned the roads into mud, causing Joe's bike to break down before he made it back to Springfield. After Karl's confession, it was learned that the total amount the brothers made off with was closer to $700. Karl was convicted and spent time in the state penitentiary.[11]

John D. Rockefeller and the University of Chicago

While celebrity culture, then as now, reached across the class spectrum, the bicycle boom was driven predominately by middle- and upper-class white men. For this demographic, selectivity and elitism were part of the allure of bicycling. It was thus notable when oil mogul John D. Rockefeller, one of the wealthiest people in the world during the Gilded Age, became an ardent cyclist and strong advocate of the health benefits of cycling. During the mid-1890s, Rockefeller was known to bring friends to his New York country estate on the Hudson River and give them riding lessons. Rockefeller would then give bikes to the friends that he converted to the sport. He later built his own quarter-mile cinder bicycle track at his estate, where he announced a goal of riding a mile in under three minutes (20 mph).

Part of Rockefeller's philanthropic legacy was funding the creation of the University of Chicago in 1889. In July of 1896, Rockefeller was on campus to visit with William Rainey Harper, the university's first president. Since bicycling was all the rage in Chicago, a forty-person-strong morning group ride was coordinated with Rockefeller, Harper, faculty members, and students. This group went from the campus to Jackson Park, where they toured the remnants of the World's Fair and stopped off at the Columbian Museum.[12] On the return trip, a friendly race broke out among the group. University of Chicago coach and American football legend Amos Alonzo Stagg came out ahead in the race. Reporting on this event, the *Chicago Daily Tribune* noted, "The man of many millions, and he to whom the university is due, not only can ride a bicycle, but he does ride. And, as in all his other doings, he is in earnest when he is on his bicycle. John D. Rockefeller is noted for his manner of giving. If he were in a different sphere of life he might be noted for his bicycle riding. At least, so said some of the men who tried to keep his pace yesterday."[13]

Cycling Around the World

Other Illinois bicycle characters gained their notoriety from riding great distances, including cycling around the globe. Most Americans in the nineteenth century rarely left their home states, let alone traveled to another country. Around-the-world travel, replete with tales from strange foreign lands, had long captured people's attention. In 1884, Thomas Stevens rode his ordinary-style bicycle from his home in San Francisco to New York. The ride took him 103 days and involved pushing his bike for one-third of the total distance. Once in New York, Stevens laid out an ambitious plan to circumnavigate the globe on his bicycle. Over the course of the next two years, Stevens made good on his promise to ride around the world. He traveled from Europe through the Middle East and finally arrived in Yokohama, Japan, on December 17, 1886. Over the course of his journey, Stevens estimated that he rode about 13,500 miles.[14]

Stevens' ride around the world inspired an entire generation of adventurers, many of whom had Illinois ties. Not long after Stevens' book was published, two students at St. Louis's Washington University declared their intentions to complete an around-the-world bicycle trip. William Sachtleben was from Alton, Illinois, and his good friend Thomas Allen was from Ferguson, Missouri.[15]

In 1890, Allen and Sachtleben were finishing up their studies at Washington University and dreaming of adventure. They claimed that "the idea of a trip around the world had been conceived by us as a practical finish to a theoretical education; and the bicycle feature was adopted merely as a means to that end."[16] This "practical finish" was not a particularly hurried endeavor, as it would end up taking the pair three years to complete. They started out on new cushion-tire safety bicycles provided by Chicago's Iroquois Cycle Company but would utterly destroy multiple bicycles over the course of their journeys. Wasting no time, the friends left for New York the day after graduation and then sailed for Liverpool on June 23, 1890. Following the same sponsorship model as Stevens, Allen and Sachtleben received financial support from London's *Penny Illustrated Paper* in return for regular dispatches on their progress. Allen and Sachtleben also embraced advances in photography that had recently led to portable (by 1890s standards) Kodak cameras. Over the course of their trip, they would take 2,500 photos that were used for news stories and then later for their book documenting part of their journey: *Across Asia on a Bicycle* (1894). Their story was resurrected and recounted in detail in the engaging book *The Lost Cyclist: The Epic Tale of an American Adventurer and His Mysterious Disappearance* by bicycle historian David Herlihy.[17]

Crossing through so many foreign countries required passports and letters of introduction from multiple foreign ministers. While in London, Allen and Sachtleben called upon Robert Todd Lincoln, who was serving as American Minister to Britain. Lincoln was skeptical of the entire plan and indicated that if he signed their papers, he would have some responsibility for the outcome. Allen and Sachtleben assured him that they were attempting this undertaking with the consent of their parents. They left Lincoln's office with an essential letter to the Chinese minister, although he told the pair, "I would much rather not have written it."[18]

They began their journey with a rather casual and circuitous tour of Europe, including Britain, France, Italy, and then Greece. Clearly, they were enjoying themselves on this portion of the trip and not out to set any speed records. They spent the winter in Athens before embarking on the most ambitious, and perilous, portion of their trip through the heart of Asia. In particular, Central Asia was mostly unknown to Europeans at the time. As Allen and Sachtleben would later write, "Never since the days of Marco Polo had a European traveler succeeded in crossing the Chinese empire from the west to Peking."[19]

The trans-Asia portion of their journey began in April of 1891 from Constantinople (modern-day Istanbul). Much of their route through Turkey followed rough caravan roads that were challenging to navigate on loaded bicycles.

Everywhere they went, they drew inquisitive crowds that had never seen a bicycle, let alone an American. Not content with a mere ride around the globe, Allen and Sachtleben paused for a mountaineering detour in Armenia. Although they were "entirely inexperienced at mountain-climbing," they succeeded in summiting the 16,854-foot-tall Mount Ararat, a feat accomplished by only a few mountaineers before them.

The most difficult part of their journey still lay ahead. Even though multiple officials warned them against it, in the spring of 1892, Allen and Sachtleben headed across western China. They eventually arrived in the Gobi Desert, where they battled unrideable sand roads, fleas, lice, and extreme heat. *Harper's Weekly* reported that the pair "had to fight for their vehicles often, and once or twice had to stand with their backs to the wall and point their six-holed Colorado logic at the mob."[20] Not long after reaching the far western edge of the Great Wall of China, one of their bicycle frames broke entirely in half. They made crude repairs with an iron bar and telegraph wire and plodded on. Finally, on November 3, 1892, the haggard pair made their way into Peking, marking the eastern terminus of their bicycle trip across Asia.

In December of 1892, Allen and Sachtleben took a steamship to San Francisco, where they would complete the last leg of their journey, crossing the United States. Outfitted with new bicycles, the final leg of their journey was something of a victory lap compared to the hardships they had been through. At every major city they passed through, local wheelmen rode with them and hosted gatherings in their honor. In June of 1893, nearly three full years after

THROUGH WESTERN CHINA IN LIGHT MARCHING ORDER.

Allen and Sachtleben, from their book *Across Asia on a Bicycle*, 1894.

their departure, they finally reached New York, completing their circumnavigation of the globe. On their train trip back home, they took a detour to take in the World's Columbian Exposition in Chicago, where they were feted by Chicago wheelmen.[21] Although the friends repeatedly claimed not to be interested in settings records, their book specifies that they covered 15,044 miles on their bicycles and that the trans-Asia portion of their trip was the longest continuous land journey ever made by bicycle.[22]

Annie Londonderry

The following June, another bicyclist embarked on an around-the-world trip, claiming the title of the first woman "globe-girdler." Annie Kopchovsky, age twenty-three, was a Latvian immigrant living in Boston. Perhaps most surprisingly, she was also the mother of three young children. At a time when strict Victorian social norms still constrained women, the idea of a young mother leaving her children to ride around the world alone was downright scandalous; it thus made for good press. Even more incredibly, Annie had only learned to ride a few days before taking on her around-the-world journey.[23]

Although Annie wasn't from Illinois, Chicago played a pivotal role in her story. In this era of the second industrial revolution, more than a few robber barons had enough surplus wealth to fund publicity stunts, including outrageous physical challenges. Annie's story ostensibly began with a $10,000 wager between two Boston businessmen that a woman wasn't capable of circumnavigating the globe on a bicycle in a span of fifteen months. (Notably, it took both Thomas Stevens and the Allen/Sachtleben duo three years to complete their respective rides around the globe.) To add another layer of difficulty to the bet, the woman cyclist attempting this feat would also need to earn $5,000 along the way. From the very beginning of her story, important details were fuzzy. Annie never specified who was putting up the $10,000. Newspapers noted that she left Boston on a Columbia bicycle. Pope Manufacturing was known to spend extravagantly on all sorts of advertising, but it's not clear that there was any deal in place with Annie.[24]

Even before leaving, Annie started to make good on the requirement that she earn $5,000 en route by securing sponsorship from the Londonderry Lithia Spring Water Company of Nashua, New Hampshire. The spring water, which supposedly contained substantial amounts of lithium bicarbonate, was touted as a treatment for indigestion, gout, rheumatism, dyspepsia, heart disease, insomnia, and other ailments. For $100, Annie put a placard advertising the company on her bicycle and even changed her last name to Londonderry for the duration of the trip. Significantly, this represented one of the first times in history that a woman athlete was paid for selling advertising space on her body.

The best male athletes at the time were often sponsored by bicycle-related companies, but Annie had secured a lucrative sponsorship from a company with only a nominal relationship to cycling. During her trip, she earned money in a variety of other ways, including obtaining more sponsorships, selling postcards with her likeness, selling souvenirs, and giving lectures about her trip.[25]

A crowd of five hundred cheered as Annie left Boston and her family on June 25, 1894. She headed west on her heavy, forty-pound Columbia women's drop frame bicycle, carrying only a change of clothes and a revolver. The beginning of her trip was not auspicious, as it took Annie three months to reach Chicago. Pushing further west would have her crossing the great plains and the Rockies during the winter. Annie said of the first part of her trip, "When I left Boston . . . I rode a 42-pound wheel and was attired in skirts. The result was that when I reached Chicago I was completely discouraged."[26]

Something in Chicago gave Annie a second wind. First, she spent time with some of Chicago's women cyclists, who convinced her to adopt modern bloomer-style pants, which were much more conducive to long-distance cycling. The second important change in Annie's fortunes was gaining a new sponsorship from Chicago's Sterling Cycle Works. Sterling made popular high-grade bikes and used the marketing slogan "Built like a Watch." According to an article in the *Buffalo Courier*, "The Sterling Cycle Company came forward

Annie Londonderry aboard her Chicago-made Sterling bicycle. (*Referee*, October 12, 1894.)

with an offer of a light 20-pound diamond frame machine in exchange for the ice wagon she was riding, and also made a lucrative advertising contract with her to carry the Sterling banner on her tour."[27] Annie's new Sterling Light Roadster was a men's bike with the traditional "double-diamond" style frame, which was both substantially lighter and stronger than her previous Columbia women's bicycle. Sterling wasted no time capitalizing on their investment. In October, multiple cycling magazines featured advertisements that pictured Annie and her new Sterling.[28] Annie also secured a tire sponsorship and advertising contract from Chicago's Morgan and Wright tire company.

With winter approaching, Annie made the difficult decision to ride back to New York and then complete her around-the-world trip by continuing to the east. On October 14, she left Chicago City Hall with a large escort of women cyclists. The *Inter Ocean* reported that as Annie rode south through Chicago, she was joined by "several hundreds" of additional local cyclists, some of whom rode with her all the way to Hammond, Indiana.[29] Annie continued to earn money through additional sponsorships, which dotted her riding outfit. In November, the *Buffalo Morning Express* reported, "The young woman is a sort of a riding advertising agency. She wears ribbons advertising various goods and will receive $400 for one firm's ad that graces her left breast. On her right bloomer leg she carries $100 worth of advertisements and she has just closed a contract to cover her left arm. She says her back is for rent yet and she hopes to get $300 for it."[30] Reassuringly, her return journey to the East Coast only took a month.

In contrast to the relatively unhurried Stevens and Allen-Sachtleben, who maximized the riding portion of their trip, Annie took a route that relied heavily on steamships, a choice that would be denounced by armchair cycling critics. A steamship across the Atlantic brought her to northern France in December, leaving her only eleven months to complete her journey. From France she went to North Africa, the Middle East, Sri Lanka, Singapore, and Asia. The terms of the wager required check-ins at various United States consulates along her route. Beyond that accountability, Annie had a great deal of leeway to utilize steamships, railroads, and carts when it suited her. She seemed to revel in telling increasingly implausible stories of her journey around the world. Among other tales, she claimed to have been shot in the Sino-Japanese War, to have hunted and killed a tiger, and to have killed Chinese robbers. While such stories of derring-do helped draw in paying audience members to her talks along the way, their veracity did not seem particularly important to Annie. The newspapers and cycling magazines began to take note of Annie's far-fetched tales regarding her ride. "The woman globe girdler has not thus far proved her right to the title by riding the necessary 25,000 miles. Miss Annie Londonderry is now completing an alleged bicycle ride around the world, but has made such astounding time through Europe and

Asia that her riding must have been done on steamers and railroads."[31] It is clear that whatever riding Annie did in the Middle East and Asia consisted mainly of (relatively) short stints when she disembarked from steamships. What is documented is that she sailed from Yokohama on March 9, 1895, and arrived in San Francisco on March 23, a mere two months after leaving France. Cycling purists were quick to point out that the same journey, done mostly overland, took Stevens and Allen and Sachtleben years to complete.

Unlike her predecessors, Annie had a rough go of it during her journey from San Francisco to Chicago. Not far from San Francisco, a runaway horse and wagon knocked Annie and a companion off their bicycles. Very likely exaggerating, she told a newspaper "she'd been knocked unconscious and carried to a hospital in Stockton where she coughed up blood for two days."[32] Then, in Iowa near the end of her journey, she ran into some pigs and broke her wrist.

Whether you begin counting from when she left Boston or Chicago, Annie completed her trip around the globe in under fifteen months, arriving back in Chicago on September 12, 1895. She claimed to have ridden 10,600 miles over the course of her trip.[33] She was welcomed back with "a rousing reception by the wheelmen of the city under the auspices of the Sterling Cycle Club." The Sterling Cycle Works company purchased her bicycle for $400 to use in future advertising. This sum helped put Annie over the $5,000 she was to earn over the course of her ride. Shortly after, she boarded a train to Boston, where she presumably collected her $10,000 prize. Here again, the details are scant; it is altogether possible that there was no wager, and Annie just concocted the tale to help legitimize her trip around the globe. Regardless, a woman completing a solo trip around the world was an amazing accomplishment. The *New York World* called Annie's ride "the most extraordinary journey ever undertaken by a woman."[34]

The McIlraths

Before the end of the bicycle boom of the 1890s, two more Chicagoans would complete an around-the-world bicycle trip. Hattie Boyer met H. Darwin McIlrath in 1893 at the Chicago World's Fair, and they were married later that year. Both had journalism experience that they leveraged into funding for their globe-girdling attempt. The *Inter Ocean* newspaper agreed to sponsor the local couple in exchange for regular dispatches to the paper and prominent advertising on their bicycles. Also eager for advertising opportunities was Chicago's Fowler Cycle Manufacturing Company. Fowler provided the couple with lightweight "truss frame" bicycles. The truss frame design featured a seat tube that split into a "Y" and attached to both sides of the bottom bracket. Fowler claimed this design created a stronger frame. The Palmer

Pneumatic Tire Company, also of Chicago, stepped up with a tire sponsorship. In a move that would impress modern-day "bikepackers," Darwin whittled the total weight of their equipment—which included a change of underwear, extra bicycle parts, tools, camera, medical supplies, and three revolvers—to under fifty pounds. The original plan had been for Darwin to attempt this journey solo, but Hattie, who was surely familiar with Annie Londonderry's trip, convinced him to take her along. The couple later wrote a book about their travels, *Around the World on Wheels for the Inter Ocean.* Throughout the book, Darwin took a patriarchal and condescending tone in regard to his wife, "a brave little girl," while conversely praising her vital assistance as "an expert wheelwoman" and "an unerring shot."[35]

The McIlraths began their journey from the offices of the *Inter Ocean* on April 10, 1895, departing a few months before Annie would complete her ride. Always interested in the next bicycling spectacle, Chicagoans came out in droves. The McIlraths left town with an escort of over a hundred cyclists from the Knickerbocker, Lakeview, and Illinois cycling clubs. Extra police were on hand to help control the crowd of several thousand spectators, but still the couple was forced to push their bikes for the first half-mile due to the press of the crowds.[36]

The McIlraths chose to travel west in their circumnavigation of the globe. After a series of mishaps, they reached San Francisco and departed for Yokohama, Japan, on October 12, 1895. Unlike Annie, the McIlraths chose the long and dangerous four-thousand-mile overland route across China. Along the

Illustration of the McIlraths on their around-the-world bicycle trip. (*Around the World on Wheels for the Inter Ocean*, 1898.)

way, they acquired an ornery monkey that they named Rodney. Rodney rode either on the bicycle handlebars or underneath the coat of one of the McIlraths. He had a penchant for thievery at village markets and developed a problematic taste for bicycle tires. At another point in their journey across China, Darwin claimed that he was forced to witness a woman's execution by "seng chee," death by thirty-six cuts. Ultimately, it would take the couple nine months to cross China.

From there, the McIlraths traveled across Burma (Myanmar) and then made good time on the smooth roads of the Grand Trunk Highway in India, often averaging 15 mph despite their heavily ladened single-speed bicycles. Near the ruins of Persepolis, Hattie suffered severe frostbite on her feet, requiring Darwin to amputate two of her toes. Then, in Constantinople, Rodney met an untimely death in a hotel room. Soon after, the McIlraths met the king of Romania in his palace, and by July 1898, they had reached Vienna. In Vienna, they called upon Mark Twain, who was on an extended stay in that city with his wife and daughters. They arrived in London as celebrities, leaving on October 15 and arriving in New York on the 27th.

Fighting through the early winter weather, they finally returned to Chicago on December 1, 1898, more than three and a half years after they left. They were escorted back into town by a platoon of police, hundreds of cyclists, and a brass band. Thousands of Chicagoans turned out to welcome the McIlraths home. "It has been a long and tiresome trip and we have passed through experiences enough for an ordinary lifetime," Darwin was quoted as saying. "Frequently in troublesome portions of the journey I wished we were safe back home again, but my wife was firm in her determination to accomplish the task we had outlined." The *Chicago Daily Tribune* commented, "The tour of the McIlraths has given the world a splendid sample of grit and pluck on the part of an American woman."[37]

Thomas Davis, Centurion

Thomas William Davis of Peoria, Illinois, never rode around the world, but he did have a solid claim of having ridden the most miles of anyone in the world. Given his meticulous documentation and the coverage of his exploits by contemporary cycling magazines, his claims are likely accurate. Thomas Davis was born in England in 1828 and later recalled seeing an early Draisine there before moving to Peoria in 1864. He found work as a machinist and fathered four children.[38]

His earliest bicycle experiences were on machines that he built himself. First, he used carriage wheels to create a primitive tricycle. Following that successful experiment, he bought a velocipede that he converted into a lever-driven machine. He next rode a velocipede with wooden wheels and iron rims.

In 1889, at age sixty, he bought a fifty-inch ordinary bicycle and began logging his daily rides.

There is ample documentation of Davis as one of the country's first high-mileage cyclists. In a newspaper article, he pointed out that his League of American Wheelmen member number was 1313, his L.A.W. lifetime membership number was 158, and his Century Road Club number was 7 (all were numbered sequentially). Davis rode his first century in 1891 as part of one of the first events organized by the Century Club of Chicago. Out of 160 starters, sixty-three-year-old Davis finished in thirty-ninth place. A decade later, he returned to Chicago at age seventy-three and again held his own with much younger riders. It was during that intervening decade that Davis began to receive attention for the astounding annual mileage totals that he reported.

From 1889 to 1893, Davis kept a detailed logbook with each of his rides. The Century Road Club of America began keeping records of riders' annual mileage and awarding certificates with mileage totals. Davis's yearly totals were as follows:

1895	6,509	miles
1896	10,615	
1897	12,465	
1898	10,518	
1899	12,016	
1900	11,024	
1901	7,501	
1902	6,821	
1903	6,219	
1904	8,242	
1905	6,802	
1906	5,503	
1907	5,405	
1908	5,133	
Total:	108,554	

During his peak years, Davis averaged over thirty miles per day, assuming he rode a full seven days a week year round. Given the severity of Illinois winters, there were surely many days where he was unable to ride, requiring him to ride much further on any given day in the warmer months. Remember, too, that these rides were mostly over the rough rural roads surrounding Peoria, making his feat all the more remarkable. His 1902 total of 8,030 miles was the highest recorded in the country by the Century Road Club. Sometime when he was in his early eighties, Thomas Davis surpassed 100,000 miles, an event significant enough that it was reported in the *Journal of the American Medical Association*. "In regard to my cycle ride of 100,000 miles," he told the *Peoria Star* newspaper, "I would like to say a word or two. There is no guess work about it as the record of the cyclometer has been entered each day. These daily runs have been from one to 108 miles. I have ridden two ordinaries and nine safeties and the total number of miles run by each wheel has been correctly kept."[39]

Many newspaper and magazine articles substantiated Davis's amazing feat, and it should also be noted that the Century Road Club had strict requirements for logging mileage. Among these requirements were supporting signatures from witnesses to the riding, as well as daily mileage logs to be submitted to the chairman of the Road Records Committee before the fifth of every month. Official centuries required a check-in every twenty-five miles. Not only did Davis keep records of his daily mileage, but he also noted how many miles he got out of each bike and each tire. *The Bicycling World* reported that he routinely got 5,000 miles out of a rear tire and once had a front tire last for 10,606 miles. His bicycle saddle held up for more than 70,000 miles of riding, and he got 25,202 miles out of one pair of pedals.

During the height of his career, Davis patronized local Peoria bicycle companies. He rode 34,441 on a Patee bicycle. An advertisement for Peoria Tires lists Davis completing 6,233 miles on their tires.[40] Apparently, he kept riding on these tires after the ad went to print because he crossed out that total in his scrapbook and amended it to 6,563 miles.

Thomas W. Davis died at age eighty-nine on April 9, 1917. By the time of his death, his lifetime total miles ridden was over 142,000. Riding around the world is certainly a remarkable accomplishment, but the majority of the miles

Illustration of Thomas W. Davis. His bicycle features curved crankarms made by Peoria's F. F. Ide Manufacturing Company. (*Chicago Chronicle*, March 22, 1896.)

covered during an around-the-world bicycle trip would be by boat or plane. Davis's lifetime total equals five and a half times around the circumference of the planet.

As a true bicycle character, Davis had one final thing to add to his cycling legacy. Before his death, he had a tombstone engraved by Merkle & Sons with the image of a bicycle and a blank space to enter his final lifetime mileage. Records show that his grave and marker should be in the Bluff Division, Lot 932 of Peoria's Springdale Cemetery. Unfortunately, Thomas W. Davis's unique tombstone is nowhere to be found today.[41]

Bicycle Culture: Bicycle Clubs

Given the widespread popularity of bicycle riding in the 1890s, a rich bicycle culture developed in Chicago and other areas of the state. Notable bicycle characters like Baby Bliss, Allen, Sachtleben, Annie Londonderry, and the McIlraths all contributed to American bicycle culture. Bicycle culture, in all its forms, was the true driving force behind the bicycle boom of the 1890s. Culture is a tricky term to pin down and can mean different things in different contexts. For our purposes, bicycle culture is defined as the shared social habits, beliefs, customs, behaviors, language, and dress of Illinois cyclists.

Bicycle clubs were perhaps the greatest drivers of bicycle culture, since their members shared specific clothing, customs, language, and rules. Clubs of all types were important to Victorian society. They served to clearly delineate select groups or classes of people from outsiders. In 1888, the Chicago Club (a social club, not a bicycle club) had exorbitant admission fees of $300 along with $160 in annual dues, while the Calumet Club charged a $100 admission fee and $80 for their annual dues.[42] The Chicago Club is one of only a few nineteenth-century Chicago clubs that still exists today. Its membership remains by invitation only, with initiation fees of $8,500 and annual dues of $4,350.[43]

Membership in a bicycle club was a means of indicating one's social standing. Clubs provided a sense of belonging for members and spread bicycle culture to new riders. In line with the excesses of the Gilded Age, elaborate bicycle clubhouses became the norm in Chicago, as more than fifty bicycle clubs tried to one-up each other. The largest clubhouses featured smoking rooms, libraries, billiard rooms, theaters, masseurs, training rooms, bicycle storage, and more. The clubs hosted balls, theater productions, smokers, and live music. When riding, members could be identified by uniforms specific to their club.

Illinois was an early player in bicycle club culture. Recall that the Chicago Bicycle Club (founded in 1879) and the Peoria Bicycle Club (founded in 1880) were some of the earliest such organizations in the country. A few other Illinois bicycle clubs formed during the high-wheel era, but they were relatively small in membership and social impact.

The Associated Cycling Clubs of Chicago was organized in 1890 to leverage the growing numbers and political clout of Chicago's cycling clubs. This association's stated objectives were

> to secure harmonious and concerted action in all matters of general interest to wheelmen in Chicago and vicinity, particularly in such matters as municipal legislation, improvements of streets and roads, the prevention of the theft of wheels, to spread a knowledge of the rights, duties and privileges of wheelmen, to promote road and track racing, to foster fraternal club intercourse and, as far as possible, to aid the state and national organizations of the League of American Wheelmen.[44]

As the bicycle boom progressed, both the number of clubs and club memberships exploded. An 1896 *Chicago Tribune* article listed fifty-four clubs that belonged to the Associated Cycling Clubs and estimated that there were an additional fifty clubs outside the organization. Total club membership numbers are difficult to verify but were certainly over ten thousand. Among the larger clubs was the Lake View Cycling Club, which reported 750 members in 1898. The Peoria Bicycle Club was the largest outside of Chicago, with membership peaking at around 450 members.[45]

Bicycle clubs in Chicago were formed around a variety of characteristics. Unsurprisingly, many clubs formed based on geographical proximity (Calumet,

Peoria Bicycle Club members and clubhouse, circa 1890. (Peoria Historical Society Collection / Bradley University Library. Not to be reproduced without consent of Society.)

Englewood, Lake Park, North Shore, South Side, West Side). Others gathered together based on the brand or model of bicycle they rode (Columbia, Thistle, Rambler, Sylph, Sterling), a few were women-only (Unique, Knickerbocker, Ravenswood, Woman's Cycling Club), while the names of others suggested an economic or sociological affinity (Bankers, Board of Trade, Polish, Chicago Public Library).[46]

A "Colored Cycling Club" for Black Chicago cyclists was formed in 1888, making it one of the first of its kind in the country. The club officially incorporated in 1892 and soon thereafter applied to be admitted to the Associated Cycling Clubs of Chicago. Despite lofty Chicago rhetoric about racial equality, the Colored Cycling Club's application was voted down by an eight to two margin. This setback did not seem to stymie interest in the club as it grew to 150 members in 1893.[47]

At times, bicycles seemed almost secondary to the slate of amenities and attractions offered by some clubs. The Illinois Cycling Club built an immense three-story stone clubhouse on Washington Boulevard at a cost of $50,000 (nearly $2 million in 2023). The club's astonishing list of amenities were available for a $10 initiation fee and dues of $2 per month:

1. Acquaintance of, and association with, a large body of wheelmen.
2. Use of six best quality billiard tables and two first-class pool tables, fully equipped. If you play, these alone will save you more than your annual dues each year.
3. Use of three excellent bowling alleys, regulation length.
4. A good gymnasium, fully equipped, and in which handball may be played. Professional instructor in winter twice each week.
5. Shower and tub baths on gymnasium floor. Towels are furnished.
6. Admission to all entertainments at clubhouse, including athletic exhibitions, dances, minstrel and private theatricals.
7. An opportunity to be a member of foot-ball, base-ball, bowling and indoor teams, also the glee and mandolin clubs.
8. Advantages of cafe and also barbershop.
9. Handsome parlor, choice library and reading rooms where magazines, illustrated papers, cycling journals, etc., are regularly furnished.
10. Club runs to points of interest and storage of wheels.
11. Annual century medal (If you ride for It.) Privilege of competing in popular club races, and especially in our famous annual handicap.
12. A monthly paper "Illinois Cycling: Club Life."

> In short about all you can get from any other club for twice the money. Initiation fee, $10. Dues, $2 per month.[48]

Illinois Cycling Club's clubhouse, services, and events apparently gave it an edge over competing clubs. By 1897, they had around 600 members and claimed to be the largest bicycling club in the world.[49]

Many clubs promoted the idea of the Renaissance man who stayed physically fit by riding a bicycle and maybe playing a little football while cultivating his mind by learning an instrument, attending the theater, and reading in the club library. Various Illinois bicycle clubs each fielded their own football, baseball, and bowling teams that played against each other. So it was that you might find the Peoria Bicycle Club traveling by train to Chicago to play football against the Lakeview Cycling club.

As a testament to the widespread popularity of bicycles during this period, there were hundreds of pieces of music written about bicycles. Music, of course, is an important element of any culture. The Chicago Cycling Club had their own march for two mandolins and a guitar written by J. H. Bell in 1894. Peoria bicycle manufacturer Patee Bicycles published their own two-step "Patee Bicycle March" in 1896. The Bicycle Museum of America's sheet music collection includes at least fifty different pieces of bicycle club sheet music.[50] From this era, the only piece of bicycle music that has had any staying power is Henry Dacre's 1892 "Daisy Bell (A Bicycle Built for Two)."

Shared styles of clothing and fashion contribute to building a culture. Within the bicycle club structure, there were specific rules regarding colors and styles that helped distinguish one club from another. Take, for example, the incredibly detailed dress code spelled out by Chicago's Hermes Cycling Club:

> The club's colors were blue and silver gray; its uniforms consisted of a light brown corduroy coat buttoned to the neck, breeches of the same material, a white flannel shirt with blue lacing, dark blue stockings and belt, low blue shoes with yellow leather trim, and a dark blue hat with a visor and two ornamental bands around the crown. The club's badge depicted Hermes, the winged messenger of the gods, engraved on a gold disc the size of a quarter.[51]

Every club would have had similar specifications for their uniforms. Bicyclists themselves were a distinct subculture of everyday Americans. In an era replete with private associations, they also desired further distinction from other clubs.

Two Chicago bicycle clubs from the 1890s, the Century Road Club of Chicago and the Saddle and Cycle Club, have survived in some form into the early twenty-first century. The Century Road Club of Chicago was first organized in 1891. The idea behind the club came from Chicagoan F. E. Spooner, who wanted to establish a club limited to those who had completed a known century ride. Here again a different sort of elitism was at play. Some clubs cultivated their membership through charging fees beyond the reach of average citizens. The Century Road Club, on the other hand, only wanted to recognize serious cyclists who had completed a grueling one-hundred-mile ride. A total of 140 riders started the club's first official century ride on September 12, 1891, and 112 finished the entire route. Since there were a limited number of paved roads in and around Chicago in the 1890s, bicyclists had to contend with rough brick streets, poorly maintained gravel roads, and muddy, rutted, country roads. Riders were awarded a military-style bar for each official century completed.

Shortly after the initial successes of the club in Chicago, efforts began to make the club national in scope. As part of this expansion, the name was changed to the Century Road Club of America. In two short years, membership increased to six hundred members, a number that grew to over three thousand by 1896. The century bar awards were crucial to the success of the Century Road Club of America. Worn as part of a cyclist's outfit, they became a cultural status symbol signifying oneself as a serious cyclist.[52] The 1898 *Century Road Club of America Manual* lists R. E. O'Connor as the State Champion for Illinois, with a total of eighty-two centuries. E. E. Fricke of Chicago had the highest total mileage with 13,780 miles and was followed by Mrs. George Bunker of Chicago with 11,000 miles.[53] The Century Road Club still hosts annual rides today.

The most elite Chicago bicycle club in the 1890s was the Saddle and Cycle Club. The club was founded in 1895 by Chicago cyclists Bert Erskine and Frank Remington, who "felt the necessity of having some place where they and their friends might be able to rest after a spin without being obliged to patronize the public gardens."[54] Clearly, the idea from the very beginning was to create a highly selective club that would cater to Chicago's upper-class cyclists and equestrian riders. Erskine and Remington counted among their friends the Chicago architect Jarvis Hunt, who volunteered his services for designing the new clubhouse. Hunt gained renown in the architectural world when he designed the Vermont Building for the World's Columbian Exposition. Over the course of a productive career, he also designed splendid clubhouses for the Chicago Golf Club and National Golf Links of America. His public projects included Union Stations for Joliet, Kansas City, and Dallas. The first Saddle and Cycle Club clubhouse was completed in Edgewater at Kenmore and Bryn Mawr. Invitations to join were sent to one hundred of Chicago's leading citizens. In 1898, when the city forced the Saddle and Cycle Club to move, a new location was secured on nearby Foster Avenue. This time Hunt designed a more elaborate clubhouse for the new five-acre lakefront site, which included "a veranda overlooking a pool, stables, boathouse, pier, and three-hole golf course."[55] The cost of the lakefront property alone was $60,000, or more than $2 million in 2024. Initiation fees to the club were a steep $100 per family. The Potter Palmer family, of State Street and Palmer House Hotel fame, were early members and wouldn't have batted an eye at the membership fees.[56] Not long after the new clubhouse was built, the *Chicago Daily Tribune* lauded the club as perhaps the most successful one in Chicago, writing that "now it bids fair to outrival all the town and many of the country clubs."[57]

During the 1890s, it would appear, many of the Saddle and Cycle Club members actually were—at least occasionally—bicyclists. Horseback riding is mentioned with far less frequency in early accounts of the club. Early club member Mary Ayer Chase later recounted the high society culture of the club: "I don't remember seeing any cocktails there.... The men could have whiskey and water, or a glass of beer, and the ladies, who were LADIES in those days, with one or two glaring exceptions, quenched their thirst after their dusty bicycle ride with a lemonade, root beer or 'horse's neck'."[58] The aptly named "horse's neck" was a tall ginger ale drink garnished with lemon.

After the bicycling fad began to wane around the turn of the century, the club kept its original name and continued to be a gathering place for Chicago's high society. The club persists to this day, as does the Hunt-designed clubhouse. It is a popular wedding venue for the well-to-do, but only if you are a member or sponsored by one.

It should be remembered that Chicago had nearly one hundred bicycle clubs at this time, and only a few of these built elaborate clubhouses and charged steep initiation fees. The majority had no clubhouses. They existed simply to bring various groups of bicyclists together and to advocate for bicycling. At times, all the bicycle clubs under the umbrella of the Associated Cycling Clubs banded together for philanthropic causes. One major philanthropic event orchestrated by Chicago's cycling clubs was a six-day-long "Grand Cycle Concert and Carnival." Proceeds from this charity event went to the Waif's Mission and Training School, which had recently built a new home on East Washington Street. The *Chicago Chronicle* reported that the event would include "parades, contests, trick and fancy riding, orchestral vocal and brass band music; comedy features . . . and competitions for a large number of prizes." There were also children's bicycle competitions and awards for the best-dressed women cyclists, as well as the expected exhibits of bicycles and bicycle accessories. The paper went on to note that "over 150 of the most prominent ladies in the city" were working on the event. The Grand Cycle Concert and Carnival was held in the Battery D and Second Regiment Armory, one of Chicago's largest venues at the time; the event drew thousands of attendees.[59] The tradition of bicyclists banding together to address social issues clearly has deep roots.

Illinois bicycle clubs, many based in Chicago and others scattered across the state, were instrumental in spreading bicycle culture. They were part of a club-based landscape that left a legacy that endured into the twentieth century and beyond. In *For Members Only: A History and Guide to Chicago's Oldest Private Clubs*, journalist Lisa Holton notes,

> It's tempting to write these exclusive clubs off the way that so many of these institutions wrote off large parts of Chicago's population at their inception. Yet virtually every major political, business, or civic milestone in Chicago—

both good and bad—can be traced back to the members and activities of many of these invitation-only city clubs. Sometimes they led, sometimes they followed, albeit reluctantly—but Chicago's private clubs were always a part of the changing landscape and culture of the city.[60]

The Bicycle Press

In the final years of the nineteenth century, more than one hundred bicycle periodicals nationwide helped spread bicycle culture.[61] Bicycle advertising in mainstream newspapers and magazines was big business. Advertising agent Charles Austin Bates claimed that American bicycle companies shelled out one billion dollars for advertising in the year 1897 alone. Supporting evidence for this claim was scant (and remains so), but more recent historical scholarship has shown that 10 percent of all newspaper and magazine advertising was related to bicycles in the mid-1890s.[62]

Chicago was home to many of the most widely-read cycling magazines of the day, namely *Bearings* (1890–1897), *Referee and Cycle Trade Journal* (1892–1897), *Cycle Age and Trade Review* (1897–1901), and *Cycling Life* (1893–1897). Illinois was not only the leading producer of bicycles, but American bicycle culture also emanated from the state. On a local level, during the mid-1890s, Chicago even had a weekly newspaper, *Dash: A Society and Club Paper*, that focused exclusively on Chicago cycling-related news. Yearly publications, such as the *Chicago Cyclers' Guide for 1896*, listed pertinent bicycling information about the city, including information about fifty-four bicycle clubs, the best streets and routes for cycling, precise distances between landmarks, and advice for what to do in case of an accident. In 1898, the Illinois Cycling Club was printing up to 1,200 copies a month of their newsletter, *Illinois Cycling Club Life*. The South Side Cycling Club published *The Scorcher: A Hot Paper for Hot Cyclists*, available for five cents per issue or fifty cents per year.[63]

A deep and pervasive bicycle culture thus helped drive the American bicycle boom of the 1890s. Well-built and affordable bicycles (most of them built in Illinois) were important, as was the development of comfortable bicycle clothing. Bicycle culture, however, helped to create community and engendered a sense of belonging. Illinois bicycle clubs were instrumental in bringing cyclists together in like-minded groups. Bicycle music compositions and bicycle publications further enhanced the mystique of the bicycle. Some of the unique Illinois characters mentioned here took bicycling to extremes and further added to bicycle culture. With so many Americans taking to the wheel, bicycle culture had an impact on American society well beyond the immediate cycling communities.

7

Scorchers and Cracks

Bicycle Racing

By the mid-1890s, a good portion of the country had gone mad over bicycles, and bicycle races might have been the pinnacle of the insanity. Top racers were major celebrities and earned salaries that would make most modern professional bicyclists jealous. The best long-distance bicycle racer of the day was Chicagoan Charlie Miller. Born in Germany, Miller moved to Chicago in 1892. He was promptly caught up in the bicycle craze and learned to ride on Chicago's streets and racetracks. His promise as a racer was first noted in 1892, when he set the American amateur five-mile record with a time of 10:07 (29.5 mph). Miller soon figured out that his real potential lay in riding longer distances. During an 1896 indoor race at the Chicago Coliseum, Miller broke the 50- and 100-mile records. In 1897, he participated in his first six-day race at Tattersall's in Chicago, where he went up against twenty-nine top riders. (Notable among these riders was George B. Iliff of Aurora, Illinois. In 1893, a horrific railroad accident resulted in the amputation of both of Iliff's feet, but he learned to ride using the crude prosthetics of the day.) Over the course of the event, Miller gradually pulled ahead of most of the competition, eventually finishing a close second to Fred Schinneer, another standout Chicago racer. Schinneer won with 1,788 miles, while Miller amassed 1,764. Many riders dropped out, but Iliff persisted in finishing all six-days, riding a total of 461 miles.[1]

In December of 1897, Miller entered the premier six-day race of the era at Madison Square Garden, where he would again face off against top international riders. The sixteen-man field once again included Schinneer. The *New York Times* reported that 10,000 spectators turned out for the opening day. The format was come-as-you-go, meaning the riders chose when to take breaks (if they did so at all) over the course of six days. The crowded field on the small

Six-day racer Charles Miller. (Charles Miller scrapbooks. Courtesy of Chicago History Museum.)

track caused one competitor to smash his head into a fence that encircled the track. He was hauled off to the hospital but returned three hours later to continue racing. Miller, though, was in his element and gradually built a lead over the rest of the field. The racing remained close, and 3,000 spectators stayed overnight in the Garden to ensure they didn't miss any critical changes in the race. At the end of six days, Miller was victorious, setting a new world record of 2,093 miles, which had required nearly 19,000 revolutions around the one-ninth-mile track. It was later determined that the track was about twenty-two feet short per lap; however, Miller's revised total of 2,013 miles still eclipsed the previous record.[2]

The race was equal parts grueling and lucrative for Miller. To maintain his stamina during the race, Miller consumed "3½ pounds of rice, 1 pound of barley, 1 pound of oatmeal, 4 ounces of beef extract, 60 pints of kumis [a fermented milk drink similar to kefir], 1 orange, 4 dozen apples, 3 pounds of grapes, 6 eggs, 3 quarts of barley broth, 4 quarts of coffee and 9 quarts of milk." Miller described the race as "the hardest ride I've ever been in. Perhaps the dust was the worst thing I had to fight against. The smoke and the dust go into my lungs and made them sore, as well as filling my eyes." His reported earnings of $3,550 ($127,000 in 2024) likely helped compensate for six days of suffering.

Miller earned $1,300 for first place, $1,000 for a theatrical engagement, $500 from a tire sponsorship, $250 from a bike sponsorship, $200 for breaking the world record, $200 from a saddle sponsorship, and $100 from a handlebar sponsorship. At the end of 1897, in addition to his six-day titles, Miller held all paced records between 5 and 30 miles and all unpaced records between 50 and 100 miles.[3] At the peak of his career, Miller was racing an "Eldredge" model bicycle built by the National Sewing Machine Company in Belvidere, Illinois.[4]

Miller's fame continued to grow. In June of 1898, he traveled to Paris, where he defeated all the best European riders in a seventy-two-hour race. At the end of the 1898 racing season, Miller returned to the Madison Square Garden six-day race as both the previous champion and the race favorite. This year, Miller had an additional incentive to win. He had been courting Miss Genevieve Hanson of Chicago for some time. The papers reported that Miss Hanson would finally accept a marriage proposal if Miller won the race. This arrangement was surely orchestrated with the race promoters and promptly leaked to the press. As it turned out, this was a wildly successful publicity stunt that helped pack the Garden to capacity. On the final day of racing, Miller had amassed a comfortable lead. He took a break from racing and retired to his tent. He soon reemerged in a brightly colored orange and white bathrobe while his fiancée appeared in a dove-colored broadcloth dress. They met on a stage in front of the roaring crowds and Miller tore off his robe to display a new cycling suit that featured one bright pink pant leg and one white, with the colors alternating on his shirt. An eagle was embroidered on the back of his shirt and around his waist was an American flag. Alderman Wentz of Brooklyn began the ceremony: "Ladies and gentleman, I have been asked to unite Charles W. Miller and Miss Genevieve Hanson, both of Chicago, in marriage. I wish your close attention while the ceremony is being performed, and have been requested by the management to be as expeditious as possible, as Mr. Miller is anxious to return to the track to finish his grand ride."[5] At the time of the ceremony, Miller had completed 1,970 miles. Following the exchange of vows and rings, the newlywed returned to the track, ultimately winning with a total of 2,007 miles.

Miller's win was momentous for a reason other than his mid-race wedding. It signaled the beginning of the end for twenty-four-hours-a-day, six-day races, which reformers for years had condemned as inhumane and immoral. These claims were not unfounded. After hundreds of miles of riding with little-or-no sleep, riders would frequently crash their bikes, begin hallucinating, and suffer bouts of vomiting. The spectacle of the suffering riders was, of course, part of what drew in spectators. After the 1897 Madison Square Garden six-day race, the president of the New York Board of Health stated, in highly racialized

Charles Miller wedding ceremony during a six-day race. (Charles Miller scrapbooks. Courtesy of Chicago History Museum.)

terms, "I think it is a beastly exhibition, and one that no white man should look upon. The suffering of the men as described in the last race was so inhuman that I feel that the authorities ought to step in and prevent it. You cannot call it an exhibition of this kind of sport, when men become crazy on the track." In 1897, Illinois Representative David E. Shanahan introduced House Bill 425 to prohibit "long continued and brutal bicycle riding." His bill required at least six hours of rest following every twelve hours of racing, effectively ending "go-as-you-please" six-day races. The 1897 races at Tattersall's had been particularly brutal, causing the *Chicago Tribune* to come out in favor of the Shanahan bill, writing, "The spectacle is still fresh in the public mind of that procession of weary wheelmen, emaciated, stupefied in some cases, with senses partly dulled by frequent potions, yet sticking to the pedals, although every revolution was attended by an anguish that made the humane spectators shudder in sympathy." The bill passed 100 to 7 in May of 1897. In 1898, New York Governor Theodore Roosevelt followed Illinois's lead with a similar ban on racing more than twelve hours a day.[6] The era of round-the-clock six-day races was coming to an end, with Miller as the reigning champion.

The last continuous six-day race in the United States was held in San Francisco in February of 1899. Miller, apparently fully recovered from his efforts a mere two weeks earlier in New York, rode the first eighty-one hours without a break. In a dazzling demonstration of strength and stamina, Miller showed off for a crowd of 12,000 spectators when he rode his 2,000th mile in 2:25 (24.8 mph). Miller secured another win with a record finish of 2,192 miles and made $1,700 for his efforts. From San Francisco, Miller traveled to Roubaix, France, where he bested all the European riders in a one-hundred-hour race.[7]

With the new bans on twenty-four-hour racing in place, race promoters quickly switched to a new format of two-man teams, each racing the maximum of twelve hours per day. For the 1899 team six-day race at the Garden, Miller partnered up with a former competitor, Frank Waller. The team format seemed to increase the competitiveness of the event. Miller and Waller triumphed with a combined total of 2,733 miles, but the next five teams all finished within one mile of the winners. The Miller–Waller performance was so exceptional that their record stood until 1908.[8]

Charlie Miller was certainly one of the country's most well-known racers during the bicycle boom, but his story is only a small part of Illinois bicycle racing during the Gilded Age. At the peak of the boom, the National Racing Board of the League of American Wheelmen argued that bicycle racing was the most popular form of entertainment in the United States. They shared a report on the 1897 season that showed eight million spectators had spent $3.6 million ($129 million in 2023) on tickets to 2,912 bicycle races. Over the same period, 9,000 riders had competed for $1.6 million in prizes.[9]

While bicycle ownership itself remained largely the prerogative of the middle and upper classes, racing fandom had few financial barriers to entry. In the United States, bicycling grew to be as popular as baseball. Children collected trading cards featuring their favorite cyclists. During this period, it was reported that an astounding 200,000 spectators came out to watch contestants in Chicago's Pullman Road Race. Despite growing moral concerns about racing for six days, marquee six-day races would pack 10,000 spectators into the country's largest indoor venues.

Racing Venues

Big-dollar racing required big-dollar venues. In the 1890s, Chicago had three outdoor tracks that were used primarily for bicycle racing. The Parkside Track, built in the late 1880s, was located at Seventy-Second Street near Jackson Park. It was a quarter-mile cinder track with cement corners and featured a grandstand and clubhouse. The Spring Lake Track was located at Eighty-First Street and also featured a grandstand and training quarters. It was a one-third-mile track constructed of "black cement." Chicago's premier bicycle racetrack was the half-mile Garfield Park Track. The track was built in 1896 by the West Park

Commissioners at the end of Jackson Boulevard.[10] For this task, they hired William Jenney, who would later become known for building Chicago's first skyscrapers. The construction of the track was noted as "the most graft-filled enterprise in the city," a remarkable achievement in 1890s Chicago.[11]

The Garfield Track was only surpassed by a few tracks in the country, one of which was the half-mile Lake View Track in Peoria. The Lake View Track, located on the banks of the Illinois River, was made of a dense clay that created an exceptional record-setting surface. As early as 1890, the national cycling press was lauding Peoria's track as "the best half-mile clay track in America, if not in the world." It had "a perfectly hard and smooth surface," as well as "spacious dressing rooms which are fitted up with every modern convenience, including cots and sulphur baths."[12] The Lake View Track would go on to host multiple L.A.W. national championship races, where more records would fall.

There was year-round demand for bicycle racing in the 1890s. During the long Illinois winters, temporary racetracks were set up in some of Chicago's premier indoor facilities. A typical indoor track was made from 60,000 board feet of spruce or pine and took workers many days to assemble and disassemble. Track design was rapidly evolving as well. By 1898, the best tracks were about twelve feet wide, with a steep eight feet of banking (forty-two degrees) on the end corners and four feet (nineteen degrees) of rise on the sides. Twenty-first-century velodromes are surprisingly similar, with forty-

Poster advertising the Peoria Bicycle Club's second annual race. (Virginius H. Chase Special Collections Center, Bradley University.)

three degrees of slope on the corners and fifteen degrees on the straightaways.[13] The steep banking helped to counter centrifugal forces and allowed racers to increase their speeds far beyond the flat tracks of the early high-wheel era.

One of the most popular venues for indoor racing was the Chicago Coliseum. Remarkably, the building itself began life in 1845 as a warehouse in Richmond, Virginia, where it was later used as a Confederate prison for Union soldiers. In 1889, Chicago confectioner Charles Gunther purchased the prison and had the entire structure shipped by rail to Chicago. Gunther added a medieval-castle-style facade and renamed the building the Libby Prison War Museum. In the early 1890s, Gunther converted the museum into a 15,000-seat auditorium, which he called the Coliseum. In addition to bicycle races, the Coliseum would host early auto shows, six national political conventions, and the first roller derby. It served as the home stadium for the Chicago Blackhawks from 1926 to 1929 and the Chicago Bulls in 1967, before finally being demolished in 1982.[14] The two other Chicago venues used for indoor racing during the 1890s were the Battery D Armory and Tattersall's. At the time, Tattersall's was the second-largest indoor exhibition building in the country.

Road Racing

Road racing also thrived in this decade, despite opposition from the L.A.W. As early as 1887, the L.A.W. passed resolutions against road racing.[15] Nominally, the L.A.W. claimed that road racing was ungentlemanly and that the disruptions caused by road races could bias the general public against bicycling. One must consider that the L.A.W. realized substantial revenue from its near-complete control of track cycling events but earned no fees from unsanctioned road races. Given the state of the country's roads at this time, most of the "road" races that took place more closely resembled a modern gravel race than the Tour de France. They invariably featured some sections of high-quality urban streets but also traversed the muddy and rutted rural roads that surrounded all big cities.

Arguably, the most famous road race in the country was Chicago's Pullman race. George Pullman made his fortune building luxurious Pullman Palace railcars. The town of Pullman on Chicago's South Side was one of America's first planned communities, and even in the 1890s, it featured miles of paved streets. The origins of the famous Pullman race hearken back to the high-wheel era. In the mid-1880s, the Chicago Bicycle Club began organizing a "hare and hound" chase on Thanksgiving Day. A hare and hound race is essentially a handicapped race, with the slowest riders starting first and the fastest riders starting last and attempting to catch them. The 1886 hare and hounds chase ran from the Chicago Cycling Club's headquarters near the Leland Hotel down to the Florence Hotel in Pullman, a distance of 14¾ miles. The following year, the Club hosted the first officially sanctioned Pullman race. In hopes of more favorable racing weather, the event was moved to spring on Decoration Day (now Memorial Day). In the first year, thirty-five starters competed for their share of a rich $700 prize purse.[16]

The Pullman race quickly grew in length, participants, spectators, and prizes. Most large road races in the 1890s utilized a handicap system. The L.A.W. had officially designated handicappers for each state that reviewed racers' previous finishes and assigned them a handicap time. "Scratch men" were the top racers and received no handicap. This format inevitably led to exciting and dangerous finishes, as the handicapped riders were overtaken near the finish. The 1890 Pullman race featured 129 contestants and was won by Charles Knisley, who started with a ten-minute handicap.[17]

In 1891, 10,000 spectators on Michigan Avenue witnessed 160 cyclists starting the Pullman. A local newspaper proclaimed, "In the number of contestants and value of prizes it was far ahead of any similar event in the world."[18] The *American Cyclist* provided its readers with a detailed description of the Pullman course.

> The first 8½ miles of the course is good, being over macadamized boulevards and park drives. Then come several miles of narrow, rutty road that was once macadamized, but which is now in miserable condition. Two miles of the course is merely a wagon track through the fields over 'the sand hill' and across 'the potato patch,' almost the whole of which, in 1889 when it rained, was covered on foot by every rider. The last part of the road is over the macadamized streets of Pullman, but is interrupted by frequent turns and many bad street car crossings.[19]

Even with these challenging conditions, N. H. Van Sicklen of Chicago managed to cover the fifteen-and-three-quarter-mile course in 50:17 (nearly 19 mph). Van Sicklen had opted for an additional four-minute time penalty over the scratch men in order to race on a bicycle with newly developed pneumatic tires. (In 1892, the penalties for pneumatic tires were removed as racers adopted the new technology en masse.)

The pervasive racism of the day also reared its ugly head prior to the 1892 event. During the 1880s and early 1890s, Black cyclists were few and far between. As the bicycle boom began to pick up speed, many people of color took an interest in cycling, and some set their sights on competing. Prior to the 1892 race, members of Chicago's Colored Cycling Club expressed interest in competing. The potential inclusion of Black cyclists in the race divided the cycling aristocracy. The *American Cyclist* ran a story that bluntly summed up the opposition: "If niggers ride, I don't!" Other cyclists argued for allowing the Black cyclists to compete, noting, "We can not in one breath talk of the race, and in the next talk about our equality and democracy and all that." George Barrett, a top racer, was more pragmatic, telling the *Inter Ocean* that he did not want to "trail in the tracks of an Ethiopian." These racist sentiments exposed a deep-seated fear that if Black men were allowed to compete with white men, then the myth of physical (and moral and mental) superiority of the white race could be shattered.[20] The status quo prevailed, and Black riders were again banned from that year's race. Nonetheless, in a few short years, a Black cyclist would indeed triumph over all cyclists.

Free to watch and spread out over many miles, bicycle road races could draw huge numbers of spectators. During an economically precarious decade, the lack of a cost barrier certainly helped to explain the appeal of attending a race. The 1892 Pullman Race drew massive crowds that lined the course well before the start of the race. According to one account,

> windows, balconies, doorsteps and housetops were crowded with sightseers, and hundreds of residents displayed the colors of the different cycling clubs represented in the race. . . . Boys were perched in trees and on telegraph poles and lamp-posts. Carriage, express wagons and other vehicles had been pressed into service, and afforded sitting or standing room for spectators, and finally the sidewalks were crowded with a surging mass of humanity.[21]

In 1894, the management of the race was turned over to the Associated Cycling Clubs of Chicago, which changed the name to the Chicago Road Race. The race continued to grow in popularity with both competitors and spectators. By 1895, the race had grown to nearly five hundred participants, and the new course from Wheeling to Garfield Park now covered twenty-four miles. The next-largest race in the country, New Jersey's Millburn-Irvington race, never drew more than two hundred competitors.[22] *The Wheel and Cycling Trade Review* estimated 100,000 spectators packed Lincoln Park for the 1894 race and that "probably three or four times that many lined the course its entire length." The *Detroit Free Press* reported that there were 200,000 spectators at the 1895 event and that 250 policemen were needed to control the finish area.[23] To put these numbers in proper perspective, the population of the entire city of Chicago was only about 1.5 million at the time.

In an 1897 interview, professional racer Arthur Gardiner summed up the reputation of the Chicago Road Race: "This is the biggest contest of its kind in the country, and the winner gains more prestige than the man who is first to cross the tape in one of the national championships."[24] The program for that year's race gives a sense of how the race had evolved and become more

CHICAGO BICYCLE ROAD RACE, MAY 30, 1894.
Scene along the course.

Chicago Road Race, 1894. (Author's collection.)

commercialized over time. A total of 498 entrants competed for the first-place prize of a Baumeister piano valued at $400. Overall, the program lists one hundred different prizes, including eighteen bicycles. Chicago's Fowler bicycle manufacturing company offered $300 to anyone who won the race using one of its bicycles. The recently formed Postum Cereal Company, from Battle Creek, Michigan, offered a special $25 prize to the winner if they had used Postum Cereal Flakes as part of their training diet. How a racer would prove this technicality was not specified.[25] As the bicycle boom ended rather abruptly, so too did the Chicago Road Race. The last event was held around 1900. It was resurrected in 1909, but this time the contestants were all in automobiles.

For the long-distance riders, Chicago also had two official century courses. The aforementioned Century Road Club of America maintained records for the Chicago centuries. Through 1897, the record for the Chicago-Libertyville-Waukegan century was 5:04 (19.7 mph). The record for the more difficult Elgin-Aurora century was set in 1894 by H. Kohl with a time of 5:57:30 (16.8 mph). When comparing these efforts to modern road century times, it should be noted that century rides of the 1890s were challenging affairs on poor roads using only fixed-gear bicycles. The Century Road Club of America stipulated "that no more than one-tenth of the entire distance ridden shall be on asphalt, wood-block, stone or brick pavement, or park boulevards."[26]

In addition to these Chicago century routes, the Century Road Club of America also recognized a few popular routes in other parts of the country. Far and away, the most impressive of these was the 1,017-mile route from Chicago to New York. In the mid-1890s, a Chicago postal delivery worker named Arthur E. Smith (better known by his nickname, Letter Carrier Smith) completed the full route at least five times. In 1894, he established a record of seven days, twenty hours, fifteen minutes over the Chicago–New York course. In the following years, he lost and regained the record several times. Competition had become fierce by 1896, so in his next record attempt, Smith rode from Chicago to Erie, Pennsylvania, without sleeping. Over the course of the entire ride, he slept about twenty hours total. This strategy proved effective, helping him establish a new record of five days, seventeen hours, fifteen minutes. In addition to his Chicago–New York record, Smith also set an American record for most miles ridden in twenty-four hours (295 miles) and for 500 miles (two days, eight hours, five minutes). Rounding out Illinois's dominance of ultralong-distance racing, Joseph F. Gunther, another Chicagoan, set the American record in 1894 for 1,000 miles with a time of four days, seventeen hours, forty-five minutes.[27]

Chicago was the national center of century riding. "There is something in Chicago air which makes century riders," *The Referee* noted in 1894, "for no city in America can boast of centurions who have as many bars to their credit as those of the Windy City." In just that year, Chicagoans C. M. Fairchild and J. F. Gunther rode sixty-one and sixty centuries, respectively. The following year, Gunther improved on his total, finishing eighty-five centuries; thirty-five of these were ridden over a period of thirty consecutive days. In 1896, Chicagoan E. N. Roth blew these totals out of the water when he rode 146 centuries. His total mileage for the year of 34,388 was contested and then rejected by the Century Road Club officials. Roth and friends blamed a rival tire manufacturer's sponsorship of a competitor for the discrepancy. The Chicago century riding competition was fierce in 1897, with John Gintowt riding ninety-two centuries and R. E. O'Connor close behind at eighty-two centuries and 18,225 miles. Recall that Chicago women cyclists' totals weren't far behind, with Mrs. George Bunker completing eighty-two centuries and 18,225 miles in 1897.[28]

Track Racing

The Gilded Age remains associated with profit-hungry monopolies asserting control over major industries like oil and railroads. The L.A.W. also got in the game, exerting control over nearly all the track racing that occurred during the

1890s. For a track race to be official, race promoters had to pay sanctioning fees to the L.A.W. and agree to adhere to the forty-three pages of rules published in the *League of American Wheelmen Racing Rules*. Racers who participated in unsanctioned events could be banned from all L.A.W. events.

These *Racing Rules* also took great pains to delineate three classes of racers: Class A amateurs, Class B amateurs, and professionals. Intense debates had swirled around defining and enforcing amateurism since the earliest days of ordinary racing. Many American and British cyclists adhered to an aristocratic ideal of the gentleman cyclist who raced only for love of sport, not money. In practice, this ideal worked fine for well-off men of a certain social class but inhibited the masses of working-class riders who took up cycling during the boom. In 1893, the L.A.W. hoped they had struck upon a solution with new rules for Class A and B amateurs. Class A amateurs were forbidden from teaching cycling for money; competing against professionals or Class B amateurs; accepting prizes over $50 in value; selling, pawning, or bartering prizes; and racing more than two hundred miles from home. Class B "amateurs" were allowed to be employed by bicycle-related companies, have traveling and training expenses paid, and accept prizes up to $150. However, they could not accept actual prize money or a portion of ticket sales. They, too, were banned from selling any of their prizes but were allowed to barter them for anything other than cash. They were prohibited from racing against professionals or pacing professionals in races. The gaping loopholes in the Class B category allowed many of these racers to earn an excellent living while maintaining their amateur status. Professionals had no restrictions placed on them regarding sponsorship and prize money. Toward the end of the century, these draconian regulations caused the L.A.W. track monopoly to crumble, as the new, more liberal National Cycling Association (nicknamed the "cash league") took over sanctioning most United States track events.[29]

While Chicago could lay claim to one of the premier road events in the country, Peoria, Illinois, was a top destination for increasingly popular short-distance track events. In the 1890s, a "Grand Circuit" of L.A.W.-sanctioned track races developed that saw top national and some international talent-breaking records and winning big prizes. The Grand Circuit started in the northeast in May and worked its way across the country over the spring and summer. According to *Spalding's Official Bicycle Guide,* "The three big meets of the year were Louisville, Springfield [Massachusetts], and Peoria," with many less prestigious stops in between.[30] Peoria won out over Chicago because of its extremely fast, banked half-mile clay track and strong local support from the 450-member strong Peoria Bicycle Club and multiple Peoria bicycle manufacturers and wholesalers. "Probably no city in the United States has occupied more prominence in the wheeling sphere than Peoria," a Chicago paper surprisingly conceded.[31]

Although the Peoria Bicycle Club had hosted earlier events, their first L.A.W.-sanctioned race on the Lake View Track occurred in 1889. However, it was the 1890 event that truly cemented Peoria as a top racing destination. Race organizers had amassed $3,500 in prizes, which included the deed to a lot in Chicago and a piano. An additional incentive was a solid gold Peoria Bicycle Club medal given to anyone who broke a world or American record. Local papers boasted that "the races here will truly be a battle of giants. The fastest men of the world are here and a combination of circumstances forces them to settle right here and now not only the question of who is the fastest man in America, but also the supremacy of England or America and the east and west." The *Wheel and Cycling Trade Review* concurred, writing, "The Peoria meet stands out prominently as the most successful meet of the year."[32]

By 1890, most racers had transitioned to safety-style bicycles with solid rubber tires. As a sign of rapidly evolving bicycle technology, English riders H. E. Laurie and E. J. Willis arrived in Peoria with bicycles equipped with new Dunlop pneumatic tires. This marked one of the first times pneumatic tires were used in the United States. They were banned from competing against hard-tire safeties in the main events, but Laurie did an exhibition race where he bested all hard-tire racers and established a new pneumatic tire mile record of 2:27.[33] Within a year or two, the superiority of pneumatic tires was established, and most racers had made the switch.

What the 7,000 spectators really came to see were the showdowns between the undefeated champion W. W. Windle and a young New Jersey amateur racer named A. A. Zimmerman. Coming into Peoria, Windle had amassed an amazing string of eighty straight victories. In a changing of the guard moment for American bicycle racing, Zimmerman defeated Windle in both the quarter-mile and ten-mile events. Newspapers across the country carried headlines about Windle's defeat. The meet was not all bad news for Windle, though, as he set a new one-mile world record for high-wheel bicycles in a time of 2:25. This time actually surpassed all safety records up to that point and still stands as the mile high-wheel record from this era. Separate record-breaking races were held before and after the main competitive events. In all, an astonishing sixteen world and American records were set in 1890 at Peoria. A detailed list of world and American bicycle records set in Illinois before 1900 can be found in the endnotes.[34]

Peoria hosted many successful L.A.W. events at the Lake View Track during the 1890s. The pinnacle may have been the event held in June 1896, during the height of the bicycle boom. Just before the beginning of the races, the *Chicago Tribune* reported, "Chicago is practically deserted today by all prominent cycling men and riders. More than 400 cyclists left last night to attend the state L.A.W. meet at Peoria and more will follow today." Those Chicago cyclists joined others from around the country for a 1,000-rider-strong parade before the main events. There were 1,200 entries for thirty races, and it was claimed that the $3,500 purse was the largest in the country. Although conditions didn't allow for the kind of record-breaking sprees of the 1891 and 1892 events, 10,000 spectators still turned out for the races. A full slate of evening festivities added to the allure of the Peoria races. There were moonlight steamboat trips on Lake Peoria that included a military band, dinner and dancing, and "smokers" at the Peoria Bicycle Club's clubhouse. The 1896 races concluded with a novel form of entertainment. Aeronauts from Chicago and Bloomington flew their balloons over the racetrack, at which point, two cyclists, mounted on their bicycles, parachuted from the balloons and tried to land on the track. At least one nearly ended up in the Illinois River.[35]

The Peoria Grand Circuit events were certainly the highlight of Illinois track racing, but there were probably over a hundred different bicycle track events annually in Illinois during the mid-1890s. Chicago's South Side Cycling Club hosted a very successful event called the Bicycle Derby on July 4, 1895. Held on the Washington Park racetrack, the Bicycle Derby garnered 248 entries for thirteen races. Newspapers reported that 25,000 spectators came out to watch racers compete for $1,500 in prizes. Chicago tire manufacturer Morgan and Wright offered a special prize of a two-pound slab of 24 karat gold valued at $750 ($28,000 in 2024) for the fastest unpaced amateur mile.[36] Track events were not limited to Illinois's largest cities, as most mid-sized towns and cities also had multipurpose racetracks. For example, the Rockford Cycling Club held an event in 1890 that attracted 500 cyclists and 10,000 spectators. The larger colleges and universities in Illinois also fielded bicycle teams that competed against each other on the track.[37]

Racers of the 1890s

Cyclists across all eras have developed their own bicycle slang. In the 1890s, racers were referred to—by fans, as well as each other—as "scorchers" and "cracks." "Scorchers" was often used in a derogatory manner by the general public to refer to cyclists who scorched around urban areas with little concern for pedestrians or carriages. An 1896 bicycling book put it this way: "Scorching is a form of bicycle intoxication, and the taste once acquired, the bicyclist craves its excitement, caring little for the other pleasures of the sport. The scorcher sees little, hears little, and is conscious of little but the exhilaration of the moment."[38] For racers, being labeled a scorcher was something of a badge of honor. The best racers, though, were called "cracks." A "crack" was a skilled racer who knew precisely when to jump out of the draft, sprinting furiously to the finish to clinch the win.

World-class racing venues, wealthy bicycle manufacturers seeking sponsored riders, and a recent history of racing success during the high-wheel era all positioned Illinois to grow many of the top racers of the 1890s.

Albert Schock

Only a small handful of high-wheel racers were able to make the transition to become successful safety racers. Chicagoan Albert Schock is one of the few who made the leap. (His high-wheel exploits, including multiple six-day world records, are outlined in chapter 1.) Schock began dabbling with safety racing in the 1890s, but he seemed to be keenly aware of the need for a career exit strategy after racing. In 1892, *Wheel and Cycling Trade Review* noted that Schock had undertaken the task of refurbishing the West Side Ball Park (home of the Chicago White Stockings), which had fallen into disrepair for use as a riding school and racing venue.[39] In this instance, Chicago cyclists picked up baseball's slack and funded the stadium's upkeep.[40]

For a time, some races held separate categories for ordinaries and safeties, while others were free-for-alls that wagered the best technology would eventually win out. One of the latter races was the December 1893 Madison Square Garden six-day. Schock was competing on a track where he already had found much high-wheel success. This time, he made the move to the safety bicycle. After only a day and a half of racing, the superiority of the safety was apparent to all, as they were, "on an average, over three miles an hour faster than the old-fashioned ordinaries used in previous contests."[41] Schock had chosen well. Leveraging his long racing background and the speed advantage of the safety bicycle, he succeeded in defeating the eighteen other contestants. Not only did he take the win, but he smashed the former six-day safety bicycle world record of 1,360 miles, ultimately riding 1,600 miles (his 1886 high-wheel record had been 1,405 miles). He took home $1,200 for his efforts.

Six-day races were big money events all around. The racers competed for rich prize purses, while race promoters raked in money from ticket sales. Bicycle manufacturers enticed top racers with generous salaries and bonuses for winning big events. Fortunes were also won and lost with the rampant betting that occurred at the races. Schock's personal scrapbook contains an account of when someone who had bet against him sabotaged his bicycle. During a race in Rochester, New York, Schock took a break to eat and get a rub-down from his trainer. While he was away from the race,

> the bearings on Schock's Rambler bicycle were filled with flour and sand. Schock quickly noticed the difference on the track, but having only one avail-

able wheel, he did not want to dismount and have repairs made. Wrenches and oilcans were brought to the track, and as quickly as possible, the stuff was emptied out and a deluge of oil poured in, and Schock was off again. That was all the repairs he would have to make to the wheel, and so he finished and won the race.[42]

During the bicycle boom, top professional racers had a wide variety of options for earning additional income beyond prize purses. The best of the best secured individual sponsorships for their frames, tires, saddles, and handlebars, but the list didn't stop there. The American public in the 1890s was also hit with an onslaught of advertising for a huge array of patent medicines with dubious health benefits. After his 1893 victory, Schock secured a sponsorship deal for Bovinine, which, according to its creators, was a "great blood-generating, life-maintaining, strength-developing, and flesh-producing product of lean, raw meat." Elsewhere, it was claimed that one bottle contained "the nourishment of ten pounds of meat."[43] Nothing was written about the taste of this product, but fortuitously, the manufacturers also claimed that in the case of very ill patients, it could be injected. Following Schock's 1893 Madison Square Garden win, a Bovinine advertisement depicted Schock on his bicycle and included the following testimonial: "I ascribe my ability to accomplish that result without breaking down under the tremendous strain, solely to the preservation of my strength and energy by constant use of Bovinine throughout the entire week."[44] If Schock truly relied on Bovinine during the race, his record is all the more impressive for his gastrointestinal fortitude.

In 1896, at age thirty-nine, Schock threw his hat in the ring for one more chance at Madison Square Garden glory. This time around, he wouldn't have the advantage of riding a safety for the whole event, as some of his competitors stuck to ordinaries. Schock may not have been at his fittest, but he still managed to surpass his previous record by riding 1,766 miles. Unfortunately, that total was only good for fifth place. Irishman Teddy Edward Hale established a new record of 1,910 miles, but he wasn't destined to hold it for long. In a changing of the Chicago racing guard, Charlie Miller won the next year's Garden six-day with a new record of 2,013 miles. There was hardly a time during the 1890s when an Illinois racer was not the six-day world record holder.

Apparently recognizing that he couldn't earn a living racing his bicycle forever, Schock had worked on earning his high school diploma by taking night classes between races in 1896. That year, he also opened another riding school in New York City, the Bicycle Riding Academy. His next big career move was in 1897 when he opened the Champion Cycle Co. near Wall Street. He further leveraged his bicycling fame when he opened a restaurant called the Champion's Rest. His later career saw him hired by Columbia bicycles to train the next generation of racers. Schock died in 1921 and is buried in the Forest Home Cemetery, Cook County, Illinois.[45]

Major Taylor

One of the most important figures in American bicycle history—and, arguably, in all of American sports history—is Marshall "Major" Taylor. In addition to being a world-champion cyclist, Taylor is notable for being a Black bicycle racer in an environment that was frequently hostile to non-whites. Major Taylor was from Indiana and later moved to Worcester, Massachusetts, but many of the major events in his racing career occurred in Illinois. This chapter can only provide a brief summary of Taylor's storied career, while paying closer attention to his connections to Illinois.

Marshall Taylor was born in Indianapolis on November 26, 1878, and he learned to ride alongside the son of the white family for whom his father worked. As a child, Taylor excelled at trick riding rather than racing. His trick-riding skills caught the attention of an Indianapolis bicycle shop owner, who hired him to work at the shop and do trick-riding demonstrations. He was given a nice uniform to perform in, which earned him the nickname "Major" Taylor. In 1890, at the prompting of his employer, he entered a local ten-mile race and was given a large handicap due to his young age and lack of racing experience. The eleven-year-old Taylor shocked everyone by taking the overall win.

That same fall, he headed to Peoria to participate in his first L.A.W. track competition. This time, he was racing against other experienced boys without any handicap. The Peoria races featured a one-mile youth high-wheel race, in which Taylor finished third in a close race. In its coverage of the Peoria races, the *Wheel and Cycling Trade Review* commented, "The Major was a bright little 'nig,' with all the snap and style of a veteran. He cried a little over his defeat, which he attributed to lack of condition."[46] In these comments, we again see the unconcealed racism of the day and get a glimpse of the social and political barriers Major Taylor would have to overcome on his path to becoming a world champion. Notably, this race actually occurred two years earlier than Taylor recalled in his own autobiography. Writing thirty-eight years later, Taylor recalled, "Peoria was the Mecca of bicycle racing in those days. On its historical track all of the fastest riders in the world struggled for fame and glory."[47]

When white racers began to learn they couldn't beat Taylor outright, they often turned to cheating to try and secure a victory. Taylor also had to contend with racism from within the L.A.W. In 1892, Colonel Watts, a delegate from Kentucky, introduced a motion to ban "the Negro" from membership, but the

Major Taylor, 1898. (New York Public Library, Wallach Division Picture Collection.)

motion failed. *Bicycling World* represented the views of many cyclists north of the Mason-Dixon line when they wrote, "When a negro sends in his name and two dollars, and asks admission to the League, I claim that by that act he exhibits symptoms of patriotism and intelligence which puts the burden of proof on the pale faced dyspeptic who would keep him out. . . . A black gentleman is infinitely superior to a white hoodlum."[48] A similar ban failed in 1893, but with some ethically questionable behind-the-scenes lobbying, Colonel Watts was successful in limiting L.A.W. membership to whites only in 1894. Many L.A.W. members from northern and eastern states were outraged and protested the amendment. In response to the amendment, League membership dropped precipitously. A sixteen-year-old Taylor spoke his mind in a rather eloquent letter to the *Bearings* cycling magazine: "We want nothing from south, north, east, or west but that which we are entitled to, and that is certainly not membership to any white man's league of wheelmen."[49]

For his part, Taylor joined the all-Black See-Saw Cycling Club and continued to win races. In 1895, by virtue of winning a local race, Taylor had earned the right to compete in a ten-mile Chicago road race hosted by the Douglass Cycling Club, which similarly was all Black. The race attracted top Black cyclists from all over the country, making it the de facto Black American

Championship. Through a combination of impeccable tactical racing skills and expert coaching from former racer Birdie Munger, Taylor defeated the stronger and far more experienced Henry Stewart of St. Louis.

From his earliest days as a racer, it was clear that Major Taylor's strength was as a crack short-distance sprinter. He became known—and feared—for his powerful "jump," that moment when a racer applies maximum force to the pedals to either sprint to the finish or drop a competitor mid-race. Throughout the 1897 and 1898 racing seasons, Taylor established himself as one of the top American sprint cyclists. Along the way, he continued to encounter racism in the cycling ranks, particularly as he began to defeat almost every white rider he faced. In 1898, he lowered the world record for a flying start (meaning he was already up to speed at the beginning of the race), paced mile with a time of 1:31 (39.6 mph). For this paced record, he followed behind other riders on tandems and sometimes triplet and quadruplet bicycles. To further lower the record, he realized he needed to be paced by newly developed motorcycles, which in those early days were mostly steam- or gasoline-powered engines mounted to a bicycle frame. Word had spread that Eddie McDuffie had lowered Taylor's paced mile record to 1:28 by drafting a motorcycle. The Stearns bicycle company built a steam-powered motorcycle specifically for Taylor to break records behind.

For his next record attempt, Taylor traveled to Chicago to take advantage of the fast tracks and enthusiastic bicycle spectators. The Stearns machine was finicky, and at first could not maintain the necessary speed for lowering the record. On August 3, 1899, Taylor made multiple attempts at the paced mile record on the cement Garfield Park Track. As the evening wore on, everything seemed to click on one particular trial. Taylor flew across the line in 1:22 (43.9 mph). The *Chicago Times-Herald* carried the story on their front page: "In the presence of a yelling, frenzied crowd, Major Taylor, the swift colored professional cyclist, rode a mile behind his steam motor in the phenomenal time of 1:22$\frac{2}{5}$, thereby beating McDuffie's time by 5$\frac{3}{5}$ seconds."[50] Previously, McDuffie and Taylor were shaving fractions of a second off each other's records. Taylor's new mark absolutely obliterated the previous record.

Taylor had a mere nine days after this record to recover and prepare for the World Championships, held in Montreal. This was his first chance to race the best in the world, and he was in peak condition. In his autobiography, he recalled, "All through my racing career my one outstanding motive was to win the world's championship—and the same desire inspires every rider to his greatest efforts at all times."[51] The bicycle craze had also hit hard in Canada. The Queen's Park track was filled to capacity with 18,000 lucky spectators, and 5,000 more were turned away. Most observers claimed that Taylor had won the half-mile race, but the judges awarded the win to another rider. Taylor was not about to let the same thing happen in the mile. On August 12, he sprinted away from the rest of the field to claim the title of world champion. This was only the second world champion title in any sport for a Black athlete (George Dixon, the bantamweight boxer, won the first title in 1888). Unfortunately, this was the only world championship that Taylor would contest in peak form. Future events were held in Europe on Sundays; Taylor, a devout Baptist, refused to race on the Sabbath.

After Montreal, Taylor returned to racing in the L.A.W. professional circuit. Going into the last races of the series in Peoria, Taylor was well-positioned to win the overall American national sprint championship title. His top rival was a former teammate, Tom Butler. Taylor continued his domination of sprint racing in 1899, winning the mile, two-mile, and five-mile races in Peoria. The five-mile race was particularly memorable for Taylor, as he sprinted away from the field and crossed the finish line in first only to realize he had miscalculated the number of laps. The field blew by him, and he had to regroup and chase them down. In a testament to his superior abilities, he overtook the field and still finished first. In his autobiography he recalled, "Even now I consider that five-mile race the climax of the most gruelling day's work I ever put in on the bicycle track during my whole racing career covering almost seventeen years on both sides of the Atlantic."[52] Taylor had added the American sprint national championship title to his world championship title. Unfortunately, an unscrupulous track manager took off with all the gate proceeds that were used to pay the racers, so Taylor had the title but earned nothing for his efforts. The theft of the gate proceeds, coupled with the decline of interest in bicycling, spelled the end of an era for racing in Peoria. Taylor lamented that this would be "the last race held on that famous track in good old Peoria. It was known throughout the cycling world as one of the finest that ever staged a bicycle race."[53]

Although it was now November, Taylor had one more accolade to add to his stellar 1899 season. Shortly after his win in Peoria, Taylor received word that Eddie McDuffie was in Chicago on the Garfield Park Track, working to break his paced one-mile world record. Taylor promptly boarded a train to Chicago to better McDuffie's efforts on the same track. This late-season showdown was a goldmine for the local press. One Chicago paper pontificated, "Chicago will be the scene of the greatest battle that has ever been fought for the mile, the blue ribbon record of the cycling path."[54] Over the course of eight days in mid-November, both McDuffie and Taylor contended with foul weather and finicky pacing motorcycles as they sought to lower the record. McDuffie had affixed a windshield to the rear of his pacing machine to improve the draft, and Taylor immediately followed suit with his own windshield. To maintain the speed necessary for a world record, Taylor had his bike fitted with a massive

121-inch gear (that is, one revolution of his cranks yielded 121 inches of forward travel). After many failed attempts, Taylor gave the record one more go late on November 15. Finally, the steam-driven pace motorcycle was functioning properly, and Taylor tucked in tight behind it. He crossed the mile marker in 1:19, averaging 45.6 mph to shave two seconds off McDuffie's short-lived record. McDuffie, knowing he was outclassed, left Chicago and announced his retirement from cycling. A local paper summarized Taylor's 1899 season: "Major Taylor is Champion. Colored Youth won L.A.W. and International Championships and set many new records, capturing 22 firsts in 29 races.... If he never had it before Major Taylor this year has gained the title of Champion Cyclist of the World. It would be presumptuous for anyone to question his standing."[55]

Taylor repeated his national American sprint champion title in 1900 and began looking for rivals in Europe. Over the next few years of his career, he would spend more and more time racing in Europe, where he faced less racism from spectators and his fellow competitors. He set more world records and made a reported $35,000 ($1.2 million in 2024) for the 1902 season.

E. E. Anderson

Just north of St. Louis, on the Illinois side of the Mississippi River, lies Granite City. That city's role in Illinois bicycle history has been nearly lost to history. In 1896, E. E. Anderson, an accomplished sprint cyclist, announced plans to do something no human had done: ride a mile in under a minute. In the days before motorcycles and automobiles, trains were the fastest things on the planet. Unladen engines could exceed the requisite 60 mph. Anderson's plan involved laying two miles of pine boards on the flat Bluff Line railroad tracks near Granite City. A four-inch white line was painted down the middle of the narrow boards to help Anderson stay centered. To reduce wind resistance, a wooden shroud was built around the rear of Engine No. 7, one of the fastest in the West. Test runs had taught Anderson that he would need to deal with the hot cinders and smoke that spewed from the train. He assembled a breathing apparatus to filter the smoke, and he also wore goggles and long black gloves as protection against flying cinders.

On August 9, 1896, Anderson was ready to make his record-breaking attempt. His nineteen-pound Stearns bicycle was geared to ninety-two inches. Anderson's bride of just one week rode on the platform at the rear of the train. The record-breaking attempt began after both the train and Anderson had reached about 60 mph. Approximately 1,000 spectators lined the tracks near his finishing point. Anderson held the necessary pace for most of the mile but dropped back partially out of the draft at one point and had to fight his way

E. E. Anderson attempts to ride one mile in under a minute. (*St. Louis Post-Dispatch*, July 18, 1896.)

back to the train. He crossed the mile mark in 1:03, a little faster than 57 mph but just short of his goal. The August heat, coupled with the heat from the steam engine, had caused the glue that held Anderson's tires to his rims to melt. The *St. Louis Post-Dispatch* reported, "He 'burned' his breathing apparatus by inhaling smoke and vapor of the engine. His tongue was skinned by the hot sulphurous atmosphere and his lungs were 'scotched.'"[56]

Anderson announced plans to take a break and make another attempt at the record at a later date. For unknown reasons, his follow-up attempt never happened. In 1899, New Yorker Charles M. Murphy mimicked Anderson's setup, laying out two miles of boards on the Long Island Railroad track from Babylon to Farmingdale. He, too, had a large shroud built around the rear of the engine. After a couple failed attempts, Murphy finally crossed the mile mark in fifty-seven seconds and was known thereafter as "mile-a-minute-Murphy." The *New York Times* lauded his efforts, reporting that Murphy "drove a bicycle a mile faster than any human being ever drove any kind of machine and proved that human muscle can, for a short distance at least, excel the best power of steam and steel and iron."[57]

John A. Nelson

One of the best motor-paced riders in the world at this time was John A. Nelson from Chicago. Toward the end of the century, motor-paced bicycle races were becoming all the rage. As motorcycle designs improved, they could be utilized to set ever-faster records by the daring cyclists who would follow in their draft. Spectators were enticed by both the danger and the chance to see new records set. The highlight of Nelson's career may have been the 1899 World Championships held in Montreal. Nelson won the 100-kilometer motor-paced race in a time of 2:04:13 (30 mph). Second place was a distant four miles behind. The following year, Nelson left the amateur ranks to chase big winnings among the professional field. In July of 1900, he set the world record for twenty-five motor-paced miles with a time of 39:46 (nearly 38 mph). In his first year as a professional, Nelson was the top earner among the 161 American professional bicycle racers with a total of $11,747 ($415,000 in 2023). In 1901, he defeated Major Taylor in multiple motor-paced races.[58]

The final act of Nelson's tragically short career came at Madison Square Garden, which remained one of the largest indoor venues for bicycle racing. On September 4, 1901, Nelson entered a fifteen-mile motor-paced race in the Garden against Welsh champion Jimmy Michael. Many early motorcycle designs would be more accurately described as motor-assisted bicycles, as the pacers still pedaled the machines. In this case, both racers were following behind their respective tandem motor-bicycle pacers. The rear tire of Nelson's pacing machine blew out, causing him to crash. His competitor's pacers then crashed into Nelson. The *Evening Express* reported, "After Michael's machine went down the motor continued to send the pedals around at lightning speed and Nelson's left leg, which was pinned down under the wreck, was literally ground to a pulp by the flying pedals. His leg was cut from the knee to the ankle, but he never lost consciousness and gamely directed the men who ran to his aid."[59] Surgeons tried to save his leg, but gangrene set in, forcing an amputation. Shortly after, blood poisoning set in, ending the young racer's life. Politicians had lobbied hard and then successfully passed legislation to stop twenty-four-hours-a-day, six-day races in Madison Square Garden to protect riders. Ironically, it was a short, fast, fifteen-mile motor-paced race where a cyclist was actually killed.

Racing Slows Down

The end of the bicycle racing boom in Illinois, as with the bicycle boom in general, was swift and severe. Overproduction was partially to blame, but the bicycle had also lost some of its allure as a status symbol. In November of 1899, the *Chicago Daily Tribune* ran an article with a headline that would have been unimaginable only a year or two earlier: "Wheelmen say Cycling Is Dead as Organized Sport." The article specifically points to the decline in club membership and club events, as well as the fact that the bicycle was no longer novel. Manufacturers had drastically reduced their investments in racers and race prize purses. Gone were the days when the Pullman and Decoration Day races were "attended by crowds so large that the racers were obliged to finish in the midst of a throng that had encroached upon the track and only left passage of a few feet."[60]

Despite its precipitous decline, the Illinois bicycle racing boom left a widespread and long-lasting impact. Nineteenth-century cyclists were at the forefront of establishing what it meant to be a professional athlete. They became savvy negotiators of contracts with sponsors and event promoters. They figured out how to leverage the media to enhance their careers. Along the way, they established bicycle racing as a major American spectator sport. Chapter 5 has already noted the profound progress women racers pushed forward in the area of women's rights. On the men's side, it is not an overstatement to say that Major Taylor altered the course of history in the United States. Systemic racism persists to this day, but through his racing performances, Taylor clearly demonstrated that the purported physical superiority of the white race—and all of white supremacy—was nothing but a racist myth. He also opened the door for the next generations of great African American athletes, such as Jack Johnson, Jesse Owens, and Jackie Robinson.

8

Demon Motors

Motorcycles, Automobiles, and the End of the Boom (1895–1920)

"The Race of the Century" occurred in Chicago on Thanksgiving Day 1895. A small assortment of early automobile prototypes converged on Chicago from around the country to participate in the first automobile race in American history. The bicycle boom was in full swing, but this particular race did not directly involve any cyclists. Even so, bicycles provided the historical foundation for this event.

Indeed, an automobile race in 1895 would have been impossible if not for the wide array of technological advances already made by bicycle manufacturers. Early automobile prototypes relied heavily on components and manufacturing techniques pioneered and perfected by bicycle manufacturers, including pneumatic tires, ball bearings, roller bearings, wire-spoked wheels, differential axles, bevel gears, chain drives, and stamped fittings, as well as weldless, seamless steel tubing. The first mass-produced automobile, Carl Benz's 1886 German Motowagen, was clearly just a two-seat "sociable" tricycle with an engine mounted on it. Sociable tricycles were developed in the high-wheel era to allow a man and woman to sit side by side. Beyond the technological advancements, bicyclists' relentless advocacy for good roads literally paved the way for American automobiles. The story of the automobile thus begins with the history of the bicycle.[1]

That connection was evident from the very moment Herman H. Kohlsaat, editor and publisher of the *Chicago Times-Herald*, announced a horseless carriage (an early name for automobiles) race with a prize purse of $5,000. The Race of the Century would cover ninety-two miles over much of the already established Chicago–Waukegan–Libertyville bicycle century route. The vehicles had to meet a number of requirements, including having at least three wheels, being motor-driven (steam, electric, and combustion were all allowed), and carrying at least two people. Eighty-three entries from aspir-

Frank Duryea and umpire Arthur White at Chicago's "Race of the Century," 1895. (From the Collections of The Henry Ford.)

ing inventors were received, but the great majority were not ready by the November 2 deadline, so a small exhibition event had to be held instead.

The rescheduled Race of the Century finally happened on Thanksgiving Day 1895. Conditions for the race would push the new vehicles to their limits since up to twelve inches of snow had fallen onto the already muddy and rutted streets. Due to the snow and freezing temperatures, the course was shortened to Evanston and back, a distance of about fifty-four miles. Even with the time extension, only six vehicles were ready to start the race. These included a Benz and a Duryea vehicle, two electric vehicles, and two additional gasoline-powered vehicles. The Duryea (driven by Frank Duryea) was the only American-made, gasoline-powered vehicle in the race.

Beginning at 8:55 a.m., the vehicles were sent off from the Midway Plaisance in Jackson Park time-trial style, with a few minutes of spacing between each car. The electric cars were particularly hampered by the deep snow. The snow foiled plans to swap out fully charged batteries en route. Still, one of the electric cars completed an admirable fifteen miles before running out of power. A few hours into the race, only the Benz, driven by Oscar B. Mueller of Decatur, Illinois, and the Duryea were still contending for the finish. Adaptability and engineering abilities turned out to be key for this event. At a bridge crossing, the Duryea's steering arm snapped, but Frank forged a repair at a nearby blacksmith's shop, only losing an hour in the process. An ignition problem later required another stop and repair at a tinsmith's shop. Frank

Duryea, however, was not the only one plagued with mechanical problems. Mueller's Benz had clutch issues, and the Benz driven by O'Connor broke its steering linkage near Evanston and had to drop out of the race. Two reporters from Chicago's *Bearings* cycling magazine, who were following the race on a tandem bicycle, had to continually brake, or come to a full stop, to avoid overtaking the Benz automobile. The tandem riders stopped for lunch, then hopped back on their bicycle and caught up to the automobiles in short order.[2] A wrong turn added two miles to Frank Duryea's route, but he still managed to win the first American automobile race when he crossed the Douglas Park (now Douglass Park) finish line ten hours after starting. The only other contestant to finish the course was the Mueller-driven Benz, which finished two hours behind the Duryea.[3]

Although hardly anyone witnessed the finish of the first automobile race, its significance to American history cannot be overstated. The terrible conditions the racers faced were actually the strongest factor to influence the eventual widespread adoption of the automobile. As slow as the finishing times were, one spectator who attempted to follow the race in a carriage pulled by horses remarked, "No horse on earth could have made those fifty-four miles."[4] As automotive historian L. Scott Bailey has written, "If any single event can be pointed to as the catalyst leading to the ultimate acceptance of the automobile in America and the impetus for the beginning of a new industry, that event would have to be the *Chicago Times-Herald* contest."[5]

Still, Illinois cyclists in 1895 paid the automobile little heed. At that point, bicycles were still gaining in popularity. That would change in just a few years, and the twentieth century would belong to the automobile.

Because of the proximity of the end of the bicycle boom and the rise of the automobile era, it is tempting to draw a causal connection between the two trends. Indeed, most twentieth-century bicycle and automobile histories have embraced this line of reasoning. As detailed below, however, contemporary statistics and data contradict the claim that the automobile was the *primary* cause of the bicycle's relative demise. The end of the bicycle boom was much more complicated than the beginning of the automobile's reign over the American imagination. To understand what happened, one must also consider the broader social context surrounding bicycles, along with trends within the bicycle industry itself like overproduction, the rise of mail order, and the formation of a near-monopoly on bicycle manufacturing. Unsurprisingly, Illinois played a central role in these developments.

Cheap Bikes by Mail

By the end of the nineteenth century, mail-order companies had grown to the point where they began to dominate the sale of nonperishable goods in rural areas across the country. Their success was fueled by a new Rural Free Delivery system that the United States Post Office began implementing in 1896. Before Rural Free Delivery, United States citizens living outside of cities had to travel to either the nearest post office or a general store to pick up their mail. Mail order, combined with Rural Free Delivery, had a profound effect on the lives of rural Americans. In 1946, New York's esteemed Grolier Club, a literary club, included a Montgomery Ward catalog in their list of the top one hundred books that had an influence on American life, writing, "The mail order catalogue has been perhaps the greatest single influence in increasing the standard of American middle-class living. It brought the benefit of wholesale prices to the city and hamlet, to the cross-roads and the prairies . . . and, above all, it substituted sound quality for shoddy."[6] By a wide margin, the country's largest mail-order companies were the Illinois-based Montgomery Ward & Co. and Sears, Roebuck & Co. By the end of the nineteenth century, Ward and Sears were massive consumer juggernauts. Even so, their decisive role in the bicycle industry has been largely overlooked by past historians.

Montgomery Ward & Co. was founded in 1872, when Aaron Montgomery Ward circulated a single-sheet catalog that listed 163 items. With little serious competition for the next twenty years, Montgomery Ward flourished. By 1897,

Montgomery Ward Hawthorne bicycle catalog, 1920. (Author's collection.)

it claimed to be the largest mail-order business in the world and was filling 6,000–16,000 orders per day from their fifteen-acre Chicago warehouse. That year, they printed and shipped 900,000 catalogs that had burgeoned to 800 pages and featured 40,000 items.[7] A few of those 40,000 items were bicycles. It's not clear when Ward first added bicycles to his catalog, but the company was advertising bicycles for sale in the 1890 Pullman Race program. In the early 1890s, Ward imported English bicycles and also sold a few domestic models. Their 1893 catalog featured an English Humber for the princely sum of $165 and a slightly cheaper $115 American-made Lovell bicycle. "Our bicycle department is one of our most prominent," Ward boasted in its 1896 catalog. It started selling its own "Hawthorne" brand of bicycles for an unheard of $25 to $49, depending on the model. Ward contracted for very large numbers of bicycles from local manufacturers in the winter off-season and then resold them through its catalogs at small profit margins. This massive price drop from 1893 to 1896 is indicative of the role of mail-order companies in accelerating overproduction and destroying what were previously generous profit margins in the bicycle industry. By 1899, a perfectly functional Ward's Hawthorne was selling for only $18, and the company was expecting to sell 20,000 bicycles. The catalog for that year bragged about how mail order was upending the American bicycle industry: "Bicycle dealers held up their hands in horror and said that no manufacturer could make wheels according to our specifications so that we could sell them at $25 and make a profit. We told them we didn't expect to make much profit, but we must, as a business proposition, make a little."[8]

Sears, Roebuck & Co. was founded in 1893, twenty-one years after Montgomery Ward. The company's founder, Richard W. Sears, was ambitious and aggressive, believing that within a few years he could outsell his Chicago rival. The first general Sears catalog came out in 1894 and featured bicycles with a one-year warranty that sold for only a one-dollar down payment, with the balance due on delivery. What is astonishing is that in 1894, Sears was able to sell bicycles that started at $17.45 and topped out at only $55.95. By comparison, Chicago-made 1894 Monarch bicycles were selling for $100-$125, while Columbia bicycles for that year ranged from $125-$160. The Sears catalog boasted, "At our prices everyone can own a bicycle."[9] From the very first year, the high-volume, low-margin mail-order business model began to upend the previously lucrative American bicycle industry.

Sears grew exponentially over the next few years by attempting to undercut Ward's prices whenever possible, including in bicycle prices. By 1898, Sears was publishing a standalone bicycle catalog that was over one hundred pages long. That year, Sears featured bicycles ranging from the $13.95 Cincinnatus to the $35 Acme King. Again, the catalog was candid about the company's business model:

> We have contracted for the entire output of two of the largest factories in America. We shall control the prices of this season, and every one who buys from us will get the best wheel ever sold for so little money. In order that the maker can maintain his high retail prices and still allow us to sell everyone everywhere on our cost basis . . . we were compelled to enter into a contract with the manufacturer not to disclose his name.[10]

In Chicago, at least, it was a poorly kept secret that one of these manufacturers was Arnold, Schwinn & Company. In 1898, Richard Sears paid a visit to Ignaz Schwinn to negotiate the purchase of bicycles for the following year. Once prices were agreed upon, Sears ordered 50,000 bicycles, to which an incredulous Schwinn replied, "Hadn't you better make it 5,000, Mr. Sears?" The mail-order magnate responded, "You just go ahead and make the bicycles. . . . We'll sell 'em."[11] Sears was true to his word. Even as hundreds of bicycle manufacturers around the country were going bankrupt, Sears sold 45,000 bicycles in 1899.[12]

By 1900, Sears had overtaken the venerable Ward in terms of overall profits.[13] The following year, as the American bicycle industry was crashing down in a spectacular fashion, Sears declared itself "the largest dealers in bicycles in the world." Their 1902 catalog boasted, "Last season we sold one-quarter of all the wheels made and sold in America. Our sales for 1901 were between 90,000 and

Sears bicycle catalog, 1901. (The Bicycle Museum of America, New Bremen, Ohio.)

100,000 bicycles, while the estimated production and sales for this country was approximately 400,000. It will thus be seen that we practically control the bicycle situation, make the price, and for like quality undersell by far any and all competition." The same catalog featured bicycles that sold for only $8.95 to $15.75; less than ten years earlier, average prices had been around $100.[14]

In addition to these two general mail-order businesses, Illinois was also home to most of the country's large bicycle-specific mail-order companies, including Chicago's Mead Cycle Company, Lewis Cycle Company, and Peoria's Rouse & Hazard.

Of these bicycle mail-order companies, the Mead Cycle Company deserves specific mention. In 1888, James L. Mead began selling used bicycles in Wichita, Kansas, under the name the Mead Cycle Company. To take advantage of the soaring urban demand for bicycles during the boom, he moved to Chicago in 1891. Once established in Chicago, Mead formed Mead & Prentiss Company with Benjamin L. Prentiss. In the mid-1890s, this new company found success selling both used and new bicycles by mail order. By 1896, Mead & Prentiss were manufacturing and selling their own line of low-priced bicycles under the brand names Ranger and Monitor. Mead & Prentiss, along with a few other bicycle-related businesses that had been started by James Mead, were all merged under the Mead Cycle Company name in 1898. The Mead Cycle Company was not swept up into the bicycle trust and continued to find success with aggressive nationwide magazine and newspaper advertising campaigns. The volume of mail leaving Mead was so great that the United States Postal Service kept a full-time employee onsite. Mead's advertisements invariably focused on the low price of its bicycles due to the direct-to-consumer mail-order model. In the first years of 1900, during the midst of the bicycle industry bust, Mead still managed to sell around 50,000 bicycles per year, rivaling Sears. In 1902, an overseas branch of the Mead Cycle Company was established in Liverpool, England.[15]

In 1900, the *Wheel and Cycling Trade Review* reported on all of Chicago's bicycle mail-order businesses. The publication cited a "very conservative estimate" that the city's mail-order houses had sold 150,000 bicycles the previous year.[16] All of the abovementioned mail-order companies either survived—or even thrived—during the bust period of the American bicycle industry. The mail-order model of selling decent-quality bikes directly to consumers at the lowest price possible had clearly triumphed over the old model of manufacturers selling high-profit-margin bicycles to dealerships and bicycle shops, which, in turn, sold them to consumers.

Cheap mail-order bikes were only partially to blame for the collapse of the American bicycle industry, however. Another important part of the puzzle was the formation, and rapid collapse, of the American Bicycle Company trust.

American Bicycle Company Trust

Many Gilded Age robber barons made—or enhanced—their fortunes by forming trusts that monopolized an industry. John D. Rockefeller's Standard Oil Company and Trust is perhaps the most familiar of these. The Standard Oil Company was an example of vertical consolidation within an industry, as Rockefeller eventually controlled oil production, transportation, refining, and retailing. The late nineteenth century also saw American monopolies in the steel, sugar, tobacco, and meatpacking industries. To rescue the free market, Congress passed the Sherman Antitrust Act in 1890, but it lacked teeth and was rarely used in the next decade or so to break up big monopolies.

The massive but decentralized United States bicycle industry of the late 1890s was ripe for the formation of a horizontal combination. Compared with vertical combinations, horizontal combinations were relatively straightforward: choose an industry, combine as many firms as possible, squeeze out any remaining competition, reduce production, and then raise prices. The possible formation of a bicycle trust was frequently discussed in the mid-1890s, but nothing came of it until March of 1899, when newspapers across the country ran stories, albeit with vague details, that a trust was amassing an estimated $50 million in capital to acquire the largest bicycle firms in the country. A.G. Spalding, who had gotten his start in the early 1880s with sporting goods and bicycles in Chicago, was the leading organizer. Over time, bicycles had become a major part of Spalding's sporting goods empire, and by 1899 he had served as the president of the nationwide Bicycle Board of Trade and had purchased his own factory to manufacture bicycles.

The American Bicycle Company (A.B.C.) was incorporated on May 12, although which firms would make up the trust was still to be determined. Spalding was elected president of the new company, with Columbia Manufacturing's Albert Pope elected vice president. Unable to raise the staggering amount of cash the trust needed, the principal investors fell back on a risky but common scheme of offering a combination of cash, stock in the new company, and debenture bonds (i.e., bonds that lacked any assets as collateral). Given that Illinois was the leading manufacturer of bicycles at the time, in-state companies unsurprisingly made up the majority of the initial forty-three companies that agreed to be bought out by the trust. The Illinois bicycle companies included Ames and Frost, H. A. Cristy, Fanning Cycle, Featherstone, Gormully & Jeffery, Hart & Cooley, Monarch, Peoria Rubber and Manufacturing, Stover Bicycle Manufacturing, George M. Thompson, and Western Wheelworks. Notably absent from the list was Schwinn, which was doing well selling lower-priced bicycles but was not yet large enough to interest the trust. Schwinn's founder, Ignaz Schwinn, also had a notorious independent streak, which might have contributed to keeping his company out of the trust.[17]

Problems arose with the trust almost immediately. On a superficial level, to be sure, the trust looked unstoppable. Since the formation of A.B.C., more than one hundred American bicycle manufacturers had quit the trade (including twenty-one companies that were acquired and closed by the A.B.C.). The fourteen remaining A.B.C. factories controlled about 65 percent of the United States bicycle trade; combined, they had earned an average of $5 million in net profits each of preceding four years. Yet A.B.C. was undercapitalized from the start, and the companies it acquired were overvalued and burdened by outstanding debts. At its formation, the A.B.C. had claimed assets of $45.4 million, but later examinations into the trust estimated that the true value was only $10-$18 million. A shake-up of the board occurred in January of 1900, and R. L. Coleman, former president of Chicago's industry-leading Western Wheelworks, took over as the new president of A.B.C. Meanwhile, demand was drying up across the bicycle industry. A few years earlier, two million bicycles were being produced annually in the United States, but the prediction for 1901 was a mere 600,000 bicycles.[18]

By September 1902, the writing was on the wall for the bicycle trust. President Coleman announced that it was entering into bankruptcy but had plans to restructure. The *Chicago Tribune* summarized the situation: "The trust was formed in the boom days and had the craze for wheeling maintained its popularity the company might have pulled through, but it has been apparent for some time that a crash was inevitable."[19] The United States bicycle market hit rock bottom between 1900 and 1905, when three-fifths of United States bicycle manufacturers were forced to close up shop.[20] The greed and subsequent value failure of the A.B.C. certainly bore some responsibility for the end of the bicycle boom. However, as the *Tribune* had pointed out, if consumer demand had stayed anywhere near peak levels, the trust may have succeeded. Clearly, far more bicycles were being produced than demand merited. The rise of the motorcycle and then the automobile also had a part to play in what had transpired. Multiple Illinois bicycle companies had a stake in those markets as well, as they contributed directly to the nascent American motorcycle and automobile industries.

Motorcycles

The first motorcycle was invented shortly after the invention of the pedal-driven velocipede. There is considerable debate among motorcycle historians about who first mounted a steam engine to a velocipede frame. Recall that velocipedes were not commercially available until Michaux began selling them in 1865. The contenders for the first steam-powered motorcycle are Michaux and French steam engineer Louis Guillaume Perreaux, who mounted an alcohol-fueled steam engine to a velocipede sometime between

1867 and 1869. They called their invention a *vélo-à-vapeur*. Over exactly the same span of years, there were at least one, and possibly two, Americans also working on a steam velocipede. Sylvester H. Roper of Roxbury, Massachusetts, was demonstrating his coal-powered steam velocipede at fairs and circuses by 1869. The Roper steam velocipede used water stored in a bladder that also served as the saddle, with the boiler sandwiched between the brave rider's legs. In 1868–69, W. W. Austin of Winthrop Massachusetts, was also demonstrating a steam velocipede, but it is unclear if it was of his own design or one made by Roper.[21] In the mid-1880s, German Gottlieb Daimler and Englishman Edward Butler both developed prototypes of gasoline-powered internal combustion engines. Daimler's 1885 *Einspur* is credited as the first gasoline-powered motorcycle.[22]

The bicycle boom of the 1890s was directly responsible for creating an American motorcycle market and spurring innovation. As the previous chapter on bicycle racing made clear, bicycle racers were forever chasing the fastest *paced* records that they could achieve by any means possible. In the early and mid-1890s, paced bicycle records were generally set by following behind a couple of pacers. Initially, these pacers were individual cyclists or a small group of cyclists that the record-setter drafted behind. Riders soon figured out that even faster speeds could be achieved with two cyclists working together on a tandem bicycle. If a tandem was good, a triplet was better, and a quadruplet better still. Chicago's Fowler Manufacturing Company entered into this arms race of pacing bicycles with the first pacing sextuplet in 1896. Ten and a half feet long with a weight of 107 pounds, it was propelled by seven chains that ran over a combination of fourteen cogs and sprockets.[23] A year later, Mayor Carter Henry Harrison IV piloted the 300-pound, ten-man tandem Oriten bicycle around Chicago's streets. The mania for human-powered bicycle-pacing madness apparently stopped there. A sextuplet was already too long to be used anywhere but straight sections of road and the largest tracks. Clearly, what cyclists who aspired to lower paced records needed was something faster and more compact to draft behind.

Prototype motorcycles were usually unreliable, custom-made machines. Like their steam velocipede predecessors, the earliest motorcycle prototypes featured a gasoline engine mounted to a bicycle frame. Early motors were severely underpowered compared to top cyclists. Thus, many designs were best-described as motor-assisted bicycles, since the rider or riders still added additional power to the system through pedaling. In a 1925 history of motorcycling, John H. Wyatt called the earliest motorcycles "merely a bicycle of rather stouter build than usual with an engine attached—one might almost say stuck on, for it was fixed in any position that seemed convenient, rather than as a part of a complete and symmetrical whole."[24]

1905 Monarch Motor Bicycle. Note that this early motorcycle is simply a bicycle frame with a motor added on. This model sold for $210. (Monarch Bicycle Catalog. The Bicycle Museum of America, New Bremen, Ohio.)

Still, prototype motorcycles caught the attention of top cyclists such as Major Taylor and John Nelson. Riders and reporters nicknamed these early motorcycle prototypes "demon motors" or "infernal machines." These terms were generally not used in a derogatory fashion, but rather with a tone of awe or excitement. The speed and erratic nature of these early machines were part of the appeal for spectators. Bicycle track racing, particularly the shorter events, always had an element of danger that was then multiplied exponentially with the addition of motorcycles. After 1900, a true motorcycle industry began to appear, and the machines were used for more than just pacing bicycles around a track. Reliability, power, and speed quickly improved.

All early motorcycles relied heavily on technologies and processes devised by bicycle manufacturers. Chicago was already one of the most important manufacturing centers in the country and, for a few firms, the transition from manufacturing bicycles (or sewing machines, or agricultural implements) to motorcycles was an easy one. In 1901, the Chicago Motorcycle Club was formed, with the *Inter Ocean* reporting, "As there is a growing number of users of motorcycles of all forms in and about Chicago, it was deemed advantageous to all concerned to organize a club for the purpose of bringing them in closer communication with one another."[25] In 1903 and 1904, bicycle and motorcycle races were held together on the Garfield Park Track under the auspices of the Century Road Club. The 1904 version of the fifteen-mile motorcycle race was won with an average speed of 13.5 mph, a speed almost every amateur bicycle racer could easily exceed.[26] In 1903, there were an estimated fifty-four substantial motorcycle manufacturers in the United States, with five of them calling Chicago home.[27]

All of the larger Illinois motorcycle manufacturers shared deep bicycle roots. The following section does not make any attempt at a comprehensive early history of motorcycles in Illinois but instead focuses on only the companies with direct ties to bicycles.

Aurora Automatic Machinery Company / Indian / Thor

In 1893, A. Levendahl and C. E. Erickson incorporated the Automatic Machinery Company in Aurora, adding the city to their official name in 1895. Although they manufactured parts for a variety of industries, bicycle parts and fittings appear to have made up the majority of their work. The company found success with the highly regarded Thor brand of bicycle hubs, cranks, and crank hangers, which were used by many companies across the country during the bicycle boom.[28] By 1903, the company's bicycle offerings included ten types of rear hubs, five front hubs, spokes, nipples, handlebars, and patented spoke washers for wooden rims.[29] Around this time, Aurora Automatic Machinery Company's history intersected with a former top bicycle racer named George Hendee. Based in Connecticut, Hendee had been one of the top American racers of the high-wheel era. He won his first one-mile amateur national championship in 1882 at age sixteen and went on to win championships at two-, five-, ten-, and twenty-mile distances. For a time, he held the world record for the one-mile. Hendee raced professionally from 1886 to 1895, winning 302 out of the 309 races he entered over the course of his career.[30] After retiring from racing, he founded the Hendee & Nelson Manufacturing company and began producing Silver King and Silver Queen bicycles. Hendee's first association with Aurora Automatic Machinery Company was when he contracted with them to supply parts for his bicycles. After his first bicycle company failed, Hendee launched Hendee Manufacturing Company and began producing a new line of bicycles called Indians.

At the Madison Square Garden bicycle races in 1900, Hendee met an engineer and former bicycle racer named Oscar Hedstrom, who had been building one-off bicycle-pacing motorcycles. Both men recognized the growing demand for motorcycles, and they formed a partnership under the name Indian Motocycle Company. This became the first major American motorcycle company, and it produced the most successful motorcycles of the early 1900s. Hedstrom had a new prototype Indian motorcycle ready for exhibition in the spring of 1901. Successful demonstrations on the streets and hills of

Springfield, Massachusetts, helped the duo secure $20,000 in funding for their new company.[31] Lacking a foundry, Hendee reached out to his old partners at the Aurora Automatic Machine Company to build Indian engines based on Hedstrom's specifications. Aurora became the exclusive engine supplier for all Indian motorcycles between 1902 and 1907. Per their initial contract, Aurora retained the right to sell surplus individual engines and motorcycle parts but not complete motorcycles. Since Aurora already had nationwide brand recognition from its Thor line of bicycle components, the new engines were also named Thor. In 1903, Auora created a spin-off named Thor Moto Cycle and Bicycle Company.[32]

Within a year or two, there was high demand both for Indian motorcycles and Thor engines. Many—perhaps the majority—of early American motorcycles began using Thor engines. Motorcycle models utilizing Thor motors included America, Apache, Chicago, Greyhound, Light/Thor-Bred, Manson, Rambler, Reading-Standard, Royal, Sears, Torpedo, and Warwick.[33] After the 1907 contract with Indian ended, Aurora wasted no time in bringing its own Thor-branded motorcycles to market. In 1910, it designed one of the first v-twin engines, which made their motorcycles faster and more powerful. By 1920, Aurora/Thor had ceased motorcycle production and moved on to a more lucrative line of Thor pneumatic power tools.

Excelsior/Schwinn/Henderson

The Excelsior Supply Company was established in Chicago in 1876 and was officially incorporated in 1884. Originally, their primary line of business was selling sewing machines and sewing machine parts from their factory and warehouse near the Randolph Street Bridge.[34] Like so many other manufacturers and wholesalers in the Midwest, Excelsior saw an opportunity to expand into bicycles during the early years of the boom. By 1894, they were selling bicycle parts and accessories and had brought their own line of Excelsior bicycles to market.[35] Changing with the times, Excelsior began selling automobile parts and machinery around the turn of the century. By 1905, they had developed a motorcycle prototype, which was then brought to market in 1907.

Excelsior found early success with their three-horsepower Auto-Cycle motorcycles. Having survived—and even thrived—through the end of the bicycle boom, Arnold, Schwinn & Company was looking to diversify its manufacturing portfolio when it acquired the Excelsior Supply Company in 1911 for $500,000. Ignaz Schwinn previously had his bicycle engineers design and build a prototype of their own motorcycle, but the opportunity to acquire a local motorcycle company was apparently too good to pass up. It turned out to be yet another savvy business move by Schwinn. Schwinn helped to infuse

Excelsior motorcycle advertisement featuring boxer Jack Johnson. (*Motorcycling*, March 28, 1912.)

cash and additional engineering capabilities into Excelsior and built a new 200,000-square-foot motorcycle factory. One of Excelsior's early customers was the Chicago Police Department, which had come to appreciate the reliability of the Excelsior machines. Excelsior got some free publicity in 1912 when a Chicago police officer on an Excelsior Autocycle was able to catch and ticket a speeder. The offender was boxing champion Jack Johnson, and he was driving an early Lozier automobile. Schwinn/Excelsior wasted no time in running advertisements that showcased the event.[36]

Similar to the evolution of bicycles, racing success was a major factor for motorcycle sales. Excelsior asserted their racing dominance in 1913 when rider Lee Humiston became the first to hit 100 mph in a sanctioned competition on the new Excelsior 1,000cc v-twin.[37] A few days later, Humiston broke every motorcycle record between two and one hundred miles, further cementing the new Excelsior's reputation as the fastest motorcycle of the day.

With demand high for Excelsior motorcycles, Schwinn further expanded his empire by acquiring Detroit-based Henderson Motorcycle Company in

1917. Henderson motorcycles were known for their powerful in-line four-cylinder motors, and after 1913 they could also lay claim to the first motorcycle circumnavigation of the globe thanks to rider Carl Stearns Clancy. Henry Ford was a fan of the Henderson design and tried to negotiate a discount on a 1917 four-cylinder. He did end up buying one of the motorcycles, but he was forced to pay full price.[38]

Ignaz Schwinn moved Henderson employees and assets to his Chicago Excelsior factories, cross-branding his new line of motorcycles as Excelsior-Henderson. Never one to let an opportunity slip by, Schwinn also produced Excelsior and Henderson bicycles. Excelsior-Henderson was the third-largest American motorcycle manufacturer (behind Harley-Davidson and Indian) in the late 1910s and throughout the 1920s. The Great Depression finally ended Schwinn's foray into motorcycles and forced them to close their motorcycle divisions to save the bicycle portion of the company. It was, again, a perceptive business decision. During the Depression and then World War II years, it was much easier to sell cheap utilitarian bicycles than it was to sell motorcycles, which were still something of a luxury item.[39]

The United States motorcycle industry followed an arc that was very similar to that of the bicycle industry, albeit on a smaller scale. Between 1900 and 1917, there were an estimated 150 American motorcycle manufacturers. Beyond the major Illinois motorcycle manufacturers with bicycle roots mentioned above, there was also Pope-founded American Cycle Manufacturing Company, which made some motorcycles in Chicago. Fred Patee from Peoria had a successful line of Patee bicycles before manufacturing Patee Motorcycles in Indiana. Although no surviving examples are known, the 1901 Patee Motorcycle deserves credit as one of the first commercially produced motorcycles made in the United States (no Indian motorcycles were sold to the public until 1902).[40] From 1905 to 1908, the Fowler-Manson-Sherman company made motorcycles in Chicago. The subsequent motorcycle industry bust occurred largely as a result of World War I; only around a dozen companies survived into the 1920s.[41]

Because of already-established manufacturing capacity and easy railway access, the Midwest led the way in American motorcycle manufacturing. Through the first three decades of the twentieth century, there were three clear leaders in American motorcycle manufacturing, and they all had Midwestern ties. Harley-Davidson was based in Milwaukee, and Excelsior-Henderson was based in Chicago. Indian, while based in Massachusetts, initially relied on engines and fittings from Aurora, Illinois. Several bicycle companies retooled their factories to make motorcycles and thereby survive the dramatically shrinking American bicycle market. Other Illinois bicycle manufacturers would cast their lots with automobile manufacturing.

Automobiles

The earliest examples of motorized vehicles that we would recognize as the precursors to today's automobiles utilized steam engines. However, most automotive historians point to vehicles utilizing the first gasoline-powered internal combustion engines as the true roots of the modern automobile. As with motorcycles, early automobile prototypes relied extensively on parts and technologies developed by the bicycle industry. The relatively quick emergence of commercial automobiles after 1900 can be attributed largely to technology transfer from the bicycle industry.

This was certainly true for Karl Friedrich Benz and Gottlieb Daimler, the two German engineers who have competing claims for inventing the first gasoline-powered automobiles. Unbeknownst to each other, both Benz and Daimler filed patents on their automobiles on the same day, January 29, 1886. Karl Benz had learned to ride on a friend's velocipede during the craze of the late 1860s. He later developed an internal combustion engine in the early 1880s, and by 1885 was endeavoring to fit the engine onto what was clearly a sociable-style tricycle. Other parts for Benz's *motowagen* were procured from Germany's largest bicycle dealer and parts supplier, the House of Bicycles. One of the early Benz patents for his invention describe it as a tricycle, and in 1886 a local paper called his invention a "Motoren Velociped," or motorized velocipede.[42]

Gottlieb Daimler began his motorized efforts with his 1885 *Einspur* motorcycle, and then in 1886 he adapted a carriage into the world's first four-wheeled automobile. Unlike Benz's, Daimler's automobile featured a more practical high-speed gasoline engine. In the 1920s, Benz & Cie and the Daimler Motoren Gesellschaft would merge to form Daimler-Benz, the precursor to Mercedes-Benz.[43]

Another connection between bicycles and early automobiles came from Hiram Percy Maxim, an 1886 MIT graduate who invented his own gasoline-powered tricycle in 1895. This invention caught the attention of Albert Pope, who hired him to work on developing an electric Columbia automobile. By 1897, Pope was successfully producing electric automobiles based on Maxim's designs. In his 1937 autobiography, *Horseless Carriage Days*, Maxim succinctly summarized the pivotal role of bicycles in developing the automobile industry:

> It has been the habit to give the gasoline-engine all the credit for bringing the automobile.... [I]n my opinion this is a wrong explanation. We have had the steam-engine for over a century. We could have built steam vehicles in 1880, or indeed in 1870. But we did not. We waited until 1895. The reason why we did not build road vehicles before this, in my opinion, was because the bicycle had not yet come in numbers and had not directed men's minds

> to the possibilities of independent long-distance travel over the ordinary highway. We thought the railroad was good enough. The bicycle created a new demand which it was beyond the ability of the railroad to supply. Then it came about that the bicycle could not satisfy the demand which it had created. A mechanically propelled vehicle was wanted instead of a foot-propelled one, and we know now that the automobile was the answer.[44]

Maxim wasn't just waxing nostalgic about bicycles, as his conclusions have also been echoed by modern automotive historians. In his definitive social history of the automobile, *The Automobile Age*, James Flink contends, "No preceding technological innovation—not even the internal-combustion engine—was as important to the development of the automobile as the bicycle."[45]

Even more than Benz and Daimler, the Duryea brothers lived out the transition from the bicycle era to the automobile epoch.

Charles and Frank Duryea

The deep bicycle roots of the Duryea brothers (Charles especially) have already been detailed. The Duryeas are also credited with inventing the first *commercially available* American automobile. There were certainly earlier American steam- and gasoline-powered vehicles, but these were all one-off prototypes that never made it into production. While both Duryea brothers contributed to their earliest designs, later years would find the two locked in a bitter squabble over who deserved credit as the inventor of the first mass-produced American automobile.

By 1890, both Duryea brothers had moved to Chicopee, Massachusetts, where Charles was overseeing the construction of his bicycles at the Ames Manufacturing Company and Frank was employed by the same company as a toolmaker. By 1891, the brothers had designs for what they believed would be a workable combustion engine. Early in 1892, Charles purchased a used "phaeton"-style carriage and additional tricycle parts from Pope Manufacturing. He then rented space to work on the new automobile in Springfield, Massachusetts.[46]

In later years, the brothers would bicker over what month in 1892 marked the first successful test run of their automobile. Charles laid claim to a successful indoor test run in the spring of 1892, when both brothers were still actively involved in working on the vehicle. In September of 1892, Charles Duryea returned to Peoria to make bicycles with his newly formed Rouse-Duryea Company. It is clear that after September, Charles was only involved remotely through correspondence with his brother, while Frank was responsible for the actual day-to-day work on the prototype. There is solid documentation that a successful test run of the Duryea automobile was made on the streets of Springfield on September 21, 1893.[47] Clearly, there were other American inventors that have plausible earlier claims to the first functioning American automobile, but most historians choose to credit the Duryeas because they were able to take an experimental design and make it commercially viable.

While Charles focused on bicycles in Peoria, Frank continued to make incremental improvements to the automobile. By 1894, he was able to complete a six-mile trial run. Later in 1894 and early 1895, Frank completely redesigned both the engine and transmission. Utilizing a new four-stroke engine, the Duryea vehicle became (relatively) faster and more reliable. This would be the car that Frank drove to win the Race of the Century in Chicago. Reflecting on the significance of the Duryea car, Henry Ford would later say, "The Duryea car was a masterpiece. It did more to start the automobile business than any other car that was ever made. With no patterns to go by, with inferior tools and machinery to make parts, with practically no financial backing, Duryea accomplished wonders."[48]

Charles first went to visit Albert Pope, of Columbia bicycle fame, to try to negotiate a contract whereby Pope Manufacturing would produce Duryea automobiles. Given that the Duryeas were poised to create an entirely new industry, Charles's proposal to Pope seemed very reasonable: "Production and a bit of the profits. A little cash to pay advances, a salary, and enough to live on and a royalty of five or ten percent." Known for always driving a hard bargain, Pope countered, "You have nothing, Duryea, but an engine. We can buy engines anywhere. Give you three dollars per engine." Exasperated, Charles walked out without making a deal. Later the same year, Pope was reported as saying, "That man Duryea knows more about horseless carriages than any other man in the world but he is one hundred years too soon."[49] Apparently, he would quickly change his mind, as Pope Manufacturing would launch their own successful electric car business in 1897.[50]

Charles and Frank decided to go it alone and formed the Duryea Motor Wagon Company in the fall of 1895. Charles held 48 percent of the stock while Frank held 33 percent. Their limited manufacturing facilities were still located in Springfield, Massachusetts. Shortly after the formation of the new company, Frank won the Race of the Century in Chicago and garnered a good deal of nationwide publicity for the new vehicle. In the following year, the Duryea Motor Wagon Company successfully built and sold thirteen Duryea Motor Carriages, clearly establishing the brothers as the first to mass-produce automobiles in America. The Duryeas deserve much of the credit for launching the venerable American automobile industry.

A Duryea brother was also involved in the first documented automobile accident. It was also the first documented example of an automobile driver hitting a bicyclist—a sign of things to come, unfortunately. On Memorial Day

1896, *Cosmopolitan* magazine (its content and target audience were a bit different in 1896) sponsored the second "large" American automobile race in New York. This was a forty-mile event, starting and finishing at City Hall. John Jacob Astor IV, a member of one of the wealthiest families in America, was one of the officials at the start. (In addition to further enhancing the family fortune in real estate, Astor also patented a bicycle brake.)[51] Four of the six cars entered were Duryeas, and this time Frank and Charles were driving separate cars. Henry Wells of Springfield, Massachusetts, was piloting another of the Duryea vehicles. As it was a pleasant spring day in the midst of the bicycle boom, New York's streets were crowded with cyclists. Miss Ebeling Thomas was riding down Western Boulevard (better known as Broadway) while the Wells Duryea was heading in the opposite direction. Eyewitnesses reported that "the motorman of the horseless wagon seemed to lose control of the wagon, which ran zig-zag and thus confused the bicyclist." Unable to regain control of the car, Wells ran into Miss Thomas, knocking her off her bicycle. She was taken unconscious to Manhattan Hospital and was diagnosed with a fractured leg. Wells was arrested and spent the night in jail, and someone else took over driving his car.[52] Frank would go on to win the New York race, with brother Charles trailing by nearly two hours.

While the Duryea Motor Wagon Company succeeded in building thirteen automobiles, it was short-lived. The brothers sold their stock shares to the other owners in 1898. With differing views of how to proceed, they then went their separate ways. Charles returned to Peoria, Illinois, where he still had connections with multiple bicycle businesses. Once there, he founded the Duryea Manufacturing Company in 1898 and retrofitted the Rouse & Hazard bicycle factory for manufacturing his new automobile. In Peoria, Charles successfully manufactured a number of three-wheel, three-cylinder "Motor Trap" automobiles. Variations of the Motor Trap include the first armored vehicle with an integrated rifle and the first delivery van. Duryea sold this factory to the St. Louis Motor Carriage Company, which then built cars in Peoria from 1905 to 1907. Charles never seemed to settle anywhere for long, and eventually he launched automobile manufacturing companies in Reading, Pennsylvania; Saginaw, Michigan; and finally, Philadelphia. Before his retirement from manufacturing in 1920, he had designed and built several hundred automobiles consisting of ten different models.[53]

Frank forged his own path in the growing automobile industry. His first effort, in 1900, was the formation of the Hampden Automobile and Launch Company in Springfield, Massachusetts. This small engineering and manufacturing shop managed to produce three prototype automobiles and one launch (a type of boat) in its first year. These prototypes caught the attention of the much larger and established Stevens Arms and Tool Company in nearby Chicopee Falls. Duryea entered into a contract to build cars for Stevens, leading to the formation of the Stevens-Duryea Company in 1904. The earliest Stevens-Duryea automobiles were built in the factories of the defunct Overman Wheel Company (makers of Victor bicycles from 1882 to 1900). Stevens-Duryea became one of the country's leading manufacturers of automobiles, finding particular success with a large, six-cylinder luxury automobile. Frank retired in 1915.[54]

Even though Charles passed in 1938, the controversy over which of them had built the first American automobile continued unabated throughout the 1940s. In 1944, Frank published a small book, *Who Designed and Built Those Early Duryea Cars? Answered in 10 Deadly Parallels*, which laid out a solid argument with documentary evidence. Still, as the *Chicago Tribune* observed in 1952, "taking sides with the Duryeas is one of the country's unlisted sports."[55] In truth, the question Frank posed in his book title likely had more than one answer. All available evidence points to Charles financing and helping with the designs of the 1892 Duryea in question, but Frank clearly supplied the great majority of the engineering, machining, and assembly work to make a functioning automobile.

On Thanksgiving Day 1945, Chicago's Museum of Science and Industry organized a fifty-year-anniversary reenactment of the Race of the Century. None of the original cars were available, but five of the earliest functioning American automobiles were selected for participation. A seventy-five-year-old Frank Duryea entered an 1896 Duryea automobile in the race. As in 1895, only two cars were able to finish; once again, Frank Duryea won the race.[56]

Thomas B. Jeffery & Co. / Rambler

Another Illinois bicycle manufacturer that successfully made the leap to automobiles was Gormully & Jeffery. The company was an early acquisition of Albert Pope's American Bicycle Trust, allowing G&J co-owners R. Phillip Gormully and Thomas B. Jeffery to walk away with a substantial fortune just before the bottom fell out of the bicycle industry.

Ever since witnessing the Race of the Century in Chicago, Jeffery had been interested in trying his hand at manufacturing automobiles. He tinkered with a few prototypes during the final years of the G&J bicycle manufacturing empire and then built a few additional prototype automobiles under contract for Pope's American Bicycle Company. Unlike Pope, Jeffery's timing was spot-on. In 1900, he took his proceeds from the sale of G&J and purchased the old Sterling Cycle Works factory in Kenosha, Wisconsin. Ironically, the Sterling factory was for sale at the bargain price of $65,000 because Pope had purchased it as part of the A.B.C. trust and then shuttered the factory in an attempt to consolidate the bicycle industry and monopolize profits. (Sterling,

Early Rambler automobile designed by Thomas B. Jeffery. (From the Archives of Kenosha County Historical Society.)

as noted earlier, was originally a Chicago-based bicycle manufacturer before relocating to a larger Kenosha factory in 1895.)

Jeffery knew that his Rambler line of bicycles had good nationwide brand recognition. Under his original agreement with Pope, Jeffery had retained the right to use the name on products other than bicycles. Diving headlong into the automotive industry, the Thomas B. Jeffery Company produced 1,500 one-cylinder, eight-horsepower Rambler automobiles in 1902. This rate of production represented one-sixth of all American automobile sales and put the Thomas B. Jeffery Company in second place nationwide behind Detroit's Olds Motor Works (Oldsmobile). Over the next fifteen years, the Thomas B. Jeffery Company would remain one of the leaders of the American automobile industry, producing more than 60,000 automobiles.[57]

After Thomas Jeffery died unexpectedly in 1910 while vacationing in Italy, his son Charles took over the company. Charles then narrowly avoided death as a passenger of the doomed Lusitania in 1915. This near-death experience prompted him to sell the company in 1916 to another native Illinoisan, Charles W. Nash. Nash had previously cofounded the Buick Motor Company. With the purchase of the Thomas B. Jeffery Company, he then created Nash Motors. Nash Motors remained one of the top American automobile manufacturers in the early and mid-twentieth century and would eventually sell 4.2 million Rambler automobiles before they were discontinued in 1969. Nash Motors would later become the American Motors Corporation (AMC), which, in turn, would become Chrysler.[58]

Eldredge

The National Sewing Machine Company was officially incorporated in Belvidere, Illinois, in 1892. Prior to this, the company had made sewing machines under the names June Manufacturing and Eldredge (after the company president, Barnabas Eldredge). The new name reflected the company's big ambitions. Like so many other manufacturers across the country, the National Sewing Machine Company saw an opportunity to diversify their production by manufacturing bicycles. The company entered the bicycle manufacturing business just before the height of the boom in 1894. The company soon went all in on bikes, purchasing the assets of a smaller bicycle company and then building a new, three-story, 100,000-square-foot bicycle factory. According to an 1896 history of Belvidere, the new facilities made the National Sewing Machine Company "the largest and most completely equipped bicycle plant in the United States as well as the second largest sewing machine factory in the world." The company made 10,000 bikes in its first full year and targeted 48,000 for the second year.[59]

Beginning in 1903, the National Sewing Machine Company pursued yet another opportunity to diversify, this time by manufacturing automobiles. Their first effort was the $750 Eldredge Runabout, a two-cylinder, eight-horsepower machine that could carry two passengers. The Eldredge Runabout is historically significant as the first production American automobile to utilize a left-side steering design instead of having the driver seated in the middle of the vehicle. It was also one of the first to utilize a sliding gear transmission. In 1903, the editors of *Automobile Review* called the Eldredge Runabout "a remarkably well designed car" and "one of the best pieces of mechanism of its kind that we have examined."[60] By 1904, the company was also offering a $2,000, five-passenger Eldredge Tonneau model with a four-cylinder, sixteen-horsepower motor. Competition was rapidly increasing in the automobile industry. Despite producing high-quality vehicles, the National Sewing Machine Company ceased automobile production around 1906, having built around six hundred cars in total.[61]

The Bicycle Bust Reconsidered

Clearly, the Illinois motorcycle and automobile industry evolved from the bicycle industry. The bicycle boom came to a rather abrupt end around the end of the nineteenth century, around the same time that early American motorcycles and automobiles were increasing in popularity. It thus stands to reason that the rise of motorized vehicles might have caused the end of the bicycle boom; however, history is messy and rarely adheres to such simple connections. What can be said definitively, is that automobiles were not the primary reason the bicycle boom ended.

Contemporary manufacturing statistics for bicycles and automobiles (there are far fewer motorcycle statistics from this period) can help clarify the relationship between the bicycle bust and the beginning of the automobile era. Some skepticism should always be applied to the output statistics reported by manufacturers in their advertising material, in newspapers, and in trade publications, but in some instances, those are the best sources we have.

While the two trends were clear (bicycle production declined and automobile production grew), they did not commence at the same time. In 1896, League of American Wheelman president Isaac Potter estimated that the total American bicycle economy was worth an astounding $75 million ($2.7 billion in 2024). This number included bicycles themselves, but also everything associated with bikes, tickets for events, bicycle repairs, bicycle clothing, and so on. His estimates were probably not far off. With more certainty, we know that Pope manufacturing produced around 60,000 bikes in 1896, while Chicago's Western Wheelworks, the country's top producer, made 70,000.[62] American bicycle export figures give us a good proxy for the health of the industry as a whole. In 1896, United States bicycle manufacturers exported $1.9 million worth of bicycles. That number nearly quadrupled when bicycle exports peaked the following year with a total of $7 million.[63] For the peak years of 1897–1898, a reasonable estimate for American production is around two million bicycles. Usually, historians can rely on decennial census data for generally reliable statistical information, but the bicycle boom hadn't yet begun in 1890 and was mostly over by 1900.[64] An additional *Census of Manufactures* undertaken in 1900 (data was actually collected in 1899) provides us with an incredible amount of detail for the American bicycle industry at the end of the nineteenth century. Given the massive growth in the industry, an additional special report on bicycles was included in 1900. In that year, the *Census of Manufactures* found that 312 American bicycle manufacturers made 1.1 million bicycles, worth a total of $32 million (a 1,143% increase over 1890). Illinois led the country with sixty large manufacturers making $9 million worth of bicycles (note that there would have been many more smaller bicycle shops assembling—but not manufacturing—their own bicycles).[65] The 1905 *Census of Manufactures* shows a continued decline in the American bicycle industry. According to the 1905 Census, 101 manufacturers now only made 257,000 bicycles worth $5.2 million. These figures represent only a little over 10 percent of peak output during the boom. Illinois's thirteen remaining manufacturers still led the country by producing 80,000 bicycles, worth $1.2 million.[66]

Automobile production in the early 1900s ramped up much more slowly than bicycles had in the 1890s. In 1899, fifty-seven firms only produced 3,723 automobiles, with a value of $4.7 million. In the same year, only 8,000 automobiles were registered across the country. The city of Chicago issued a measly 189 permits for automobiles in 1900 (90 electric, 55 gas, 44 steam). By 1904, 178 firms made 22,000 automobiles, worth $30 million. In 1904, 58,000 vehicles were registered.[67] After 1905, American bicycle production leveled out and then began to slowly grow again. Automobile production continued to grow for many years, but automobiles wouldn't match peak bicycle sales (in terms of number sold) until 1920.[68]

Looking strictly at bicycle and automobile production numbers around the turn of the century, it is clear that the rise of the automobile could not have been the primary factor that brought about the end of the bicycle boom. The bicycle boom peaked in 1897 and 1898, when there were—at best—a few thousand automobiles scattered across the country. Before 1900, the vast majority of Americans had certainly heard of automobiles but never had a chance to see one. Automobiles would have needed to be more available and affordable to have caused the end of the boom by themselves. By contrast, at this time, there were millions of bicyclists, and bicycle prices had dropped exponentially, making them accessible to most Americans.

One of the major causes of the end of the bicycle boom was a decline in the relative cost of bicycles. In the mid-1890s, bicycles were still a luxury item, selling for around $100 at a time when the average worker only made about $1,000 per year. The tens of thousands of Americans who bought bicycles at this time were by and large from the upper ranks of society. During most of the 1890s, the bicycle actually reinforced class status, rather than bridging divides between social classes, as so many claimed. As competition increased drastically in the late 1890s (particularly from Illinois mail-order companies), bicycle prices dropped accordingly. Based on the 1900 *Census of Manufactures*, the average price of a bicycle in the United States was now only around $19. Overproduction and flagging demand certainly contributed to these drastic price drops. Working-class Americans were now using bicycles for their work commutes, and racial and ethnic minorities started cycling in ever greater numbers. In 1905, *Scientific American* specifically pointed to the rise of cheap and widely available bicycles as a chief cause of the bicycle bust: "Another . . . cause of the decline was the introduction of cheap bicycles, and the placing of the wheel within reach of everybody . . . Bicycling became unfashionable."[69] To put it another way, not only were bicycles seen as "unfashionable," but they had also ceased to be a status symbol.

While bicycles had declined drastically in price and were within the economic reach of most Americans, early automobiles were clearly a luxury item. In 1899, the average price of an automobile was a lofty $1,559. In 1906, the *Washington Post* reported, "Not more than one-hundredth of the people who formerly rode wheels can now afford automobiles."[70] In 1906, Woodrow Wilson, an avid cyclist who was then president of Princeton University, warned in a speech of spreading socialism due to the high prices of automobiles, "Nothing has spread socialistic feeling in this country more than the use of automobiles. To the countryman they are a picture of arrogance of wealth, with all its independence and carelessness."[71] Even Ford's Model T, which would later be renowned for bringing the automobile to the masses, was definitely a luxury item, as it sold for $850 when it was introduced in 1909.[72]

Contemporary cyclists drew similar connections with the changing social dynamics of bicycles. In 1899, the *Chicago Tribune* reported, "The first sign of the passing of the wheel as a fad was given by society. In 1896 and 1897, wheeling parties were well attended by society and cycling was the recreation for many society women. Now the wheel is dropped almost entirely by the society men and women and wheeling parties are things of the past. Golf, of course, has been responsible for a great deal of the falling off of the popularity of the bicycle among society people, but the cheapening of cycles also has been a cause."[73] The word "society" was used by the *Tribune* to refer to the white middle and upper classes who had taken to the bicycle. It wasn't the automobile that was the primary cause for the end of the bicycle boom, but rather the fickleness of the leisure class. When bicycles became accessible to everyone, those with financial means moved on to a variety of other pursuits that could better highlight their social status, including golf, motorcycles, automobiles, and airplanes.[74]

In terms of practical sources of transportation, the biggest new competitor to bicycles during the 1890s and early 1900s were electric streetcars, not automobiles. Chicago's first streetcars were installed in 1882, and by 1894 there were eighty-six miles of track in the city. By 1900, streetcar use had expanded around the country to the point where urban-dwelling Americans took an estimated five billion rides per year. By 1916, there were more than 15,000 miles of streetcar tracks around the country. For cyclists who used bicycles for transportation, the electric streetcar became an easy and inexpensive alternative to the bicycle and played a role in the end of the cycling boom.[75]

It should also be remembered that the turn-of-the-century automobile was far from universally embraced. In 1903, residents around Evanston, Illinois, banded together to form the Farmers' Anti-Automobile League. The focus of this league was on scorching automobile drivers, who were terrorizing horse-drawn carriages and wagons. The *Chicago Tribune* quoted one of the founding members, who declared, "We have decided that this scorching business must stop. We don't want to get into trouble, but we are going to use force if necessary. I carry a shotgun myself, and I know of others that do." The organization does appear to have engaged in some vigilante justice against automobiles in the rural areas surrounding Chicago. While never large in numbers, the organization did establish something of a nationwide presence through at least 1909.[76]

In the end, the rise of the automobile is only one part of a larger and more complex explanation for the end of the bicycle boom. Automobiles and motorcycles certainly caught American's attention, but they were both too expensive and too few in number around the turn of the century to topple the era of the bicycle on their own. Overproduction and the resulting glut of cheap bicycles led to the end of an era where the bicycle was a status symbol. Bicycling as a sport joined a well-established American pattern of intense fads followed by extreme busts.

America was not done with bicycles by any means. The bust at the beginning of the twentieth century was the worst in American bicycling history. The bicycle industry rebounded in the 1920s, but (despite later booms) never achieved quite the level of mass appeal as they did in the 1890s. If the boom-and-bust cycle was a recurring pattern in American bicycling history, so too was the ongoing role of Illinois in leading the nation in bicycle production and bicycle culture.

9

Booms and Busts

Illinois Bicycling in the Twentieth and Twenty-First Centuries

"Less gas, more ass" is a popular slogan used by cyclists who participate in Chicago's World Naked Bike Ride (WNBR). Held every June, the WNBR covers a fourteen-to-fifteen-mile route around downtown Chicago. Organizers say that, officially, the ride is "bare as you dare," since full nudity could still land you a public indecency fine. In this bicycling-related spectacle, Chicago once again was out front. The first Chicago WNBR was held in 2003, one year prior to the official organization of a series of naked bike rides around the world under the umbrella of WNBR. The WNBR is a form of peaceful protest, with nude or semi-nude riders demonstrating the vulnerability of bicyclists in an automobile-centric culture, raising awareness of climate change, and advocating for green transportation options and infrastructure. Over time, the events have spread to seventy cities in twenty different countries.

The nudity does seem to be effective in gaining media attention for the issues the protesters care about. Local newspapers and TV news channels routinely promote the event before it occurs and then run stories afterwards. The Chicago WNBR saw an estimated 4,000 participants on a particularly nice night in 2017. The riders took a leisurely cruise through the city at night, shouting, "Can you see me now?," "Nude not crude!," "Burns fat not oil!," and "Put some fun between your legs!"[1]

There is nothing in contemporary bicycle culture that stands in such stark contrast to the strict, puritanical standards of Victorian society that overlapped with the bicycle boom of the 1890s than the WNBR. Recall that in 1894, Chicagoan Hattie Strage was arrested and fined for disorderly conduct for the offense of riding down Dearborn Street in a sweater and tights. The tights were considered indecent. By contrast, in an official statement regarding the 2018 WNBR event, the Chicago Police Department stated, "The ride has

Poster for the 2013 Chicago World Naked Bike Ride. (Courtesy of Chris Lai.)

been taking place in Chicago for years, and the organizers work very closely with CPD to ensure a safe and orderly event." In the 1890s, Illinois women cyclists were routinely criticized and publicly ridiculed for simply wearing bloomers instead of the respectable Victorian corsets and skirts. To some twenty-first-century Chicagoans, the mass of naked riders participating in the WNBR has become commonplace enough not to merit a second glance. Still, WNBR participants must contend with sexist catcalls, unwanted filming, and aggressive drivers who try to assert their presumed automotive dominance over the cyclists.[2] Clearly, lack of fretting about bloomers does not equate to the arrival of the bicycling utopia that 1890s wheelers had envisioned.

Many bicyclists of that era had genuinely believed that bicycles were the answer to creating a more perfect society. "It is safe to say that few articles ever used by man have created so great a revolution in social conditions as the bicycle,"[3] the United States Census proclaimed in 1900. For bicycling's many advocates, bicycles were agents of progress. Chicago's *Inter Ocean* newspaper painted a Walt Whitman–like portrait of a city awheel:

> The boulevard is crowded with wheels, and their riders are from every walk and avocation of life. The merchant prince, the mistress of fashion, the minister of the gospel, the miller, the milliner, the butcher, the baker, and the candlestick-maker, roll along in one grand procession. Indifferent to all social and business distinctions, each feeling a fraternal interest in all the rest and each yielding a cheerful obedience to the code of ethics that governs the democracy of the wheel.[4]

As the preceding chapters have shown, the utopian vision of bicycles so frequently expressed in the 1890s had profound limits. More specifically, it was overwhelmingly a middle- and upper-class white male vision of cycling. Cycling reinforced restrictive gender norms far more often than it challenged them. In some respects, these cultural and political limitations have remained. At the same time, the dream of a bicycle democracy has evolved in ways that inspire hope. The history of Illinois cycling since the 1890s boom is a story of both dynamics.

This concluding chapter considers the next one hundred years (1920–2023) of Illinois cycling history. This book has established that the 1890s boom was foundational for all subsequent bicycling history. That era continues to shape the modern bicycling economy and culture alike. Its legacy is striking, not least because, for much of the twentieth century, there was simply less Illinois bicycle history being made than during the 1890s. For decades, fewer Illinoisans (per capita) were riding, and fewer bicycles were being manufactured in the state. Bicycle infrastructure vanished to the point where it had to be recreated almost from scratch a century later. Bicycling and bicycle culture followed a now familiar boom-and-bust cycle. Throughout the twentieth century, the majority of American-made bicycles were still produced in Illinois by Chicago's Schwinn Bicycle Company. That story has been expertly told by other bicycle historians.[5] Through it all, then, Illinois remained central to the American bicycle booms and busts, the dreams voiced and dreams deferred, that characterized the last 125 years.

Booms and Busts in the Bicycle Industry

Frank V. Schwinn, the grandson of Schwinn's founder, Ignaz Schwinn, and third-generation president of the company, once remarked that the difference between a good year for bicycle sales and a poor one was "how many days of rain we get in April."[6] While most likely uttered in exasperation, Schwinn's comment expressed a common lament among American bicycle manufacturers about the industry's extreme lack of consistency. From the very beginning, American bicycling has been characterized by dramatic fluctuations in interest and demand. The first velocipede craze was intense but fizzled out in two years. Interest in bicycling slowly re-grew over the 1870s and 1880s until it exploded during the 1890s. The bust that followed nearly wiped out the United States bicycle industry. In 1909, the bicycle industry hit its lowest point with only 169,000 bicycles produced nationwide, with the majority of these being produced by Schwinn.[7]

Schwinn, Mead, Sears, and Ward dominated the United States bicycle industry in the early decades of the twentieth century. Prior to World War I, 35 to 75 percent of Schwinn's sales came from Sears. In the 1920s, one-third of all Schwinns sold went to Montgomery Ward. Schwinn also began supplying bicycles to the Chicago-based Mead Cycle Company, the only other large-scale Illinois bicycle manufacturer that survived from the 1890s. During World War I, Schwinn factories assisted the war efforts by manufacturing plane motors, bomber plane parts, and other items needed by the United States military.[8] Sears and Ward continued to sell massive quantities of bicycles through their catalogs but outsourced manufacturing to other bicycle companies.

The economic fallout from World War I and then the Great Depression, coupled with sustained interest in automobiles, kept United States bicycle production below 500,000 until 1935. Led by Schwinn designers, the development of more durable and comfortable "balloon" tire bicycles helped to create a new children's and teens' market that began to bolster the bicycle industry. Despite decent sales, Schwinn closed their Excelsior-Henderson motorcycle division in 1931 to refocus on bicycles. Schwinn's Aerocycle, Cycleplane, and Motorbike models took design cues from the airplanes and motorcycles of the day and were exceedingly popular with children and teens. For a time, children's bike sales accounted for more than 80 percent of the total market. During the 1930s, Schwinn also moved away from selling to mail-order companies and department stores in favor of selling in bicycle shops.

The decade also saw the creation of Monark Silver King, Inc., the first new large bicycle manufacturer to arise in Illinois since the 1890s. Part of what distinguished Monark was its innovative use of aluminum. Formed in 1934, the company had no relationship to the 1890s Chicago Monar*ch* bicycle brand or the Swedish bicycle company of the same name. George Strong Lewis got his start in the bicycle industry working for the Mead Cycle Company but had larger ambitions of his own. In the early 1930s, he was working on prototypes for an aluminum-frame bicycle. In a familiar Midwest industrial story, Chicago's Monark Battery Company was looking to diversify by branching out into bicycle manufacturing. The Battery Company soon hired Lewis and put him in charge of the new Monark Silver King bicycle company. Monark produced some steel-framed bikes that were near-clones of Schwinn's designs, but it was Monark's aluminum Silver King models that really made a splash in the bicycle market, with company advertisements dubbing it "The Bicycle of Tomorrow." Aluminum was lighter and stronger than steel and had the additional allure of looking like the airplanes of the 1930s. The highly polished and stylized Silver Kings were a hit, and Monark quickly carved out 7 percent of the national market in its first few years. It did not hurt that Montgomery Ward contracted for a large number of aluminum bicycles to be produced under their Hawthorne brand.[9]

Meanwhile, another Illinois company was producing what it called "A New Kind of 'Bike.'" Brothers Phillip and Prescott Huyssen were inspired by the homemade scooters that they saw Chicago children cobbling together during the Great Depression. The brothers, however, put a unique twist on traditional scooter design when they designed a rear wheel with an eccentric (off-center) hub. They called the new contraption an Ingo. Instead of creating forward motion by pushing on the ground with your foot, Ingo riders pulled on the handlebars and bent slightly up and down at the knees in a bobbing motion to move forward. The brothers applied for a patent in 1934 and received it in 1938 (United States Patent 2,125,568). They worked with the Ingersoll Division of Rockford-based industrial manufacturer Borg-Warner to produce the scooters. A 1934 catalog descried the Ingo as a "'Bike' That Has Everything Except Pedals, Chain, and Sprocket."

Although quirky in design, the Ingo was quite functional. To drive home that point, Phillip Huyssen once "rode" an Ingo from Chicago to Miami over the course of twelve days in 1935. The Ingo gained national attention when Hollywood took interest in the scooters. Starlets, including Jean Chatburn,

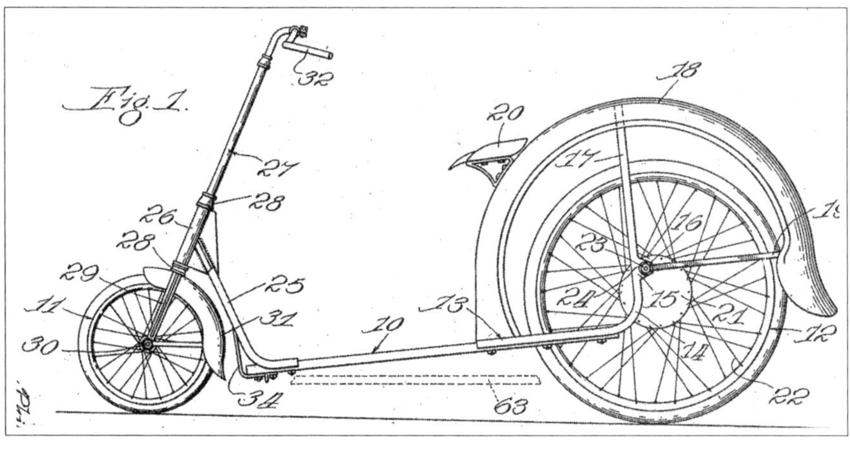

1938 Ingo Patent drawing. (US Patent Office.)

Eleanor Stewart, Maxine Doyle, and Rita Hayworth, were all pictured riding Ingos, and an Ingo was featured in a 1939 Three Stooges episode. Unfortunately, the Ingo craze was brief, and they were only produced from 1934 to 1937.[10]

The bicycle industry revived somewhat during the latter years of the Great Depression. The low price point of bicycles, which had contributed to the end of the 1890s boom, now assisted sales. So did shifting fashions. In 1937, United States bicycle production finally exceeded the highwater mark of the late 1890s, as 1.13 million bicycles were produced. Of these, more than 200,000 were Schwinns. Even accounting for the fact that the country's population had nearly doubled in size over the intervening decades, the bicycle industry had entered a new boom period. A *Popular Science* article titled "Bicycle Comes Back" attributed some portion of the boom to Hollywood stars embracing bicycles. Led by Hollywood, public perceptions of bicycle riding began to shift, and in 1936 an estimated four million Americans were again riding bicycles. This number finally approached the peak cycling participation of the 1890s, which was estimated to have been between four and five million. In 1938, a perceptive entrepreneur opened a bicycle parking lot across from Chicago's Lane Tech High School. For two cents a day, students could leave their bikes under the watchful eye of a guard. During good weather, more than 1,000 students a day took advantage of this service. At the University of Illinois, undergraduate students could not bring automobiles to campus, leading to a surge in bicycle riding. At the time, there were an estimated 1,000 bicycles and many Ingos on campus.[11]

Ironically, the recovery of the American economy did not immediately help the bicycle industry. While the economy as a whole grew during World War II, the bicycle boom of the late 1930s foundered as the War Production Board began rationing industrial use of metals and rubber. From 1942 to 1944, the War Production Board halted the production of all children's bicycles while concurrently establishing bicycle manufacturing quotas for both civilian and military use. Some bicycle manufacturers, such as Schwinn, were required to cease production of bicycles and instead contribute to manufacturing military equipment. During the war, Schwinn would manufacture 217 different items for the United States military, including shells, munitions parts, airplane parts, ship parts, gun mounts, and communication devices. Monark, likewise, was tapped to produce radar and other electronic equipment in its factory. For Schwinn's war efforts, it received the prestigious Army-Navy "E" award. At the award ceremony, a Navy commander commended Schwinn, stating, "Not only have you consistently met or anticipated your delivery schedules, but you have kept up a high standard of quality that resulted in a need for rejecting less than 1 percent of your production. That makes you practically perfect."[12]

Ignaz Schwinn's obsession with quality engineering and precise machining clearly extended to more than just bicycles.

Amid these wartime conversion directives, the War Production Board did recognize bicycles as essential transportation, since they helped conserve gasoline and required far less metal and rubber than automobiles. Other manufacturers were allowed to produce a certain number of "Victory Bikes." Like their better-known counterpart, Victory Gardens, Victory Bikes were part of a patriotic effort on the home front to support war efforts. Specifications were drawn up to build lightweight bicycles that conserved steel, nickel, and rubber. In 1943, two approved Victory Bike manufacturers produced 154,000 bicycles. Of those, 73,000 were sold to civilians, while the rest went to military personnel.[13]

Victory Bikes and government control of the United States bicycle industry likely contributed little to the overall war efforts, but they did link bicycle riding with patriotism. In Chicago, bicycle ridership and sales quadrupled in 1942, leading the *Chicago Daily Tribune* to declare, "Previously accepted as a child's plaything or an exercise device for fresh air enthusiasts, the bicycle is expected to come into its own as a result of conversion of the auto industry to war production and the severe rationing of tires." Due to increased bicycle traffic, the *New York Times* suggested that some streets in Rockford, Illinois, should "be reserved for bicycle traffic during specified hours every day."[14]

At the end of World War II, pent-up demand, renewed patriotic interest in bicycling, increases in disposable income, and a strong children's market all contributed to ignite the next American bicycle boom. In 1947, 2.8 million bicycles were sold in the United States, drastically eclipsing all previous records. One in every four bicycles sold was a Schwinn. Schwinn sales received a boost from Whizzer engines, which converted a bicycle into a 125-miles-per-gallon motorcycle. The engines claimed a universal fit but were most easily mounted to many Schwinn frames. In 1948, for the first time in company history, Schwinn stopped producing bicycles for other companies to sell under their own brand name. That year also marked the passing of Ignaz Schwinn.

Predictably, this boom was not meant to last. As would later happen to American automobile companies, United States bicycle manufacturers faced new competition from the foreign countries that the United States government was helping to recover after World War II. In 1953, Gabriel Hauge, President Eisenhower's economic advisor, communicated a message from the president to the American Bicycle Manufacturers Association. To assist in our ally's economic recovery, import duties on British bicycles were to be cut from 30 to 7.5 percent. Despite the American bicycle industry's substantial contributions to the war effort, they were undercut by the executive branch. "The President believes you can do other things," Hauge bluntly stated. "You are expendable." For the first time since the high-wheel era, imports began to make up a significant portion of the American bicycle market. Domestic bicycle sales were cut in half in a single year. In 1947, 25,000 bicycles were imported to the United States, and by 1954, that number had skyrocketed to 850,000, many now coming from Britain. This trend would continue to grow in the following decades until imports eventually came to dominate the American bicycle market.[15]

The 1950s marked the end of the road for both Mead and Monark. In 1944, Mead had been sold to bicycle shop owner James Lynch, who operated the company on a far smaller scale than in its heyday. Lynch sold Mead in 1954, but the company never resurfaced after the sale. Monark was bought out in 1957 by the Huffman Manufacturing Company based in Dayton, Ohio.

Schwinn was then left as the only sizable bicycle manufacturer in Illinois. It continued to thrive, in part by pulling their bikes out of department stores and instead only selling bicycles through authorized dealers—a new concept at the time. The move to the authorized dealer network allowed Schwinn to better control prices, marketing, and post-sale bicycle service. Regular advertising plugs from *Captain Kangaroo*, along with sales from the extremely popular Schwinn Black Phantom, helped Schwinn retain 25 percent of the United States market in the 1950s.[16]

Bicycle sales, both import and domestic, climbed steadily throughout the 1960s. The Bicycle Manufacturers Association of America estimated the total domestic sales for 1960 at 2.6 million. Although light on methodological details, the association also estimated that there were 23.5 million bicycles in use, spread across 35.2 million riders.[17]

Schwinn continued a pattern of innovation that left the rest of the American bicycle industry to play catch-up. In 1960, they introduced two "lightweight" road bikes, the Varsity and Continental. Although not an immediate hit, their time was coming. Also in the early 1960s, a Schwinn employee reported that kids in Southern California were taking bicycles with small twenty-inch wheels and adding polo seats and huge handlebars to them, mimicking the popular chopper-style of motorcycle. Schwinn took a chance on this new style of bicycle and created the Sting-Ray in 1963. Despite some skepticism from Schwinn management, the initial production run of 45,000 Sting-Rays sold out in a matter of months. Schwinn had a new hit model. It would go on to sell an astounding two million Sting-Rays between 1963 and 1968. As other manufacturers scrambled to produce knockoffs, Schwinn Sting-Rays made up 60 percent of all American bicycle sales. Powered by the Sting-Ray, Schwinn set a new record by selling more than one million bicycles in 1968.[18]

The 1960s also saw the emergence of the first new major bicycle manufacturer in Illinois since Monark. The roots of the American Machine and

Foundry Co., or AMF, date back to 1900, when the company made automatic cigarette manufacturing machines and automatic bowling pinsetters. Looking to diversify its manufacturing base, AMF purchased rights to well-known Roadmaster bicycles from the Cleveland Welding Company in 1950. The AMF Roadmasters were first manufactured in Hammond, Indiana, but AMF moved operations to the southern Illinois town of Olney in 1962. Large-scale manufacturing in major urban centers had become prohibitively expensive, so AMF welcomed the opportunity to build a new factory on 122 acres that were provided free of charge by the Olney Chamber of Commerce. The new 420,000-square-foot factory cost $5 million to build and featured two miles of automatic overhead conveyors. Unlike Schwinn, AMF focused on building the cheapest bikes possible to compete with the influx of similarly cheap imports. For a time, AMF would find great success with this business model.[19]

If the 1960s saw steady growth in bicycle sales, then the early 1970s saw an outright boom. In 1970, a *Time Magazine* article proclaimed that bicycling was experiencing its "biggest wave of popularity in its 154-year history." They weren't wrong. From 1960 to 1970, total United States bicycle sales had averaged around five million. From 1971 to 1974, sales skyrocketed to between fourteen and fifteen million annually. In 1972, more bicycles were sold than cars for the first time since the early years of the twentieth century. That year, a federal report estimated that there were eighty-five million cyclists in the country, constituting one out of every two people between the ages of seven and sixty-nine. If these figures were accurate, more than 42 percent of the total population rode a bicycle at least occasionally. For the first time since the 1890s, women began riding in substantial numbers. In 1971, the boom caused Schwinn to sell out all its year's supply of 1.2 million bicycles by May. In 1974, they sold a record 1.5 million bicycles. On the University of Illinois campus in Champaign-Urbana, throngs of bicycle-riding college students caused pedestrians to wait up to fifteen minutes to cross some busy streets.[20]

Not only were far more Americans riding, the demographics of those riders had also shifted radically. The great majority of bicycles sold in the 1950s and 1960s were juvenile bicycles, mostly made by Schwinn. By 1971, the trend had completely reversed itself, with adult lightweight bicycles now accounting for a strong majority of sales. By 1974, 75 percent of bicycles being sold were adult bicycles. Schwinn's Varsity model road bicycles sold very well, but the company had a hard time moving beyond the child/teen market that had been their bread and butter for the past few decades. Schwinn could not meet the surging demand for bicycles that forced Schwinn dealers to import high-quality European and Asian ten-speeds with names like Cinelli, Raleigh, Peugeot, Nishiki, and Motobecane. In 1972, Schwinn did what was previously unthinkable and began importing European bicycles to sell under its own name. By 1975, 200,000 out of 900,000 bicycles sold by Schwinn were imported from Europe and Japan. Schwinn was following an outsourcing pattern familiar to many of the other Midwest manufacturing companies, hastening the formation of the industrial "rust belt."[21]

The 1970s boom was rooted in a blend of lifestyle preferences and evolving socio-political priorities. In a 1973 *National Geographic* article titled "Bikes Are Back—and Booming," Noel Grove laid out what he saw as the main factors contributing to the boom: "Glutted roadways, ecological concern, the quest for healthful recreation, and the sophistication of geared machines have all contributed to a flood of cycling activity." In hindsight, Grove's analysis was spot-on. The first Earth Day occurred in 1970, fueled by the counterculture movements of the 1960s. The Arab oil embargo began in 1973 and quickly led to extreme price increases in gasoline, federal rationing, and lowering of speed limits. Americans were beginning to wake up to the problematic environmental and health impacts of a car-centric culture and turned again to bikes as a solution.

In 1970, a group of Chicago cyclists organized Bicycle Ecology, likely the country's first major organization to link bicycling with environmental issues. In an era of successful "sit-ins" to raise awareness about social issues, Bicycle Ecology organized a "pedal-in" in October of 1970. An estimated 1,500 to 2,000 riders took part in the pedal-in, setting the stage for the critical mass bicycle movement of the 1990s and 2000s.[22]

The 1970s also saw a surge of interest—primarily among the baby boom generation—in improving physical fitness. Jogging and bicycling to improve one's health became popular pastimes and further contributed to the bicycle boom. Lastly, advances in bicycle design also played a role in this boom. Beginning in the mid-1960s, ten-speed bicycles became increasingly popular. Prior to the ten-speed, most bicycles sold in the United States were heavy, single-speed models with a coaster brake. By contrast, the new ten-speeds were far lighter and could easily cover a variety of terrain thanks to their gearing system. For a few years in the early seventies, baby boomers who had grown up riding balloon-tired cruisers and high-rise-style bikes moved on to ten-speeds en masse.

AMF's investment in their bicycle division in Olney had come along at just the right time. AMF was selling more than a million of their cheap ten-speed Roadmaster bicycles during the peak of the 1970s bicycle boom. Two major German bicycle parts manufacturers, Union Frondenberg and Weinmann, followed AMF's lead and built large manufacturing facilities in Olney. In 1979, the Japan-based KHS bicycles also opened a bicycle factory in Olney.[23]

The "invention" of the mountain bike in the 1970s depended upon modified Chicago Schwinns. In the mid-seventies, a small group of Southern California off-road cycling enthusiasts, led by Joe Breeze and Gary Fisher, began heavily modifying old bicycles, usually Schwinns. In *Fat Tire Flyer: Repack and the Birth of Mountain Biking*, author and mountain bike pioneer Charlie Kelley explains, "The ideal Marin County Klunker started with a Motobike frame manufactured by Schwinn in the '30s. . . . These frames were tough and elegant and had the high bottom bracket and handling characteristics necessary for our use."[24] Eventually, Breeze and Fisher began to create their own mountain-bike frames, setting up the next significant evolution of the bicycle.

Like all the previous booms, the level of interest in bicycling seen in the early seventies did not last. By as early as 1975, bicycle sales had decreased by 50 percent. Many bicycle shops around the country closed. A Schwinn executive reported that "dealers were saying, stop, we can't take it anymore. For the next few years, the mindset of the bike industry was that it would come back. Well, it didn't."[25]

While total United States bicycle sales wouldn't reach the numbers seen in the early 1970s until the early 1990s, two new developments in bicycle design prevented the bicycle market from completely bottoming out. Both involved bicycles designed to go off-road. First, BMX bicycles became popular with children and teens in the late 1970s and early 1980s. As soon as the BMX fad began to wane, it was replaced by ever-increasing mountain bike sales in the 1980s and 1990s. In the mid-1980s, 60 percent of bicycles being sold were mountain bikes. Neither BMX nor mountain bike sales ever triggered a boom, but they were enough to sustain the industry.[26]

Schwinn had built its reputation on innovation and quality, but by the 1980s, both of these features were slipping. The dominant force in American bicycling for most of the twentieth century owned only 15 percent of the market in 1980. By 1983, Schwinn was forced to close its storied Chicago factory. The company had played the wait-and-see game with both BMX and mountain bikes and missed critical sales as a result. Schwinn's first chromoly mountain bikes were introduced in 1984 and won races beneath mountain bike legend Ned Overend. They sold well, but unfortunately, Schwinn had outsourced the manufacturing of these bikes to a rival manufacturer, Giant. Schwinn's saving grace during the 1980s was the hugely popular Schwinn Air-Dyne exercise bike, which leveraged Americans newfound fascination with physical fitness and managed to gross up to $25 million per year.

As Schwinn's star was waning, the next big Illinois bicycling industry giant was just getting its start. Stan Day graduated from Northwestern University's Kellogg School of Management in 1984. In 1986, he was training for a triathlon on Chicago's rough streets and had an idea for a new shifting system that wouldn't require taking your hands off the handlebars to reach down-tube shifters. After designing and prototyping with friends Scott King and Sam

Patterson, Grip Shift was invented. The novel, and mechanically simple, twist-shift design relocated bicycle shifting to the handlebars. A company name was needed to promote the new shifter, and SRAM was settled on through creative use of the founders' names: **S**cott King, Stan **RA**y Day, Sa**M** Patterson. In 1987 SRAM was officially incorporated in Chicago. The fledgling company got an early boost when Illinois-born cyclist Bob Mionske used a Grip Shift system en route to a fourth-place finish at the 1988 Olympic road race in Seoul, Korea. A few weeks later, another major success came when American Scott Molina won the Ironman World Championship using the Grip Shift system. Early Grip Shift manufacturing took place in Chicago but was soon outsourced to Taiwan.

In another important evolution for the American bicycle industry, SRAM filed an antitrust lawsuit against the component manufacturing giant Shimano. The essence of the case was that Shimano penalized bicycle manufacturers and shops that wanted to purchase individual bicycle components rather than a complete set of Shimano parts. Shimano settled with SRAM in 1990 and modified its practices, opening up the component market for SRAM and others. SRAM was on the rise.[27]

Schwinn, by contrast, continued to decline. The company closed its last remaining manufacturing facility in Greenville, Mississippi, in 1991. Its market share had fallen to a dismal 7 percent that year. Schwinn filed for bankruptcy in 1992, three years short of what would have been their one-hundredth anniversary. Competitor Scott Sports Group purchased Schwinn's naming rights and assets and promptly relocated all operations to Boulder, Colorado, thus ending the Illinois heritage of America's most famous bicycle brand.

The 1990s, and the continued shift to cheap foreign bicycles, likewise were hard for AMF's bicycle division. Ironically, AMF/Roadmaster, which focused on producing the cheapest bicycles possible, purchased the legendary Columbia Manufacturing plant in Westfield, Massachusetts, in 1990. The remnants of the company that built the American bicycle industry were sold on the cheap, only for the purchaser to discover that the environmental contamination at the site was too severe for continued operation. The Environmental Protection Agency eventually razed the original factory. Despite excellent sales of Roadmaster mountain bikes in the mid-1990s, the Roadmaster division was sold in 1997 to the Brunswick Corporation, which turned around and sold it to Pacific Cycle. Under Pacific Cycle, manufacturing in Olney ceased, with the factory turned into a warehouse for cheap, low-quality, imported bicycles from Taiwan and China. The end of AMF/Roadmaster manufacturing marked the demise of large-scale bicycle manufacturing in Illinois.[28]

While Illinois bicycle manufacturers struggled in the 1990s, SRAM continued to innovate and grow. In the early 1990s, up-and-coming companies

Trek and Specialized decided to spec Grip Shift on some of their bicycles. In 1992, SRAM sold 300,000 Grip Shift sets, a number that rocketed up to 8.6 million by 1996. SRAM brought their first rear derailleur to market in 1995. The company continued their upward trajectory by acquiring the venerable German bicycle component maker Sachs in 1997. Strategic acquisitions would become part of SRAM's business model in the following years.[29]

The ever-volatile American bicycle industry found a period of relative stability in the early 2000s through 2020. The biggest disruptor was the rise of e-commerce platforms that eroded sales of bicycles and bicycle accessories at traditional specialty bike stores. These specialty bike stores (as opposed to a department or sporting goods store) decreased from around 6,200 in 2000 to 3,800 in 2015. Where people were purchasing bicycles was changing, but the total value of bicycle sales over the same period remained consistent at $5 to $6 billion annually. The trend away from domestic production continued. Bicycles imported from Asia now comprise almost 99 percent of the market.

There was also good news about cycling participation in the first two decades of the twenty-first century. The bicycle advocacy group PeopleForBikes pioneered a new methodology to quantify bicycle riding in the United States. In 2014, they estimated that more than one hundred million Americans (or 34 percent of the population) rode a bicycle at least once in the past year. The League of American Bicyclists found that from 2000 to 2012, bicycle commuting rose 61 percent.[30]

In terms of national and international significance, SRAM was now single-handedly keeping the heritage of the Illinois bicycle industry on the map. In order to expand its offerings beyond shifters and derailleurs, SRAM continued to acquire more companies. In 2002, they acquired bicycle suspension leader RockShox, and then two years later added both bicycle brake specialist Avid and drivetrain manufacturer Truvativ. With these additions, SRAM was able to bring three full road component groups (Rival, Force, Red) to the market by 2007. These groupsets featured an innovative "double-tap" shifting system, and the Force/Red groups were lighter than anything else on the market. SRAM components were soon being used by top road, mountain, and cyclocross professionals. In the 2009 Tour de France, the top three riders all used SRAM components.

SRAM continued a successful pattern of innovation and acquisition. The company single-handedly did away with the need for front derailleurs on mountain bikes when they introduced a wide gear range 1X11 drivetrain in 2012. This technology was quickly applied to road and cyclocross drivetrains. In 2015, in another industry first, SRAM debuted a fully wireless road-shifting groupset. This wireless technology would be applied to SRAM mountain groupsets in 2019. By 2022, SRAM employed more than 3,200 people across its divisions and saw a revenue of over one billion dollars. SRAM remains headquartered in Chicago, with most of the company's manufacturing taking place overseas. Having perhaps learned something from Schwinn's missteps, SRAM continues to drive innovation in the bicycle component market.[31]

While the period from 1975 and 2020 was the most stable era in United States bicycle industry history, the COVID-19 pandemic saw a reversion to the boom-bust cycle. As the pandemic spread and social distancing was recommended (and often enforced), people looked to a variety of outdoor activities for socializing and stress relief. Bicycle commuting rose drastically as an alternative to crowded public transportation options. A bicycle boom was inevitable. From mid-2020 to mid-2021, overall bicycle sales jumped a massive 65 percent. Some bicycle shops were nearly empty, and supply-chain disruptions meant that new inventory was nearly impossible to come by. In the summer of 2020, Mike Welte, owner of Bike Works in Peru, Illinois, reported, "We have sold almost all of our new bikes and would be able to sell more if we could get them. We do have over one hundred bikes on order and already over half have names on them ready to pick up when they come in." PeopleForBikes found that American bicycle ridership had increased to 108 million during the pandemic. In absolute terms, that represented a new record for the total number of American bicyclists; however, there were a few more riders per capita during the boom of the 1970s.[32]

Of course, a global pandemic couldn't be expected to prop up bicycle sales indefinitely. In the later years of the bicycle boom of the 1890s, overproduction saturated the bicycle market just as demand fell off a cliff. Similarly, in late 2022 and 2023, manufacturers of bicycles and bicycle accessories scrambled to ramp up production to fill empty shops just as the pandemic came under control and bicycle demand dried up. In the spring of 2023, *Bicycle Retailer and Industry News* wrote, "Let's face it. The first couple months of 2023 were some of the worst the industry has seen in years, if not ever. Sales were down, inventory was up, and even heavily discounted product wasn't moving off retailers' floors."[33] The boom-and-bust pattern of the United States bicycle industry had repeated itself once again.

What remains in 2023 of the once-great Illinois bicycle manufacturing heritage? As noted above, nearly all the bicycles sold in the United States are now imported. In the last two decades, however, there has been a resurgence of interest in high-quality, handmade American bicycles. Handmade bicycles can be custom-made for a rider or built in stock sizes. Steel is the building material of choice, but handmade builders also work in aluminum, carbon, titanium, wood, and bamboo. Illinois bicycle builders have embraced the handmade trend. Handmade bicycles can currently be purchased from the following Illinois companies: Heritage, Humble Frameworks, Legacy Frameworks,

Method Built, Pachyderm Bikes, Patton Frames, RRB Cycles, Wan Gerin, and Wiseman Frameworks.[34]

Despite the effective end of Illinois bicycle manufacturing, economic connections to that history endure. Manufacturing has moved out of Olney, Illinois, but the former factories there are now important distribution hubs for the bicycle industry. Pacific Cycle owns the old AMF/Roadmaster facility and uses it to distribute cheap Asian-made Schwinn and Mongoose bicycles to Amazon, Walmart, Target, and Dick's Sporting Goods. The Roadmaster bicycle trademark is also owned by Pacific Cycle and sold exclusively through Walmart. Highway Two is another major distributor for the American bicycle industry. The company is headquartered in California but has a major warehouse in Olney for distributing top bicycle brands, including Abus, Brooks, Crankbrothers, Continental, Fizik, Knog, and Selle Royal. In Elgin, Taiwan-based Giant Bicycles has also maintained one of the largest distribution centers (180,000 square feet) in the United States. During the 2000s, BRG Sports in Rantoul, Illinois, produced up to 4.5 million Bell, Giro, and Blackburn bicycle helmets, which accounted for 42 percent of the global helmet market. The factory also assembles 100,000 child bicycle seats and 70,000 bicycle car racks annually.[35]

Material culture connections to Illinois's bicycle industry endure as well, not least in the state's large number of historically significant bicycle-related buildings, many of which date back to the nineteenth century. A partial list of surviving buildings in Chicago includes Schwinn's earliest factory at the corner of Lake and Peoria Streets, currently home to the Lake Street Lofts. Another Schwinn factory, located on North Kostner Avenue in Chicago's Hermosa neighborhood, is the current home of Right Bee Cider. Although Ignaz Schwinn's elaborate Palmer Square mansion is long gone, the nearby Shakespeare Apartment building he constructed for his employees has survived. Also, the 1904 Gothic and Moorish revival mansion of Schwinn cofounder Adolph Arnold is still standing (barely) and was listed as one of Illinois's most endangered landmarks in 2015.[36]

After Western Wheel Works went under in the early 1900s, its massive factory on Wells Street was purchased by the Dr. Scholl's company, which utilized the space through 1981. After extensive renovations, the factory was converted into upscale apartments known as Cobbler Square Lofts. Gormully & Jeffery's 1888 factory building has survived and currently houses office spaces at 213 West Institute Place in Chicago's River North neighborhood. The 1884 home of company founder R. Philip Gormully still stands in the Gold Coast neighborhood at 1245 N. Dearborn Street.[37]

The Mead Bicycle Company used many different buildings in Chicago for manufacturing, warehousing, and sales. Their six-story building at 168 North Clinton Street, used for general offices and manufacturing in the 1910s and

1920s, is still in use today. The 75,000-square-foot Monark Silver King factory that features a six-story tower remains at 1240 North Homan Avenue.[38]

Belgian frame-builder Emil Wastyn opened his bike shop in Chicago in 1910. The business has been handed down through generations of Wastyns including Oscar Wastyn Sr., Oscar Wastyn Jr., and now Scott Wastyn. Today, Oscar Wastyn Cycles remains in business at 2634 West Fullerton Avenue and is one of the oldest continually operating bicycle shops in the country. The shop features a bicycle museum that highlights both Wastyn and Chicago bicycle history. The Century Road Club of America, founded in Chicago in 1891, still organizes races and group rides in New Jersey.

Incredibly, a few sections of the wood-block Nicolson pavement that helped launch Chicago's nineteenth-century bicycle boom have remained in service all these years. One section is part of an alley off West Roscoe Street near Lake Shore Drive, and another restored section is behind the Archbishop of Chicago's mansion on North State Parkway. Far more sections still exist beneath Chicago's concrete and asphalt streets.[39]

If you know where to look, additional remnants of Illinois's bicycle heritage can be found scattered throughout the state. The Rockford Watch Company capitalized on the bicycle boom for a brief period when it built bicycles at a huge factory on 325 S. Madison Street. The dilapidated building still stands in 2024, and the city is seeking a developer to refurbish the space. The nearby Belvidere factory of the National Sewing Machine Company, which made the very popular Eldredge model bicycle, was not so fortunate, as the building was razed in 2021. (Intriguingly, fans of Eldredge bicycles in faraway Tonawanda, New York, formed the Eldredge Bicycle Club in 1898 and the club is still thriving today.) Portions of the original Stover Bicycle Manufacturing Company factory in Freeport have been incorporated into the current Honeywell Plant 1, directly east of the Pecatonica River.[40]

In Illinois during the 1890s, Peoria was second only to Chicago when it came to bicycle manufacturing. In Peoria Heights, the Rouse & Hazard bicycle factory, built in 1895, is currently occupied by Trefzger's Bakery, which dates back to 1861. A couple of Rouse & Hazard bicycles are on display in the bakery. Rouse & Hazard's large warehouse and showroom, located at the corner of Harrison and Adams Street in downtown Peoria, is currently seeking new tenants. Peoria's Illinois Cycle & Fitness bike shop is still in operation and traces its earliest roots back to Rouse & Hazard in the 1870s.[41]

The Enduring Popularity of Bicycle Racing

While the 1890s were the heyday of American bicycle racing, the sport saw booms and busts that were roughly aligned with the industry as a whole. In

1946 program for the 45th International Six-Day Race at the Chicago Coliseum. (Author's collection.)

1902, bicycle racer Dottie Farnsworth died of injuries from a bicycling-related accident. Cycling was already on the wane at the time, and the League of American Wheelmen, which had long been opposed to women racing bicycles, banned women's competitions altogether. Women's bicycle races of any substantial size would not return until the 1970s.[42]

Even though the United States bicycle industry was in a downturn during the 1920s and early 1930s, six-day racing grew in popularity. In 1926, *Popular Mechanics* wrote, "The mad moments of a cycling jam have kept bicycle racing alive years after the majority of the people have given up the sport. They bring out thousands in New York and Chicago every winter to sit through days and nights of the 144-hour races, watching hour after hour of listless pedaling to await the few brief moments of sprinting or lap stealing." During sprints, the racers flew around the steeply banked tracks at speeds of up to 40 mph. During this era, six-hundred American riders called themselves professionals. Chicago held one or two premier six-day races nearly every year between 1915 and 1957. The Chicago Stadium on West Madison Street and the Chicago Coliseum on Wabash Avenue were two of the most popular venues in the country for six-day races, regularly hosting the Six Days of Chicago and other six-day races. Outdoor track racing got a boost when the Humboldt Park velodrome was built in 1928.[43]

Six-day racing became a highly lucrative endeavor for both racers and promoters. In the early decades of the twentieth century, it was estimated that a million spectators paid more than a million dollars annually to attend six-day races. Good racers were making up to $15,000 per year, and the best racers cleared $100,000 (about $1.7 million in 2024) at a time when top NHL salaries were $7,500 and professional football players only made $5,000 per year. Drug use among racers was a common (and legal) practice. Over the course of six days of racing, trainers gave racers concoctions of caffeine, strychnine, and cocaine. The riders needed the drugs because six-day racing was a brutal sport. Not only did teams of two race for six days straight, but accidents were part of the spectacle. Bobby Walthour Sr., a top six-day and track racer in the early 1900s, accumulated forty-six collarbone fractures, thirty-two broken ribs, and sixty stitches over the course of his career. He was once mistaken for dead and taken to a Paris morgue. Reggie McNamara, an Australian cyclist from the same period, estimated that he survived 1,500 crashes in the course of riding 135,000 miles during the 108 six-day races he competed in.[44]

Betting on races and dangling substantial "primes" (pronounced *preems* after the French word for gift) for the tired cyclists attracted a veritable who's who of celebrities from the era. Ernest Hemingway wrote the end of *A Farewell to Arms* while attending a six-day race. Babe Ruth was a regular at Chicago six-day races and once paid for $700 worth of sprint primes in one night of racing. Actress Peggy Joyce outdid Ruth when she once offered a single $1,000 prime. Bing Crosby was known to pay the hospital bills of injured riders. Bob Hope, Jimmy Durante, and John Dos Passos could all be found at six-days. All the cash flowing through the Chicago six-day races also got the attention of the Chicago mafia. Although solid historical documentation is scarce—this is the mob, after all—Al Capone is known to have taken an interest in Chicago six-days. At first, Capone was just in on the betting, sometimes buying off racers to increase his winnings. Later, Capone was the financial backer for a new six-day race in Chicago that reportedly made $100,000. Capone sent his gang after the race organizer, who had to flee town hidden in a laundry basket.[45]

Although Illinois riders did not dominate six-day racing to the same extent that they did during the 1880s and 1890s, the state was still home to a number of top athletes. Carl Stockholm was born in Wisconsin but grew up in Illinois. While serving in the Army during World War I, he took friendly fire to his knee, and a doctor recommended bicycling for rehabilitation. It was a fortuitous recommendation, as Stockholm took to cycling, strengthened his knee, and qualified for the 1920 Olympics. He turned professional in 1922 and went on to finish more than twenty six-day races, including overall wins at the 1923 and 1927 Chicago six-days. Following his cycling career, Stockholm founded a successful chain of dry-cleaning businesses in Chicago that incorporated a bicycle into the company logo.[46]

William "Cecil" Yates was born in Texas but raised on Chicago's South Side. Yates turned professional in 1932 and specialized in six-day racing. Considered one of the best sprinters in the world, he managed to win nineteen out of the eighty-one six-day events he entered and finished on the podium a total of twenty-six times.[47]

In the early 1930s, another famous bicycle racer made his way back to Chicago, although his racing days were long past. Major Taylor had retired from his groundbreaking career in 1910 at age thirty-two. In 1928, Taylor wrote and self-published his autobiography, *The Fastest Bicycle Rider in the World: The Story of a Colored Boy's Indomitable Courage and Success Against Great Odds: An Autobiography*. Amid financial difficulties, Taylor split from his wife in 1930 and moved to Chicago to continue selling his autobiography. Plagued with heart problems, Taylor underwent surgery performed by pioneering Black heart surgeon Daniel Hale Williams at Provident Hospital. He survived the surgery but succumbed to his illnesses on June 21, 1932. Taylor's death went largely unnoticed in a city where the papers used to publish detailed accounts of his cycling exploits. Only the city's Black newspaper, the *Chicago Defender*, ran a story on Taylor's passing: "Major Taylor. Famous Bike Rider, Dies Penniless. Dies Here in Charity Ward." With no one claiming his remains, Taylor was buried in an unmarked pauper's grave in Mount Glenwood Cemetery. In 1948, Frank W. Schwinn provided funds to move Taylor's remains to a better location in the cemetery. A new plaque was also installed over his grave that reads, "World's champion bicycle racer who came up the hard way without hatred in his heart, an honest, courageous and God-fearing, clean-living gentlemanly athlete. A credit to his race who always gave out his best. Gone but not forgotten."[48]

Tillie "The Terrible Swede" Anderson also returned to Chicago a number of times, but under happier circumstances than Taylor. Tillie had wrapped up her racing career at the end of the nineteenth century but remained keenly interested in cycling throughout her life. In 1934, Tillie returned to Chicago to participate in the "Bicycle Day" that was part of the 1934 Century of Progress World's Fair. She apparently buried the hatchet with the L.A.W., as she also attended some of their reunions. In 1941, a new club called "Bicycle Racing Stars of the 19th Century" was formed in Chicago. Word went out in papers across the country seeking surviving racers from the heyday of bicycling. The men—they had neglected to reach out to any women riders—all gathered at a golf club near Northbrook to reminisce about their glory days. Tillie drove from her home in Minnesota and crashed the men's party. According to the *Chicago Tribune's* reporting on the event, when Tillie introduced herself, "a hush fell over the old-timers as one by one, they stepped forward to shake her hand and tell her how well she looked 'after all these years.'" It was clear that Tillie had not completely forgotten her poor treatment at the hands of many male cyclists in the 1890s; she gloated to a reporter that she was one of the few in attendance that had retained her racing figure over the years. Tillie died in 1965 and was inducted into the United States Bicycling Hall of Fame in 2000.[49]

American-made bicycles dominated domestic racing during the 1890s, but during the first decades of the twentieth century, racers gravitated toward European racing bicycles. The few surviving American companies, like Schwinn, focused on the children and teen markets. That all changed with the creation of the above-mentioned Schwinn Paramount chromoly bicycle in 1938. The roots of this storied racing bicycle actually date back to 1910, when a Belgian immigrant and frame builder, Emil Wastyn, opened his bicycle shop in Chicago. Emil's high-end racing frames were sought out by the Schwinn racing team. Along the way, Emil taught his son, Oscar Wastyn Sr., the craft of frame building. Emil built the first Schwinn Paramounts in his shop in the late 1930s, and Oscar took over following World War II. Paramounts got a publicity boost in 1939 when the six-day team of Bobby Thomas and Gustav Killian won the Buffalo six-day on Schwinn Paramounts. Their win marked the first time in thirty years that a six-day race was won using an American-made bicycle. The Schwinn-sponsored racer Alfred Letourner used a Paramount to set a new bicycle speed record. On May 17, 1941, Letourner rode his Paramount on a closed stretch of flat highway behind a race car equipped with a rear awning to shield him from the wind. The front chainring of Letourner's Paramount nearly touched the ground and yielded an absolutely massive 252 gear inches. The end result was a new bicycle speed record of 108.92 mph and tons of publicity for Schwinn.[50]

Outside of a handful of high-profile American six-day races, though, the epicenter of international bicycle racing had clearly shifted to Europe. In the 1920s and 1930s, few Americans attempted to race in the highly competitive European road race circuit. Still, a nearly forgotten Illinois rider named Joseph Magnani managed to break into the top ranks of European cycling during the late 1930s and early 1940s. Magnani was born into an Italian immigrant family and was raised in central Illinois. Due to family hardships, he was sent at age sixteen to live with relatives in the south of France. In his early twenties, Magnani began winning local amateur races and he was offered a professional contract with the Urago Cycles team in 1935. That year, he notched his first professional win at the prestigious Marseille–Nice race. In the next few years, Magnani backed up that performance with overall wins at Marseille–Toulon–Marseille, Circuit de Lourdes, Lyon–St. Etienne, and the Tour de Porto Allegre. Those were not the premier European races of the day, but Magnani also notched respectable finishes at classics, such as the Tour of Switzerland, Paris–Nice, and Milan–San Remo. Back home, writers at the *American Bicyclist*

Alfred Letourner was featured on the cover of a 1949 Schwinn comic book. (Author's collection.)

were dumbfounded at the reports of a successful American cyclist that were trickling in from Europe: "If anyone knows who he is or where he came from to represent America, we would like to hear about it."[51]

As an American in German-occupied France, Magnani was taken to a concentration camp, where his weight fell from 170 pounds to 98 pounds. After liberation in 1944, Magnani returned to racing and finished seventh overall in the 1947 World Championships in Reims, the best American finish in thirty-three years. In 1948, Magnani returned home to Illinois for the first time since he had left at age sixteen. After a brief stint as a six-day racer for Schwinn, he retired from racing and took a permanent position with the company assembling Schwinn Paramounts. He went on to spend some time coaching other cyclists, including his son Rudy.[52]

The next major racing event to occur in Illinois was the third Pan American Games, which were held at Soldier Field in the fall of 1959. Former star cyclist Carl Stockholm served as chairman of the games. The Pan Am games featured three cycling track events and a road race. Chicagoan James (Jim) Rossi took home a gold medal in the 4,000-meter team pursuit event. Rossi followed up that performance with a silver medal in the 1,000-meter match sprint at the 1963 Pan Am games in São Paulo, Brazil. Rossi competed in the 1956 and

1960 Olympics, and he also amassed six national titles over the course of his career.[53] In 1960, the Ed Rudolph Velodrome was built in Northbrook, Illinois. The velodrome was one of only a handful of remaining outdoor tracks in the country and would go on to host many state and national championships.

The early 1960s also saw another important addition to American bicycle racing: cyclocross. The first American national cyclocross championships were held in 1963 at Palos Park, Illinois. The race was dominated by an unknown twenty-three-year-old rider from Rockford, Illinois, named Leroy "Tyger" Johnson. Tyger had only begun racing in the spring of 1963, but his victory at nationals was not due to lack of top competition. The race featured the reigning national road champion as well as multiple Olympians. Not only did Tyger take the win, he did so in a decisive fashion, finishing two minutes ahead of second place. Tyger went on to win additional national cyclocross titles in 1966 and 1967. Over the fall and winter of 1974–1975, Tyger qualified to race cyclocross in Europe with the United States national team. Tyger finished forty-sixth at the 1975 World Championship, the best American finish up to that point.[54]

The bicycle boom of the 1970s extended into bicycle racing. By 1976, the United States Cycling Federation, the organization that sanctioned and coordinated American bicycle racing, saw its membership grow to include 8,000 men and 500 women.[55] Once again, Illinois had a rider in the mix of the top American cyclists: John Vande Velde. As an amateur, Vande Velde won three national track championships in the 4,000-meter individual pursuit and then won a bronze medal as part of the 4,000-meter team pursuit at the 1971 Pan Am Games. He would later hold the American record for the 4,000-meter with a time of 4:53:02. Vande Velde participated in the 1968 and 1972 Olympics. Following the 1972 Olympics, he turned professional and joined the ranks of the Shimano Pro Cycling Team, the first modern American professional cycling team. As a professional, Vande Velde primarily raced six-day team races both domestically and in the ultra-competitive European circuit. In 1979, after retiring, he scored a role alongside fellow Illinoisan Eddy Van Guyse as part of the villainous Cinzano bicycle team in the Academy Award–winning film *Breaking Away*.

The most accomplished Illinois cyclist of the modern era was the track specialist Mark Gorski. Born in Evanston, Gorski won overall national titles in 1980, 1983, 1984, and 1985. Over the course of his career, he qualified for the United States Olympic teams in 1980, 1984, and 1988, winning a gold medal at the 1984 games in Los Angeles. Gorski earned a spot in the United States Cycling Hall of Fame in 1995.[56]

As it turned out, racing ran in the blood of the Vande Velde family. John's son, Christian Vande Velde, raced professionally from 1998 to 2013 on top teams such as the United States Postal Service, Liberty Seguros, Team CSC, and Garmin-Sharp. He raced in many European classics, such as the Tour de France, Vuelta a España, and the Giro d'Italia. Christian later admitted to being part of the rampant doping scandals that rocked professional cycling. Christian's sister, Marisa Vande Velde, won multiple junior national track championships and later raced professionally for a year. In addition to the Vande Veldes, the 1990s also saw the ascension of track sprinter William "Bill" Clay from Vernon Hills, Illinois. Bill won a bronze medal at the World Track Championships in 1995, took an overall win in a World Cup event in 1996, and then competed in the 1996 Olympics.[57]

By the late 1990s and early 2000s, triathlon had rocketed past cycling in terms of the overall number of licensed racers and number of events. Illinois embraced triathlon, hosting what was, at the time, the largest triathlon in the world, Mrs. T's Triathlon (named after race sponsor Mrs. T's Pierogies). Now called the Chicago Triathlon, the event still draws thousands to race every summer on Chicago's lakefront. In 2015, Chicago hosted the ITU World Triathlon Series Grand Final, which also served as an Olympics qualifier for United States athletes.

Thanks, in part, to strong youth developmental programs, Illinois has churned out several top professional triathletes. Ben Kanute of Geneva, Illinois, participated in the 2016 Olympics and then placed second overall at the half-Ironman world championships in 2017 and 2022. Kevin McDowell, a former teammate of Kanute's, placed second at the 2015 Pan American Games and then finished sixth overall at the 2020 Olympics. Andrew Starykowicz, from Long Grove, Illinois, has long been one of the strongest cyclists in triathlon. Starykowicz turned pro in 2005 and eventually found success at the half-Ironman and Ironman distances. In 2015, at a half-Ironman in Miami, he set a new world record of 1:56:11 for the 56-mile bike leg (28.9 mph), a feat that he followed up with an even more impressive world record for the full Ironman bike split 3:54:59 (28.6 mph for 112 miles) in 2018 at Ironman Texas. At the Texas race, he became the first American to break the eight-hour overall time barrier. As a professional, Starykowicz has accumulated seventeen overall wins and thirteen second-place finishes, and he was first off the bike sixty times.[58]

Dating back to the 1890s, Illinois's bicycle racing legacy remains strong today. The Intelligentsia Cup is Illinois's premier road racing event, featuring ten consecutive criterium (races consisting of several short laps on a closed road course) races in and around Chicago. Compared to the 1970s and 1980s, road racing participation has declined as off-road cycling disciplines and triathlon have grown. The seven races in the ChiCrossCup cyclocross series see hundreds of participants in each race. Mountain bike racing and gravel racing have attracted large numbers of riders to suburban and downstate venues.

On September 12, 1895, Annie Londonderry became the first woman to ride around the globe. Her eleven-month long ride started and ended in Chicago, allegedly covering 10,600 miles in the process. On September 11, 2024 (almost 129 years to the day later), American ultracyclist Lael Wilcox substantially improved upon the previous fastest women's around-the-world bicycle ride when she finished her GPS-documented ride of 18,125 miles in an astonishing 108 days. Like Londonderry, Wilcox chose Chicago as the beginning and endpoint of her circumnavigation. Londonderry finished her ride at the Wellington Hotel (corner of Jackson Boulevard and Wabash Avenue), while Wilcox's ride started and ended at Grant Park's Buckingham Fountain, a few short blocks from the former site of the Wellington Hotel.[59]

Clearly, the legacy of bicycle racing and record-setting in Illinois remains strong. Compared to the 1890s, the United States population is now more equally spread across the fifty states. Illinois produces some top riders on occasion, but the competition is stiff. No single state consistently produces top cyclists. The Ed Rudolph Velodrome in Northbrook is one of the few remaining locations left in the country for track racing. Whereas track and road racing dominated Illinois bicycling history from the 1860s through the 1980s, new types of racing have supplanted those old stalwarts. BMX and mountain bike racing increased in popularity in the 1980s and 1990s. Triathlon grew by leaps and bounds in the late 1990s and early 2000s. Cyclocross and gravel racing are where you will find the majority of Illinois bicycle racers today.

Bicycle Infrastructure

One of the most striking trends in recent American bicycle history has been the revival of interest in bicycling infrastructure. At the end of the nineteenth century, building and improving bicycle infrastructure was still a popular idea, particularly in urban areas. In 1909, famed Chicago architect Daniel Burnham published the *Plan of Chicago*, the most ambitious and comprehensive urban planning document created up to that point. One of the best examples of the Progressive City Beautiful movement, Burnham's plan called for quadrupling Chicago's parkland and ensuring public access to the entire Lake Michigan shorefront, only 25 percent of which was publicly accessible at the time. Burnham's plan was also directly responsible for the Magnificent Mile and Navy Pier, along with Wacker Drive's double-decker design. What was not in the plan was bicycles. The word bicycle only appears once in the entire document—a testament to just how much the city had moved on from the bicycle craze that had peaked only a few years earlier. Nevertheless, Burnham's *Plan of Chicago*, with its focus on greenspaces and lakefront access, would shape modern Chicago and benefit cyclists through today.[60]

By the 1920s and 1930s, bicycles were an afterthought when it came to transportation planning. Yet the focus on cars and motorcycles did have the benefit of Illinois continuing the work of the Good Roads Movement by building the largest network of permanent roads in the country. By 1930, 65 percent of the state's 10,098 miles of highway were covered with concrete. In Chicago, though, the boulevards that had once been dominated by bicycles were now hostile spaces crowded with cars. In 1935, amid the Depression-era bicycle boom, 165,000 Chicagoans signed a petition demanding the creation of bike paths. Chicago Mayor Edward Kelly supported the idea, declaring, "There isn't anything that soothes the nerves more than a ride on a bicycle. I'm glad people are getting back to old fashioned thoughts and recreations." A plan was put forward to establish one hundred miles of bike paths in forest preserves and to possibly dedicate some underutilized rural roads that surrounded the city for bicycle-use only. Action fell short of words, so that by 1938, only forty miles of forest-preserve bicycle paths had been established, a far cry from the city's extensive bicycle infrastructure of the 1890s.[61]

By the 1960s, there was a resurgence of interest in bicycle infrastructure across the state. In 1963, Chicago Mayor Richard J. Daley officially designated most of the lakefront trail as a pedestrian/bicycle path. Planning for the Illinois Prairie Path trail in DuPage County began in 1963. The creation of the Illinois Prairie Path was a community-driven effort to reclaim twenty-seven miles of the abandoned Chicago, Aurora and Elgin Electric rail line. Although it predated the official Rails-to-Trails organization, the successful establishment of this trail marked one of the country's first projects to convert old railroad corridors into pedestrian paths.[62]

By 1970, though, the City of Chicago still only had about eighteen miles of bicycle paths, mostly along its lakefront. From 1970 to 1971, amid the latest bicycle boom, Chicago designated additional bicycle routes in and around the city, with the stated goal of 250 miles by the end of the decade. Rather than the result of new construction, these paths were almost entirely on existing streets, the Lakefront Trail, forest preserve trails, and even sidewalks that were shared with pedestrians. Due to surging demand, Mayor Daley also established rush-hour bicycle lanes on Clark and Dearborn Streets, the same streets that had seen heavy bicycle traffic during the counts undertaken in 1896 and 1898. In 1978, the Northeastern Illinois Planning Commission published a bicycle map with 532 miles of bike paths in Cook, Lake, McHenry, DuPage, Kane, and Will Counties. There, as well, the majority of these paths were still sections of road with bicycle signage.[63]

Chicago-area cycling infrastructure got a major boost with the incorporation of the Chicagoland Bicycle Federation in 1985. It was the first significant bicycle advocacy organization in Illinois since the Associated Bicycle Clubs of Chicago in the 1890s. The organization's missions for 1985 included "improv[ing] the bicycling environment and thereby the quality of life in the region" and "recogniz[ing] the synergies between promoting bicycling and promoting walking and public transit. We align our advocacy with social equity and community improvement and we embrace the power of a broad multimodal coalition to achieve our mission." The Chicagoland Bicycle Federation's early focus on bicycling and social justice would lead it to become one of the nation's largest and most influential bicycle advocacy groups. In 2008, the organization would be renamed the Active Transportation Alliance.[64]

Chicago bicycling got another major boost in 1991, when recently elected Mayor Richard M. Daley (son of former Chicago mayor Richard J. Daley) created an official Mayor's Bicycle Advisory Council. Daley, himself a cyclist, stated, "My goal is to make the City of Chicago the most bicycle-friendly city in the United States." In 1992, the Mayor's Bicycle Advisory Council created Chicago's first comprehensive bicycle plan, *The Bike 2000 Plan*. It would be the first in a series of increasingly ambitious bike plans. The stated goal of *The Bike 2000 Plan* was to make Chicago bicycle friendly by the year 2000. The council intended to accomplish this goal by having 10 percent of trips under five miles be made by bicycle by 2000, improving air quality, reducing congestion, developing 300 miles of bicycle paths, and increasing bicycle safety and awareness. *The Bike 2000 Plan* put Chicago on track to regain status as the heart of American bicycling. It was followed by plans with far more detail and more measurable goals, including the *Bike 2015 Plan* (published in 2002), the *Chicago Streets for Cycling Plan 2020* (2012), and *Chicago Cycling Strategy* (2023).

Other efforts to promote biking continued in Illinois. A statewide bicycling advocacy organization, the League of Illinois Bicyclists, was formed in 1992. The mid-1990s also saw the early planning stages for the Grand Illinois Trail. The Illinois Department of Natural Resources, along with cycling enthusiasts from various northern Illinois counties, began to envision a five-hundred-mile loop from Lake Michigan to the Mississippi River, then back along the Illinois River and Hennepin Canal. Today, the Grand Illinois Trail features three hundred miles of dedicated bicycle path connected by two hundred miles of low-traffic rural roads.[65]

Peorian Ray LaHood, the United States Secretary of Transportation under President Barack Obama, was a huge booster of bicycling. In 2010, as Transportation Secretary, LaHood, a former Illinois member of the House of Representatives, announced "the end of favoring motorized transportation at the expense of non-motorized." Since the dawn of the automobile, the vast majority of federal funding had gone toward automobile-oriented projects. Arguing for increased spending on bicycle infrastructure, LaHood said, "Look, bike projects are relatively fast and inexpensive to build and are environmentally sustainable; they reduce travel costs; dramatically improve safety and public health; and reconnect citizens with their communities."[66] Utopian bicycling ideas were again on the rise.

In 2011, Rahm Emanuel succeeded Richard M. Daley as mayor of Chicago. Emanuel, like his predecessor, was an advocate for bicycling. In his introduction to *Chicago Streets for Cycling Plan 2020* (2012), Emanuel wrote,

> My vision is to make Chicago the most bike-friendly city in the United States. The Streets for Cycling Plan 2020 helps bring this vision to reality by identifying a 645-mile network of on-street bikeways that will encourage all Chicagoans to ride their bikes. Over the next few years, we will build more protected bike lanes than any other city in the country, redesign intersections to ensure they are safer for bicyclists, and improve hundreds of miles of residential streets for bicyclists, pedestrians, and the people that live on them.

In 2011, Chicago's first barrier-protected bike lane was installed on Kinzie Street. A follow-up study found that 53 percent of total rush hour traffic on Kinzie was from bicycles. Emanuel specifically called on the city to build an additional one hundred miles of these protected bike lanes, which are far safer than other styles of on-street lanes. The city claimed to have met this mark for protected lanes in 2015, but they had to stretch the definition of what qualifies as "protected" to make the assertion.[67]

One major Chicago bicycle infrastructure project that opened to the public during this period was The 606 trail. The origins of The 606 date back to before the Great Fire, when the Chicago & Pacific Railroad installed tracks down Bloomingdale Avenue. The tracks were elevated in the early 1900s and were utilized through the 1990s, receiving heavy use by Schwinn's Kostner Avenue factory. The tracks were eventually abandoned and became an eyesore during the early 2000s. A $95 million investment converted the old elevated railway into a new 2.7-mile bicycle and pedestrian trail, which opened in 2015. The opening of The 606 is one of the dreams of the 1890s cyclists that actually came true. In 1897, Chicagoan D. A. Engstrom proposed building bicycle paths on top of Chicago's existing elevated railroads. Although completely taking over a railroad right of way wasn't exactly what Engstrom envisioned, the project was certainly a significant addition to Chicago's bicycle infrastructure. One downside to the opening of The 606 is that it accelerated gentrification in surrounding northwest neighborhoods. Today's urban homebuyers clearly want good bicycle infrastructure.[68]

Overhead view of part of The 606 Trail. (Courtesy of Colin Hinkle, Soaring Badger Productions.)

In 1883 *The Wheelman* cycling magazine wrote the following about Chicago,

> Chicago is . . . the most wide-awake, energetic, progressive city in the land. Everything here is on a gigantic scale. . . . [T]he system of parks and boulevards surpasses anything yet attempted in that line in any other place. The time will soon come when Chicago wheelmen can ride around the entire city on the finest boulevards ever constructed. There will be a continuous drive-way, extending from South park to Lincoln park, and from there through Humboldt, Central, and Douglass parks back to South park, the total length being between fifty and sixty miles.[69]

From the perspective of 2024, this prediction about Chicago bicycle infrastructure looks remarkably prescient. In 2024, Chicago had 423 miles of on-street bikeways and off-street paths. Illinois cyclists can, indeed, utilize these bikeways and paths to connect Chicago's major parks. Chicago's forward-thinking boulevard system helped bicycling to thrive during the 1890s, but soon after they were overrun by automobiles. In 2021, the Chicago Department of Transportation began coordinating a series of day-long "Open Boulevards," where designated streets are once again closed to automobiles. Across the state, you can ride more than one thousand miles on eighty-eight different Rails-to-Trails projects.[70]

The demographics of Illinois bicyclists from the 1890s through today have seen extreme swings. Nineteenth-century bicycling was predominately the sphere of white men. From a bicycling participation standpoint, the first two decades of the twentieth century were a clear low point. From the 1920s through the 1960s, bicycling became most closely associated with kids and teens, although six-day racing remained a popular spectator sport. The environmental movement of the 1970s and the fitness movement of the 1980s brought adults back to bicycles.

In the twenty-first century, bicycling demographics are slowly beginning to reflect the demographics of the country as a whole. Bicycling continues to be a male-dominated sport, but a 2015 nationwide survey by the advocacy group PeopleForBikes found that one-third of the United States population rode a bike in the previous year, and 43 percent of those riders were women.[71] In Illinois and around the country, bicycle advocacy groups and some municipalities are working to improve these demographics and achieve the long-sought-after bicycle equality.

Epilogue

A Bicycling Dream Deferred

In 1896, the New York *Evening Post* published a story about the many effects of the bicycle craze on American society. Reflecting widespread beliefs about bicycles creating a more egalitarian society, the paper wrote,

> As a social revolutionizer it has never had an equal. It has put the human race on wheels, and thus changed completely many of the most ordinary processes and methods of social life. It is the great leveller, for not till all Americans got on bicycles was the great American principle, that every man is just as good as any other man, and generally a little better, fully realized. All are on equal terms, all are happier than ever before."[1]

While the sentiments the article expressed remain laudable, even the language used ("every man") suggests that this particular concept of creating a better society through bicycles was actually limited mostly to upper- and middle-class white men and some women. For the better part of the twentieth century, the prevailing social norms dictated that bicycles weren't even for women.

In the twenty-first century, bicycle advocates returned to the idea that bicycles can, in fact, be used to help create a more just and equitable society. In doing so, they echoed much of the rhetoric from the nineteenth century but made strides in applying it more equally across all genders, races, and socioeconomic classes.

This closing of the bicycling gender gap did not happen on its own; it took a great deal of effort from a variety of organizations and initiatives. In 2012, the group Women Bike Chicago was formed with a mission of "educating, encouraging, and empowering every woman in the Chicago region to enjoy biking for transportation and recreation." Two years later, the women-owned and women-specific BFF Bikes shop opened in Chicago's Bucktown neigh-

A group of riders at a Slow Roll Chicago group ride. (Courtesy of Slow Roll Chicago.)

borhood. It was the first women-specific bike shop in the Midwest, and its opening garnered national media coverage.[2] Improving bicycling inclusivity requires this sort of direct outreach in order to subvert patterns that have been in place for more than a century.

In the twenty-first century, USA Cycling sanctions and promotes most bicycle races in the United States. In a 2020 survey of their membership, the organization found that 80 percent of members were male and 86 percent of members were white. In the 1890s, Major Taylor began the work of breaking down barriers for BIPOC (Black, Indigenous, Person of Color) communities to participate in bicycle racing, but clearly his work remains unfinished. In recent years, a Chicago Elite Women's Cycling team was created to "elevate women's cycling in the Chicago region." SRAM has invested over $100,000 in BIPOC-specific initiatives, one of which subsidizes race entry fees. A cycling organization called Chicago United was formed to "nurture and create access for the Chicago BIPOC cycling community" and help introduce riders from these communities to bicycle racing. Chicago-area Team Veloz is also working to increase diversity in track racing. As is true of many areas of bicycle culture, this work has a way to go.[3]

Progressing toward the goal of getting "all Americans"—or even all Illinoisans—on bicycles will require greater efforts to make the sport more inclusive than it has been in the past. Since 1992, the Windy City Cycling Club has been working toward the goal of increasing LGBTQ+ cycling participation in the Chicago area. The Windy City Cycling Club currently coordinates a variety of group rides, participates in bicycle advocacy, and provides bicycle-related educational opportunities.[4] The Major Taylor Cycling Club Chicago was founded in 2008 "to promote good health by supporting recreational and social cycling activities in the community." In the spirit of the club's barrier-breaking namesake, the group welcomes all cyclists "regardless of race, creed, or skill level." Slow Roll Chicago was founded in 2014 and modeled after Slow Roll Detroit, which popularized the concept of community-building through slow-paced group rides open to all. The mission of Slow Roll Chicago is "to connect a diverse group of people, transform lives, and improve the condition of communities by organizing community bicycle rides and other bicycling-related programs throughout the greater Chicago area."[5]

Project Mobility, based in St. Charles, Illinois, is working to make bicycling more inclusive for those with a range of disabilities. Project Mobility got its start when bike shop owner Hal Honeyman's son Jacob was born with cerebral palsy. Hal wanted to make sure Jabob was included on family rides, and this experience with adaptive cycling led to the formation of Project Mobility. The organization's mission is "to provide the services, resources, and equipment needed to promote better health, independence, and the freedom of mobility through adaptive cycling." If bicycles are going to be the great social leveler envisioned in the nineteenth century, they need to be widely and cheaply accessible for those with disabilities. While previous generations of Illinois cyclists talked about bicycles improving social conditions in abstract terms, the above organizations are practicing what they preach, and in the process improving social justice through bicycles.

Perhaps the greatest force for true bicycle equality in the twenty-first century is the rise of bicycle cooperatives/community bike shops. Bicycle cooperatives and community bike shops build the bicycling community through a wide range of programs and events. All are nonprofit organizations predominately run by volunteers. Most focus on bicycle education, both how to ride and how to repair bicycles. At most bicycle co-ops, anyone can earn a free bicycle by volunteering and fixing up a donated bicycle. Many provide low-cost or free bicycle tune-ups to their local communities.

Chicago is home to numerous large bicycle co-ops. Chicago's Blackstone Bicycle Works has roots dating back to 1994, when it was part of the Resource Center, a recycling initiative. For a time, Blackstone Bicycle Works operated a full-service community bike shop, but it now focuses on programming that "empowers youth through bicycle education and provides a space to develop problem-solving, leadership, and life skills." Chicago's Working Bikes community bike shop was founded in 1999 and has evolved into a full-service bike shop that sells affordable refurbished bicycles and accessories. The shop's various donation programs take donated bicycles from around the Midwest, refurbish them, and then give them away to those in need. Since 1999, Working Bikes has donated more than 100,000 refurbished bicycles to those who need them both in the Chicago area and in Latin America and Africa. West Town Bikes, in Chicago's Humboldt Park neighborhood, is another bicycle co-op with a special focus on youth bicycle programs. Its youth offerings include bicycle mechanic apprenticeships, a girls' bike club, afterschool programs, a 606 Trail Ambassador program, and a cyclocross team. Speaking about the youth programs, Alex Wilson, West Town Bikes founder, has said, "I have high hopes for the young people who have been involved at West Town Bikes and believe that it has made a better world for all of them."[6] Wilson's rhetoric regarding the bicycle's ability to improve society are similar to nineteenth-century claims, but in this case, the actual community-building work is being done to make it happen. Chicago is home to the largest bicycle co-ops in the state, but the idea has taken hold and one can find a burgeoning bicycle co-op culture across Illinois in cities large and small.

One organization thinks of bicycle equality in global terms. Chicago-based World Bicycle Relief was founded in 2005 by F. K. Day (SRAM founder Stan Day's brother) and his wife Leah Missbach Day in response to the devastating 2004 Indian Ocean tsunami. The long-term vision of the organization "is to inspire all sectors to address the transportation needs for nearly 1 billion

Blackstone Bicycle Works students listen to an instructor. (Courtesy of Experimental Station/Blackstone Bicycle Works.)

who need to get to school, work or healthcare. We will work with companies, governments, collaborators and competitors to scale the availability of quality bicycles, especially for women and girls." With support from SRAM and a wide array of bicycle industry supporters and other charitable organizations, the World Bicycle Relief has now donated 700,000 new, high quality, exceptionally durable bicycles to individuals in need from twenty-one countries.[7]

Another major project that SRAM has helped fund is the creation of Chicago's 280-acre Big Marsh Park. Big Marsh offers hope that bicycles and bicycle infrastructure can play a role in redressing inequality in American society. Big Marsh should be looked to as a case study in urban environmental justice. Big Marsh Park is located adjacent to Lake Calumet, on the city's south side. Throughout much of the twentieth century, Chicago's South Side, and particularly the Lake Calumet and Calumet River areas, was the site of industrial pollution and landfills. Much of Chicago's waste was foisted upon the Black and immigrant communities that called the South Side their home. Part of the Lake Calumet area was declared a Superfund cleanup site by the Environmental Protection Agency in 2010. In December of the following year, the area that is now Big Marsh Park was acquired by the Chicago Park District, which began remediating the area. SRAM executives drew attention to the area as a potential bike park and ended up donating substantial sums to the effort. As of 2023, the bicycle areas of the park contained three miles of off-road single-track trail, two world-class bicycle pump tracks, and a more challenging jump track. Much of the park was built over slag waste from the nine steel mills that operated in the area. The pump and jump track areas were all covered in a layer of clay soil to encapsulate the contaminants. Parts of the single-track trails ride directly over the old slag waste heaps. Big Marsh has successfully taken an environmentally degraded area and created recreational activity options for the same communities that have long been disproportionately affected by environmental injustice.[8]

The 2012 *Chicago Streets for Cycling Plan 2020* called for establishing a bike share program. Bike share systems allow for greater access to bicycling without the need to own and maintain a bicycle. By that point, Chicago was behind the curve globally and, to a lesser extent, domestically in creating such programs. Chicago's Divvy bike share officially launched on June 28, 2013, with 750 bikes spread across 75 stations. In its first year, Divvy bikes were checked out 1.1 million times and ridden a total of 2.2 million miles. The program was a success, and by 2015, Chicago had more docking stations (476) and covered a larger area than any other bike share in the country. That year, Divvy had 4,760 bicycles, ranking second in the nation to New York City's Citi Bike share. In January of 2017, Divvy hit a major milestone when its ten millionth ride was recorded. According to Divvy, that equated to "20,345,107 miles ridden,

13,834,673 lbs. of CO2 reduced, 874,839,673 calories burned . . ., and 834,149 gallons of gasoline saved." In 2021, amidst the ongoing social distancing era of the COVID-19 pandemic, Divvy set another record when it surpassed four million rides for a single year.[9]

Despite these successes, critics astutely pointed out that since its inception, the majority of Divvy stations (along with bicycle lanes) had been built near the city's wealthiest areas, and ridership, in an age-old story, continued to skew heavily toward middle- and upper-class white men. Chicago's communities of color, as well as citizens from lower socioeconomic classes—particularly those on the city's South Side—could have realized greater benefits from access to cheap, reliable transportation but were overlooked in Divvy's early years. In some ways, Divvy was replicating the errors of the bicycle boom of the 1890s, when bicycle advocates claimed bicycling was the great social leveler, even though it was, in fact, reserved mostly for a narrow demographic.

The first program that began to right these wrongs was called Divvy for Everyone, or D4E. Launched in 2015, D4E drastically cut the cost of a Divvy membership from $75 to $5 for low-income residents. D4E also removed the barrier of needing to have a credit card to be able to use the system. D4E signed up 1,300 riders in its first year and has grown to 8,000 by 2023. A 2017 study found that 28 percent of D4E riders were Black, and 27 percent were Asian.[10]

Chicago's Divvy bike share program. ("Bicycles," by Martin Baumgärtel, https://www.flickr.com/photos/martin_baumgartel/30481836807/, CC BY-SA 2.0.)

D4E was certainly a big step in the right direction, but bicycle equity and advocacy organizations, such as Slow Roll Chicago and the Major Taylor Cycling Club Chicago, continued to point to a lack of bicycle infrastructure in the city's less affluent neighborhoods. It took time and a great deal of effort, but the city eventually got the message. By 2023, Divvy stations were finally made available in all fifty of Chicago's wards. Reassuringly, this expansion wasn't just Divvy stations dropped down randomly to generate a good press release. The city also drastically shifted investment in bicycle infrastructure, with 75 percent of new projects since 2019 occurring in the city's South and West Sides. The Chicago Department of Transportation's 2023 bicycle plan, *Chicago Cycling Strategy*, notes, "Chicago has a rich history of bicycling. By working together we can build a better transportation system today and an equitable cycling network for generations to come." The plan lays out a vision for adding another 150 miles of bicycle infrastructure, which will put the city over the 500-mile mark. Learning from history, the plan also specifies that Chicago "must continue to expand our network and grow the visibility of cycling in all communities, particularly those that have historically had less bike infrastructure."[11]

In another move toward improving social justice through bicycling, in 2022, the Chicago Department of Transportation announced a new "Bike Chicago" program that will distribute five thousand free new bicycles to low-income residents fourteen and older. In announcing the program, Chicago Mayor Lori Lightfoot said, "Every resident in our city deserves equitable access to safe, reliable, and affordable clean transportation options. *Bike Chicago* accelerates both the City's climate and equity goals by providing new workforce pathways, bikes and supportive resources that promote safe biking and a healthy low-carbon transportation ecosystem for all Chicagoans."[12] Mayor Carter Henry Harrison IV, the "cyclists' champion" of the 1890s would be proud to know that bicycles are again an important issue in Chicago politics and city planning.

Learning from history requires not only celebrating progress but also taking a hard look at the whole picture, including areas where progress is not so apparent. In 2023, a bicycle commuter, Divvy user, or racer is still likely to be a middle- or upper-class white man, the same demographic that ruled the bicycle boom of the 1890s. Through the hard work of many, particularly community-based bicycle advocacy groups, the demographics of bicycling in Illinois are beginning to be more reflective of the make-up of local communities. As noted above, a 2015 national survey found that 43 percent of bicyclists were women. That doesn't mean these women cyclists have found equality on the streets that they ride. In 2016, the Women's Bike Messenger Association found it necessary to launch a video campaign called "Cut the Catcalling" to speak out against the persistent sexism and racism women bicycle messengers encounter on the street every day.[13]

Even when affordable bicycles reach communities of color, they still face additional barriers to cycling. In 2017, the *Chicago Tribune* analyzed bicycle tickets from 2008 to 2016 and found that "twice as many citations are being written in African-American communities than in white or Latino areas." Even though there are more cyclists in predominately white areas of the city, not a single one of these areas was in the top ten in terms of ticketing bicyclists. Most of the tickets were for riding illegally on sidewalks, a problem directly caused by lack of equitable investment in safe, on-road bicycling infrastructure. These citation statistics are also problematic for other reasons. As Slow Roll founder Oboi Reed points out, "[I'm] confident this type of enforcement strategy in predominantly black and brown neighborhoods on the South Side and West Side is racial profiling under a new name, being used as subtext to stop people to check for warrants and search people for guns and drugs." *Arrested Mobility,* a 2023 nationwide analysis of the barriers to walking, biking, and e-scooter use, found that "Black Americans and other people of color, traveling by foot, bicycle, or e-scooter can be fraught with obstacles and risks that reflect structural racism and White supremacy."[14]

Clearly, Illinois has yet to achieve the egalitarian, bicycle-driven society dreamed of by so many cyclists in the 1890s. Work remains to be done both inside and outside the bicycling community before we reach the point where, as the *Inter Ocean* envisioned, "[a]ll are on equal terms, all are happier than ever before." The good news is that there are now more bicycle advocates and bicycle advocacy organizations than at any other time in history. Thanks to them, and to the work of Chicago's bicycle infrastructure planners, *Bicycling Magazine* rated Chicago as the best city for cycling in the United States in both 2001 and 2016. In a nod to the state's extensive bicycle history, bicycling became the official state exercise through the passage of House Bill 2895 in 2018.[15]

For those who know where to look, Illinois's bicycle heritage runs deep. Certainly, a few of the nineteenth-century bicycles made in the state have survived and are still being ridden by collectors today. The surviving factories used to build those bicycles all serve other purposes now. More significantly, the manufacturing technologies pioneered by Illinois bicycle manufacturers—Western Wheel Works in particular—helped drive a now bygone golden era of Midwest manufacturing dominance. Without technologies first pioneered by many of those manufacturers, functional automobiles may never have been invented. The National League of Good Roads was founded in Illinois in 1892, and the efforts of that organization were primarily responsible for creating our nationwide network of roads that are built and maintained by federal, state, and local governments instead of individual landowners. Notably, Illinois women cyclists of the 1890s were at the forefront of the Progressive Era, which led directly to changing American social norms in regard to women's dress, freedom of movement, participation in sports, gender roles, and eventually, women's right to vote in 1920. Through his many victories in Illinois, and around the globe, Major Taylor single-handedly shattered racist ideas about the physical superiority of the white race.

A truly egalitarian society underpinned by bicycling remains a dream of Illinois cyclists today, much as it was for cyclists in the nineteenth century. If the first two decades of the twenty-first century are any indication of the trajectory of bicycling in American society, then Illinois cyclists another hundred years from now will be much closer to experiencing a safe and equitable bicycle utopia.

Notes

A Note on Primary Sources

1. Christopher A. Sweet, "A Comprehensive Bibliography of Nineteenth-Century Bicycling Periodicals," *American Periodicals* 29, no. 1 (2019): 76–95.

2. Christopher Sweet, "Nineteenth Century Illinois Bicycle Brands, Manufacturers, Assemblers, And Jobbers," Internet Archive, archived November 13, 2024, https://archive.org/details/nineteenth-century-illinois-bicycle-brands-manufacturers-assemblers-and-jobbers, and "Nineteenth Century Men's World and American Bicycle Records Set in Illinois," Internet Archive, archived November 13, 2024, https://archive.org/details/nineteenth-century-mens-world-and-american-bicycle-records-set-in-illinois. Alternatively, contact the author at csweet@iwu.edu.

Introduction

1. "The Wheel in Politics," *The New York Journal*, April 18, 1897, 29; "The Wheel in Politics," *The Indianapolis Journal*, April 27, 1897, 6.

2. Carter H. Harrison, *Stormy Years* (New York: Bobbs-Merrill Co., 1935), 104–6.

3. "Mayor in Cycle Crash," *Chicago Chronicle*, October 7, 1897, 12; Alexander Schwalbach and Julius Wilcox, *The Modern Bicycle and Its Accessories* (New York: The Commercial Advertiser Association, 1898), 136.

4. United States. Bureau of the Census, *Foreign Commerce and Navigation of the United States, 1897–1898* (Washington: U.S. Govt. Print. Off.), xxx.

5. Newspaper stories mentioned in this section were selected from the *Chicago Daily Tribune* and *Inter Ocean*, October 7 and 8, 1897.

6. "It Carries the Injured," *Chicago Daily Tribune*, May 30, 1897, 35; "Policemen Ride the Wheel," *Chicago Tribune*, November 25, 1892, 8; "Chicago, Ill," *Postal Record* 7, no. 7 (July 1894): 169.

7. "Ravages of the Bicycle Craze," *Evening Post* (New York), June 2, 1896.

8. Joseph Bishop, "Social and Economic Influence of the Bicycle," *The Forum* XXI (August 1896): 683.

9. "Greatest in the World," *Inter Ocean* (Chicago), June 16, 1895, 6.

10. Axel Josephsson, "Bicycles and Tricycles," 1900 Census, vol. 10, Manufactures, part 4, in Special Reports on Selected Industries (Washington, DC: US Government Printing Office, 1902), 329.

11. "Ravages of the Bicycle Craze."

12. *Chicago Bicycle Directory: A Reference Book of the Trade, 1898* (Chicago: Carr and Mensch, 1898), 2.

13. 1900 Census, vol. 7, Manufactures, part 1, in United States by Industries (Washington, DC: US Government Printing Office, 1902), 325.

14. *Wheel Talk* 2, no. 22 (March 1896): 176.

15. Data documenting more than 500 Illinois bicycle companies between 1869 and 1900 was compiled by the author. The starting point was the Bicycle Brands spreadsheet maintained by *The Wheelmen*. The author's data is available through the Internet Archive: "Nineteenth Century Illinois Bicycle Brands, Manufacturers, Assemblers, And Jobbers," Internet Archive, archived November 13, 2024, https://archive.org/details/nineteenth-century-illinois-bicycle-brands-manufacturers-assemblers-and-jobbers.

16. "Passing Hour," *Bicycling World and L.A.W. Bulletin* 25 (Dec. 30, 1892): 272.

17. For a general overview of bicycle history, see David Herlihy, *Bicycle: The History* (New Haven, CT: Yale University Press, 2004) and Andrew Ritchie, *King of the Road: An Illustrated History of Cycling* (Berkeley, CA: Ten Speed Press, 1975). For an overview of bicycle social history, see Robert Smith, *A Social History of the Bicycle: Its Early Life and Time in America* (American Heritage Press, 1972). The bicycle history summary is derived primarily from these sources.

18. Nick Clayton, *Birth of the Bicycle* (Gloucestershire: Amberley Publishing, 2016), 27–34.

19. *Galaxy*, April 1869; and "The Human Wheel and Its Rival—The Velocipede Mania," *Scientific American*, January 9, 1869, 25.

20. Bruce Epperson, *Peddling Bicycles to America: The Rise of an Industry* (Jefferson, NC: McFarland, 2010), 24.

21. Epperson, *Peddling*, 28–31.

22. Isaac Potter, "Bicycle Outlook," *The Century Illustrated* 52 (May–October 1896), 789.

23. J. E. Clausen, "Rediscovering the Bicycle," *Outing* 60 (Sept. 1912).

24. This summary of bicycling in the twentieth and twenty-first centuries is my own. A detailed timeline of bicycle history can be found in James L. Witherell, *Bicycle History: A Chronological Cycling History of People, Races, and Technology* (Cherokee Village, AR: McGann Publishing, 2010).

25. "How to Calculate the Power Used by a Bicycle," Better Bicycles, accessed November 24, 2024, https://betterbicycles.org/bicycle-power-calculations/.

26. Smith, *A Social History of the Bicycle*, 47.

Chapter 1. Boneshakers and High-Wheels

1. "Evolution of the Cycle," *L.A.W. Bulletin and Good Roads* 27 (1898): 110.

2. "Non-Academic," *The Harvard Graduates' Magazine* 20 (1911–1912): 544–45.

3. *Chicago's First Half-Century, 1833–1883* (Chicago: The Inter Ocean Publishing Company, 1883), 31.

4. "The Velocipede: One of the Novel Vehicles Introduced in this City," *Chicago Tribune*, August 26, 1868.

5. Multiple Illinois newspapers carried a one-line report about Wheeler's ride in Chicago. For example, see "Illinois Items," *The Quincy Whig and Republican*, August 29, 1868.

6. *New Haven Daily Palladium*, April 5, 1866.

7. Early velocipede history was summarized from the following sources: David Herlihy, *Bicycle: The History* (New Haven: Yale University Press, 2004), 75–102; Nick Clayton, *Birth of the Bicycle* (Gloucestershire: Amberley Publishing, 2016), 27–34.

8. David Herlihy, "Cycling with the Tsars: Four Generations of Rolling Romanovs," *Adventure Cyclist*, June 2019, 12.

9. Donald L. Miller, *City of the Century: The Epic of Chicago and the Making of America* (New York: Simon & Schuster, 1996); Robert Cromie, *A Short History of Chicago* (San Francisco: Lexikos, 1984).

10. "The Human Wheel and Its Rival: Velocipede Mania," *Scientific American*, January 9, 1869, 25; "Velocipedomania", *The College Courant* 4, no. 7 (February 1869): 111.

11. Andrew Ritchie, *King of the Road: An Illustrated History of Cycling* (Berkeley, CA: Ten Speed Press, 1975), 62.

12. J. T. Goddard, *The Velocipede: Its History, Varieties, and Practice* (New York: Hurd and Houghton, 1869), 34.

13. Margaret Guroff, *The Mechanical Horse: How the Bicycle Reshaped American Life* (Austin: University of Texas Press, 2016), 18–19.

14. Arthur Judson Palmer, *Riding High: The Story of the Bicycle* (New York: E. P. Dutton, 1956), 58.

15. *Velocipedist* 1, no. 3 (April 1869); "Progress of the Velocipede," *Scientific American*, March 20, 1869.

16. "Evolution of the Cycle," *L.A.W. Bulletin and Good Roads* 27 (1898): 110.

17. E. K. W. Blake. Velocipede. US Patent 84163, issued November 17, 1868.

18. John Lauer. Velocipede. US Patent 92976, issued July 27, 1869.

19. "News Brevities," *Detroit Free Press*, January 22, 1869, 3.

20. Helen Sikuta, "Loring & Keene: Manufacturers of a Bicycle Made in Chicago," nd, Chicago Museum of History.

21. I based annual salary estimates off of the ten-hour days and six-day work weeks that were common at the time. Goddard, *Velocipede*, 62; Christopher Hanes, "Comparable Indices of Wholesale Prices and Manufacturing Wage Rates in the United States, 1865–1914," *Research in Economic History* 14 (1992): 269–92.

22. "Velocipedes," *Chicago Tribune*, April 6, 1869, 4.

23. "Chicago Letter," *St. Cloud Journal*, April 29, 1869, 2.

24. "Sporting Gossip," *Chicago Tribune*, April 25, 1869, 3.

25. "Our Chicago Letter," *Nebraska Advertiser* (Brownville, Nebraska), April 8, 1869, 1.

26. Ritchie, *King of the Road*, 63–64.

27. Louis Moeser, *Velocipede March* (Chicago: Molter and Wurlitzer, 1869); Newberry Library and Frank Howard, *Velocipedia* (Chicago: Root and Cady, 1868); Lester S. Levy sheet music collection at Johns Hopkins University, https://jscholarship.library.jhu.edu/handle/1774.2/2085.

28. Earnest Travers de Vere, "Correspondence," *Velocipedist* 1, no. 2 (March 1869): 3.

29. "Velocipede Notes," *Scientific American*, May 29, 1869, 343.

30. "Converted," *The Pantagraph* (Bloomington, IL), February 11, 1869, 4.

31. "The Greatest Velocipede Exploit on Record," *The Daily Milwaukee News*, April 22, 1869, 3.

32. Earnest Travers de Vere, "Correspondence," 3.

33. J. F. B., *The Velocipede, Its Past, Its Present & Its Future* (London: Marshall & Co., 1869), 76.

34. "The Velocipede Rink," *The Daily Milwaukee News*, April 21, 1869, 5.

35. "Local Brevities," *Chicago Evening Post*, March 3, 1869, 4.

36. "Interesting Exhibitions," *The Evening Argus*, May 20, 1869, 4.

37. "Wabash Av. Velocipedrome," *Chicago Evening Post*, May 29, 1869, 4; "Wabash Av. Velocipedrome," *Chicago Evening Post*, May 31, 1869, 1; "Sporting," *The Missouri Republican*, September 11, 1869, 3.

38. Donald L. Miller, *City of the Century: The Epic of Chicago and the Making of America* (New York: Simon & Schuster, 1996), 15–16.

39. David Herlihy, *Bicycle*, 124.

40. St. Nicholas Toy Company, *Catalogue of American Wheels*, circa 1885, Bicycle Museum of America.

41. St. Nicholas Toy Company, *Illustrated Catalog and Price List*, 1878, Chicago History Museum.

42. Bruce Epperson, *Peddling Bicycles to America: The Rise of an Industry* (Jefferson, NC: McFarland, 2010), 43–44.

43. Advertisement, *Bicycling World*, March 17, 1882, 226.

44. George W. Marble. Bicycle. US Patent 328499, filed October 22, 1884, and issued October 20, 1885.

45. "Half a Century in the Development of the Bicycle," *Scientific American*, February 10, 1900, 88–89.

46. *Bicycling World*, March 26, 1886; *Bicycling World and L.A.W. Bulletin*, May 11, 1888, 32.

47. Christopher Thale, "Haymarket and May Day," in *The Encyclopedia of Chicago*, ed. James Grossman, Ann Keating, Janice Reiff, and Michael Conzen (Chicago: University of Chicago Press, 2004), 375–77.

48. "Trouble May Come Yet," *Chicago Tribune*, May 1, 1886, 2.

49. "Mr. Bruschke's Pistol," *Chicago Tribune*, May 12, 1886, 2.

50. Hans Erhard-Lessing, "Adolph Schoeninger: The Henry Ford of the Bicycle Industry?" in *Bicycle History 18: Proceedings of the 18th International Cycling History Conference* (Van der Plas, 2009), 59–64.

51. "A Great Bicycle Plant and Its Founder," supplement, *The Wheel and Cycling Trade Review*, March 27, 1891.

52. Western Toy Company, catalog, 1879, Chicago History Museum.

53. Epperson, *Peddling*, 43–44.

54. Western Toy Company, *Price List for Spring 1887*, Bicycle Museum of America.

55. Luther Porter, *Wheels and Wheeling, an Indispensable Handbook for Cyclists* (Boston: Wheelman Co., 1892), 4.

56. Epperson, *Peddling*, 44.

57. Gary Sanderson, "The Gormully and Jeffery Manufacturing Co. and Its Founders," *Cycle History 26: Proceedings of the 26th International Cycling History Conference: Entraigues-Sur-La-Sorgue, France 2015* (San Francisco: Cycle Publishing, 2016), 218–27; Gormully & Jeffery, *Rambler Bicycles*, 1895 catalog from the Henry Ford Museum Archives, 3.

58. Sanderson, "Gormully and Jeffery," 221.

59. Epperson, *Peddling*, 45.

60. *American Athlete and Cycle Trades Review* 3, no. 5 (May 1888): 55.

61. Peter Levine, *A.G. Spalding and the Rise of Baseball* (New York: Oxford University Press, 1985), xi–xii.

62. A.G. Spalding & Bros., *Bicycles*, catalog, 1883, Wheelmen collection; *General Sporting Goods*, catalog, 1888, author's collection.

63. A. J. and F. S. Beavis, Velocipede, US Patent 318,532, filed August 2, 1884, and issued May 26, 1885.

64. "Cycling 'Round the Circle," *The Wheelman* 2, no. 6 (September 1883).

65. C. E. Hawley, "Uses of the Bicycle," *Wheelman* 1, no. 1 (October 1882): 24.

66. *Bicycling World*, November 15, 1879, 4; Paul M. Angle, "The Golden Age of Cycling," *Chicago History* 8, no. 4 (1967): 107; Gerald R. Gems, *Windy City Wars: Labor, Leisure, and Sport in the Making of Chicago* (Lanham, Maryland: Scarecrow Press, 1997), 38.

67. *The Bicycling World*, June 12, 1880, 258.

68. "The Wheel," *Inter Ocean*, January 22, 1884, 3.

69. "Chicago's Lady Riders," *L.A.W. Bulletin*, October 16, 1885, 282.

70. Steven A. Riess, *Chicago Sports Reader: 100 Years of Sports in the Windy City* (Urbana: University of Illinois Press, 2009), 8.

71. Edith Abbott, "The Wages of Unskilled Labor in the United States, 1850–1900," *Journal of Political Economy* 13 (June 1905): 363; E.A.P., "The Price of Bicycles," *Wheelman* 1, no. 2 (November 1882): 111–12.

72. *Streator Daily Free Press*, May 30, 1882, 1; "Aesthetic Athletes," *Chicago Tribune*, May 30, 1882, 12; "League Meet at Chicago," *Wheelman* 1 (October 1882): 115–25.

73. Academy of Music, program, February 10, 1881; Sprague's Olympic Theatre, program for week ending February 1882, Chicago Public Library, Chicago Theater Collection.

74. "Letter from Harry Etherington," *The American Bicycling Journal* 1, no.18 (November 1879): 6.

75. "Bicycle Tournament Postponed Again," *Boston Globe*, November 3, 1879, 1; "Five Days Bicycle Race," *Boston Globe*, November 6, 1879, 3.

76. "Sporting," *Sunday Daily Telegraph* (Chicago), November 23, 1879, 4.

77. Andrew Ritchie, *Quest for Speed: A History of Early Bicycle Racing 1868–1903* (El Cerrito, California: Andrew Ritchie, 2011): 111–50; *The Cyclist and Bicycling and Tricycling Trade Review* 1, no. 9 (December 1879): 75–88; I also consulted all newspaper articles published from November 1 to December 10, 1879, in the *Chicago Tribune*, *Inter Ocean*, and *Chicago Daily Telegraph*.

78. "Polite Athletics," *Chicago Daily Tribune*, April 17, 1881, 19.

79. "Wheeling," *Chicago Tribune*, November 7, 1885, 12.

80. Laurent Pernot, *Before the Ivy: The Cubs' Golden Age in Pre-Wrigley Chicago* (Urbana: University of Illinois Press, 2015), 51–52.

81. Peter Nye, *The Six-Day Bicycle Races* (San Francisco: Van Der Plas Publications, 2006), 31.

82. Susan Gray, "Albert Schock—Champion of the World," *Wheelmen* 93 (November 2018): 12–13.

83. Gray, "Albert Schock," 13.

84. "Schock the Champion," *The Saint Paul Globe*, March 14, 1886, 6; "Prince of Riders," *Star Tribune*, May 16, 1886, 2.

85. Charles Meinert, "Six-Day Bicycle Races," *Wheelmen* 53 (November 1998): 5; "Schock Succeeds," *The Cycle*, December 31, 1886, 181.

86. M. Ann Hall, *Muscle on Wheels: Louise Armaindo and the High-Wheel Racers of Nineteenth-Century America* (Chicago: McGill-Queen's University Press, 2018), 109–10.

87. Unless otherwise noted, the section on Louise Armaindo was summarized from the following sources: Hall, *Muscle on Wheels*, 76; Wells, S. Michael, "Ordinary Women: High Wheeling Ladies in Nineteenth Century America," *The Wheelmen* 43 (1993): 5.

88. Wells, "Ordinary Women," 5.

89. Hall, *Muscle on Wheels*, 76.

90. *Arizona Silver Belt*, June 2, 1883, 2.

91. Francis P. Prial, *The Best American and English Path & Road Cycle Records* (New York: W. N. Oliver & Co., 1885).

92. Hall, *Muscle on Wheels*, 99–110.

93. "Athletic Louise Armaindo," *Omaha Herald*, March 24, 1889, 7, cited in Hall, *Muscle on Wheels*, 132.

94. "Here and There," *Bicycling World and L.A.W. Bulletin*, December 21, 1888, 119.

Chapter 2. The Great Bicycle Boom of the 1890s

1. "Almighty Bicycle," *Chicago Daily Tribune*, June 14, 1896, 17; Robert A. Smith, *A Social History of the Bicycle* (New York: American Heritage Press, 1972), 51; "Hard Blow at Horses," *Chicago Daily Tribune*, May 24, 1896, 38.

2. "The Bicycle," *Scientific American* July 25, 1896, 68–69; Evan Friss, *The Cycling City* (Chicago: University of Chicago Press, 2015), 37; Philip P. Mason, *The League of American Wheelmen and the Good Roads Movement*, 1880–1905 (PhD diss., University of Michigan, 1957), 63; *Bicycling and Walking in the United States: 2018 Benchmarking Report*, May 16, 2023, https://data.bikeleague.org/past-benchmarking-reports/.

3. Gary Allan Tobin, "The Bicycle Boom of the 1890's: The Development of Private Transportation and the Birth of the Modern Tourist," *Journal of Popular Culture* 7, no. 4 (1974): 839; Carlton Reid, *Roads Were Not Built for Cars* (Washington, DC: Island Press, 2015), 192; "Fifth Annual Directory of the Cycle Trade of the United States," *The Referee*, January 7, 1897.

4. "Ravages of the Bicycle Craze," *Scientific American*, June 20, 1896, 391; Joseph Bishop, "Social and Economic Influence of The Bicycle," *The Forum* 21 (August 1896): 680–89; "The Almighty Bicycle"; Smith, *A Social History*, 52.

5. R. K. Keating, *Velodrome Racing and the Rise of the Motorcycle* (Jefferson, North Carolina: McFarland, 2021), 36; Gary Richardson and Tim Sablik, "Banking Panics of the Gilded Age, Federal Reserve History, accessed May 16, 2023, https://www.federalreservehistory.org/essays/banking-panics-of-the-gilded-age.

6. Joseph Gustaitis, *Chicago's Greatest Year, 1893* (Carbondale: Southern Illinois University Press, 2013), 8.

7. "Cycling Chicago," *Philadelphia Inquirer*, July 27, 1890, 8.

8. "Reign of the Bicycle," *Chicago Tribune*, May 17, 1896, 38.

9. "Figures on Wheels," *Chicago Daily Tribune*, September 18, 1898, 32. Friss, *Cycling City*, 154.

10. Isaac B. Potter, *Cycle Paths* (Boston: League of American Wheelmen, 1898), 7.

11. Thomas E. Hill, *Hill's Souvenir Guide to Chicago and the World's Fair* (Chicago: Laird and Lee, 1892), 175–76; "Streets Used by Riders," *The Chicago Chronicle*, January 24, 1897, 30; "Nicolson Pavement," Chicagology, accessed May 16, 2023, https://chicagology.com/prefire/prefire011/; "Chicago: Wood Block Street Pavement," Historic Pavement, accessed May 16, 2023, http://www.historicpavement.com/chicago-wood-block.

12. "Chicago Parks and Boulevards," *Chicago Chronicle*, January 24, 1897, 30; Julia S. Bachrach, *The City in a Garden: A History of Chicago's Parks* (Chicago: Center for American Places, 2012), 8–12.

13. Joseph D. Kearney and Thomas W. Merrill, *Lakefront: Public Trust and Private Rights in Chicago* (Ithaca, NY: Cornell University Press, 2021), 85.

14. Latham, *A Century of Serving*, 54–56; Dennis H. Cremin, *Grant Park: The Evolution of Chicago's Front Yard* (Carbondale, IL: Southern Illinois University Press, 2013), 75–77.

15. "Topics About Town," *Canonsburg Daily Notes* (Pennsylvania), March 24, 1906, 4.

16. "An Asphalt Bicycle Road from New York to Chicago," *The Manufacturer and Builder* 24, no. 11 (November 1892): 247; Robert McCullough, *Old Wheelways: Traces of Bicycle History on the Land* (Cambridge, MA: MIT Press, 2015), 181; Robert Bruce, "Bicycle Side-Path Building in 1900," *Outing*, May 1900, 182; Friss, *Cycling City*, 104–5.

17. "Elevated Bicycle Road," *Chicago Chronicle*, July 14, 1895, 6; "To Pedal Up in the Air," *Chicago Tribune*, June 7, 1897, 4; "Chicago's Elevated Cycleway," *L.A.W. Bulletin and Good Roads*, May 26, 1899.

18. Friss, *Cycling City*, 105–7.

19. "Bicycle Row and Other Trade Centers," *Chicago Tribune* June 9, 1895, 46.

20. Christopher George Sinsabaugh, *Who, Me? Forty Years of Automobile History* (Detroit: Arnold-Powers, Inc., 1940), 27; Peter Nye, *Hearts of Lions: The History of American Bicycle Racing* (New York: W. W. Norton, 1988), 33.

21. Gary Sanderson, "The Gormully and Jeffery Manufacturing Co. and Its Founders," 218–27; Friss, *Cycling City*, 25. The 2023 Chicago calculations are the author's, based off contemporary directories.

22. Forrest Crissey, *Since Forty Years Ago: An Account of the Origin and Growth of Chicago and Its First Department Store* (Chicago: Privately Printed by The Fair, 1915); "The Fair Department Store II," Chicagology, accessed May 16, 2023, https://chicagology.com/goldenage/goldenage017/; Jeffrey A. Brune, "Department Stores," in *The Encyclopedia of Chicago*, ed. James R. Grossman et al. (Chicago: University of Chicago Press, 2004), 238–39.

23. "Close of the Week's Bicycle Show," *Chicago Daily Tribune*, January 13, 1895, 4.

24. "Hotels are Forced to Use Cots," *Chicago Tribune*, January 9, 1896, 1.

25. "Beats all Bike Shows," *Chicago Tribune*, January 12, 1896, 4; "Faint at the Bicycle Show," *Chicago Tribune*, January 11, 1896, 3; "Opening Their Big Show," *New York Times*, January 5, 1896,

25; "Aftermath of the Show," *Bearings*, January 16, 1896; "The New York Cycle Show," *Bearings*, January 23, 1896.

26. Lewis Bates, "The Political Power of the L.A.W.," *Wheelman*, May 1883, 98–100.

27. Joseph Flinn, *Chicago, the Marvelous City of the West: A History, an Encyclopedia, and a Guide 1892* (Chicago: Standard Guide Co., 1892), 224.

28. "Cycling Clubs Unite," *Chicago Tribune*, November 21, 1890, 6; "Chicago's Cycling Clubs," *Chicago Daily Tribune*, May 17, 1896.

29. George D. Bushnell, "When Chicago Was Wheel Crazy," in *The Chicago Sports Reader*, ed. Steven A. Riess and Gerald R. Gems (Urbana, IL: University of Illinois Press, 2009), 86.

30. Friss, *Cycling City*, 93–95.

31. Michael Taylor, "The Bicycle Boom and the Bicycle Bloc: Cycling and Politics in the 1890s," *Indiana Magazine of History* 104, no. 3 (2008): 217.

32. Reid, *Roads Were Not Built*, 176–78; Taylor, "The Bicycle Boom," 217.

33. "Run Led by Carter," *Chicago Daily Tribune*, May 24, 1897, 3.

34. "Mayor Heeds Appeal of Cyclists," *Chicago Tribune*, June 13, 1897, 1.

35. "Boulevard Soon to Be," *Chicago Tribune*, June 13, 1897, 43; "Jackson Boulevard," *Inter Ocean*, April 5, 1897, 6.

36. "Favors the Wheel Tax," *Chicago Tribune*, July 14, 1897, 5.

37. "Approves the Wheel Tax," *Chicago Chronicle*, July 20, 1897, 8; "Bicycle Tax is Void," *Chicago Tribune*, August 8, 1897, 30.

38. Friss, *Cycling City*, 89.

39. "Woe Follows the Bicycle," *Chicago Daily Tribune*, August 1, 1897; "Bicycle Accidents," *Inter Ocean*, November 7, 1897, 21.

40. Smith, *A Social History*, 48–49; "It Carries the Injured," *Chicago Daily Tribune*, May 30, 1897, 35; "Chicago Bicycle Ambulance," *The Times* (Philadelphia), November 15, 1896, 19; "Local Bicycle Derby Today," *Chicago Daily Tribune*, July 4, 1895, 4.

41. "Chicago, Ill," *Postal Record* 7, no. 7 (July 1894): 169; Smith, *A Social History*, 48.

42. "Policemen Ride the Wheel," *Chicago Tribune*, November 25, 1892, 8; "Bikes Defy Old Sol," *Chicago Tribune*, June 3, 1895, 1; James Whiteside, "'It was a Terror to the Horses': Bicycling in Gilded-Age Denver," *Colorado Heritage*, Spring 1991, 14; "Plan a Big First Night," *Chicago Tribune*, August 12, 1897, 8.

43. Jim Fitzpatrick, *The Bicycle in Wartime* (Washington, DC: Brassey's, 1998), 18; Epperson, *Peddling*, 86.

44. George Niels Sorensen, *Iron Riders: Story of the 1890s Fort Missoula Buffalo Soldier Bicycle Corps* (Missoula, MT: Pictorial Histories Publishing Co., 2012), 17–20; William T. May, *Cyclists' Drill Regulations* (Boston: Pope Manufacturing Co., 1892).

45. Sorensen, *Iron Riders*, 18; Robert S. Kohn, *Bicycle Troops* (Columbus, OH: Remote Area Conflict Information Center, Battelle Memorial Institute, 1965), 8; Perry Duis, *Challenging Chicago: Coping with Everyday Life, 1837–1920* (Urbana: University of Illinois Press, 1998), 179; "The Great Bicycle Relay Race" *Wilkes-Barre Record*, May 19, 1892, 1; Pete Ehrmann, "The Great Bicycle Relay Race of 1892," *BikeReport*, August 1991, 9–11; "Chicago to New York by Relays," *Wheel and Cycling Trade Review*, May 27, 1892, 18.

46. "Strikers Come to Grief," *Los Angeles Herald*, June 10, 1893, 1; "Chicago," *American Cyclist*, August 1, 1893, 402; "Second Regiment Bicycle Corps," *Inter Ocean*, March 31, 1895, 15; "Lemont Strike Ends," *Chicago Tribune*, June 15, 1893, 8.

47. Sorensen, *Iron Riders*, 32–48; Kay Moore, *The Great Bicycle Experiment: The Army's Historic Black Bicycle Corps* (Missoula, MT: Mountain Press Publishing Co., 2012), 21–23; David McCormick, "The Buffalo Soldiers Who Rode Bikes," HistoryNet, accessed May 15, 2023, https://www.historynet.com/the-buffalo-soldiers-who-rode-bikes/.

48. Sorensen, *Iron Riders*, 72.

49. Sorensen, *Iron Riders*, 49–74; "On Wheels from Montana," *The Kansas City Star*, August 17, 1897, 1.

50. Micah Toll, "These Powerful Electric Bicycles Are Now Serving with the Special Forces," October 6, 2021, https://electrek.co/2021/10/06/these-powerful-electric-bicycles-are-now-serving-with-the-special-forces/.

51. Portions of this section are derived from one of my earlier publications that focused on the religious institutions and the bicycle boom across the United States. See Chris Sweet, "'The Church or the Wheel?': Religious Institutions Contend with the American Bicycle Boom," *Cycle History 27: Proceedings of the 27th International Cycling History Conference* (San Francisco: Van der Plas: North Haven, CT, 2016), 16–23.

52. "The Bicycle," *Portland Daily Press*, June 16, 1897, 3.

53. Thomas Hughes, *Tom Brown at Oxford* (London: Macmillan, 1861), 83.

54. "Wheels Should Rest Sunday," *Chicago Daily Tribune*, June 17, 1895.

55. *Britannica Academic*, s.v. "Dwight L. Moody," accessed August 30, 2016, http://academic.eb.com/levels/collegiate/article/53595.

56. Dwight Lyman Moody, *Works of Dwight L. Moody*, vol. 14 of *Moody's Latest Sermons* (Chicago: Fleming H. Revell Company, 1900), 117–18.

57. "Rev. Dwight L. Moody Discovers Tillie Anderson," *Cincinnati Enquirer*, March 12, 1897.

58. "Pastor Johnson and His Wheel," *Chicago Daily Tribune*, October 29, 1894.

59. "Rev. F. M. Johnson," *Sandusky Register*, October 31, 1894.

60. As a historical note, the Rev. Jones was an influential figure for his nephew Frank Lloyd Wright. His ideas about religious architecture heavily influenced his young nephew. See Joseph Siry, "Frank Lloyd Wright's Unity Temple and Architecture for Liberal Religion in Chicago, 1885–1909," *The Art Bulletin* 73, no. 2 (1991): 257–82.

61. "Bikes in the Church," *Chicago Daily Tribune*, April 16, 1896.

62. "Take Issue with Stone," *Chicago Daily Tribune*, February 27, 1896.

63. "Fifield on the Bicycle," *Chicago Daily Tribune*, September 27, 1897.

64. "Bicycles and the Liquor Trade," *The Topeka Daily Capital*, August 27, 1897.

65. A. O. Downs, "Clergymen and the Bicycle," *Wheelman*, December 1882, 219.

66. Michael Taylor, "Rapid Transit to Salvation: American Protestants and the Bicycle in the Era of the Cycling Craze," *Journal of the Gilded Age and Progressive Era*, (2010): 337–63.

67. "Evangelists on Bicycles," *The Daily Republican*, August 12, 1895.

68. Taylor, "Rapid Transit," 363.

69. Elmer L. Johnson, *The History of YMCA Physical Education* (Chicago: Association Press, 1979), 50.

Chapter 3. "Two-Thirds of All Bicycles"

1. George W. May, *Charles E. Duryea Automaker* (Chillicothe, IL: River Beach Publishing, 1996), 31; Charles W. Carey and Ian C. Friedman, *American Inventors, Entrepreneurs, and Business Visionaries* (New York: Facts on File, 2011), 103–5.

2. Gormully & Jeffery, *American Cycles*, 1888, catalog, Bicycle Museum of America Archives; Gormully & Jeffery, *American Cycles*, 1891, catalog, author's collection.

3. Carl Wideman, "Frank and Charles Duryea—Transportation Pioneers," *Wheelmen* 44 (May 1994): 2–8.

4. "Hubless and Spokeless," *The Bearings*, January 2, 1892; May, *Charles E. Duryea*, 36.

5. Sylph catalog, 1892, Smithsonian Trade Literature Collection.

6. Parker Morell, *Diamond Jim: The Life and Times of James Buchanan Brady* (New York: Simon and Schuster), 96–97.

7. Smith Hempstone Oliver and Donald H. Berkebile, "Wheels and Wheeling: The Smithsonian Cycle Collection," *Smithsonian Studies in History and Technology* 24 (1974): 25.

8. "Evolution of the Cycle," *L.A.W. Bulletin and Good Roads*, October 14, 1898, 296.

9. "The Sylph," *Bicycling World and L.A.W. Bulletin*, November 29, 1889, 101.

10. Luther H. Porter, *Wheels and Wheeling; An Indispensable Handbook for Cyclists* (Boston: Wheelman Company, 1892), 198–99.

11. "New Corporations," *Inter Ocean*, December 21, 1889, 9.

12. "A Selected List of Patents," *Wheel and Cycling Trade Review*, March 17, 1893, 36.

13. *World's Columbian Exposition: List of Awards*, Chicago History Museum Archives.

14. Democratic State Central Committee, *A Brief History of Peoria*, 1896, 38.

15. Democratic State Central Committee, *A Brief History of Peoria*, 38.

16. David A. Hounshell, *From the American System to Mass Production 1800–1932* (Baltimore: John Hopkins University Press, 1984), 189–215.

17. David Herlihy, *Bicycle: The History* (New Haven, CT: Yale University Press, 2004), 250.

18. "A Million Bicycles," *Harper's Weekly*, August 17, 1895, 769; "The Industry: How It Grew Up," *Bicycling World*, December 18, 1902, 323–31.

19. Isaac Potter, "Bicycle Outlook," *Century Illustrated* 52 (May–Oct. 1896): 789.

20. *Bicycling World*, May 27, 1898, 21.

21. Bureau of the Census, *Census of Manufactures: 1905* (Washington, DC, GPO, 1908), 287–97; "Export Trade Matters," *Wheel and Cycling Trade Review*, January 26, 1899, xii.

22. *Foreign Commerce and Navigation of the United States,1897–98* (Washington, DC: GPO, 1898), xxx–xxxiii; Bruce Epperson, "How Many Bikes? An Investigation into the Quantification of Bicycling 1878–1914," *Cycle History 11: Proceedings of the 11th International Cycling History Conference* (San Francisco: Van der Plas Publications, 2001), 42–45.

23. Herlihy, *Bicycle*, 278.

24. "Chicago Report," *American Athlete and Cycle Trades Review*, November 28, 1890, 727.

25. Herlihy, *Bicycle*, 282.

26. Gary Sanderson, "The Gormully and Jeffery Manufacturing Co. and Its Founders," *Cycle History 26: Proceedings of the 26th International Cycling History Conference: Entraigues-Sur-La-Sorgue, France 2015* (San Francisco: Cycle Publishing, 2016), 218–27.

27. "Trade Directory of the United States," *The Referee*, 1897, 1–4, Bicycle Museum of America Archives.

28. *Chicago Bicycle Directory: A Reference Book of the Trade, 1898* (Chicago: Carr and Mensch, 1898), 3.

29. Axel Josephsson, "Bicycles and Tricycles," 1900 Census, vol. 10, Manufactures, part 4, in Special Reports on Selected Industries (Washington, DC: US Government Printing Office, 1902), 325.

30. A list of Illinois bicycle brands and manufacturers was compiled by the author: "Nineteenth Century Illinois Bicycle Brands, Manufacturers, Assemblers, And Jobbers." https://archive.org/details/nineteenth-century-illinois-bicycle-brands-manufacturers-assemblers-and-jobbers

31. "Importance of the Assemblers," *Cycle Age and Trade Review*, June 29, 1899, 211.

32. Epperson, *Peddling*, 198–99.

33. "Retail Notes," *Sporting Goods Dealer*, June 1900.

34. *Half-Century's Progress of the City of Chicago* (Chicago: International Publishing Company, 1887), 349.

35. "Featherstone's Pneumatics," *Wheel and Cycling Trade Review*, February 27, 1891, 5; "Featherstone Dunlop Pneumatic Tire," *Bicycling World and L.A.W. Bulletin*, November 6, 1891, 44.

36. Christopher Hanes, "Comparable Indices of Wholesale Prices and Manufacturing Wage Rates in the United States, 1865–1914," *Research in Economic History* 14 (1992): 269–92.

37. For more on the American Bicycle trust, see chapter eight. Advertisement, *Passaic Daily News*, March 3, 1891, 3; A. Featherstone & Co., catalog, 1893, Chicago History Museum archives; *A History of the City of Chicago*, 247.

38. *The Cycle*, June 11, 1886, 203; "New Factories," *The Cycle*, July 23, 1886, 291–93.

39. "The Manufacture of Bicycles and Tricycles in America," *Frank Leslie's Illustrated Newspaper*, July 30, 1887, 393–94.

40. "The American Rambler," *Bicycling World*, January 27, 1888, 205.

41. American Cycles, Gormully & Jeffery, 1891, catalog, author's collection; *Bicycling for Girls from a Medical Standpoint* (Chicago: Gormully & Jeffery Mfg. Co., 1891), 7.

42. G. Donald Adams, *Collecting and Restoring Antique Bicycles* (Blue Ridge Summit, PA: TAB Books, 1981), 206; Henry C. Pearson, *Pneumatic Tires, Automobile, Truck, Airplane, Motorcycle, Bicycle* (New York: India Rubber Pub. Co, 1922), 40; Sanderson, "The Gormully and Jeffery Manufacturing Co.," 218–27.

43. Epperson, *Peddling*, 54; "Pope to Use G & J Tires," *The Referee*, December 8, 1893, 1.

44. Gormully & Jeffery, *Rambler Bicycles*, 1895, catalog, 4, Henry Ford Museum Archives.

45. "Compact Road Design," Giant Bicycles, accessed April 7, 2023, https://www.giant-bicycles.com/us/about-us/our-history/compact-road-design.

46. Gormully & Jeffery, *Rambler Bicycles*; "Boom in Business Is Apparent," *Chicago Chronicle*, October 20, 1895, 10.

47. Advertisement, *Chicago Tribune*, May 10, 1896, 10; William Herbert Mariboe, "The Bicycle in America to 1900" (master's thesis, Oberlin College, 1940), 39.

48. Sanderson, "Gormully and Jeffery," 218–27.

49. "Monarch Cycle Company," *Wheel and Cycling Trade Review*, April 1, 1892, 24; *Monarch Bicycles*, 1895, catalog, Henry Ford Museum Archives; Monarch Bicycles, 1896, catalog, Northwestern University Archives; "A Wonderful Record," *Mitchell Capital* (Mitchell, SD), April 9, 1897, 5; Monarch Bicycles, 1900, catalog, Bicycle Museum of America Archives; *The Modern Bicycle and Its Accessories* (New York: Commercial Advertiser Association, 1898), 14–15.

50. Frank S. Presbrey, *The History and Development of Advertising* (New York: Doubleday, Doran, and Company, 1929), 413; Ross D. Petty, "Peddling the Bicycle in the 1890s: Mass Marketing Shifts into High Gear," *Journal of Macromarketing* (Spring 1995): 34; "Notes," *Printers' Ink* XVI, no. 13 (September 1896): 21.

51. This statement, which has since been repeated verbatim in many subsequent histories, is misleading. Since "Hill & Moffat" never actually existed as a bicycle company, what Ignaz was likely recalling, more than a half century later, was that he worked for businessmen Mark W. Hill and George D. Moffatt. Moffatt was president of Moffatt (sometimes spelled with only one "t") Cycles, which was incorporated in Chicago in 1891. And Hill was the company's treasurer. Arnold, Schwinn and Company, *Fifty Years of Schwinn-Built Bicycles* (Chicago: Arnold, Schwinn & Company, 1945) 7–9.

52. Judith Crown and Glenn Coleman, *No Hands: The Rise and Fall of the Schwinn Bicycle Company: An American Institution* (New York: Henry Holt, 1996), 15–24; Arnold, Schwinn and Company, *Fifty Years*, 7–9; "Arnold, Schwinn & Co." *The Referee*, October 17, 1895.

53. "New Corporations," *Chicago Tribune*, September 22, 1895, 14.

54. Arnold, Schwinn & Co., *The "World" Is Mine* (Grand Rapids: Dickinson Bros., 1897), catalog, 4, Bicycle Museum of America Archives; *Fourth Annual Report of the Factory Inspectors of Illinois* (Springfield, IL: Phillips Bros., 1897), 121.

55. Jay Pridmore and Jim Hurd, *Schwinn Bicycles* (Osceola, WI: MBI Publishing, 1996), 27–31.

56. Crown and Coleman, *No Hands*, 15–24; Arnold, Schwinn and Company, *Fifty Years*, 7–9.

57. "Greatest in the World," *Inter Ocean*, June 16, 1895, 6.

58. "New Corporations," *Inter Ocean*, July 23, 1889, 9; "Greatest in the World," *The Inter Ocean*, June 16, 1895, 6.

59. *Crescent Bicycles*, 1898, catalog, 19, Howie Cohen's Everything Bicycle Collection, accessed April 7, 2023, https://proteanpaper.com/scart_results.cgi?comp=howiebik&part=CatAntqBike-C-023; "Chicago Trade," *Wheel and Cycling Trade Review* 6, no. 18 (1890): 474.

60. *Rand McNally & Co.'s A Week at the Fair Illustrating the Exhibits and Wonders of the World's Columbian Exposition* (Chicago: Rand McNally, 1893) 54; "Greatest in the World," *Inter Ocean*, June 16, 1895, 6.

61. Erhard-Lessing, "Adolph Schoeninger," 59–64; "Greatest in the World," *The Inter Ocean*, June 16, 1895, 6; Thomas Burr, "Markets as Producers and Consumers: The French and U.S. National Bicycle Markets, 1875–1910" (PhD diss., University of California Davis, 2005), 230.

62. "Bicycle Figures," *Sibley Journal* (Sibley, IL), July 23, 1897, 3.

63. Hounshell, *From the American System*, 189–215; "Making the Crescent," *Minneapolis Daily Times*, February 21, 1897, 11; "Bicycles by the Trainload," *New York Times*, March 15, 1896; *4me Salon du Cycle: Exposition Internationale de Vélocipédie et d'Automobiles* (Paris: F. Thévin & Ch. Houry, 1896), 71.

64. *Crescent Bicycles*, 1898, catalog; *Crescent Bicycles*, 1899, Howie Cohen's Everything Bicycle Collection, accessed April 7, 2023, https://www.proteanpaper.com/scart_results.cgi?comp=howiebik&framed=0&part=CatAntqBike-C-023d&scat=1&scatord=desc&scatall=&skey=norm; "Bicycle Trust Collapses," *Buffalo Review* (Buffalo, NY), April 25, 1899, 1; "The Bicycle Leads the Way," *Brooklyn Citizen*, January 23, 1900, 4.

65. "Historical Review of Prominent Companies," *Cycle Age and Trade Review*, September 7, 1899, 464; "Cycle Trust Punctured," *Chicago Tribune*, September 3, 1902, 1.

66. Hounshell, *From the American System*, 189–215.

67. "The Mechanical Side," *New York Times*, January 21, 1896, 7.

68. Hounshell, *From the American System*, 189.

69. *Crescent Bicycles*, 1897, catalog, author's collection; *Crescent Bicycles*, 1898, catalog.

70. Hounshell, *From the American System*, 189–208.

71. "Greatest in the World," *Inter Ocean*, June 16, 1895, 6; supplement, *Wheel and Cycling Trade Review*, March 27, 1891, i.

72. "Making the Crescent," *Minneapolis Daily Times*, February 21, 1897, 11.

73. Glen Norcliffe, "Popeism and Fordism: Examining the Roots of Mass Production," Regional Studies 31, no. 3 (1997): 267–80; Hounshell, *From the American System*, 208–12.

74. Epperson, *Peddling*, 198.

75. The best resource on John Deere bicycles is a research packet compiled by the Deere & Co. library in 1972. Reproductions of this document are available upon request. Other sources consulted for this section include Wayne G. Broehl, *John Deere's Company: A History of Deere & Company and Its Times* (New York: Doubleday, 1984), 219–26; "Capitol Pickings," *Saint Paul Globe*, November 2, 1893, 4; "The Deere and Webber Co. Minneapolis, Minn," *Farm Implement News*, February 22, 1894, 32.

76. Broehl, *John Deere's Company*, 219–26; "Capitol Pickings," *Saint Paul Globe*, November 2, 1893, 4; "The Deere and Webber Co. Minneapolis, Minn," *Farm Implement News*, February 22, 1894, 32.

77. Broehl, *John Deere's Company*, 219–26; *Farm Implement News*, March 19, 1896, 34; *Executive Documents of the State of Minnesota for the Fiscal Year Ending July 31, 1896, Vol. III* (St. Paul, MN: Pioneer Press Co., 1897), 319–24; "The Big Deere and Webber Company," *The Referee*, August 29, 1895.

78. "Trade at Minneapolis," *Farm Implement News*, June 3, 1897, 1; "From Minneapolis," *Farm Implement News*, November 18, 1897, 17.

79. "Chicago Cycle Show," *American Machinist*, January 30, 1896, 130–6; "Finest Bicycle in the World," *Inter Ocean*, January 10, 1896, 4; "Cycle Show Statistics," *Iron Age*, January 16, 1896, 216; "Confusion Courted," *The Wheel*, November 15, 1895; *Elgin King*, 1897, catalog, Bicycle Museum of America archives.

80. Adams, *Collecting*, 222–23.

81. "Aluminium" was at the time a common spelling for what in American English is now usually spelled "aluminum," with the former spelling prevailing in British English.

82. "Trade in Chicago," *Wheel and Cycling Trade Review*, October 16, 1891, 235; "Breezy Notes," *The Bearings*, January 22, 1892; Luther Porter, *Wheels and Wheeling*, 372–80.

83. "Back-Pedaling Brakes," *Wheel and Cycling Trade Review*, March 24, 1898, 42–43; "The Owners of the Original Patent," *Bicycling World and Motorcycle Review*, April 3, 1902, 13.

84. "The Stover Bicycle Mfg. Co.'s Catalogue," *Wheel and Cycling Trade Review*, February 26, 1892, 19.

85. Joseph Kirkland and John Moses, *History of Chicago, Illinois* (Chicago: Munsell & Company, 1895), 447; Advertisement, *Chicago Tribune*, June 7, 1896, 39; US Patent 581,973, filed September 9, 1895, and issued May 4, 1897; *Old Hickory* circa 1898, catalog, Bicycle Museum of America Archives; Adams, *Collecting*, 219.

86. Frank J. Berto, *The Dancing Chain: History and Development of the Derailleur Bicycle* (San Francisco: Cycle Publishing, 2017), 45.

87. "Sporting News Department," *Elmira Gazette and Free Press* (Elmira, New York), November 23, 1892, 6; "Trade Notes," *The Bearings*, November 23, 1894.

88. "New Incorporations," *Chicago Tribune*, April 15, 1893, 13; "Two-Speed Bicycle Company," *Iron Age*, December 28, 1893, 1189.

89. I am unaware of any source that has definitively documented the first freewheel mechanism in a safety bicycle. There were earlier freewheel mechanisms in high-wheel bicycles, and there are earlier patents for safety bicycles that incorporated a freewheel mechanism. To the best of my knowledge, the American Hill-Climber was the first production safety bicycle to include a freewheel mechanism.

90. "Trade Notes," *The Bearings*, November 23, 1894; "Why They Like Their Wheels," *Chicago Tribune*, May 11, 1895, 7.

91. Advertisement, *Harper's Round Table*, June 22, 1897, 827.

92. William Zimmerman Jr., *William Wrigley, Jr., The Man and His Business, 1861–1932* (Chicago: Lakeside Press, 1935); *Good Bicycles from a Good House at Makers' Prices*, 1898 Wrigley bicycle catalog, Northwestern University Library Archives.

93. *First Annual Report of the Factory Inspectors of Illinois for the Year Ending December 15, 1893* (Springfield, IL: State Printers, 1894), 127–34; *Fifth Annual Report of the Factory Inspectors of Illinois for the Year Ending December 15, 1897* (Springfield, IL: Phillip Bros., 1898), 25–33.

94. "Chronic Poisoning by Benzine," *New Orleans Medical and Surgical Journal* 50, no. 5 (November 1897): 319–20.

95. Inter Ocean, *A History of the City of Chicago: Its Men and Institutions* (Chicago: Inter Ocean, 1900), 225–58.

Chapter 4. All the World Awheel

1. "The Columbian Exposition Cranks," *Chicago Daily Tribune*, June 15, 1890, 12.

2. Richard Weingardt, *Circles in the Sky: The Life and Times of George Ferris* (Reston, Virginia: American Society of Civil Engineers Press, 2009), 5–6.

3. Weingardt, *Circles in the Sky*, 135.

4. "The American-Ormonde Cycle Co.," *The Bearings*, January 5, 1894.

5. Luther V. Rice, *Report of the Committee on Awards of the World's Columbian Commission* (Washington, DC: GPO, 1901), 479.

6. "Cycling Soldiers," *The Bearings*, October 28, 1892.

7. Chicago Cycling Club, "World's Fair Dedication Tournament," 1892, University of Wisconsin-Madison Library Archives.

8. "The Chicago Cycling Club's Dedication Tournament," *The Bearings*, October 28, 1892.

9. Joseph Gustaitis, *Chicago's Greatest Year, 1893: The White City and the Birth of a Modern Metropolis* (Carbondale: Southern Illinois University Press, 2013), 18.

10. Rand McNally and Company, *Rand, McNally & Co.'s a Week at the Fair: Illustrating the Exhibits and Wonders of the World's Columbian Exposition* (Chicago: Rand, McNally & Co., 1893), 210.

11. "Two Courts Established," *Daily Inter Ocean*, February 23, 1893, 7.

12. John Flinn, *Best Things to Be Seen at the World's Fair* (Chicago: Columbian Guide Company, 1893), 105–6; Jesse Gant and Nicholas Hoffman, *Wheel Fever* (Wisconsin Historical Society Press, 2013), 96–97; "Bicycles at the Fair," *The Referee*, May 5, 1893, supplement.

13. Tony Hadland and Hans-Erhard Lessing, *Bicycle Design: An Illustrated History* (Cambridge, MA: The MIT Press, 2014), 186.

14. Katharine M. Rogers, *L. Frank Baum, Creator of Oz: A Biography* (New York: St. Martin's Press, 2002), 115.

15. Flinn, *Best Things*, 111, and "Bicycles at the Fair," supplement.

16. R. K. Keating, *Velodrome Racing and the Rise of the Motorcycle* (Jefferson, NC: McFarland, 2021), 38; *Boston with Its Points of Interest* (New York: Mercantile Illustrating Company, 1895), 276.

17. *Report of the Committee on Awards of the World's Columbian Commission: Special Reports Upon Special Subjects or Groups* (Washington: G.P.O., 1901).

18. "Ready to Withdraw," *Sunday Inter Ocean*, July 30, 1893, 1.

19. *World's Columbian Exposition, List of Awards (Domestic), as Copied for Mrs. Virginia C. Meredith, Chairman, Committee on Awards, Board of Lady Managers, from the Official Records in the Office of Hon. John Boyd Thacher, Chairman, Executive Committee on Awards,* 1893, Department G—Transportation, Group 83, Chicago History Museum Archives.

20. Andrew Ritchie, *Quest for Speed: A History of Early Bicycle Racing 1868–1903* (El Cerrito, California: Andrew Ritchie, 2011), 297.

21. "Good State for Cyclists," *New York Times*, June 30, 1893, 3.

22. Ritchie, *Quest for Speed*, 297.

23. "America vs. The World . . . International National, and State Championships," *The Referee and Cycle Trade Journal*, advertisement, July 21, 1893, 32.

24. Ritchie, *Quest for Speed*, 307.

25. "Where are the Champions?" *The Bearings*, August 11, 1893, 6.

26. The best coverage for the International Tournament can be found in "The International Meet," *The Bearings*, August 11, 1893, and *The Referee*, August 11, 1893, and August 18, 1893.

27. Ritchie, *Quest for Speed*, 301.

28. *Record of the 1893 International and National Bicycle Race Meet*, Chicago History Museum Archives.

29. "Like a River of Fire," *Chicago Tribune*, August 11, 1893, 3, and "Better Days Here," *Daily Inter Ocean*, August 11, 1893, 1.

30. *The World's Fair Album: Containing Photographic Views of Buildings . . . at the World's Columbian Exposition, Chicago 1893* (Chicago: Rand, McNally & Co, 1893), 47.

31. Karen Abbott, *Sin in the Second City: Madams, Ministers, Playboys, and the Battle for America's Soul* (New York: Random House, 2007).

32. "Holmes as Bicycle Swindler," *Chicago Daily Tribune*, July 26, 1895, 2.

33. "Light on the Plot," *Daily Inter Ocean*. November 20, 1894, 1–2.

34. Lew Freedman, *Buffalo Bill Cody: The Man Who Shaped the Wild West Legend* (Jefferson, NC: McFarland, 2020), 148.

35. Matt Braun, "Buffalo Bill Goosed the World's Fair," *True West Magazine*, April 22, 2014, accessed November 11, 2022, https://truewestmagazine.com/article/buffalo-bill-goosed-the-worlds-fair/.

36. Robert A. Carter, *Buffalo Bill Cody: The Man Behind the Legend* (Edison, NJ: Castle Books, 2005), 277.

37. "Miss Annie Oakley," *The Bearings*, August 17, 1894.

38. Walter Havighurst, *Annie Oakley of the Wild West* (Edison, NJ: Castle Books, 2003), 168.

39. Glenda Riley, *Life and Legacy of Annie Oakley* (Norman: University of Oklahoma Press, 1994), 141.

40. Riley, *Life and Legacy*, 138–39.

41. "Cycling and the Wild West," *Campfire Chats*, Buffalo Bill Museum and Grave, vol. 2, 2017, 1–3, accessed November 11, 2022, https://goldentoday.com/wp-content/uploads/2017/05/2017-vol-2_newsletter.pdf.

42. "A Talk with Cody. Buffalo Bill Believes that Women Should Be Athletes," *Topeka Weekly Capital*, January 4, 1894.

43. "Buffalo Bill Exhibition Leaves Mark," *Jacksonville Journal Courier*, September 17, 2016, 3A.

44. Freedman, *Buffalo Bill Cody*, 151.

45. "Want Good Roads," *Daily Inter Ocean*, October 21, 1892, 6.

46. Phillip Mason, "The League of American Wheelmen and the Good Roads Movement, 1880–1905" (PhD diss. University of Michigan, 1957), and Carlton Reid, *Roads Were Not Built for Cars* (Washington, DC: Island Press, 2015), 153–54.

47. "A Roadway for the Fair: Exhibit of National League for Good Road," *New York Times*, May 12, 1893.

48. *Rand, McNally & Co.'s A Week at the Fair*, 96–97.

49. Gustaitis, *Chicago's Greatest Year*, 1.

50. Chaim Rosenberg, *America at the Fair: Chicago's 1893 World's Columbian Exposition* (Charleston, SC: Acadia Publishing, 2008), 260–79.

Chapter 5. The Great Emancipator

1. Joseph Gustaitis, *Chicago's Greatest Year, 1893* (Carbondale, IL: Southern Illinois University Press, 2013), 84.

2. Frances E. Willard, *A Wheel within a Wheel: How I Learned to Ride the Bicycle, with Some Reflections by the Way* (Chicago: Women's Temperance Publishing Association, 1895), 12–13.

3. "Bicycles and the Liquor Trade," *Topeka Daily Capital*, August 27, 1897.

4. Willard, *A Wheel*, 25–26.

5. Ross D. Petty, "Women and the Wheel," *Cycle History: Proceedings of the 7th International Cycle History Conference* (San Francisco: Van Der Plas, 1997), 124.

6. "A Cycling Prima Donna," *Evening World* (New York), November 29, 1888, 3.

7. "Girls Who Ride Wheels," *Chicago Daily Tribune*, August 3, 1890.

8. "Great Endurance on the Bicycles," *San Francisco Call*, January 17, 1892, 16.

9. "Fair Faces on Wheels: Women Riders No Longer a Novelty," *Chicago Daily Tribune*, August 16, 1891.

10. "Chicago," *The Cyclist*, May 1890, 58.

11. "In Their New Home," *Chicago Daily Tribune*, July 19, 1895, 5; "Chicago Cycling Clubs for Women," *Chicago Daily Tribune*, March 22, 1896, 42.

12. "The Almighty Bicycle," *Chicago Daily Tribune*, June 14, 1896.

13. Sarah Hallenbeck, *Claiming the Bicycle: Women, Rhetoric, and Technology in Nineteenth-Century America* (Carbondale: Southern Illinois University Press, 2016), 35.

14. Hallenbeck, *Claiming*, 35.

15. "She Makes Bicycles: A Woman Who Is an Expert in This Line of Work," *Detroit Free Press*, August 24, 1895, 4, cited in Christin Neejer, "The Bicycle Girls: American Wheelwomen and Everyday Activism in the Late Nineteenth Century" (PhD diss., Michigan State University, 2016), 191.

16. *Fifth Annual Report of the Factory Inspectors of Illinois for the Year Ending December 15, 1897* (Springfield, IL: Phillips Bros, 1898), 24–33.

17. "Champion of Her Sex: Miss Susan B. Anthony," *The New York World*, February 2, 1896.

18. "A Bifurcated Being," *The Examiner*, September 16, 1896.

19. *Rational Dress Society Gazette* 1 (April 1888): 1.

20. For a more in-depth discussion of the differences between dress reform and women's bicycle clothing, see Caitlin Cohn, "Wheelwomen: Women's Dress in a Transatlantic Cycling Culture, 1868–1900" (master's thesis, University of Minnesota, 2016).

21. "Their Wheels Spin," *Chicago Daily Tribune*, April 15, 1894.

22. "Health, Beauty, and Dress," *The Women's Tribune* 12, no. 25 (June 22, 1895): 100.

23. "Have Come to Stay," *Chicago Daily Tribune*, October 28, 1894.

24. "Bloomers and Bloomer Etiquette: How the Unique Club Disciplined Two Members Who Appeared in Skirts," *Journal of the Illinois State Historical Society* 34, no. 3 (September 1941): 378–79.

25. "Edict Against Bicycle Suits," *Chicago Daily Tribune*, September 7, 1895.

26. Julia Christie-Robin, Belinda T. Orzada, and Dilia López-Gydosh, "From Bustles to Bloomers: Exploring the Bicycle's Influence on American Women's Fashion, 1880–1914," *Journal of American Culture* 35, no. 4 (December 2012): 315.

27. "Bloomer Ball," *The Referee*, July 25, 1895; Robert A. Smith, *A Social History of the Bicycle: Its Early Life and Times in America* (New York: American Heritage Press, 1972), 104; Jim Hurd and Jay Pridmore, *Schwinn Bicycles* (Osceola, WI: MBI Publishing Company, 1996), 64.

28. Robert McCullough, *Old Wheelways: Traces of Bicycle History on the Land* (Cambridge, MA: MIT Press, 2015), 17.

29. "Scarlet Women on Wheels," *Denver Evening Post*, August 23, 1895, 1.

30. "Bathhouse John's Bloomer Ordinance," *Chicago Daily Tribune*, May 28, 1895.

31. Steven A. Riess and Gerald R. Gems, *The Chicago Sports Reader: 100 Years of Sports in the Windy City* (Urbana: University of Illinois Press, 2009), 9.

32. Arabella Kenealy, "Woman as Athlete," *The Nineteenth Century*, April 1899, 645.

33. E. D. Page, "Woman and the Bicycle," *Brooklyn Medical Journal* 11 (1897): 81–87.

34. Amy Drake, "Rubbing the Pommel: Women and Bicycling in the 1890s" (master's thesis, Oneonta, State University of New York, 2011).

35. Iland Leibovitch and Mor Yoram, "The Vicious Cycling: Bicycling Related Urogenital Disorders," *European Urology* 47, no. 3 (2005): 277–87.

36. Jean Bethke Elshtain, *Jane Addams and the Dream of American Democracy* (New York: Basic Books, 2002), 124.

37. "Woman and Her Bicycle," *Chicago Daily News*, October 17, 1894.

38. Francis Nash, "A Plea for the New Woman and the Bicycle," *The American Journal of Obstetrics and Diseases of Women and Children*, 33 (1896): 556–60.

39. Robert N. Tooker, *Bicycling for Girls from a Medical Standpoint: A Paper Read Before the Chicago Academy of Homeopathic Physicians* (Chicago: Gormully & Jeffery Mfg. Co., 1891).

40. "Their Wheels Spin: Eight Chicago Women Who Have Made Bicycle Centuries," *Chicago Daily Tribune*, April 15, 1894, 35; "Chicago's Noted Centurions," *The Referee*, August 31, 1894; Mary Ann Parker, "Bicycle in American History" (master's thesis, Urbana, University of Illinois, 1947), 114; "Girls of Great Endurance," *Streator Daily Free Press*, January 26, 1892; "Chicago Ladies Ride Centuries," *The Bearings*, June 29, 1894.

41. "They Ride 100 Miles," *Chicago Tribune*, August 6, 1894, 1; "Chicago's Champion Lady Century Rider," *Akron Daily Democrat*, August 18, 1894, 5; "Lowers a Century Record," *Chicago Chronicle*, September 20, 1895, 4.

42. "Young Girl 'Shoots the Chutes,'" *Chicago Chronicle*, October 8, 1896, 4.

43. Tammy Haley, "She Wore White Duck Bloomers: Annis Burr Porter's 1897, 1,100 Mile Summer Outing," *The Wheelmen* 93 (November 2018): 2–11; "In White Duck Bloomers," *Daily News* (Batavia, NY), June 12, 1897.

44. "Miss Bunker Rides the Woman's Century Down," *The Bearings*, October 10, 1895; "Century Road Club Records," *Chicago Tribune*, March 12, 1897, 8; Century Road Club of America, *C.R.C. Manual* (Terre Haute, Indiana: Moore & Langen Printing Co., 1898), 77.

45. *Stillwater Messenger* (Minnesota), April 1896, quoted in Roger Gilles, *Women on the Move: The Forgotten Era of Women's Bicycle Racing* (Lincoln: University of Nebraska Press, 2018), 112.

46. "Women's Bicycle Races," *Courier-Journal* (Louisville, KY), September 23, 1894, 13; *League of American Wheelmen Racing Rules, 1895.*

47. "Women's Cycle Races Come Next," *Chicago Tribune,* September 6, 1896, 7; "Charity Bicycle Races Tonight," *Chicago Daily Tribune,* September 23, 1899.

48. "Miss Tillie Anderson," *Referee Cycle and Trade Journal,* February 6, 1896; Heather Drieth, "Tillie Anderson, the Terrible Swede," *The Wheelmen* 56 (May 2000): 2–3.

49. "Ride Like the Wind," *Chicago Tribune,* January 29, 1896, 7; "Tillie Wins by a Lap," *Chicago Tribune,* February 2, 1896, 7; Drieth, "Tillie Anderson, the Terrible Swede," 4–5; Hall, *Muscle on Wheels,* 159.

50. "Challenged by Miss Anderson," *Chicago Chronicle,* May 16, 1896, 6; "Will Race Tillie Anderson" *Chicago Chronicle,* May 17, 1896, 11.

51. "Wants to Ride in Road Race," *Chicago Chronicle,* May 5, 1896, 5.

52. Drieth, "Tillie Anderson, the Terrible Swede," 2.

53. Drieth, "Tillie Anderson, the Terrible Swede," 2; Gilles, *Women on the Move,* 73.

54. "Tillie Anderson's Views," *Chicago Chronicle,* April 11, 1897, 30.

55. Gilles, *Women on the Move,* 67–68.

56. "Women Injured in a Race," *Chicago Chronicle,* March 17, 1897.

57. "Glaw Wins at Chicago," *American Wheelman,* March 25, 1897.

58. Gilles, *Women on the Move,* 141–42; *St. Louis Republic,* Sunday, December 12, 1897.

59. Fanny Darling, "Bicycle Racing Transforms Lovely Woman from a Pale Beauty into a Perfect Fright," *St. Louis Post-Dispatch,* December 5, 1897, 16.

60. Gilles, *Women on the Move,* 197–198.

61. "Tillie Anderson," U.S. Bicycling Hall of Fame, accessed February 20, 2023, https://usbhof.org/inductee/tillie-anderson-2/; "Victoria Bussi Reclaims the UCI Hour Record," UCI, accessed October 11, 2024. https://www.uci.org/pressrelease/vittoria-bussi-reclaims-the-uci-hour-record-timed-by-tissot-and-breaks-the/3oM6jKT0yM32oSnCwyuTRI.

62. "Big Handicap Century Road Race," *Chicago Tribune,* October 19, 1895, 6; Gilles, *Women on the Move,* 5.

63. Darling, "Bicycle Racing Transforms."

64. "Glaw the Winner," *Toledo Commercial,* July 29, 1897.

65. *Chicago Journal,* November 29, 1898, quoted in Gilles, *Women on the Move,* 245.

66. "Miss Bayne Finished Fourth," *Brooklyn Citizen,* April 28, 1902, 4; Gilles, *Women on the Move,* 282–83.

67. Gilles, *Women on the Move,* 165–66.

68. "Don'ts for Women Riders," *Illinois State Journal,* July 15, 1895.

Chapter 6. Larger than Life

1. Edward Wilson, "Edward Wilson Diary," November-December 1895, McLean County Museum of History.

2. Christopher Sweet, "Baby Bliss: World's Heaviest Cyclist," *Wheelmen* 92 (May 2018): 2–7; "Baby Bliss' Top Weight, 565," *Daily Pantagraph,* June 5, 1942; *McLean County, Illustrated* (Brookhaven Press, 1899), 715–17.

3. "The Chicago Road Race," *The Referee* 15, May 31, 1895, 192.

4. "Morgan and Wright Victories," *The Referee,* July 1895.

5. "Baby Bliss on a Wheel," *The Upper Des Moines,* June 17, 1896, 5.

6. *McLean County, Illustrated,* 715–17.

7. "'Baby' Bliss, Bloomington's Giant, Dead," *Weekly Pantagraph,* January 5, 1912, 6.

8. "Big Cycle Show Is on Wheels! Wheels! Wheels!" *Inter Ocean*, January 24, 1897, 7; "At the Start of the Great Race," *Chicago Tribune*, July 6, 1897.

9. Francine Hornberger, *Carny Folk: The World's Weirdest Sideshow Acts* (New York: Citadel Press, 2005), 76–77.

10. "Prodigies in Conference," *New York Times*, April 13, 1903, 6.

11. The story of the Buffalo bicycle bank robbers was well documented in Illinois newspapers published May 14–25, 1896. The following papers had the best coverage: *Decatur Weekly Republican, Decatur Daily Republican, Decatur Herald*, and *Chicago Chronicle*.

12. This section on John D. Rockefeller and bicycles was compiled from the following sources: "Rockefeller on a Wheel," *Inter Ocean*, July 4, 1896, 1; "John D. Rockefeller on Wheels," *Chicago Tribune*, March 3, 1895, 43; "Money Kings Scorch," *Fort Wayne News*, July 17, 1897, 1.

13. "Man of Wealth A Wheel," *Chicago Daily Tribune*, July 4, 1896, 8.

14. Thomas Stevens' ride was summarized from his book, *Around the World on a Bicycle* (New York: C. Scribner's Sons, 1888).

15. This section on Allen and Sachtleben's trip was summarized from Thomas Gaskell Allen and William Lewis Sachtleben, *Across Asia on a Bicycle* (New York: Century Co., 1894); David Herlihy, *The Lost Cyclist: The Epic Tale of an American Adventurer and His Mysterious Disappearance* (Boston: Mariner Books, 2010); Irving A. Leonard, "A Trans-Asia Bike Tour in 1890," in *The Best of Bicycling*, ed. Harley Leete (New York: Trident Press, 1970), 335–38.

16. Allen and Sachtleben, *Across Asia*, 83.

17. Herlihy, *The Lost Cyclist*.

18. Allen and Sachtleben, *Across Asia*, 1894, 84.

19. There are multiple versions and editions of Allen and Sachtleben's book. This quote comes from *Across Asia on a Bicycle* (London: T.F. Unwin, 1895), xi.

20. "Round the World on Bicycles," *Harper's Weekly*, January 14, 1893, 46.

21. Herlihy, *Lost Cyclist*, 144.

22. Allen and Sachtleben, *Across Asia*, 1895, xi.

23. Most of the documentation for this section comes from Peter Zheutlin, *Around the World on Two Wheels: Annie Londonderry's Extraordinary Ride* (New York: Kensington, 2007). Zheutlin, the great-grandnephew of Annie, did extensive research and compiled a compelling story of Annie's travels. For this section, I also consulted David Herlihy, "A Tale of Two Annies," *Adventure Cyclist*, June 2021, 10–49.

24. Zheutlin, *Around the World*, 6–27.

25. Zheutlin, *Around the World*, 42.

26. Zheutlin, *Around the World*, 39.

27. "Miss Londonderry," *Buffalo Courier*, November 1, 1894, 10.

28. Zheutlin, *Around the World*, 39–40.

29. "Miss Londonderry Departs," *Inter Ocean*, October 15, 1894, 8.

30. "Round the World," *The Buffalo Express*, November 1, 1894, 11, cited in Zheutlin, *Around the World*, 49.

31. Zheutlin, *Around the World*, 94.

32. Zheutlin, *Around the World*, 89.

33. "Miss Londonderry Near Home," *Chicago Chronicle*, September 10, 1895, 2.

34. Zheutlin, *Around the World*, 131.

35. Mr. and Mrs. H. Darwin McIlrath, *Around the World on Wheels for the Inter Ocean* (Chicago: Inter Ocean Publishing Co., 1898), 9.

36. McIlrath, *Around the World*, 6; Duncan R. Jamieson, *The Self-Propelled Voyager: How the Cycle Revolutionized Travel* (Lanham, Maryland: Rowman & Littlefield, 2015), 85.

37. "McIlraths Reach Home," *Chicago Daily Tribune*, December 2, 1898, 4.

38. The majority of the material for this section comes from the Thomas Davis scrapbooks held in the Special Collections of the Cullom-Davis Library at Bradley University, Peoria, Illinois.

39. Thomas Davis scrapbooks.

40. *Bicycling World*, June 2nd, 1906.

41. Judy Rosella Edwards, *Underground@Springdale: True stories about Springdale Cemetery* volume 1 (lulu.com: 2008), 19.

42. Cleveland D. Miller, *The Chicago Clubs Illustrated* (Chicago: Lanward Publishing Company, 1888).

43. Lisa Holton, *For Members Only: A History and Guide to Chicago's Oldest Private Clubs* (Chicago: Lake Claremont Press, 2008), 268.

44. Joseph Flinn, *Chicago, the Marvelous City of the West: A History, an Encyclopedia, and a Guide 1892* (Chicago: Standard Guide Co., 1892), 224; "Cycling Clubs Unite," *Chicago Tribune*, November 21, 1890, 6.

45. "Chicago's Cycling Clubs," *Chicago Daily Tribune*, May 17, 1896; Allyson Hobbs, "Bicycling," in *The Encyclopedia of Chicago*, ed. James Grossman, Ann Keating, Janice Reiff, and Michael Conzen (Chicago: University of Chicago Press, 2004), 78; Steven Streight, *Bicycle Fever: Peoria Bicycle Races from the 1890s to the 1990s* (Peoria, IL: Ruppman Marketing Services, 1990), 30.

46. Information on specific clubs can be found in *Bicycle Directory and Chicago Cycler's Guide for 1896*.

47. "Flotsam and Jetsam," *The Freeman* (Indianapolis), September 15, 1888, 1, as found in Robert J. Turpin, *Black Cyclists: The Race for Inclusion* (Urbana: University of Illinois Press, 2024), 37; "New Incorporations," *Chicago Tribune*, June 21, 1892, 14; "Will Have No Colored Members," *Chicago Tribune*, September 9, 1892, 7; "The Cycle Thief in Chicago," *Wheel and Cycling Trade Review*, June 16, 1893, 29.

48. *Illinois Cycling Club Life Newsletter* 4, no. 2 (June 1896), Chicago History Museum.

49. "Leads on the West Side," *Chicago Chronicle*, January 24, 1897, 36.

50. The original pieces of sheet music are held in the collections of the Bicycle Museum of America in New Bremen, Ohio. The Wheelmen website has digital images of many of these: https://www.thewheelmen.com/sections/memorabilia/covers/default.php.

51. George D. Bushnell, "When Chicago Was Wheel Crazy," in *Chicago Sports Reader*, ed. Steven Riess and Gerald Gems (Urbana: University of Illinois Press, 2009), 86.

52. "Like a Masonic Charm," *Chicago Tribune*, May 24, 1896, 5.

53. Century Road Club of America, *C.R.C. Manual* (Terre Haute, Indiana: Moore & Langen Printing Co., 1898), 77, https://catalog.hathitrust.org/Record/002020917.

54. Patrick Butler, *Hidden History of Uptown and Edgewater* (Charleston, SC: The History Press, 2013), 73.

55. Butler, *Hidden History*, 73.

56. Eleanor Page, "Saddle and Cycle Recalls Early Days as Bicycle Club," *Chicago Tribune*, October 11, 1965, C7.

57. "Saddle and Cycle Club," *Chicago Daily Tribune*, May 14, 1899, 42.

58. "Looking Backward Around Town with the Saddle and Cycle Club," *Chicago History: The Magazine of the Chicago Historical Society* 11, no. 2 (Summer, 1982): 112.

59. "Cyclists to Act for Charity," *Chicago Chronicle*, November 17, 1895, 5.

60. Lisa Holton, *For Members Only*, viii.

61. Christopher Sweet, "A Comprehensive Bibliography of Nineteenth-Century Bicycling Periodicals," *American Periodicals* 29, no. 1 (2019): 76–95.

62. Charles Bates, *Art and Literature of Business*, vol. 4 (New York: Bates Publishing Co., 1902), 241; Ross D. Petty, "Peddling the Bicycle in the 1890s: Mass Marketing Shifts into High Gear," *Journal of Macromarketing* 15, no. 1 (1995): 32–46.

63. Copies of *Chicago Cyclers' Guide for 1896*; *Dash: A Society and Club Paper*; *Illinois Cycling Club Life*; and *The Scorcher: A Hot Paper for Hot Cyclists* are held by the Chicago History Museum.

Chapter 7. Scorchers and Cracks

1. *Wheel Talk*, March 1897, 57; Charlie Miller, scrapbooks, Chicago History Museum; "McIliff Enters the Race," *Chicago Tribune*, February 7, 1897, 7.

2. Robert Smith, *A Social History of the Bicycle: Its Early Life and Time in America* (New York: American Heritage Press, 1972), 135–36.

3. "Miller Finishes a Winner," *New York Times*, December 12, 1897, 2.

4. Andrew M. Homan, *Life in the Slipstream: The Legend of Bobby Walthour Sr.* (Washington, DC: Potomac Books, 2011), 41; "Miller Finishes a Winner"; Advertisement, *Sunday Inter Ocean*, February 19, 1899, 10.

5. Homan, *Life in the Slipstream*, 41–43; Michael Leccese and Arlene Plevin, *The Bicyclist's Sourcebook* (Rockville, MD: Woodbine House, 1991), 326–27.

6. Homan, *Life in the Slipstream*, 41–43; "No More Endurance Bicycle Races," *Chicago Tribune*, March 11, 1897, 6; "Enter for Road Race," *Chicago Tribune*, May 13, 1897, 4; Lou Dzierzak, *The Evolution of American Bicycle Racing* (Guilford, Connecticut: FalconGuides, 2007), 20.

7. Charlie Miller, scrapbooks.

8. Charlie Miller, scrapbooks.

9. Dzierzak, *Evolution of American Bicycle Racing*, 20.

10. *Cycling Record Book* (Cleveland, OH: Emil Grossman & Co., 1898), 25.

11. Todd Balf, *Major: A Black Athlete, a White Era, and the Fight to Be the World's Fastest Human Being* (New York: Crown Publishers, 2008), 139.

12. *The Cyclist*, August 1890.

13. Peter Nye, *The Six-Day Bicycle Races* (San Francisco: Van Der Plas Publications, 2006), 101; Roger Gilles, *Women on the Move: The Forgotten Era of Women's Bicycle Racing* (Lincoln, NE: University of Nebraska Press, 2018), 58.

14. John Paulett and Ron Gordon, *Forgotten Chicago* (Charleston, SC: Arcadia, 2004), 42–43; "Libby Prison Museum," Chicagology, accessed February 17, 2023, https://chicagology.com/goldenage/goldenage118/.

15. League of American Wheelmen, *League of American Wheelmen Racing Rules*, 1895, 34. https://catalog.hathitrust.org/Record/100598269.

16. "Winners of Decoration Day Races," *Chicago Tribune*, May 23, 1897, 37; Smith, *A Social History of the Bicycle*, 145–47.

17. "Await the Big Road Race," *Chicago Chronicle*, May 24, 1896, 23; Pullman, *Road Race Souvenir Program*, 1890, Henry Ford Museum Archives.

18. Paul M. Angle, "The Golden Age of Cycling," *Chicago History* 8, no 4 (Summer 1967): 107.

19. "Pullman Road Race," *American Cyclist*, June 1891, 126.

20. "Chicago," *The American Cyclist*, May 1892, 124; "The Color Line in Cycling," *Inter Ocean*, April 26, 1892, 6.

21. "Pullman Road Race," *The American Cyclist*, June 1892.

22. Smith, *A Social History of the Bicycle*, 145–47; Michael C. Gabriele, *Golden Age of Bicycle Racing in New Jersey* (Charleston, SC: History Press, 2011), 21.

23. "The Chicago," *Supplement to the Wheel and Cycling Trade Review*, June 1, 1894, iv; "Won by a Dark Horse," *Detroit Free Press*, May 31, 1895.

24. "Big Race Should Be Open," *Chicago Chronicle*, April 11, 1897, 30.

25. *Eleventh Annual Chicago Road Race*, 1897, Chicago History Museum.

26. Century Road Club of America, *C.R.C. Manual*, 77.

27. "Letter Carrier Smith Returns," *Chicago Tribune*, September 15, 1894, 7; "Road Records Accepted," *Boston Post*, September 20, 1896, 18; *C.R.C. Manual*, 1898, 97; S. A. Nelson, *Spalding's Official Bicycle Guide for 1897* (New York: American Sports Publishing Co., 1896), 70.

28. "Chicago's Noted Centurions," *The Referee*, August 31, 1894; "Century Road Club Records," *Chicago Tribune*, March 12, 1897, 8; Noman L. Dunham, "The Bicycle Era in American History" (PhD diss., Harvard University, 1956), 462; *C.R.C. Manual*, 1898, 35–43.

29. Ari C. de Wilde, "'The Dizzy Race to Nowhere:' The Business of Professional Cycling in North America, 1891–1940" (PhD diss., Ohio State University, 2010), 83–84; *League of American Wheelmen Racing Rules*, 1895.

30. Nelson, *Spalding's Official Bicycle Guide for 1897.*

31. "Peoria a Cycling Center," *The Chicago Chronicle,* March 22, 1896, 16; Steven Streight, *Bicycle Fever: Peoria Bicycle Races from the 1890s to the 1990s* (Peoria, IL: Ruppman Marketing Services, 1990).

32. "Concerning the Peoria Meet," *Wheel and Cycling Trade Review* 5, no. 26 (August 1890): 776; *History of the Peoria Bicycle Club*, circa 1941, 5, Bradley University Library, Special Collections; Streight, *Bicycle Fever*, 47; "Peoria," *Wheel and Cycling Trade Review*, September 19, 1890, 99.

33. "Bicycle Records Broken," *Inter Ocean,* September 14, 1890, 3; *Peoria Journal Transcript,* December 7, 1930, 6.

34. The author's compiled list of nineteenth-century world and American bicycle records can be found in the Internet Archive, https://archive.org/details/nineteenth-century-mens-world-and-american-bicycle-records-set-in-illinois. Specific information about the records broken in Peoria can be found in the following sources: "Bicycle Records Broken," 3; "Peoria," *Wheel and Cycling Trade Review*, 99; "World Records for Penny Farthing Bicycles," The International World Record Breakers' Club, accessed February 20, 2023, http://www.recordholders.org/en/list/pennyfarthing.html; "Peoria Tournament," *American Cyclist*, August, 1891.

35. "Chicago Cyclists Go to Peoria," *Chicago Tribune*, June 25, 1896, 8; "Riders Are at Peoria," *Chicago Chronicle*, June 25, 1896, 5; "The Illinois Meet," *Chicago Chronicle*, June 22, 1896, 5; *Spalding's Official Bicycle Guide for 1897*; *Illinois Cycling Club Life* 4, no. 2 (June 1896); "No Records Broken," *Inter Ocean*, June 27, 1896, 4.

36. "Grand Bicycle Fete," *Inter Ocean*, July 5, 1895, 3; *Bicycle Derby*, 1895, Chicago History Museum; Morgan & Wright, advertising catalog (Chicago: C.H. Morgan Co., 1896), 99.

37. Amanda Becker, *Rockford's Forgotten Driving Park: Racing Politics & Circuses* (Charleston SC: History Press, 2019), 25; *Chicago Record*, May 2, 1897, 6.

38. Maria Ward, *Bicycling for Ladies* (New York: Brentano's, 1896), 78–79.

39. "Concerning Chicago Trade," *Wheel and Cycling Trade Review*, April 22, 1892, 23.

40. Glenn Stout, *Cubs* (Boston: Houghton Mifflin, 2007), 5.

41. Charles Meinert, "Six-Day Bicycle Races," *Wheelmen* 53, November 1998, 8.

42. Susan Gray, "Albert Schock—Champion of the World," *Wheelmen* 93, November 2018, 19.

43. "Diphtheria," *Fall River Daily Evening News*, February 25, 1895, 2; Gray, "Albert Schock," 20.

44. Gray, "Albert Schock," 20.

45. Gray, "Albert Schock," 12–23.

46. "Peoria," *Wheel and Cycling Trade Review*, 99.

47. Marshall Taylor, *Fastest Bicycle Rider in the World* (Worcester, MA: Commonwealth Press, 1928), 5.

48. Andrew Ritchie, *Major Taylor, "The Fastest Bicycle Rider in the World* (San Francisco: Van der Plas Publications, 2010), 29.

49. "The Other Side," *Bearings*, February 9, 1894.

50. Ritchie, *Major Taylor,* 85.

51. Taylor, *The Fastest Bicycle Rider*, 86.

52. Taylor, *The Fastest Bicycle Rider*, 106.

53. Taylor, *The Fastest Bicycle,* 106.

54. Balf, *Major: A Black Athlete*, 138–42.

55. Ritchie, *Major Taylor,* 90.

56. Homan, *Life in the Slipstream*; "Made the Mile in 'One Three,'" *St. Louis Post-Dispatch,* August 10, 1896, 5.

57. "Beat A Mile A Minute," *New York Times,* July 1, 1899.

58. "John Nelson's Great Ride," *Ottawa Journal,* August 11, 1899, 3; "Broke Twenty World's Records," *The Indianapolis Journal,* July 5, 1900, 2; "Cycle Racing Records," *Boston Globe,* November 19, 1900, 4; "Major Taylor Beaten," *Hartford Courant,* July 23, 1901, 2.

59. "Arena of Sports," *Evening Express* (Portland, ME), September 10, 1901, 7.

60. "Wheelmen Say Cycling Is Dead as Organized Sport," *Chicago Daily Tribune,* November 19, 1899, 8.

Chapter 8. Demon Motors

1. For this account of the 1895 Race of the Century, I consulted the following sources: Richard P. Scharchburg, *Carriages Without Horses: J. Frank Duryea and the Birth of the American Automobile Industry* (Warrendale, PA: Society of Automotive Engineers, 1993), 101–117; Cord Scott, "The Race of the Century: 1895 Chicago," *Journal of the Illinois State Historical Society* 96, no. 1 (Spring 2003): 37–48; Russel H. Anderson, "The First Automobile Race in America," *Journal of the Illinois State Historical Society* 47, no. 4 (1954): 343–59; George May, "The Thanksgiving Day Race of 1895," *Chicago History* (October/November 1982): 177; Albert R. Bochroch, *American Automobile Racing: An Illustrated History* (New York: Viking Press, 1974), 12–16.

2. Christopher George Sinsbaugh, *Who, Me? Forty Years of Automobile History* (Detroit: Arnold-Powers, Inc., 1940), 39–40.

3. May, "The Thanksgiving Day Race of 1895," 177; Bochroch, *American Automobile Racing,* 12–16.

4. Stephen W. Sears, *The American Heritage History of the Automobile in America* (New York: American Heritage Publishing Company, 1977), 26.

5. *The American Car Since 1775: The Most Complete Survey of the American Automobile Ever Published* (New York: L. S. Bailey, 1971).

6. Frank Brown Latham, *1872–1972: A Century of Serving Consumers: The Story of Montgomery Ward* (Chicago: Montgomery Ward, 1972), 2.

7. *Our Silver Anniversary* (Chicago: Montgomery Ward & Co, 1897).

8. Montgomery Ward & Co., *Price List of Safety Bicycles, Sundries, Etc.*, 1893; Wheelmen collections, *Montgomery Ward Bicycle Catalog,* 1896; Wheelmen Collections, *Montgomery Ward Bicycle Catalog,* 1899, Bicycle Museum of America.

9. Joseph Gustaitis, *Chicago's Greatest Year, 1893* (Carbondale, IL: Southern Illinois University Press, 2013), 60; *Sears, Roebuck & Co., Consumer's Guide for 1894* (New York: Skyhorse Publishing, 2013), 180–84.

10. Sears, Roebuck & Co., *Models of 1898,* catalog, Baker Library, Harvard Business School, Harvard University.

11. Frederick Asher, *Richard Warren Sears, Icon of Inspiration* (New York: Vantage Press, 1997), 12; Charles W. Carey Jr., *American Inventors, Entrepreneurs, and Business Visionaries* (New York: Facts On File, 2011), 317–19.

12. "Sales through the Mail," *The Wheel and Cycling Trade Review,* January 25, 1900, 94.

13. Gustaitus, *Chicago's Greatest Year,* 67.

14. *The 1902 Edition of the Sears Roebuck Catalog* (New York: Bounty Books, 1975), 276.

15. Gary Sanderson, "James L. Mead and the Mead Cycle Company: 1888 to the 1940s," *Cycle History 24: Proceedings of the 24th International Cycling History Conference* (Birmingham, England: Cycling History Ltd., 2014), 97–120; "Sales through the Mail," 94; George S. Lewis, "Story of the Mead Cycle Company," *Mahin's Magazine* 2, no. 10 (January 1904): 924–28.

16. "Sales through the Mail," 94.

17. "Finally Form Bicycle Trust," *Chicago Tribune*, September 1, 1899, 1; Bruce Epperson, *Peddling Bicycles to America* (Jefferson, NC: McFarland, 2010), 171–78; Arthur S. Dewing, *Corporate Promotions and Reorganizations* (Harvard University Press, 1914), 249–68.

18. Epperson, *Peddling*, 180–81; Dewing, *Corporate Promotions*, 249–68.

19. "Cycle Trust Punctured," *Chicago Tribune*, September 3, 1902, 1.

20. Roland C. Geist, *Bicycling as a Hobby* (New York: Harper Brothers, 1940), 159.

21. Alan Dowds, *The Encyclopedia of Motorcycles: From 1884 to the Present Day* (San Diego: Thunder Bay Press, 2007), 11; *Bicycling World*, January 10, 1901, 370; Michael Partridge, *Motorcycle Pioneers: The Men, the Machines, the Events 1860–1930* (New York: Arco, 1977), 6.

22. Dowds, *Encyclopedia*, 11; Steven E. Alford and Suzanne Ferriss, *An Alternative History of Bicycles and Motorcycles: Two-Wheeled Transportation and Material Culture* (Lanham, MD: Rowman & Littlefield Publishing Group, 2016), 33.

23. "First of Its Kind on the Market," *Chicago Daily Tribune*, January 4, 1896, 7.

24. John H. Wyatt, *Motor Cycling* (London: George G. Harrap & Co., 1925), 10–11.

25. "Motorcycle Club Formed," *Inter Ocean*, April 24, 1901, 7.

26. "Garfield Park Cycle Races," *Chicago Tribune*, July 5, 1903, 9; Cord Scott, "Harley's Wayward Cousins: A History of Chicago Motorcycle Makers," *Journal of the Illinois State Historical Society* 98, no. 4 (2005): 290.

27. Cord Scott, "Harley's Wayward Cousins: A History of Chicago Motorcycle Makers," *Journal of the Illinois State Historical Society* 98, no. 4 (Winter 2005/2006): 287.

28. Rodolphus W. Joslyn and Frank W. Joslyn, *History of Kane County, Ill.*, vol. 1 (Chicago: The Pioneer Publishing Company, 1908), 593; Advertisement, *Chicago Tribune*, May 7, 1899, 15.

29. Greg Walter, "History of the Thor Motorcycle Company," Police Motor Units, accessed March 13, 2023, http://policemotorunits.com/history-of-thor-motorcycle-company/.

30. "George Mallory Hendee," U.S. Bicycle Hall of Fame, accessed March 13, 2023, https://usbhof.org/inductee/george-mallory-hendee/.

31. Tod Rafferty, *The Complete Illustrated Encyclopedia of American Motorcycles* (Philadelphia: Courage Books, 1999), 124; Tod Rafferty, *The Indian: The History of a Classic American Motorcycle* (London: Salamander, 2001), 7–17; R. K. Keating, *Velodrome Racing and the Rise of the Motorcycle* (Jefferson, NC: McFarland & Company, 2021), 304–13.

32. Keating, *Velodrome*, 304–13; "Remembering the Aurora Automatic Machine Company," Hemmings, accessed March 13, 2023, https://www.hemmings.com/stories/2015/08/24/remembering-the-aurora-automatic-machine-company; Rafferty, *Indian*, 7–17.

33. Rafferty, *Indian*, 7–17; Rafferty, *Encyclopedia*, 124–65.

34. "Licensed to Organize," *Chicago Tribune*, August 7, 1884, 6.

35. Advertisement, *Chicago Tribune*, June 24, 1894, 24.

36. Advertisement, *Motorcycling*, March 28, 1912; Jay Pridmore and Jim Hurd, *Schwinn Bicycles*, (Osceola, WI: MBI Publishing, 1996), 35–45.

37. Rafferty, *Encyclopedia*, 48; M. D. Henry, "Chicago Colossus," *Cycle*, March 1962, 34–37.

38. Rafferty, *Encyclopedia*, 116–118.

39. Rafferty, *Encyclopedia*, 50; Pridmore and Hurd, *Schwinn*, 109–11.

40. "The Vehicle Trade," *Indianapolis Journal*, May 26, 1901, 20; "Patee, Morris, and Their Remodeling of Tandems," *Bicycling World*, May 23, 1901, 199; "Lobby Chatter," *Dayton Daily News*, May 10, 1902, 5.

41. Rafferty, *Indian*, introduction.

42. Carlton Reid, *Roads Were Not Built for Cars: How Cyclists Were the First to Push for Good Roads & Became the Pioneers of Motoring* (Washington, DC: Island Press, 2015), 10–17.

43. Sears, *Automobile*, 19; Reid, *Roads*, 282–83.

44. Hiram Percy Maxim, *Horseless Carriage Days* (New York: Harper & Bros., 1937), 4–5.

45. James Flink, *The Automobile Age* (Cambridge, MA: MIT Press, 1990), 5.

46. George W. May, *Charles E. Duryea, Automaker* (Chillicothe, IL: River Beach Publishing, 1996), 52–55.

47. May, *Charles E. Duryea,* 53–70.

48. *Springfield Union*, June 24, 1923, cited in May, *Charles E. Duryea*, 70.

49. May, *Charles E. Duryea*, 72–73.

50. Epperson, *Peddling*, 131.

51. John Jacob Astor, Bicycle Brake, US Patent 417,401, December 17, 1889.

52. Bob Mionske, *Bicycling & the Law: Your Rights as a Cyclist* (Boulder, CO: VeloPress, 2007), 4–5.

53. Carey, *American Inventors*, 103–5; May, *Charles E. Duryea*, 126–76.

54. Richard P. Scharchburg, *Carriages Without Horses*; Carey, *American Inventors*, 103–5.

55. "Wanted to Stick to the Bicycle Business," *Chicago Tribune*, October 5, 1952, 12.

56. May, *Charles E. Duryea*, 97.

57. Beverly Rae Kimes, "Thomas B. Jeffery Company," in *Encyclopedia of American Business History and Biography*, ed. Keith L. Bryant (New York: Facts On File), 271–72.

58. David M. Young, "Automobile Manufacturing," in *The Encyclopedia of Chicago*, ed. James R. Grossman et al. (Chicago: University of Chicago Press, 2004), 55–56. Pridmore and Hurd, *Schwinn*, 108; Jesse J. Gant and Nicholas J. Hoffman, *Wheel Fever: How Wisconsin Became a Great Bicycling State* (Madison: Wisconsin Historical Society Press, 2013), 187.

59. *Belvidere Illustrated* (Belvidere, IL: Daily Republican, 1896), 30–67.

60. "The New Eldredge Runabout," *Automobile Review*, December 1, 1903, 207–9.

61. *Automobiles of 1904* (Scotia, NY: Americana Review, 1967), reprinted from *Frank Leslie's Popular Monthly*, January 1904; Mike Doyle, "The First Auto to Be Built in Boone," *Rockford Register Star*, January 18, 2012.

62. Isaac Potter, "Bicycle Outlook," *The Century Illustrated* 52 (May-October 1896), 789; David A. Hounshell, *From the American System to Mass Production 1800–1932* (Baltimore: John Hopkins U.P., 1984), 201–224.

63. Bureau of the Census, *Census of Manufactures: 1905* (GPO, 1908), 287–97.

64. Bruce Epperson, "How Many Bikes? An Investigation into the Quantification of Bicycling 1878–1914," *Cycle History 11: Proceedings of the 11th International Cycling History Conference* (2000), 42–50.

65. 1900 Census, vol. 10, Manufactures, part 4, in Special Reports on Selected Industries (Washington, DC: US Government Printing Office, 1902), 325–39.

66. 1905 Census, Census of Manufactures: 1905 (Washington, DC: Government Printing Office, 1908), 287–97.

67. Greg Borzo, *Where to Bike Chicago* (United States: Where to Bike LLC, 2011), 37; 1909 Census, vol. 10, Manufacturers, "Automobile Industry," (Washington, DC: Government Printing Office, 1913), 807–19; *Statistical Abstract of the United States 1923* (Washington, DC: Government Printing Office, 1924), 379.

68. Karl Hodges, "Did the Emergence of the Automobile End the Bicycle Boom?," *Proceedings of the 4th International Cycle History Conference* (San Francisco: Bicycle Books, Inc., 1994), 39–42.

69. "The Bicycle and the Automobile," *Scientific American*, September 23, 1905, 234.

70. "The Death of a Fad," *Washington Post*, December 16, 1906, 2.

71. "Wilson Blames Speeders," *New York Times*, February 28, 1906.

72. Hodges, "Did the Emergence," 39–42.

73. "Wheelmen Say Cycling is Dead as Organized Sport," *Chicago Tribune*, November 19, 1899, 8.

74. Thomas Burr, "Markets as Producers and Consumers: The French and U.S. National Bicycle Markets, 1875–1910" (PhD diss., University of California Davis, 2005), 283–316.

75. Frank J. Berto, "The Electric Streetcar and the End of the First American Bicycle Boom," *Cycle History 17: Proceedings of the 17th International Cycling History Conference* (San Francisco: Van der Plas Publications, 2006), 91–100; James J. Flink, *The Automobile Age* (Cambridge, MA: MIT Press, 1990), 3.

76. "Form Anti-Automobile League," *Chicago Tribune*, August 5, 1903, 5; Reid, *Roads*, 46.

Chapter 9. Booms and Busts

1. "About the World Naked Bike Ride: Chicago," ChicagoNakedRide, accessed June 21, 2023, http://chicagonakedride.org/about; Brett Lunceford, *Naked Politics: Nudity, Political Action, and the Rhetoric of the Body* (Lanham, MD: Lexington Books, 2012), 74–89; "How Nude," *Chicago Tribune*, February 8, 2013, 6–7.

2. Julia Christie-Robin, Belinda T. Orzada, and Dilia López-Gydosh, "From Bustles to Bloomers: Exploring the Bicycle's Influence on American Women's Fashion, 1880–1914," *Journal of American Culture* 35, no. 4 (December 2012): 315; "Naked Bike Ride Set to Roll Across City," *Chicago Tribune*, June 9, 2018, 3.

3. Axel Josephsson, "Bicycles and Tricycles," 1900 Census, vol. 10, Manufactures, part 4, in Special Reports on Selected Industries (Washington, DC: US Government Printing Office, 1902), 329.

4. "Greatest in the World," *Inter Ocean* (Chicago, IL), June 16, 1895, 6.

5. Judith Crown and Glenn Coleman, *No Hands: The Rise and Fall of the Schwinn Bicycle Company, an American Institution* (New York: Henry Holt and Company, 1996); Jay Pridmore and Jim Hurd, *Schwinn Bicycles*, (Osceola, WI: MBI Publishing, 1996); Arnold, Schwinn & Company, *Fifty Years of Schwinn-Built Bicycles* (Chicago: Arnold, Schwinn & Company, 1945).

6. Crown and Coleman, *No Hands*, 142.

7. Solomon Fabricant, *The Output of Manufacturing Industries, 1899–1937* (New York: National Bureau of Economic Research, 1940), 590.

8. Crown and Coleman, *No Hands*, 30; Schwinn, *Fifty Years*, 78.

9. George Strong Lewis, *My Early Life in Wichita and Other True Stories* (self-pub., 1954); "Bicycle Firm Enlarges Its Chicago Plant," *Chicago Tribune*, October 29, 1944, 44; "Monark Silver King Inc, Est. 1934," Made in Chicago Museum, accessed June 21, 2023, https://www.madeinchicagomuseum.com/single-post/monark-silver-king/.

10. *Ingo-Bike*, 1934, catalog, author's collection; *Popular Mechanics*, May 1987; Mary Miller, "Ingo Bicycle," *Wheelmen* 14 (May 1979): 2–4.

11. Fabricant, *Output of Manufacturing*, 590; John Lodge, "Bicycle Comes Back," *Popular Science*, July 1936, 40; "The Bicycle," *Scientific American*, July 25, 1896, 68–69; Evan Friss, *The Cycling City* (Chicago: University of Chicago Press, 2015), 37; Philip P. Mason, *The League of American Wheelmen and the Good Roads Movement*, 1880–1905 (PhD. diss., University of Michigan, 1957), 63; Lorin Ellsworth, "Riding to Learn," *American Bicyclist and Motorcyclist*, January 1939.

12. Arnold, Schwinn & Company, *Fifty Years*, 78–79.

13. ACME Newspictures, Inc., "Bike Parking Lot," Commercial press photograph and description. 1938. Author's collection; Mary Ann Parker, "Bicycle in American History" (master's thesis, University of Illinois, 1947), 134; James Longhurst, *Bike Battles: A History of Sharing the American Road* (Seattle: University of Wisconsin Press, 2015), 123–49; Jay Pridmore, *Classic American Bicycles* (Osceola, WI: MBI Pub. 1999), 50; Arnold, Schwinn & Company, *Fifty Years*, 78–79; "Progress Within the Bicycle Industry," *American Bicyclist and Motorcyclist* 68 (1947).

14. Longhurst, *Bike Battles*, 141–42; "Bicycles: They Come Back into American Life," *Consumers' Research Bulletin*, April 1942, 3–10.

15. Bruce Epperson, *Peddling Bicycles to America: The Rise of an Industry* (Jefferson, NC: McFarland, 2010), 223; Crown and Coleman, *No Hands*, 37; Pridmore, *Classic American Bicycles*, 50.

16. "People and Events," *Chicago Tribune*, May 28, 1944, 21; "Wagon Wheel Store Rolls Right Along for Lisle Man," *Chicago Tribune,* October 20, 1957, 29; Pridmore, *Classic American Bicycles,* 62–63.

17. Certain Tariff and Trade Bills: Hearings Before the Subcommittee on Trade of the Committee on Ways and Means, vol. 4, 485, H.R., 98th Cong., 1983.

18. Pridmore, *Classic American Bicycles*, 73; Crown and Coleman, *No Hands*, 74.

19. "New Plant at Olney Training Employees," *Evansville Courier and Press*, February 9, 1962, 22; "Expansion of Operation Is AMF Anticipation," *Evansville Courier and Press,* August 15, 1965, 2; Jason Norman, "Roadmaster Leaves Distribution Legacy," Bicycle Retailer and Industry News, February 1, 2010, https://www.bicycleretailer.com/north-america/2010/02/01/roadmaster-leaves-distribution-legacy.

20. "They Like Bikes," *Time Magazine* 97, no. 24 (June 14, 1971): 81; Certain Tariff and Trade Bills, 485; Frank J. Berto, "The Great American Bicycle Boom," *Cycle History 10: Proceedings of the 10th International Cycling History Conference* (San Francisco: Van der Plas, 2000), 133–141; Stefan Kanfer, "The Full Circle: In Praise of the Bicycle," *Time Magazine* 105, no. 17 (April 1975): 61; Margaret Guroff, *The Mechanical Horse: How the Bicycle Reshaped American Life* (Austin: University of Texas Press), 135–36.

21. Crown and Coleman, *No Hands*, 102.

22. Noel Grove, "Bikes Are Back—and Booming," *National Geographic*, May 1973; Carlton Reid, "Pedal-ins and Car Burials: What Happened to America's Forgotten 1970s Cycle Boom?" *The Guardian*, June 16, 2017, https://www.theguardian.com/cities/2017/jun/16/pedal-ins-patchouli-bikeology-americas-forgotten-1970s-cycle-boom.

23. "Bicycle Move Adds 500 Jobs in Olney," *Herald and Review* (Decatur, IL), October 25, 1980, 5; "Bike Parts Firm to Be First in Olney Park," *Herald and Review* (Decatur, IL), August 22, 1978, 6; Bicycle Retailer and Industry News, "Roadmaster Leaves Distribution Legacy."

24. Charlie Kelley, *Fat-Tire Flyer: Repack and the Birth of Mountain Biking* (Boulder, CO: Velo Press, 2014), 36.

25. Jeff Mapes, *Pedaling Revolution: How Cyclists are Changing American Cities* (Corvallis: Oregon State University Press, 2009), 29–30.

26. Crown and Coleman, *No Hands*, 106–13; Pridmore and Hurd, *Schwinn*, 140–44.

27. SRAM, *SRAM 25th Anniversary* (Chicago: Classic Color, 2012), 8–32; "A History of Innovation," About SRAM, SRAM, accessed June 22, 2023, https://www.sram.com/en/company/about/history; Mike Levy, "From the Top—SRAM CEO Stan Day"; Pinkbike, April 7, 2014, https://www.pinkbike.com/news/sram-ceo-stan-day-interview-2014.html.

28. "Roadmaster Industries, Inc.," Reference for Business, accessed June 22, 2023, https://www.referenceforbusiness.com/history2/53/Roadmaster-Industries-Inc.html#ixzz83syl95Fq; "Columbia Manufacturing Seeks Chapter 11 Protection," AP News, March 5, 1991, https://apnews.com/article/cfbd64b8e7823319346d144363592db1.

29. SRAM, "SRAM 25th Anniversary," 35; SRAM, "A History of Innovation"; Pinkbike, "From the Top."

30. "Bicycle Industry Overview 2015," National Bicycle Dealers Association, accessed June 22, 2015, https://nbda.com/bicycle-industry-data-overview/; Breakaway Research Group, "U.S. Bicycling Participation Benchmarking Study Report," PeopleForBikes, March 2015, https://prismic-io.s3.amazonaws.com/peopleforbikes/ea52c570-a114-4962-aa26-c7cf72aeb331_2014_Participation_Study.pdf.

31. "Sram LLC Company Profile: Financials, Valuation, and Growth," PrivCo; SRAM, "A History of Innovation."

32. "Bicycle Shortage Hits Local Shops," *The Times* (Streator, IL), July 28, 2020, A3; CORONAINSIGHTS, "2022 U.S. Bicycling Participation Study," accessed June 22, 2023, https://prismic-io.s3.amazonaws.com/peopleforbikes/22d4a9f5-f114-4c5e-a40d-a32c7fa1567f_2022+PeopleForBikes+US+Bicycling+Participation+Study.pdf; Dick Sorenson, "The Cycling Mar-

ket Pedals Ahead in 2021," NPD Group, accessed June 22, 2023, https://www.npd.com/news/blog/2021/the-cycling-market-pedals-ahead-in-2021/.

33. Rick Vosper, "Vosper: 2023 Is Shaping Up to Be the Year of the Double Whammy," Bicycle Retailer and Industry News, May 15, 2023, https://www.bicycleretailer.com/opinion-analysis/2023/05/13/vosper-2023-shaping-be-year-double-whammy#.ZGzW5HaZO3A.

34. Kristin Ostberg, "A Bicycle Built for You," *Crain's Chicago Business* 35, no. 35 (August 2012): 0025; Coco Johnson, "Chicago Handmade Bike Show Is a Sign that the Local Scene Is Picking Up Speed," Streetsblog, May 26, 2017, accessed June 22, 2023, https://chi.streetsblog.org/2017/05/26/chicago-handmade-bike-show-is-a-sign-that-the-local-scene-is-picking-up-speed/.

35. "About Highway Two," Highway Two, accessed June 22, 2023, https://highwaytwo.com/; "Brands," Pacific Cycle, accessed June 22, 2023, https://www.pacific-cycle.com/; Epperson, *Peddling*, 228; TRD Staff, "Giant Bicycle Signs Big Industrial Lease Renewal and Expansion in Elgin," The Real Deal, December 26, 2018, https://therealdeal.com/chicago/2018/12/26/giant-bicycle-signs-big-industrial-lease-renewal-and-expansion-in-elgin/; Don Dodson, "BRG to Hire 30 More for Rantoul Facility," *News-Gazette* (Champaign, IL), August 14, 2014.

36. "The Lost Mansion," Lost Houses of Lyndale, accessed June 22, 2023, https://www.wurlington-bros.com/Marvelous/Lyndale/LostMansion.html; "Most Endangered Historic Places in Illinois," Landmarks Illinois, accessed June 22, 2023, https://www.landmarks.org/preservation-programs/most-endangered-historic-places-in-illinois/; John Morris, "Uncertain Future for a Vacant Gothic Mansion Built for Co-founder of Schwinn Bicycle Company," Chicago Patterns, November 18, 2015, http://chicagopatterns.com/uncertain-future-vacant-gothic-mansion-built-co-founder-schwinn-bicycle-company/.

37. "Western Toy Company," Chicagology, accessed June 23, 2023, https://chicagology.com/rebuilding/rebuilding186/; "History," 213 West Institute, accessed June 23, 2023, https://www.213westinstitute.com/history; "R. Philip Gormully House Façade on N. Dearborn Street," Explorest, accessed June 23, 2023, https://www.explorest.com/places/illinois/chicago/r-philip-gormully-house-facade-on-n-dearborn-street.

38. Made in Chicago Museum, "Monark Silver King."

39. "Chicago—Wood Block Street Pavement," Historic Pavement, accessed June 23, 2023, http://www.historicpavement.com/chicago-wood-block.

40. Lindsey Holden, "City Redevelopment of Rockford Watch Co. Remains in Limbo," *Rockford Register Star* (Rockford, IL), March 28, 2016, https://www.rrstar.com/story/news/politics/county/2016/03/29/city-redevelopment-rockford-watch-co/32052270007/; "Eldredge Bicycle Club, Tonawanda," Forgotten Buffalo, accessed June 23, 2023, http://www.forgottenbuffalo.com/privateethnicclubs/eldredgebicycleclub.html; Harriett Gustason, "Freeport Brews 100 Years of History," *Journal-Standard* (Freeport, IL), October 11, 2009, accessed June 23, 2023, https://www.journalstandard.com/story/entertainment/local/2009/10/11/freeport-brews-100-years-history/45160331007/.

41. "Cycling's Roots Run Deep at Illinois Cycle & Fitness," *Journal Star* (Peoria, IL), August 27, 2013, accessed June 23, 2023, https://www.pjstar.com/story/news/2013/08/27/cycling-s-roots-run-deep/41995137007/.

42. Roger Gilles, *Women on the Move: The Forgotten Era of Women's Bicycle Racing* (Lincoln, NE: University of Nebraska Press, 2018), 281.

43. "Six-Day Races Supreme Test of Grit," *Popular Mechanics*, February 1926, 251–54; David Herlihy, *Bicycle: The History* (New Haven, CT: Yale University Press, 2004), 382; Chris McAuliffe, *Cycling in Chicago* (Charleston, SC: Arcadia Publishing, 2017), 33–86; Peter Nye, *Hearts of Lions: The History of American Bicycle Racing* (New York: W. W. Norton, 1988), 102.

44. "Six-Day Races Supreme Test," 251–254; "Six Day Bicycle Racing, with a Million Dollar 'Take,'" *Literary Digest* 125, January 8, 1938, 22; Nye, *Hearts of Lions*, 72; Peter Nye, *The Six-Day Bicycle Races* (San Francisco: Van der Plas, 2006), 183.

45. Edward Harper, *Six Days of Madness* (Ontario: Pacesetter Press, 1993), 16–17 and 71–72; Nye, *Hearts of Lions*, 108; Nye, *The Six-Day*, 87; Scott Martin, "The Grand Game," *Bicycling*, May 1990, 58–64; Arch Ward, "In the Wake of the News," *Chicago Daily Tribune*, November 23, 1940, 15; James C. McCullagh, *American Bicycle Racing* (Emmaus, PA: Rodale Press, 1976), 42; Richard Browne, "The Concept of the 6-Day Cycling Show-Circus in the 1930's the Star Showman, 'Torchy' Peden," *Canadian Journal of History of Sport* 17, no. 2 (1986): 85–96.

46. "'From College to Bike Rider,' in One Act, by Stockholm," *Chicago Tribune*, October 26, 1927, 23; "Clean Up Man on a Bike," *International Trail* 20, no. 5 (January 1951): 8–9; Erica Gunderson, "Ask Geoffery," WTTW, accessed June 22, 2023, https://news.wttw.com/2016/03/02/ask-geoffrey-whats-history-telenews-theater-state-street.

47. "William 'Cecil' Yates," U.S. Bicycling Hall of Fame, accessed June 22, 2023, https://usbhof.org/inductee/william-cecil-yates/; "Cecil Yates," 6 Day Racing, accessed June 22, 2023, http://www.6dayracing.ca/USriders/yatesc/index.html.

48. Andrew Ritchie, *Major Taylor, "The Fastest Bicycle Rider in the World"* (San Francisco: Van der Plas, 2010),181–89, 181–89; Michael Kranish, *The World's Fastest Man: The Extraordinary Life of Cyclist Major Taylor* (New York: Scribner, 2019), 289–93.

49. Heather Drieth, "Tillie Anderson, the Terrible Swede," *Wheelmen* 56 (May 2000): 9–10; "Lady Champion Turns Stag into a Surprise," *Chicago Tribune*, September 6, 1941, 9; Gilles, *Women on the Move*, 287–88.

50. "History," Oscar Wastyn Cycles, accessed June 22, 2023, http://www.wastyn.com/history.html; W. T. Farwell, "The American Racing Bicycle Comes Back," *American Bicyclist and Motorcyclist*, January 1939, 42; Schwinn, *50 Years*, 53, Pridmore and Hurd, *Schwinn*, 123–25.

51. Peter Nye, "Joseph Magnani: Illinois Rider Challenged Coppi and Bartali in Giro d'Italia," Cycling Revealed, March 2011, https://www.cyclingrevealed.com/Mar11/Mar_feature11_PN_Magnani.html.

52. "Joseph Magnani," U.S. Bicycle Hall of Fame, accessed June 22, 2023 https://usbhof.org/inductee/joseph-magnani/; Peter Nye, "Joseph Magnani: The Illinois Rider Who Challenged Coppi and Bartali in the Giro d'Italia," Bike Race Info, accessed June 22, 2023, http://bikeraceinfo.com/riderhistories/JosephMagnani.html.

53. "Jim Rossi Olympic Cyclist," *Chicago Tribune*, September 6, 2005, 3–5; "Jim Rossi," Olympedia, accessed June 22, 2023, https://www.olympedia.org/athletes/16378.

54. Lou Dzierzak, *The Evolution of American Bicycle Racing* (Guilford, CT: FalconGuides, 2007), 56; "The 1963 US Cyclocross National Championships," CVCC Bike, accessed June 22, 2023, http://cvccbike.com/50th_Anniversary_US_CX/The%201963%20US%20Cyclocross%20Championships.html; Gabor L. Konrad, "'The Tyger': America's Cyclo-Cross Champion, Leroy Johnson," *Cycle History 11: Proceedings of the 11th International Cycling History*, 137–46.

55. McCullagh, *American Bicycle*, 89; Dzierzak, *Evolution*, 38.

56. "Mark Gorski," Cycling Archives, accessed June 23, 2023, http://www.cyclingarchives.com/coureurfiche.php?coureurid=9362.

57. "John Vande Velde," U.S. Bicycle Hall of Fame, accessed June 22, 2023, https://usbhof.org/inductee/john-vandevelde/; "For the Vande Veldes Success Goes in Cycles," *Chicago Tribune*, December 31, 1995, 1–6; Nye, *Six-Day*, 208–11; Dzierzak, *Evolution*, 59; "William Clay," Olympics, accessed June 23, 2023, https://olympics.com/en/athletes/william-clay.

58. "About Me," Andrew Starykowicz, accessed June 22, 2023, https://www.andrewstarykowicz.com/about-me/; "Kevin McDowell," USA Triathlon, accessed June 22, 2023, https://www.teamusa.org/usa-triathlon/athletes/kevin-mcdowell; "Ben Kanute," USA Triathlon, accessed June 22, 2023, https://www.teamusa.org/usa-triathlon/athletes/ben-kanute.

59. Peter Zheutlin, *Around the World on Two Wheels: Annie Londonderry's Extraordinary Ride* (New York: Citadel Press Books, 2007); Caroline Kubzansky, "Cyclist Completes World-Record Attempt in Downtown Chicago," *Chicago Tribune*, September 12, 2024.

60. Daniel Burnham and Edward H. Bennett, *Plan of Chicago* (Chicago: Commercial Club, 1909).

61. "The Wheels Go Round and Round," *Recreation*, June 25, 1941, 204; "Cyclists to Get a Break! Plan on Pathways," *Chicago Tribune*, July 18, 1935, 1; David R. Wrone, "Illinois Pulls Out of the Mud," *Journal of the Illinois State Historical Society*, 58, no. 1 (Spring, 1965): 76.

62. "A Mini-Bike History from Daley to Daley," *Chicago Tribune*, June 25, 2000, 13; "History," Illinois Prairie Path, accessed June 22, 2023, http://www.ipp.org/history/.

63. "A Mini-Bike History"; Grove, "Bikes Are Back"; Allyson Hobbs, "Bicycling," in *The Encyclopedia of Chicago* ed. James R. Grossman et al. (Chicago: University of Chicago Press, 2004), 78; "Figures on Wheels," *Chicago Daily Tribune*, September 18, 1898, 32; "NIPC Offer Bike Path Map," *The McHenry Plaindealer* (McHenry, IL), July 19, 1978, 8.

64. "Chicago Bicycle Federation," Bike Collectives Wiki, accessed June 23, 2023, https://www.bikecollectives.org/wiki/Chicago_Bicycle_Federation; J. Harry Wray, *Pedal Power: The Quiet Rise of the Bicycle in American Public Life* (Boulder, CO: Paradigm Publishers, 2008), 116–21; "Our Accomplishments," Active Transportation Alliance, accessed June 23, 2023, https://activetrans.org/about-us/our-organization/our-accomplishments.

65. "How Bike Friendly Cities Got That Way," *Pittsburgh Post-Gazette*, May 18, 2003, 9; Mayor's Bicycle Advisory Council, *The Bike 2000 Plan*, 1992, City of Chicago, accessed June 23, 2023, https://www.chicago.gov/dam/city/depts/cdot/bicycling/publications/bike2000plan.pdf; "Grand Illinois Trail," Openlands, accessed June 23, 2023, https://openlands.org/explore/regional-trails/grand-illinois-trail/.

66. Luis A. Vivanco, *Reconsidering the Bicycle: An Anthropological Perspective on a New (Old) Thing* (New York: Routledge, 2013), 6.

67. Vivanco, *Reconsidering the Bicycle*, xvii-xix; Chicago Department of Transportation, *Chicago Streets for Cycling Plan 2020,* City of Chicago, accessed June 23, 2023, https://www.chicago.gov/content/dam/city/depts/cdot/bike/general/ChicagoStreetsforCycling2020.pdf; "Initial Findings: Kinzie Street Protected Bike Lane," City of Chicago, September 21, 2011, https://www.chicago.gov/city/en/depts/cdot/provdrs/bike/news/2011/sep/initial_findingskinziestreet protectedbikelane.html.

68. "History," The 606, accessed June 22, 2023, https://www.the606.org/about/history/; "To Pedal Up in the Air," *Chicago Tribune*, June 7, 1897, 4; "606 Trail Scores Mixed Reviews," *Chicago Tribune*, June 5, 2016, 12.

69. "Cycling 'Round the Circle,'" *Wheelman* 2, no. 6, September 1883.

70. "Mayor Lightfoot Joins CDOT and DCASE to Announce 'Open Boulevards' Series as Part of Open Streets Program," City of Chicago, September 17, 2021, https://www.chicago.gov/city/en/depts/mayor/press_room/press_releases/2021/september/CDOTDCASEOpenBoulevards.html; "CDOT Bike Network," City of Chicago, accessed June 22, 2023, https://www.chicago.gov/city/en/depts/cdot/provdrs/bike/svcs/cdot-bike-network.html; "Illinois," Rails-to-Trails, accessed June 22, 2023, https://www.railstotrails.org/our-work/united-states/illinois/#state.

71. PeopleForBikes, "U.S. Bicycling Participation Benchmarking."

Epilogue

1. "Ravages of the Bicycle Craze," *Evening Post* (New York), June 2, 1896.

2. "Our Mission," Women Bike Chicago, accessed June 22, 2023, http://www.womenbike chicago.org/who-we-are/.

3. "USA Cycling Demographics Survey 2020 Results," USA Cycling, accessed June 22, 2023, https://s3.amazonaws.com/usac-craft-uploads-production/documents/Demographics-Report-2020.pdf; "It's Time to Support These Cycling Orgs Pushing for More Racial Diversity" *Bicycling*, June 25, 2020, https://www.bicycling.com/culture/a32937508/racial-diversity-cycling/.

4. "Club History," Windy City Cycling Club, accessed June 22, 2023, https://wccc.clubexpress.com/.

5. "Mission," Major Taylor Cycling Club—Chicago, accessed June 22, 2023, https://www.majortaylorchicago.com/; "About," Slow Roll Chicago, accessed June 22, 2023, https://slowrollchicago.tumblr.com/about.

6. Amy Walker, *On Bicycles: 50 Ways the New Bike Culture Can Change Your Life* (Novato, CA: New World Library, 2011), 236.

7. "Who We Are," World Bicycle Relief, accessed June 22, 2023, https://worldbicyclerelief.org/who-we-are/.

8. "The Story of Big Marsh," Big Marsh, accessed June 22, 2023, https://bigmarsh.org/history/; Ben Schulman, "How Chicago Turned an Industrial Waste Site Into a Nature Lovers' and Cyclists' Paradise," Bloomberg, July 27, 2016, https://www.bloomberg.com/news/articles/2016-07-27/how-chicago-s-big-marsh-transformed-from-an-industrial-waste-site-into-a-nature-loving-cyclist-s-paradise; "Bike Park Project Aims to Invigorate South East Side," *Chicago Tribune*, July 7, 2015, 2.

9. "City Peddles Biking Image," *Chicago Tribune*, May 25, 2014, 14; Anna Clark, "Why Chicago Is Claiming Bike-Share Bragging Rights," Next City, April 30, 2015, https://nextcity.org/urbanist-news/chicago-bike-share-stations-added-divvy-expansion-airport-suburbs; John Greenfield, Divvy Riders Made 10,519 Trips in 4.5 Days to Reach the 10 Million Mark, Streetsblog Chicago, January 3, 2017, https://chi.streetsblog.org/2017/01/03/divvy-riders-made-10519-trips-in-4-5-days-to-reach-the-10-million-mark; Mike Claffey, "CDOT Announces Divvy Tops 4 Million Rides in 2021," City of Chicago, September 24, 2021, https://www.chicago.gov/city/en/depts/cdot/provdrs/bike/news/2021/september/cdot-announces-divvy-tops-4-million-rides-in-2021--shatters-annu.html.

10. John Bryne, "Divvy at a Discount: Mayor Hopes to Get Poor onto Bikes," *Chicago Tribune*, July 8, 2015, 6; John Greenfield, "Regular Divvy Membership Is Still Heavily White, But Divvy for Everyone Is Diverse," Streetsblog Chicago, January 15, 2018, https://chi.streetsblog.org/2018/01/15/regular-divvy-membership-is-still-heavily-white-but-divvy-for-everyone-is-diverse; Amanda Woodall, Divvy for Everyone: Addressing Financial Barriers in Bikeshare, Better Bikeshare Partnership, accessed June 23, 2023, https://betterbikeshare.org/wp-content/uploads/2016/07/Amanda-Woodall-Chicago-Divvy-for-Everyone.pdf.

11. Cameron Bolton, "Divvy Has Expanded to the Entire City," Streetsblog Chicago, May 3, 2023, https://chi.streetsblog.org/2023/05/03/divvy-has-expanded-to-the-entire-city/; Chicago Department of Transportation, "Chicago Cycling Strategy," City of Chicago, Spring 2023, https://www.chicago.gov/content/dam/city/depts/cdot/bike/2023/2023_Chicago%20Cycling%20Update.pdf.

12. Erica Schroeder, "CDOT Launches Program to Distribute 5,000 Free Bikes and Safety Equipment by 2026," City of Chicago, July 11, 2022, https://www.chicago.gov/city/en/depts/cdot/provdrs/future_projects_andconcepts/news/2022/july/cdot-launches-program-to-distribute-5-000-free-bikes-and-safety-.html.

13. Breakaway Research Group, "U.S. Bicycling Participation Benchmarking Study Report," PeopleForBikes, March 2015, https://prismic-io.s3.amazonaws.com/peopleforbikes/ea52c570-a114-4962-aa26-c7cf72aeb331_2014_Participation_Study.pdf; "Cut the Catcalling," Women's Bicycle Messenger Association, accessed June 22, 2023, https://vimeo.com/155497525.

14. Mary Wisniewski, "Minority Areas See the Most Bike Tickets," *Chicago Tribune*, March 19, 2017, 1; Mary Wisniewski, "CPD Data Show Racial Disparity in Bike Tickets," *Chicago Tribune*, February 12, 2018, 1–4; Charles T. Brown, J'Lin Rose, and Samuel Kling, "Arrested Mobility," Better Bikeshare Partnership, March 2023, https://betterbikeshare.org/wp-content/uploads/2023/03/Arrested-Mobility-Report_web.pdf.

15. Joseph Bishop, "Social and Economic Influence of The Bicycle," *The Forum* 21 (August 1896): 683; Alan Coté and Sean Coffey, "The Best Cycling Cities," *Bicycling Magazine*, November 2001, 38. "Mayor Emanuel Announces Chicago Named America's Top City for Cycling," City of Chicago, September 20, 2016, https://www.chicago.gov/city/en/depts/mayor/press_room/press_releases/2016/september/Top-City-For-Cycling.html; John Greenfield, "New State Bike Laws Kick In and Cycling Becomes Illinois' Official State Exercise," January 5, 2018, https://chi.streetsblog.org/2018/01/05/new-state-bike-laws-kick-in-and-cycling-becomes-illinois-official-state-exercise/.

Index

Page numbers in *italic* refer to photographs or figures.

CHRISTOPHER SWEET is a professor and the Information Literacy and Scholarly Communications Librarian at Illinois Wesleyan University's Ames Library.

The University of Illinois Press
is a founding member of the
Association of University Presses.

Composed in 10/13 Mercury Text G1
with Roboto display
by Kirsten Dennison
at the University of Illinois Press
Manufactured by Sheridan Books, Inc.

University of Illinois Press
1325 South Oak Street
Champaign, IL 61820-6903
www.press.uillinois.edu